REGIONAL ANALYSIS

Volume II
Social Systems

STUDIES IN ANTHROPOLOGY

Under the Consulting Editorship of E. A. Hammel,
UNIVERSITY OF CALIFORNIA, BERKELEY

REGIONAL ANALYSIS

Volume II
Social Systems

EDITED BY

Carol A. Smith

Department of Anthropology
Duke University
Durham, North Carolina

ACADEMIC PRESS   New York   San Francisco   London

A Subsidiary of Harcourt Brace Jovanovich, Publishers

ACADEMIC PRESS, INC.
111 Fifth Avenue, New York, New York 10003

United Kingdom Edition published by
ACADEMIC PRESS, INC. (LONDON) LTD.
24/28 Oval Road, London NW1

Library of Congress Cataloging in Publication Data

Main entry under title:

Regional analysis.

      (Studies in anthropology)
      Includes bibliographies and index.
      CONTENTS: v. I.   Economic systems.—v. II.   Social
systems.
          1.   Underdeveloped areas—Commerce—Congresses.
2.   Central places—Congresses.   3.   Social systems—
Economic aspects—Congresses.   I.   Smith, Carol A.
HF1413.R428   380.1'09172'4   75-30474
ISBN 0–12–652102–6 (v. II)

Contents

Section B   MARRIAGE AND KINSHIP

Section D **POLITICAL ECONOMY:
SOCIAL ASPECTS OF
ECONOMIC SYSTEMS**

Chapter 11 Export Monoculture and Regional Social
Structure in Puno, Peru   291
Gordon Appleby

Chapter 12 Exchange Systems and the Spatial
Distribution of Elites: The Organization
of Stratification in Agrarian Societies   309
Carol A. Smith

List of Contributors

Numbers in parentheses indicate the pages on which the authors' contributions begin.

Johns W. Adams (149, 175), Department of Anthropology, University of South Carolina, Columbia, South Carolina

Gordon Appleby (291), Department of Anthropology, Stanford University, Stanford, California, and Institute for Scientific Analysis, 210 Spear Street, San Francisco, California

Brenda E. F. Beck (255), Department of Anthropology and Sociology, University of British Columbia, Vancouver, British Columbia

Lawrence W. Crissman (123), Department of Anthropology, University of Illinois at Urbana-Champaign, Urbana, Illinois

Richard G. Fox (95), Department of Anthropology, Duke University, Durham, North Carolina

Julia Day Howell (229), Department of Anthropology, Stanford University, Stanford, California

Jean E. Jackson (65), Anthropology Program, Massachusetts Institute of Technology, Cambridge, Massachusetts

Alice Bee Kasakoff (149, 175), Department of Anthropology, University of South Carolina, Columbia, South Carolina

Stephen M. Olsen (21), Department of Sociology, Stanford University, Stanford, California

Carol A. Smith (1, 309), Department of Anthropology, Duke University, Durham, North Carolina

Katherine Verdery (191), Department of Anthropology, Stanford University, Stanford, California

Preface

More than a decade ago G. William Skinner proposed that the way in which regional settlement systems organized and structured social intercourse in traditional China shaped cultural as well as economic institutions in that society. Since then much has happened to deepen and widen certain aspects of the approach he pioneered, an approach we term here *regional analysis*. Economic geography, the home of the spatial models which undergird the approach, has had a veritable renaissance, reflected in its newly sophisticated methodology and techniques of analysis. Central-place theory, which provided the spatial models basic to geographers' conceptualization of regional systems and also basic to Skinner's socioeconomic analysis, has been questioned, clarified, and revised, and alternative spatial models have been fashioned from it. Careful field studies of markets and regional economies carried out in different parts of the world have identified regional patterns not predicted by central-place theory or any of the other standard locational theories, thereby stimulating the development of new regional system theories. In addition, social scientists other than geographers, economists, and regional scientists now evince interest in the implications of rural–urban relations and regional settlement patterns, among them social anthropologists, archeologists, sociologists, and political scientists.

In short, regional models today are much more sophisticated than they were 15 years ago; and, on the basis of interest, regional analysis now holds promise as a general integrating framework for many of the social sciences. Yet little work has been done to relate the new theories of regional settlement systems to types and levels of socioeconomic systems, the other major element of regional analysis. And this must be done before its general promise can be realized.

In light of the growing disparity between the specialized and the generalized versions of regional analysis, I organized a conference for the purpose of discussing ways to bring the two together again. Scholars from several disciplines who had utilized locational or other territorial models to investigate either economic or social processes in real-world systems constituted the conference group. All had done field work in non-Western areas and together represented many parts of the world and many types of societies. The plan was to concentrate on various regular and irregular patterns of settlement-system organization uncovered by field work, and to discuss them as living, growing systems in order to discover the manner in which they influenced and were influenced by sociocultural systems.

The conference was held in Santa Fe, New Mexico in the fall of 1973, and most of the papers in these two volumes were first drafted for it. The effect of interaction and discussion at the conference and afterward was significant enough, however, that none of the final essays in either of the volumes bears close resemblance to its conference draft. I encouraged general theoretical formulations, which most of the essays now display; and to round out the presentation of our findings, I solicited additional papers from others whose field work was more recent than that of most of the conferees (Adams and Kasakoff, Appleby, Bromley, Olsen, Verdery). As they presently stand, the studies in these two volumes represent the most current thinking about the general applications of the regional framework for analyzing socioeconomic systems.

The two volumes are linked by a general interest in exploring the interconnectedness of economic and social systems as they exist and develop in territorial–environmental systems, but each has a different emphasis. Most of the studies in Volume I concentrate on developing and refining models of trade and urban evolution. While this concern places Volume I squarely within the realm of economic geography, the focus on evolutionary models and the relationship between economic and political subsystems in the developmental process makes it relevant to almost any student of the economy. The studies in Volume II are concerned with social systems; primary emphasis is given to showing the interrelationships among the institutional components of complex societies, including marriage and kinship, political organization, the formation of ethnic and cultural–territorial groups, and stratification systems—all as they are affected by regional–environmental variables. Hence, those who would be interested in Volume I are likely to be interested in Volume II as well; in addition, Volume II should be relevant to anyone concerned with complex sociocultural systems and the relationships among the organizational subsystems within them.

Many people and institutions were instrumental in the preparation and publication of these studies. The conference was supported by the Mathematics in the Social Sciences Board of the National Science Foundation; I would like to thank Roy D'Andrade for putting me in touch with them. The University of New Mexico gave additional assistance in holding the conference, primarily in the form of organizational help. The conference also benefited from the presence of several people from the University of New Mexico, especially Del Dyreson, Henry Harpending, and Robert Hitchcock. Duke University provided ample secretarial and copying services for preparing many of the manuscripts, tables, and figures; I am particularly grateful for the help given by Dina Smith and Sylvia Terrell. Dina Smith deserves special thanks for the exceptional work she did setting up and typing the tables, as does Ronald Smith who drew many of the figures. I am most grateful to the contributors to these volumes; all of them made useful suggestions to one another and to me and withstood cheerfully my novice editorship.

Contents of Volume I

Section A

INTRODUCTION:
THE REGIONAL APPROACH
TO SOCIAL SYSTEMS

Anthropology and sociology are the major fields from which the following contributions were drawn. But the papers reflect cross-disciplinary interests and are thereby also germane to the concerns of some geographers, historians, political scientists, and economists. The two introductions that comprise this section take into account this potentially diverse audience and define the applications of the regional approach as widely as possible. While in the first chapter I review the approach as it applies primarily to anthropology, my home discipline, I am concerned with any of the social sciences that relate human institutional systems to environmental systems. In Chapter 2 Stephen Olsen introduces the approach from a social science perspective broader than mine, providing a definitive study of the origins, problems, and methodology of regional analysis as it relates to social systems. In his treatment of methodology, Olsen points out several of the paths available for those who would do regional analysis—ways to integrate the intensive field work tradition with a broader perspective, ways to link data collection to analysis. He also discusses the pitfalls and dangers of a regional approach that gives insufficient attention to problem definition and data control. While he makes a convincing case for the regional framework utilized here, the utility of this framework must ultimately be judged by its substantive contributions, which follow this introductory section.

1

Chapter 1

Analyzing Regional Social Systems

Carol A. Smith
Duke University

I think we shall come to study regional systems. We shall study such systems, not, as we now tend to do, from the viewpoint of some one small local community looking outward, but from the viewpoint of an observer who looks down upon the whole larger regional system [Redfield 1956:28].

It has been 20 years since Redfield made this prediction, yet the attempt to grapple with regional systems of social organization has been at best scattered and desultory. Anthropologists for the most part continue to take a worm's-eye rather than a bird's-eye view of social systems, presupposing that the limits of day-to-day interaction bound the relevant social units. They rely on other social scientists to provide information about the regional and national contexts of their communities, information they then supply in several paragraphs or a chapter about the community, and pay relatively little attention to that context in their analysis of the community. Historians, political scientists, economists, and other social scientists working from the apparent centers of decision making, on the other hand, either lose sight of rural areas altogether or assume that they are composed of an undifferentiated aggregate of small communities such as those studied by anthropologists. Everyone acknowledges that there is more to the organization of social and cultural systems, something between the community and national levels, but few attempt to deal with it.

Redfield, one of the first to point out the analytical gap, tried to bridge it with the notion of a folk–urban continuum (1941). His approach was clearly inadequate to the task as is evidenced by his paucity of structural terms—family, community, region, nation—and by his confusion of time with space in the continuum he posited. But while his model is outdated, his concern is not. It is increasingly recognized that the standard anthropological monograph on a small community suffers theoretical limitations because of its narrow parochialism, and that studies of large-scale, national systems do little to illuminate the lives of people who live in small rural communities—the majority of mankind. What is lacking is a method for integrating the microperspective with the macroperspective—a coherent framework for understanding how local communities are linked to others forming intermediate and higher levels of social organization.

I will argue here that the geographers' concept of region may provide the framework and the implicit methodology called for. To geographers, regions are more than passive receptacles of human activities; they are meaningful partitions of space that subdivide large portions of the earth's landscape. Functionally defined regions represent several levels of integration, within a hierarchy of human settlements, that theoretically culminate in a single all-inclusive system—the nation, a continent, the world. Lower-level regions are seen as transactionally defined components of larger systems. Levels and patterns may be studied by means of network analysis on systems of nodes (Haggett 1966) or by functional analysis of hierarchical or central-place organization (Christaller 1966). Such modes of analysis, together with various locational theories, allow geographers to describe human groups and communities of any scale as systemic entities that occupy space, exploit resources, and interact with one another and the environment in patterned ways. These systemic entities supply the analytical units needed for describing and comprehending the levels and linkages between community and nation in a complex socioeconomic system. There is no single regional level of analysis, but rather many different regional levels of analysis.

The generalizations that can be made from regional patterns of social organization are clearly of greater comparative relevance than those drawn from community or national studies alone. On the one hand, a regional perspective makes it possible to control for local environmental or idiosyncratic variability and to discover how these might systematically affect higher-level systems, thus allowing one to observe localized and environmental effects more completely than one sees them at either the community or the national level. On the other hand, by viewing complex societies as nested regional systems, discrete in some aspects and overlapping in others at each level, with level-specific institutions, functions, and processes, analysis can also be focused directly on the higher-level or organizational determinants of societal integration. A regional analysis will not result in something that necessarily contradicts findings from local community or national studies, but it should provide a framework in which those findings can be compared and more generally understood. With other approaches, generalization requires one to assume that what is true of a part is roughly true of the whole or that what is true of the whole is also true of the parts. Regional analysis can build system variability into its models of explanation, so that generalization is neither far-fetched nor banal.

The utility of a regional approach for students of social systems has been demonstrated by a number of studies carried out by nongeographers: Leach (1954) examined political relations in highland Burma in a specifically regional context; Geertz (1963) analyzed community, ecology, and economic relations in Indonesia as they formed integrated regional systems; and Skinner (1964, 1965) used locational models to build and analyze regional systems in his study of rural Chinese social organization. These works are considered theoretical triumphs in their respective problem areas, but they do not provide clear maps of the theory and methodology required for regional analysis so that others might follow their lead. (Indeed, some seem to have been written because detailed community field notes had been lost.) As a result of this and the fact that regional analyses of social structure are by definition difficult to undertake, the regional classics have not yet stimulated in other scholars the efforts that would seem warranted by their analytical successes. The various obstacles have not, however, prevented most students of social organization from attempting to generalize to higher or lower levels of organization. I suggest that by providing a clear conceptualization of the levels and systems involved, the methods and theories or regional analysis will make it more profitable, and perhaps less difficult, to do so.

Representing this philosophy, the papers in the volume attempt to develop a regional approach to social systems that will have wide applicability, to provide clearer guides than our predecessors to the requisite theory and methodology, and to define new problem areas for which regional analysis is useful. To do so, we have borrowed eclectically from various fields for theory and applications and, where possible, have noted methodologies that might facilitate both field work and analysis (see in particular Chapter 2 in this volume, by Olsen). While many of the models and methods we use come from outside the social sciences proper, our explicit concern is with social organization. To show how regional analysis addresses this basic concern, it will be helpful to compare it with certain other approaches to social organization to which it is most akin: geography and regional science, cultural ecology and systems theory, and modern conceptualizations of complex societies.

GEOGRAPHY AND REGIONAL SCIENCE

> Regional science aims to identify and expose simple, basic principles of spatial organization—principles that govern equilibrium and organizational structure and relate to efficiency, equity, and social welfare [Isard 1975:5].

> There have been practically no attempts [by anthropologists] to correlate spatial configurations with the formal properties of other aspects of social life [Lévi-Strauss 1953:533].

Aided by the sophisticated tools of locational analysis, geographers and regional scientists are now well ahead of other social scientists in their formal and conceptual ability to handle complex levels of organization. But geographers, largely concerned with problems of landscape regularities and irregularities in and of themselves, rarely deal with sociocultural systems except as the "outside forces" that impinge on spatial–territorial systems; that is, they tend to deal with the human component as a given—much as we deal with *their* subject matter as a given. And regional science, though developed as a specialized subfield of geography and economics for the very purpose of generalizing spatial models and making them applicable to social organization, pays primary attention to normative efficiency and practical applications of its knowledge; thus regional science still has far to go to make its models relevant to those who are concerned with real-world rather than normative or ideal systems. With modification, however, the analytical tools of geographers and regional scientists can be powerful ones for uncovering "the diverse organizational and institutional structures of society as they govern the behavior and spatial distribution of population and economic activity [Isard 1975:5]." In both this and the previous volume, such tools provide a basic foundation for regional analysis.

Regional analysis, then, is based on locational analysis. But we retain a descriptive rather than a normative or applied approach to locational models—they are not for us the center of attention. We consider locational analysis to be a method that can reveal the patterned movements of people, goods, services, and information that underlie and express the structure of a given regional system, processes that *are* for us the center of attention; hence we use locational models wherever they illuminate such processes. We use, for example, central-place theory, originally set forth by Christaller (1966) in the form of a theory of economic organization as it is affected by locational constraints. While this theory is very specifically addressed to a limited subset of economic problems, it can with judicious use be applied to the analysis of social systems. Christaller himself was aware of some of the social implications of locational models, and G. William Skinner, in the articles that stimulated much of the present effort (1964, 1965), developed the point much further. In Volume I, *Economic*

Systems, the various locational theories of economic geography are described in full, particularly in my introductory paper. Here I will only suggest the general features of the locational models embodied by central-place theory that are relevant to social systems.

Central-place theory views the structure of economic systems in terms of retailer location and consumer behavior. The theory holds that the location of service centers, other things being equal, will be central for the people who use them; and that the lowest-order, more commonly used functions will be located in numerous smaller centers, while higher-order functions will be located in fewer centers having correspondingly larger hinterlands. Such distribution creates a hierarchy of centers, with discrete hinterlands at any one level, and thus groups populations in terms of their relations to particular central places. In more general terms, central places are the organizing features of territorial systems (regions) that tie communities to one another through both hierarchical and horizontal links. They may have diverse functions—economic, administrative, ideological—but in any case they are central because they provide services that allow communication of information, division of labor, exchange of goods, and delegation of authority and control, all of which are important to sustaining the places and territories dependent upon them. Central-place systems will take various forms, depending on inherent properties of the space economy as well as on the forces—the organizing impetus in a territory— that gave rise to them. Most important for social organization, the particular patterns and forms in which central-place systems are organized will have direct consequences for the adaptation, identity, and survival of the communities linked together by the central places that define a regional system. The central-place model, in short, yields typologies of regional systems that can ultimately explain a great deal about the social as well as the economic order. Several papers in this volume are concerned with these general aspects of the model: Crissman (Chapter 5) and Adams and Kasakoff (Chapters 6 and 7) deal with it as a means to delineate cultural groupings that intermarry in complex societies; Appleby (Chapter 11) and I (Chapter 12) are concerned with the social effects of irregular central-place systems.

Central-place theory calls to mind highly complex societies organized by urban centers and heavy market dependence and at first glance seems entirely irrelevant to the analysis of simpler societies. This view of it stems from the fact that the geographers who elaborated the theory were concerned mainly with industrialized, urban societies and did little to generalize the model for application to simpler societies. (For an exception, see Brookfield with Hart 1971, on Melanesia.) Yet significant cultural groupings are always defined by some kind of centralizing institution, be it as lowly as the household; and in all societies, communities organized at least by households are placed in spatial systems of interaction with one another. Therefore, we take the position that spatial analysis is useful for understanding the place of a community in *any* society and that central-place theory provides a basis for developing spatial models for nonurban as well as urban systems, which may ultimately provide keys to many aspects of both economics and social organization.

In simpler societies the household may be the *only* centralizing institution, sex and age groups constituting the main divisions involved in labor and administration that are articulated by the household alone. Ties outside the household would exist but might be formed by networks of relationships without nodal centers. (See Jackson, Chapter 3, and Fox, Chapter 4, for analyses of just such cases.) But the fact that the only centralizing institution is the family or household is of significance, and anthropologists have long recognized the nodal points of households and the networks formed by marriage and kinship, rather than other institutions, to be basic to the way in which such societies function. What they have often failed to recognize, however, is that the place of a community within a network system is one of the most important determinants of community organization, and the network itself must often be considered in defining the proper social units for analysis (see Jackson for a discussion of the problem). Developing a general interactional model that will encompass simpler exchange and network systems, for which we have few models, as well as discovering the social concomitants of centralized and hierarchical systems, for which central-place theory provides several models, is one of our goals. For a start, Verdery (Chapter 8), Fox, and Howell (Chapter 9) discuss centralizing institutions, other than markets and trade, that organize territories; Jackson describes the spatial organization of a social order without nodal centers; and my paper suggests some variables that give rise to different kinds of social orders based on the various organizing principles of the space economy. In very different fashions we all attempt to come to grips with the problem of how various centralizing systems are organized, overlap, compete, form networks of communities and cultural groups, and create complex levels of sociocultural integration.

Although geographers and regional scientists have methodologies to identify and describe regional units and subunits as they are redefined by shifting population distribution or changing technology, many of them have treated the configuration of regional systems as though, once established, their structures were permanent and static. Users of central-place theory are especially guilty of ignoring the *flows* of goods, services, information, and people through the network of centers, even though the flows structure and maintain internodal relations. Since flows can be stopped, channeled, realigned, or redeveloped, it is important to see the integration of communities and hinterlands into larger or smaller units as a continuing process, influenced by recurrent patterns of events which themselves change and develop. In the approach taken here, therefore, interconnected systems of communities are considered spatial matrices for both sociocultural activities and temporal phenomena. While distance–cost is viewed as an important determing variable, its parameters are assumed to vary depending on the weight and development of social and political institutions. In consequence, our approach to the analysis of regional systems differs from that of most geographers and regional scientists in the following ways: (1) We assume no causal priority with respect to the natural, economic, or political features of the region—we regard these as interactive variables and wish to describe their interrelationships. (2) We concentrate on the evolution of regional systems and are interested in its processes in immature and noneconomic systems as well as developed ones with central-place hierarchies. And (3) we are concerned to incorporate sociocultural variables (such as political power, social classes, and ethnic group divisions) in our definitions and descriptions of regional system organization, and as more than exogenous features. In other words, we use spatial models as frameworks, not as determinate theories, because we expect that social and environmental conditions can and will alter the expected normative patterns with which regional scientists concern themselves.

An entire typology of spatial–territorial systems for the analysis of social organization remains to be worked out, but two of the most basic units for regional analysis are "local systems" and "regional systems." Both of these are nodal forms of organization in the sense that they define a territory dependent on some particular node (settlement), typically but not necessarily a classical "central place." That node may have a purely rural hinterland or a hinterland made up of smaller dependent centers together with their encompassed hinterlands. One may define a nodal region at any level, to include larger or smaller areas of interdependence. Local systems are those in which both material and nonmaterial exchanges are organized around at least one higher-level node that relates otherwise equivalent communities or places. Depending on the question or territory of concern, the local system may involve as few as two levels or as many as four or five levels in the hierarchy of places encompassed. Simpler societies, when they consist of communities or extended households organized by network rather than centralized linkages, may have no higher-level nodes. They are distinguished here from nodal systems as "network systems" and are expected to have certain special properties that set them apart from nodal systems (see Jackson and Smith in this volume).

Regional systems are nodal systems that include a number of levels of hierarchically organized communities. They are typically distinguished from local systems by having a truly "urban" central place, complex linkages between communities and higher-level centers, and an organized pattern of nested local systems within them. They define the most important units of analysis for so-called complex societies, in which market exchange is basic to the organization of the economy. Regional systems may or may not take on the characteristics of a regular central-place hierarchy, they may be more or less open to exchanges with other regional systems, and they may include different numbers of tiers or layers of smaller nodal systems within them (see Appleby and Smith). Determination and comparison of these variable features of regional systems is one aspect of regional analysis. The point of defining regional systems in this manner is to allow reasonable kinds of comparisons between equivalent units; any regional system can be broken down to a particular hierarchical level, systems at a given hierarchical level becoming the standard units of comparison.

The standardization of comparative units is one obvious contribution of regional analysis, necessary for comparative analysis of any social phenomena—social as well as geographical. Unless one is concerned with the comparative study of individuals, one must make comparisons of social units as they exist *within* a spatial–territorial context; and unless the social unit is properly specified in this regard, comparisons will be useless. The following example illustrates my point. In China the basic building block of rural society is often taken to be the "village," and observers have noted that the Chinese village tends to be exogamous. At the same time, the "township" is defined as the basic building block of present-day Mayan society, and the township is found to be endogamous. Chinese villages and Mayan townships are not comparable units, however. The Mayan township is made up of hamlets (often exogamous) that relate to a single higher-level political and economic center. The same unit in China would be the standard marketing community, made up of a market town and its related villages; and the Chinese standard marketing community may be just as endogamous as the Mayan township (Skinner 1964; see also Crissman and Adams and Kasakoff in this volume). Clearly, comparing Chinese exogamy with Mayan endogamy in order to explain something about marriage or about the two societies would be a useless exercise; yet such problem definition is inevitable unless social units are carefully defined along the lines suggested here.

Besides defining units for cross-societal comparison, regional analysis provides data for controlled intrasocietal comparison in large-scale societies, such as China, India, and Latin America. Hundreds of thousands of rural villages make up these major social systems, but only a handful have ever been studied. The villages investigated differ from one another considerably, and within the framework of community studies there is no way to account for the pattern of diversity such that propositions can be generated about rural Chinese, Indian, or Latin American societies as wholes. But studies that locate villages in local, regional, and even higher-level systems can capture a great deal of their diversity and explain much of it. One of the goals of regional analysis is to perform cross-sectional comparisons of large cultural systems, thereby enlightening further studies of any problem that involves highly differentiated, rural areas in complex societies. A modest beginning is made here by Beck (Chapter 10), Fox, Verdery, and Appleby. G. William Skinner has taken cross-sectional analysis much further for China (in Volume I, Chapter 10) and through use of it is able to make the world's largest society much less inscrutable.

The focus on territorial systems and spatial relationships reflects more than an interest in standardizing units of comparison, however. It reflects a commitment to understanding the relationship between environment and society in a broad sense, and to a concern with cultural ecology. Regional analysis might be considered a subfield of cultural ecology, although we differ from those in the mainstream of that field on a number of points. Cultural ecologists, in fact, might benefit from pursuing some of the problems, methods, and theories offered here and developed in the locational sciences (Netting 1974).

CULTURAL ECOLOGY AND SYSTEMS THEORY

> Although it is possible . . . to designate the territory of the local group as an ecosystem, it must not be forgotten that the environment of any human group is likely to include . . . neighboring human groups. . . . [The] supralocal relations, it seems to me, can hardly be ignored in ecological analyses [Rappaport 1968:225].

> In an ecosystem approach to the analysis of human societies, everything which transmits information is within the province of ecology [Flannery 1972:400].

These remarks are more suggestive of the present malaise in cultural ecology than they are descriptive of the present–day state of the field. Cultural ecology is now redefining itself, but it first developed as a rather narrow environmental approach and still has many narrow practitioners. The following brief review of its intellectual history is relevant to pointing up some of the problems it created for itself in the process of defining its concerns.

When the reified notion of culture, useful for combating an earlier racist bias in Western social science, was found inadequate for explaining the differences in social systems, anthropologists and other social scientists increasingly turned to environmental variables for causal explanations. Gross environmentalism and the modified geographical version of "possibilism" were rejected, and various premises about culture were worked into a new position that attended to the interaction of selected features of the environment and selected features of social organization. Known as

cultural ecology, this more rigorous approach to explanation was funda-
mentally materialistic in orientation, positing a chain of causality from
features of the environment necessary for subsistence, to human
subsistence technology, to a core of social institutions. Other aspects of culture were seen as affected by but less basic to the primary ecological
interaction (Steward 1955).

At the same time that cultural ecology rejected the modified environmentalism of cultural geography, it turned away from the human ecology
school associated with sociologists from the University of Chicago who had
made an early attempt to apply the abstract locational principles of
modern economic geography to "cultural" systems, particularly urban
systems (see Olsen for further discussion of this school). Most cultural
ecologists (Steward 1955; Geertz 1963) assessed human ecology as
mechanistic and irrelevant to their central concerns—the development
and change of cultural systems. The earliest sociological use of locational
analysis was certainly vulnerable to this criticism. But in abandoning locational analysis and modern geography, cultural ecology also abandoned
any attempt to explain with environmental variables the regular, patterned variation of social institutions and culture within any system they
wished to examine. Like functionalism, of which it is an updated version,
standard cultural ecology cannot account for differing or variable adaptations—some of which may be dysfunctional or pathological—to the same
technoenvironmental settings (Orans 1975). By failing to see the human
and institutional features of the environment as causal forces in and of
themselves, moreover, it provides a flat and unconvincing picture of complex societies and is unable to address problems now seen to be of great
significance in the modern social sciences.

Regional analysis resembles cultural ecology in that it sees environment
and economic relations as basic explanatory variables. But the economy
that concerns us is not subsistence technology alone; it is that *plus* the
complex of institutions and places that play a role in exchange. Because
we view exchange as the major articulating feature of an economy, we
recognize distance and relative location as fundamental environmental
variables. The institutions that make up an exchange system are seen as
human adaptations to certain economic–environmental facts (population
density, subsistence technology, comparative advantage, division of labor,
and regional economic interdependence), to which other institutions in
turn must adapt. The net effect of the exchange system is such that different adaptations are required in different parts of the system. The
ecosystem model of biotic energy exchange is useful here: The web of relationships brought about by energy exchange creates a particular and distinctive niche for each local system (organism) in the whole. This is more
than an analogy. Energy exchange is as basic to regional organization as it
is to ecosystem organization, for a region exists only to the extent that

human energy is exchanged. Regional systems can, in fact, be seen as particular kinds of ecosystems based on the energy produced by man. It follows that the adaptation of a part (local community) can no more be explained without reference to the system than can the adaptation of an organism be explained without reference to the web of relationships involved in defining its niche.

The standard approach of cultural ecology, however, is to focus on community adaptation, which naturally leads to the study of production (and therefore technology) in the economy. The "ecosystem" is crudely defined as a community and those aspects of the natural environment that impinge on the community—much as some biologists take a pond and describe the relationships within it. Given this orientation, variable and potentially pathological adaptations cannot be explained, nor can linkages among places—indeed, they are no longer of interest. But pondlike (naturally bounded) social systems are rather rare. Much more common, even in "simpler" societies, are open systems in which economic exchange defines the economy every bit as much as do production techniques if not more so. To the extent that a system is open, ecological considerations themselves lead one beyond the single community to considerations of the space economy. Hence, just as we must accord the natural environment and productive techniques their due importance in our models, cultural ecologists should accord spatial considerations and exchange relationships importance in their models.

The advantage of our approach over the standard approach of cultural ecology can be seen in the differing explanations for levels of sociocultural integration. With this concept, Steward was able to utilize ecological explanations for cultural systems. But Steward essentially took on faith the idea that adaptations would differ depending on the level of sociocultural integration, without being able to specify how or why. And while Steward and others (1956) made a valiant attempt to use ecological analysis in a study of a complex society, the model has not generally been fruitful. Steward's followers have focused on the interaction between environment and the tools for exploiting it to explain different levels of integration. But the interaction of man and environment is mediated by organization as well as by tools—the productive capacity of an industrial society vis-à-vis a hunting–gathering society, for instance, is much higher than could be predicted from technoenvironmental advantage alone (cf. Harris 1971:209–217). Moreover, the organizational features of industrial societies are as relevant to the adaptation of a local community as are the industrial tools. The regional approach, with explicit recognition of the organizational features of exchange economies, can specify and even measure different levels of societal integration by using spatial and economic analysis—by examining how many nodal systems are articulated with one another and how fully they are articulated to incorporate different levels of organization. It can do this while paying proper attention to the organizational features implied by different exchange economies, each with its own implications for degree and type of integration. The emphasis is on the interaction of environment and system organization, not just environment and tool, an emphasis that allows perception of and explanations for variability in adaptation to similar technoenvironmental settings.

In many respects regional analysis is more akin to the kind of total system analysis espoused by the new environmentalists (e.g., Flannery 1972; Rappaport 1971; Vayda and Rappaport 1968). Proponents of this approach, building on the conceptual advantage of examining systems rather than institutions, have more sophisticated notions of human–environmental interchange than the standard cultural ecologists and assume that no aspect of culture is less important than another in adaptation. Vayda and Rappaport (1968), for instance, observe that humans adapt not simply to habitat or to selected features of the environment but also to the "cultural" features of the environment produced by their adaptation. In this conceptualization social systems are adapted not only to God-given water but also to their own attempted solutions to problems of water control and pollution. Moreover, ideological orientation is seen to be as important to adaptation as are the subsistence basics. This emphasis on the analysis of total systems moves environmentalism from a particular materialistic position on causality to a general theory of social organization.

The analysis of a system involves examining the order imposed on certain elements connected by some kind of relationship. Complex systems are commonly ordered by hierarchical relationships, while simple systems may be organized by network relationships (Ashby 1960). Understanding the organization of a system requires understanding how, when, and where particular ordering relationships are imposed. The ultimate goal of a systems analysis is to understand these relationships, tesing this understanding by developing a series of rules by which the organization of a system can be simulated and features of it predicted. While regional systems analysis is clearly not advanced to the point of specific prediction, it addresses questions that will ultimately allow prediction, such as the following: What kind of ordering is imposed in different economic and political regimes? What are the causes and the consequences of different kinds of ordering relationships? What is the relationship between ordered systems on the one hand and environmental constraints and features of social organization on the other?

Papers in this volume that are especially concerned with general problems of systemic organization are those by Verdery, Howell, and Appleby. Verdery, in attempting to discover the determinants of Welshness as a politicized ethnic identity in Wales, finds that location in physiologically defined regions is an important predictive variable, but one that can be understood as a determinant only when seen as a component of a larger system. Welshness is not a remnant phenomenon but an emergent one that encompasses a whole process of adaptation to environment, economics, politics, and ideology—a system by which effects of these institutional subsystems are incorporated into a particular identity. Howell uses modern electoral political results to examine cultural and political orientations in a region of Java. She discovers that "primordial" cultural affiliation as well as more ephemeral political orientations can be seen as changing adaptations to complex systems of organization that interrelate economics, ecology, administration, and religion. No one of these subsystems—such as ecology—can be understood causally without attention to its relation to the organization of the other subsystems. Appleby, concerned with variable economic adaptations in a region of Peru, observes that an external economic system plays a critical role in defining the organization of that region. Drawing on historical data, he shows how several adaptations came into being by quite "rational" coping processes that can ultimately be seen as dysfunctional to the internal if not the total system. Olsen reports on other regional studies that describe similar processes of adaptation.

It is noteworthy that Verdery and Howell, by examining local-level systems of organization, find some processes not explicable in economic terms, whereas Appleby, by examining a regional system of organization, can explain some aspects of local adaptation with overarching economic variables. Had Verdery and Howell attempted a regional rather than local-level analysis, no doubt they would have found some patterns of the space economy critical to the overall adaptations in the cases they examine. And had Appleby taken a closer look at local-system adaptations, he might have found other aspects of local adaptation for which the larger regional framework did not account. This does not detract from the particular studies but shows that the full specification of any process requires one to examine *both* levels of organization *and* their interaction with one another. Most of the studies in this volume fall short of being total systems analyses, but they point in that direction insofar as they specify the interaction of many sociocultural variables at a given level of a regional environmental system.

In summary, it can be said that regional analysis espouses the goals of systems theory. It differs from most espousals of that integrating field by offering some concrete proposals about how to view systemic organization; that is, we deal with empirical cases in which the organization and development of a total social system is at issue, and we suggest a number of theoretical models useful for analyzing and comparing system organization and change in these cases. Finally, we are concerned with positive feedback processes (directional change) as well as negative feedback processes (equilibrium states). Significantly, one of the most recent proponents of a systems approach to social organization (Flannery 1972) redirects attention to evolutionary models and proposes that regional analysis and locational models, such as central-place theory, may be necessary for analyzing supracommunity organizing systems and how they change.

SOCIAL ORGANIZATION IN
COMPLEX SOCIETIES

> . . . we can achieve greater synthesis in the study of complex societies by focus-ing our attention on the relationships between different groups operating on different levels of the society, rather than on any one of its isolated segments [Wolf 1956:1074].

> Anthropological work on Chinese society, by focusing attention almost exclu-sively on the village, has with few exceptions distorted the reality of rural social structure [Skinner 1964:32].

Social scientists who deal with urbanized, stratified, "complex" societies are especially aware of the fact that there are many levels of organiza-tion in social systems. Some students of complex societies have even focused on the problem by describing the linkages between communities, cities, and nations (e.g., Adams 1970; Wolf 1956, 1966). Yet the frame-work used by most of them provides no explicit methodology for distin-guishing types and levels of linkages that may differ from institution to institution and from region to region. When faced with the obvious fact that some local systems (those including peasant communities, for example) have important ties outside the face-to-face community, they trace these ties through personal networks from the village outward. The resulting analysis thus rests the integration of the society upon individuals who operate in an organizational vacuum—system brokers who stand Janus-like at the interface of community and region, or even community and state. Such people may in fact exist, but to perform the tasks with which they are credited—integrating community and nation, for instance—in the absence of societal routes or paths through which they not only moved but were expected, brokers between different levels of a complex system would have to be the supermen that perhaps the village-dwelling peasant perceives. In other words, *systems* of supracommunity organization integrate complex societies, and insufficient attention has heretofore been paid to them.

Moreover, students of complex societies place undue emphasis on the differences between complex and simpler societies, implying that entirely different methodologies and analytical models must be utilized to understand the two very different types of societies. But all societies exist in territorial systems with links outside the face-to-face community, and these extracommunity links, which form systems, are important to the environment of any community. At the same time, local levels of organization display similarities across the full range of societal types—when anthropologists compare small peasant communities to small communities in simpler societies, they find much to be held in common (Selby 1974). Credulity is strained only by the assumption that the peasant community is the national or empire society writ small. The model of nodal systems put forth by regional analysis requires no such assumptions. It places communities in both "complex" and "simple" societies in the same analytical framework, so that they contain comparable units for analysis (local-level social systems); yet it still distinguishes societies in level of complexity along a measurable dimension of organization (*levels* of nodal development). By looking at organizational rather than personal linkages between the parts or levels of a society, it also corrects the misguided view in which villages are connected to states by special personages.

What, then, are the organizational systems and integrating mechanisms that we consider special to complex societies? Basically, they are the standard institutions that have always provided the grist for social science mills—administrative, economic, ideological, class, and kinship systems. But each of these is seen to have a hierarchical organization within a territorial system. The spatial organization of layered or nested nodal systems defines places, routes, and roles for the regulated, expected exchange of goods, people, and information, which integrate complex societies into first regional, then national, and sometimes even world systems. It is true that certain personages in the small communities at the bottom nodes of the hierarchical structure have more extensive ties than others to points outside the community; and, to be sure, people rather than territories play the integrating roles. But it is equally true, and much more important for understanding the organization of complex societies, that small communities are organized spatially, economically, administratively, and otherwise in ways that assure a certain amount of systematic input and output with respect to the larger systems of which they are a part. The pattern of community linkage, then, should reflect but should also restructure the general organization of local institutions at each higher level—local system, regional system, macroregion, nation, world.

The levels of organization defined in this view are of special import for understanding societal integration. Nodes at one level of a hierarchy may be of primary importance for integrating kinship systems, nodes at another level for defining administrative systems; but the forms of integration that are basic to simpler societies are not absent in complex ones. People in empires have kinship networks as much as people in simpler societies—there is no simple substitution of "contracts" for "personal contacts." What integrates a complex society are other higher-level systems of organization that define new social groupings, which encompass and redefine old ones. Thus, Crissman finds that the basic institution of marriage still looms large in the life of a modern Taiwanese villager, but its societal locus and import has been restructured by changing market conditions that continually redefine marriage channels as the economy expands. Marriage ties are subsumed under market ties. Jackson, who describes marriage patterns in a much simpler society, finds that marriage plays a more important integrative role in that society and that marriage exchange (rather than market exchange) defines the reach of the regional system. In both cases, marriage reflects certain aspects of the space economy; but in the complex system marriage is a secondary institution and only locally integrative, while in the simpler system it is a primary institution and regionally integrative. These differences, however, also reflect a certain regularity. Adams and Kasakoff show a general spatial pattern for marriage in all types of societies when they correlate group size, territorial range, and percentage endogamy in a cross-societal sample. What determines whether marriage will integrate a local or a regional system depends on density and complexity within the region: If the region is sparsely populated and has a simple economy, marriage ties are cast widely organizing a large undifferentiated territory; but if the region is densely populated and boasts a complex type of economy, marriage ties are confined to a limited territory organizing smaller local systems. That is, numbers of people rather than distance seem to provide the basic constraint on marriage as an integrative, organizing system. These three studies taken together, then, demonstrate the way in which the form and the function of an elementary social institution such as marriage change as a society becomes more complex.

Institutions that play one role at one level often play a different role at another level in complex societies. Beck examines caste organization at both the village and the regional level in India, finding that it is a mechanism for emphasizing status differences at the local level, while at the regional level it is a mechanism for integrating a broad politicoeconomic system. In a contrasting case, Fox finds that lineage organization in India and Scotland, which plays a familial–egalitarian role at the local level, provides the basis for stratification and political leadership at the regional level, where it undergirds the organization of complex territorial systems. Neither Beck nor Fox is able to explain fully how or why single institutions in complex societies take on different functions at different levels, although the fact that they do so plays a crucial role in their analyses. But since their studies point up several areas of inquiry rarely treated before now, to ask them for a full explanation at this point would be asking too much from them. The next step—finding cross-cultural regularities in such institutional transformations as they are redefined by the changed demands made upon them, and testing theories of explanation for them—will take the efforts of many.

In summary, the basic finding in all of the empirical studies of complex societies made here is that their integrating mechanisms are formed from the raw materials that organize all societies, but that these same raw materials take on new forms and roles at higher levels of integration. A complex system of organization is the distinguishing characteristic of complex societies—it is what makes them complex. We should be able to achieve a better understanding of complex societies, therefore, when further attention is given to the ways in which different institutional systems interplay in the context of functionally defined regional systems. It is hoped that the efforts of the contributors to this volume will stimulate similar efforts by others. Only then will the potential of a regional analysis of social systems—Redfield's vision of this endeavor that introduced this essay—be realized.

REFERENCES

Adams, Richard N.
  1970   *Crucifixion by power.* Austin: Univ. of Texas Press.
Ashby, W. R.
  1960   *Design for a brain.* New York: Wiley.
Brookfield, Harold, with Doreen Hart
  1971   *Melanesia: A geographical interpretation of an island world.* London: Methuen.
Christaller, Walter
  1966   *Central places in southern Germany.* Translated by C. W. Baskin. Englewood Cliffs, N.J.: Prentice-Hall. (Originally published as *Die zentalen Orte in Suddeutschland,* 1933.)
Flannery, Kent
  1972   The cultural evolution of civilizations. *Annual Review of Ecological Systems* **3**: 399–426.
Geertz, Clifford
  1963   *Agricultural involution.* Berkeley: Univ. of California Press.
Haggett, Peter
  1966   *Locational analysis in human geography.* London: St. Martin's Press.
Harris, Marvin
  1971   *Culture, man, and nature.* New York: Crowell.
Isard, Walter
  1975   *Introduction to regional science.* Englewood Cliffs, N.J.: Prentice-Hall.
Leach, Edmund R.
  1954   *Political systems of highland Burma.* Boston: Beacon Press.
Lévi-Strauss, Claude
  1953   Social structure. In *Anthropology today,* edited by A. L. Kroeber. Chicago: Univ. of Chicago Press. Pp. 524–553.
Netting, Robert M.
  1974   Agrarian ecology. *Annual Review of Anthropology* **3**: 21–57.
Orans, Martin
  1975   Domesticating the functional dragon: An analysis of Piddocke's potlatch. *American Anthropologist* **77**: 312–328.

Rappaport, Roy
   1968   *Pigs for the ancestors.* New Haven, Connecticut: Yale Univ. Press.
   1971   The sacred in human evolution. *Annual Review of Ecological Systems* **2:** 23–44.
Redfield, Robert
   1941   *The folk culture of Yucatan.* Chicago: Univ. of Chicago Press.
   1956   Societies and cultures as natural systems. *Journal of the Royal Anthropological Institute* **85:** 19–32.
Selby, Henry
   1974   *Zapotec deviance.* Austin: Univ. of Texas Press.
Skinner, G. William
   1964   Marketing and social structure in rural China: Part I. *Journal of Asian Studies* **24:** 3–42.
   1965   Marketing and social structure in rural China: Part II. *Journal of Asian Studies* **24:** 195–228.
Steward, Julian
   1955   *Theory of culture change: The methodology of multilinear evolution.* Urbana: Univ. of Illinois Press.
Steward, Julian (Ed.)
   1956   *The people of Puerto Rico.* Urbana: Univ. of Illinois Press.
Vayda, Andrew, and Roy Rappaport
   1968   Ecology, cultural and non-cultural. In *Introduction to cultural anthropology: Essays in the scope and methods of the science of man,* edited by J. A. Clifton. Boston: Houghton-Mifflin. Pp. 477–497.
Wolf, Eric
   1956   Aspects of group relations in a complex society: Mexico. *American Anthropologist* **58:** 1065–1078.
   1966   Kinship, friendship, and patron–client relations in complex societies. In *The social anthropology of complex societies,* edited by M. Banton. London: Tavistock. Pp. 1–22.

Chapter 2

Regional Social Systems: Linking Quantitative Analysis and Field Work

Stephen M. Olsen
Stanford University

Regional analysis, simply stated, is an attempt to understand social and cultural organization in terms of spatial differentiation and organization. As such, it bears strong relations to geography and in part owes its existence to the vigor of recent developments in human geography.[1] At the same time, regional analysis of social systems follows upon previous attempts within sociology, anthropology, and rural sociology to examine the organization of society in spatial terms. In particular, several overlapping but distinct traditions of research and thought about communities form a backdrop for current efforts in regional analysis. In addition, cultural geography, political geography, and regional sociology, heretofore regarded as of minor importance for regional analysis, can now be of considerable utility because of recent methodological advances. It is my purpose in this essay to point out the ways in which previous approaches have come to dead ends and to argue for a corrective in the self-conscious use of models built on the assumption of variation in space. As a conse-

---

[1] The "new geography" appears to have its center of gravity in economic geography, locational theory, and urban geography, for which Haggett (1966) and Berry and Horton (1970) are excellent introductions. However, useful new developments are not limited to these fields, and the outsider may get some glimpse of the variety of approaches and methods now in use in geography in the surveys by Taafe (1970) and Abler *et al.* (1971), in the journal *Economic Geography,* and in the series *Progress in Geography* (Board *et al.* 1969-).

quence of this recommendation, social scientists will be urged to develop methods that fully allow for and make comparative use of local variation in social organization.

By now, the diffusion of specific research techniques and skills among the various social science disciplines is quite rapid and extensive. It is no longer the case that anthropologists, political scientists, or historians are ignorant or frightened of quantitative techniques developed in economics, geography, or sociology. However, I would like to indicate some of the new purposes to which quantitative techniques can be put and the important new role that older, qualitative techniques can play in systematic comparative community and regional studies. The focus here will be on the organization of communities[2] into *systems* and therefore on the *variation* of local social organization related to community position in a larger system. The focus must also be comparative; a systemic approach necessarily involves comparison of all elements in the system, although a comparative study need not be systemic.

Since the purpose of the studies argued for herein is different from that of previous community-level studies, new kinds of materials and new research techniques may certainly be needed; the other papers in this volume provide a number of excellent concrete examples. I hope to make the same point in more general terms and to indicate the ways in which attitudes toward data and data units will have to change along with the adoption of new techniques. Furthermore, I believe that the standard operating procedure of intensive field work—only recently discussed in much detail or candor—will have to be adapted to accord with the wider angle of vision needed for this endeavor.

COMMUNITY STUDIES

Local communities as objects of study in their own right and as samples of patterns characteristic of a larger society (see Bell and Newby 1972 for

[2] A relatively nonspecific definition of "community" will be assumed in this paper: a population *located with regard to a territory,* but less than the total population involved in significant interaction or exchange. This definition assumes that we will be dealing with multicommunity societies or macroregions and also that two kinds of "ecological" constraints are significant in community formation in the data we will be considering. The first kind I would call purely *spatial* constraints, those involving the "friction of distance" and the benefits of relative location; the second, purely *ecological* constraints, those that localization of scarce resources present to the survival of different populations. The nonspecific definition of "community" allows for multiple levels of community organization, as in such terms as "the metropolitan community," but it is not extended to include groups having no particular territorial base, such as "the professional community" or "the American Jewish community." While leaving open the questions of what constitutes a community and how it is bounded for empirical analysis, the definition does part company with strictly cultural or sociopsychological definitions (see Hillery 1955) and with empirical arguments that spatial constraints cease to be important in community formation under certain conditions.

a comprehensive review) have been important in several social science disciplines for some time. Sociologists, anthropologists, political scientists, and historians have shared many of the same concerns and have looked to one another for comparison, methods, and theory. Despite a healthy degree of controversy among disciplines, much of the community-study literature seems to me to have been hobbled by an unacknowledged metaphor: the small community as a microcosm. Not many went so far as Warner when he said that "To study Jonesville is to study America [1949:xv]," but there is no question that the microcosm metaphor influenced much of what has been written about communities. Because of this, the problem of boundary definition has never been adequately dealt with, and emphasis was placed on the self-contained nature of the communities studied.

This state of affairs arose partly from the methodological strategy of selecting communities that could be easily studied by one or a few researchers. The investigators may have also chosen or found themselves in situations in which boundaries could in fact be sharply drawn, leading them to the conclusion that such was the normal state for communities of a certain type. Lewis has pointed out that Redfield's experience in Mexican communities, which happened to be endogamous, tended to confirm Redfield's preconception of the folk society as "inward looking." Had Redfield studied societies with wider marriage fields, for example, his conception of the folk community and its boundaries might have been very different (Lewis 1965:494). Similar observations can be made of the sociological community studies (cf. Warner and Lunt 1941:5).

The defects associated with a microcosm approach to the local community are not limited to the possible lack of representativeness of the communities studied. This way of conceiving the problem, although partially correct, tends to turn the issue into one of replication: Will similar patterns be found in subsequent studies? Yet it is entirely possible for a series of similarly designed studies to come to the same highly "reliable" but invalid (because incomplete) conclusions. In addition to calling into question the means of selecting communities, criticism of the microcosm metaphor also demands a more adequate approach to the problem of community boundaries and thus to the nature of the entity studied. For a variety of reasons, most intensive studies of small communities have tended to reify their boundaries; they have ignored or minimized relationships outside those boundaries and, partially because of the concern for community anonymity, have often failed to provide information on the importance of position in a system of communities.[3]

---

[3] As an example, Jonesville (Warner 1949) is actually Morris, Illinois, located 20 miles from the old industrial city of Joliet and within 60 miles of Chicago. It must be imagined that class structure and behavior in Jonesville were substantially affected by influences from these centers, including selective migration (cf. Thernstrom 1964) and differential participation in metropolitan culture and social networks.

Redfield's community studies and his attempt to order variation in community organization along the folk-urban continuum have been soundly criticized for their oversimplification (see Lewis 1965). Yet it must be admitted that Redfield's writings were a powerful impetus to keep alive a systemic and comparative view of communities, in his famous phrase, "the little community as a community within communities" (Redfield 1955). However, it was not until Skinner's use of central-place theory as a basis for analyzing rural social structure (1964–1965) that social scientists outside of geography came to realize that systemic and comparative community studies need not depend on the oversimplified folk-urban model. Now scholars in four or five disciplines are carrying out studies that attempt to correct the omissions and distortions of earlier work on local communities, substituting a variety of models of dynamic interconnection between community position and local social and cultural organization. These are the attempts that we collectively label regional analysis.

One group of small-community studies in the earlier period did not fall victim to the appeal of the microcosm or beg the question of community boundaries but was, unfortunately, ignored by other social scientists until recently. Rural sociologists were always confronted very directly with the question of boundaries—criteria for grouping dispersed households and settlements into functional units, degrees of community membership, and change over time. They realized that a fruitful conception of community would have to include villages, towns, open-country hinterlands, and the web of relationships among them. As early as 1915, Galpin had developed empirical methods for delineating communities and relating them in a hierarchical fashion (Galpin 1915; Nelson 1969: Chapter 4), beginning an important and active tradition within rural sociology (Loomis and Beegle 1950: Chapter 6).

Galpin's work in rural sociology predates the development of central-place theory in geography by two decades (Berry and Pred 1965: 76–77), but the professional isolation of rural sociologists from other social scientists had the effect of localizing what can now be seen as a potentially fruitful approach to studying communities and systems of communities. The current work of Frank Young (discussed later) continues this tradition, but with a very distinctively sociological orientation.

Human Ecology

"Human ecology" was long identified with the series of empirical studies of social life in urban settings carried out by the group we know as the Chicago School of urban sociology (Park *et al.* 1925; Park 1952; see Short 1971). As this group pursued its detailed, problem-oriented, and often colorful investigations of life in Chicago during the first third of the century, a few of their number tried to see a larger picture and to develop an analogy between the "natural areas" of a city and niches in an ecological community (Park 1952: Part II; McKenzie, in Park *et al.* 1925). Competition between groups of people for scarce resources and a resulting dominance hierarchy were thought to be reflected in the spatial organization of the city. A parallel was also found to the ecological notion of succession in the spatial patterning of city growth and sequential occupation by different groups. It seems important to discuss human ecology in detail because criticism and reformulation of its concerns form an indispensable context for regional analysis of social systems.

Criticism of human ecology developed along three lines. First, human ecology became identified with a very specific *locational* model derived from the Chicago data, the concentric-zone theory. This was both a theory describing the pattern of urban expansion (Burgess 1927) and the basis for a simple model explaining the distributions of indices of social disorganization (Burgess, in Park *et al.* 1925). A gradient of land values culminating in the central business district, a history of rings of urban growth, and increasing rates of "deviance" (divorce, delinquency, mental illness, and so on) from suburbs to center were thought to be intimately interconnected. Needless to say, alternative empirical models of urban growth were quickly proposed (Haggett 1966:177-181), as were alternative explanations for the ecological patternings of deviance rates.

The Burgess concentric-zone model is, in fact, a useful one if it is taken as reflecting one of several interacting tendencies in population concentration and community growth (for example, the Cambridgeshire study described in Haggett 1966:180-181). It may be thought of as a more general and dynamic version of earlier zonal location models (see Smith, Chapter 1, Volume I). Similarly, as one model of the distribution of social characteristics across space, the Burgess model has stimulated research on the dimensions of urban spatial structure and how these might form a context for social behavior. Going through an intermediate stage of social area analysis, comparative factorial ecology (discussed later) has uncovered remarkable similarity in the spatial structure of modern cities.

Second, the logic of using spatially aggregated data to make inferences about individual-level phenomena (for example, inferring causes of delinquent behavior from the correlation of delinquency rates and rates of some other individual characteristic across census tracts in a city) was soundly and legitimately attacked. Robinson (1950) coined the term "ecological fallacy" for such invalid inference, and for a long time "ecological correlation" had the same connotation. More recently, scholars in several related fields have devoted their attention to proper uses of areal covariation (Dogan and Rokkan 1969; discussed later). These discussions, if properly heeded, remove ecological analysis from the category of a poor and possibly misleading substitute for individual-level studies and demonstrate its necessity in many types of analysis.

Third and most basic, human ecology as developed by the Chicago sociologists was criticized for the way in which it applied the ecological analogy to the human condition—cultural and biological factors falsely set apart from and confused with one another (Alihan 1938; Geertz 1963:5). Hawley (1950), Duncan (1964), and others have recently attempted to restate human ecology in terms more satisfactory from this point of view and to allow for realistic relations between human ecology, biological ecology, and modern evolutionary theory. In my view, regional analysis should attempt to make maximum use of modern human ecology, with its emphasis on population, resources, and adaptive culture, while at the same time making use of models of spatial organization. Regional analysis is thus self-consciously midway between purely ecological and purely locational analysis,[4] whereas Chicago human ecology did not make a clear distinction between the two.

Finally, I would like to argue that the Chicago School's root conception of *community* is an attractive one for those trying to develop a model for regional analysis. Unlike those who sought in the little community a microcosm for a larger world, the Chicago group took as its metaphor a *mosaic*. "The urban community, upon closer inspection, turns out to be a mosaic of minor communities, many of them strikingly different from one another, but all more or less typical [Park 1952:196]." It thus avoided reification of community boundaries and the unjustifiable generalization of single-community patterns to a larger society. It did not retreat from variation in time and space but tried to build both into its basic approach. With the help of ideas and techniques derived from modern geography and other social sciences, regional analysis may go farther in this same attempt.

A final note seems in order concerning the urban studies that developed in the wake of both small-scale community studies and the ecological studies of the Chicago School. The 1950s and 1960s became the era of the large-scale sample survey, the isolated individual or household the accepted unit of analysis, and individual social psychology the dominant theoretical concern. While community structure can sometimes be partially glimpsed from the reports of individuals, more thoroughgoing analysis requires consideration of community location, membership, and actual networks of relationships. With the exception of a few studies done

[4] In Haggett's Venn diagram of the overlap among earth, social, and geometrical sciences (1966:14), human ecology is depicted as having no geometrical (i.e., purely spatial) concerns, and locational analysis no earth science (i.e., purely ecological) concerns. Regional systems analysis can therefore be located at the intersection of geometrical and earth science sets, well within the social sciences.

under the aegis of "social area analysis" (see Rees 1972:326) and some voting studies (see Linz 1969), urban studies of this period seldom made use of even the simplest information on local community location or membership. Perhaps in part because of this omission in the standard methodology, investigators often fell into a "mass society" frame of reference—wherein individuals are only tied into the total social structure directly, without any mediation of localized relationships. Standard sample-survey methodology also typically accepted municipal or census-unit boundaries, unwittingly reifying boundaries perhaps inappropriate to the study of a functioning community.[5] Only recently, the development of network approaches in several disciplines (Laumann 1973; see Southall 1973) and a revival of some of the concerns of the classic Chicago School (see Suttles 1972) have partially reversed these tendencies to ignore locality as a factor in social organization. Comparative community studies and regional analysis as proposed in this paper and volume, along with network studies and the more recent urban community studies, should help to provide a more balanced picture of social organization in complex, urbanized societies.

SPATIAL DISTRIBUTION AND EXPLANATION OF SOCIOCULTURAL PHENOMENA

While the dominant approaches in social science were treating communities and societies as though they were collections (structures, if one prefers) of characteristics having no spatial or temporal dimensions, and very little environment, several more obscure traditions worked on models directly incorporating space, time, and environment in descriptions and explanations of sociocultural organization. These studies were pursued by persons variously identified as cultural anthropologists, sociologists, political scientists, and geographers, but a variety of labeling and relabeling of their essentially similar work has occurred, so it may be easiest to refer simply to "cultural geography," "political geography," and—in between the two—"regional sociology." By brief reference to the similarity of several of these traditions and by more detailed discussion of a few specific analyses, I hope to illustrate the usefulness of both ideas and techniques developed in these diverse fields.

More generally, I hope to emphasize that models constructed to deal with variation at one level (the class structure of a given community, for example) must often be seen as special cases of orderly variation at

[5] I am indebted to Frank W. Young for this observation.

another level. Comparative analysis across cultures, societies, and nations (e.g., Naroll and Cohen 1970) has provided the most vigorous demonstration of this point in previous research. Regional systems analysis can provide an important complement to comparative cross-cultural studies by providing models of sociocultural variation within societies or culture areas.

Cultural Geography[6]

In American cultural anthropology a small group of scholars has mapped the distribution of many reported cultural traits, especially of aboriginal North American groups (see Driver 1970). From these maps it is apparent that spatially contiguous groups often share more cultural traits than those farther apart. This similarity, it has been argued, may reflect historical relatedness (for example, migration followed by separation) or contact between different groups and subsequent "borrowing" of cultural traits. Both are often called diffusion, although the diffusing element can be either culture or population. Fairly simple quantitative methods have been developed and this geographical–historical approach has been pitted against explanations that look to the functional interrelationship of two or more traits (e.g., Driver 1966). Most comparativists have been more interested in functional relationships and have therefore been concerned to *rule out* diffusional associations among traits. The developing methodology of comparative cultural and social anthropology generally tries to structure samples in such a way as to exclude the possibility of simultaneous diffusion of culture traits (Naroll 1970b). However, some proposed methods do not exclude such relationships but, rather, attempt to weigh the relative importance of diffusion and functional association.[7] Despite the use of the term "diffusion," I believe that there has been no significant influence from the large geographical literature on that subject (Olsson 1965) or from geographical methods of measuring spatial association. And yet it is clear that the comparativists have come up with measures very

[6] The terms "cultural geography" and "political geography" are used herein to describe studies that have developed mainly *outside* the geographical profession. With the exception of the diffusion studies associated with the pioneering work of Torsten Hägerstrand (1953), the field of cultural geography appears to have been dominated by its teaching function, but some attempts at more scholarly development (e.g., Wagner and Mikesell 1962) have appeared. For political geography, see Prescott (1972).

[7] Naroll (1970) describes two of his five "solutions" to Galton's problem as allowing a direct comparison of diffusional and functional associations, and he mentions two other refinements developed by others. It is Naroll's matched-pair method that comes closest to methods developed by geographers, especially if, as Naroll suggests, the number of contiguous cultures is increased from a pair to three or four in a cluster.

similar to those used by statistical geographers—for example, the contiguity ratio, which will be discussed later.

European anthropologists pursuing ethnological or folklore studies have also mapped the distribution of cultural traits, usually those of the "traditional" peasant or regional cultures of Europe and often with implicit concern for the disappearance of these cultures in the face of homogenizing influences from national and world centers. On a purely descriptive level these scholars have produced a number of massive ethnographic and linguistic atlases for various regions of several European countries (see Trudgill 1975). When they have turned to explanation, their ideas are very similar to those of the American cultural anthropologists, emphasizing diffusion processes and the reconstruction of time and place of trait origin (Weiss 1952). Perhaps because these diffusion processes are seen as occurring across a landscape differentiated by transportation routes, cities and their hinterlands, national boundaries, and so on, the connections between cultural distribution and the organization of space as studied by geographers have been more obvious than for the American Indian studies, and the European ethnological work has been retrospectively incorporated in the field of cultural geography (Wagner and Mikesell 1962). Insights and methods from both strands of the geographically relevant cultural anthropology should be of use in the development of regional analysis, a point I will return to later.

Regional Sociology

In the United States, studies somewhat similar to those of the European ethnologists were pursued, especially by a small number of sociologists in Southern universities, under the general title of "regionalism."[8] The main thrust of this movement, it seems fair to say, was to document the cultural distinctiveness of certain macroregions in the United States—particularly the Southeast—and the particular problems brought to them by uneven economic development between regions. Regionalism and regional sociology were to be concerned primarily with folkways, and the term "folk–regional society" was coined (Odum and Moore 1938:416–419). Implicitly, regional sociology was amelioristic, and even paternalistic, because the folkways of the disadvantaged region were often seen as lagging behind what was required for adaptation to a technologically changing society and Afro-American folkways in the South were a primary object of study (Odum and Jocher 1945:6–9).

[8] The classic statement is Odum and Moore (1938). Odum and Jocher (1945) give a comprehensive review ("From Community Studies to Regionalism") and bibliography ("Toward Regional Documentation") of the empirical studies on which regionalism and regional sociology were erected.

In general, this group of scholars, though prolific, do not seem to have left us much to build on in the way of ideas and methods, and regional sociology is far from active at the present time (Reed 1972b). However, there are some encouraging signs. Sociologists are once again addressing themselves to problems of regional delineation, interpretation, and change over time (Gastil 1971; McKinney and Bourque 1971), activities long left to geographers. Even more interesting, however, is sociological analysis of *regional identity*—an organization of cultural distinctiveness that is not quite reducible to the sharp regional socioeconomic discrepancies of the past or necessarily extinguished by the demonstrable narrowing of those differences in the present. Reed's study entitled *The Enduring South* (1972a) uses reanalysis of nationwide attitude surveys to examine Southern regional imagery and identification, as well as key elements of the Southern way of life. In addition to being substantively and methodologically interesting, Reed's findings bring out two pivotal meanings of a "regional effect," ones that will appear again and again as we proceed.

Reed begins by noting that there are still important socioeconomic differences between the macroregions of the United States, the most dramatic single division of which is between the southeastern states and the rest of the nation.[9] However, these discrepancies are decreasing (McKinney and Bourque 1971), and it might be imagined that as socioeconomic differences between regions are reduced to zero, cultural differences will also disappear, either immediately or with some allowance for "cultural lag." Through the technique of test-factor standardization, Reed attempts to discover whether this is in fact the case. Test-factor standardization is a method for artificially equating South and non-South on the basis of occupational distribution, rural–urban residence, and education.[10] What he finds is that this kind of statistical standardization does sometimes eliminate or reduce regional differences in attitudes and behavior. But considerable differences remain. Southerners are still "more likely than non-Southerners to be conventionally religious, to accept the private use of force (or potential for it), and to be anchored in their home-place [Reed 1972a:83]."

In statistical terms Reed has identified a pattern of residual variation— that is, variation in certain cultural patterns that is left unexplained by the direct effects of membership in major socioeconomic categories, categories that are at present unevenly distributed across regions. Reed

[9] Berry's regionalization of the U.S. economy in 1954 (summarized in Haggett 1966:255–256) yielded an initial Southeast–remainder dichotomy. It seems likely that a contemporary replication would show similar results.

[10] See "Methodological Appendix" in Reed (1972a). Test-factor standardization is a simple form of multivariate analysis and should be related to the following discussion of multivariate analysis based on correlation and regression techniques.

explains these regional residuals in terms of (1) the relative efficacy of Southern institutions of socialization to a localized cultural tradition, and (2) what Frank Young (1970) has called "reactive solidarity," the cohesiveness of a lifestyle seen as threatened by powerful forces from the "outside." Despite the plausibility of these interpretations, they share a fault of all residual arguments in that further introduction of competing variables (in this case, socioeconomic)[11] might reduce the unexplained residual to a negligible quantity. Is regional analysis of this kind, then, merely a precarious search for residual variation that cannot be attributed to the generally more powerful social structural variables, residuals that may be quickly eliminated by further structural analysis? I would take a different view, for two reasons.

First, once a spatially distributed pattern of residuals is demonstrated, specific *measures* of the hypothesized causes of regional differentiation (for example, Reed's ideas about socialization institutions or reactive solidarity) should be introduced. These variables can then be linked into a "causal model" (Blalock 1964; an example appears later) that, although concerning only correlations at one point in time, would at least suggest the independent or mediating impact of such spatial–organizational factors. This would be one meaning of a regional effect, although we might very well wish to rename it to reflect the specific process thereby identified.

Second, there is a meaning of a regional effect even simpler than this. I would argue that identifying and interrelating regional variation, socioeconomic and cultural, is a legitimate and valuable contribution in its own right. The fact that the American South *is* characterized by both socioeconomic and cultural discrepancies from the rest of the nation is an important fact and would remain so even if it were shown that the cultural differences are completely "explainable" by regional discrepancies on social structural variables. It is significant for examination of social and cultural phenomena within the region, and it is significant for understanding the system of regions that makes up the nation.

There is, then, a distinction between regional analysis as, on the one hand, the attempt to specify parsimoniously the variables underlying spatial variation and to shift attention to the abstract processes involved

---

[11] A further possibility is that there exist *indirect* effects of the original explanatory variables; for example, the effects of a concentration of poor, less well-educated people in a particular area may not be exhausted by looking at the behavior of the people who themselves have those characteristics. The richer, better educated in that area behave in a *context* set by the poor and less educated. This is known as a contextual or structural effect (see Dogan and Rokkan 1969). However, a formal contextual effect must be specified by a substantive theory of *why* the context should make a difference, and I assume that hypotheses such as those proposed by Reed can be seen as providing that specification.

therein, and, on the other hand, the more synthetic approach that argues that spatial localization of a *complex* of factors is itself an important social structural phenomenon and not simply a geographic fact.[12]

Political Geography

For want of a better term, "political geography" encompasses those studies in which it has been possible to map measures of political allegiance or opposition. Most common have been studies of election returns, sometimes called "electoral geography" or "electoral sociology," but these are clearly of a piece with research into the distribution of both "public opinion" and collective political action, such as rebellion. These studies have been a staple of French political science for many years (see Meyriat 1960:47–60), and they have received the greatest methodological sharpening by French social scientists in recent years. Although electoral geography studies have also been important in Britain, Scandinavia, and elsewhere in Europe (see Prescott 1972: Chapter 4), I will focus on some examples from the French and Anglo-American studies because their greater methodological sophistication can both act as a guide for regional analysis and make it clear how the latter may make a distinctive contribution.

Political geography has often demonstrated a localization of political support or opposition in areas that are socially or culturally distinct. The most dramatic example is the strong association in France between areas of devout Roman Catholic religious adherence and right-wing political activity (see maps in Derivy and Dogan 1971). Although the fit is close, it is also clear that the association is modified by other factors that are dis-

[12] This is similar to the distinction made by Hartshorne (1959) between regional and systematic geography. Outside geography, the divergence is often reflected in attitudes toward maps in ecological research. In one view, cartographic representation of spatially distributed phenomena is useful primarily as a means of discovering correlations between several distributions, as when one overlaps maps of two different phenomena to help account for one by the other. The relationships so spotted can then be translated into mathematical expression, and the only further use of cartographic representation is in locating errors of prediction (residuals) and thereby possibly identifying further variables to improve prediction (Dogan and Rokkan 1969:9–10). In another view, maps are of intrinsic interest because of the way they can represent several major social phenomena simultaneously (but see Marchand 1975) while at the same time retaining a rather direct connection with the phenomena of space, relative location, and natural environment. In fact, it is the presumption that these factors will make some contribution to understanding of social phenomena that a priori justifies mapping. Maps also provide a basis for continuity in social research, as when boundaries established for one phenomenon prove to be significant for another (see discussion of regionalization) or when they do not do so as they might have been expected to. For example, Weiss (1952) found that a major ethnological boundary in Switzerland, the so-called "Reuss border," coincides with neither linguistic, religious, nor contemporary political boundaries.

tributed spatially—for example, urbanization and its effect on class structure. To test for the relative effect of such variables, political geography
has adopted a whole family of multivariate statistical techniques that
allow researchers to go far beyond the conclusions that can be drawn, say,
by overlapping of maps. In fact, political geography seems to have gone
farther in development of quantitative techniques appropriate to regional
analysis than any other field in the social sciences except geography.

The most important and commonly used technique in political geography is multiple regression. Localities are treated as clusters of statistical
characteristics, each a potential predictor variable for a political outcome
or criterion variable—for example, voting for the party in power. Simple
and multiple correlation coefficients demonstrate how much the spatial
variation in the criterion variable is responsive to spatial variation in the
predictor variables. Partial correlation and regression coefficients tell
which of the predictors accounts for the greatest part of the variation in
the outcome variable and, allowing for the first predictor's effects, which
has the next greatest effect, and so on.

Most of what we mean, for example, by French political regionalism is
probably captured by the twin facts of regional differences in religious
adherence and social class composition as determined by urbanization
(Derivy and Dogan 1971; McRae 1958). However, this does not exhaust
the significance of regionalism, and a regional variable in fact manifests
itself after these facts have had their due. One way this might happen
empirically is through the residual term in a regression equation—the
variance left unexplained after the linear effects[13] of all predictor variables
have been taken into account (Thomas 1960, reprinted in Berry and Marble 1968). This residual can be dealt with in two ways: by searching for
further variables to reduce this residual or by attempting to demonstrate
statistical "interaction" effects using analysis of variance and covariance
(Dogan 1969). In the latter case we would be arguing for a regional effect
in still a different way—that a region gets its character from a specific
combination of values of several variables.

A recent attempt by an American sociologist to come to grips with
regional differences in British voting patterns, although not completely
successful, is interesting for the way it tries to make use of residual
variance in regression equations. This analysis is also substantively
interesting because the author proposes a theory of "peripheral sectionalism" and reactive ethnic solidarity based upon the culturally linked
economic disadvantage of regional minorities. Hechter (1975) began with
Conservative Party voting statistics, against which he compared census-

---

[13] There are certainly important instances of phenomena in which nonlinear bivariate relationships should be assumed. Blalock's (1967) propositional inventory of minority group relations shows, for example, that majority response to changing proportion of minority group is
very unlikely to follow a straight line.

type measures of demographic structure and industrialization, wealth, religious affiliation, and language use for the 86 countries of the United Kingdom at intervals between 1885 and 1966. Using these data, he demonstrates that 10 to 30 percent (depending on the year) of the variance in Conservative voting can be statistically attributed to an industrialization factor,[14] but that a large nonrandom residual remains after this social structural explanation has been taken into account. The residual is spatially concentrated around the "Celtic fringe" and northern regions of Britain, and it is correlated with measures of Celtic culture and religious nonconformity to the dominant Anglican Church (Hechter 1975:221–226). He thus regards this residual as itself a measure of "peripheral sectionalism," and he examines whether this phenomenon decreases over time (along with the supposedly homogenizing, class-orienting effects of industrialization); he also examines the relationship between economic disadvantage and cultural distinctiveness.

Because of the complex relationships between the set of predictors he was using to explain voting patterns and income differentials, Hechter resorted to several kinds of refinements of the more familiar multiple regression techniques already described. For example, he knew that there were positive spatial correlations between measures of industrialization and extent of nonconforming religious affiliation (one of the major indices of cultural distinctiveness) and that use of either variable would carry with it part of the variance in fact attributable to the other. Since he was interested in showing the importance of the cultural variables, however, he first predicted the values that the cultural variables would take if they were a reflection only of the industrialization variables and used the remainder (the actual values above those predicted) of the cultural variables to predict voting patterns. This is known as two-stage or stage-wise multiple regression (Blalock 1971: Part III). The purified "cultural residuals" were usually more powerful predictors of Conservative voting than all the measures of industrialization, and they were also important but declining predictors of county income (Hechter 1975:318–320).

Finally, in order to introduce some notion of a sequence of causal relationships, Hechter turns to another refinement of multiple regression, path analysis (Land 1969). This allows him to look not only at the direct and independent effects of structural and cultural variables on political outcomes but also at county income as an intermediate effect, influencing in its turn the political outcome variable (Hechter 1975:330–333).

It is clear from Hechter's analysis that the differing political orientation of the British periphery did not disappear with the industrialization of the kingdom, most of Wales in particular remaining quite distinct in its pat-

---

[14] Variables that in a factor analysis of British county data (Hechter 1975:151–153) were all part of an industrialization factor (see discussion on the interpretation of factor analysis applied to ecological data).

terns. It is also clear that the linking of economic disadvantage to cultural allegiance is a factor in this political outcome and that, unlike other British regions, the whole of Wales has slipped more and more into a peripheral relationship to the national economy and culture of Britain. Unfortunately, Hechter did not take full advantage of the potential of his data for decisively demonstrating the dynamics of the reactive theory of ethnic or regional solidarity. Although his data extend over a crucial period of transformation of the British nation, each analysis is at one point in time, and the temporal dynamics of the spread and effects of industrialization over the British national space are, if not lost, at least not clarified as they might have been. Several kinds of techniques suggest themselves as means of capturing the dynamic or sequential character of causation initially observed cross-sectionally across space. One approach developed by geographers interested in diffusion dynamics will be discussed in detail, but the format of Hechter's data[15] suggests that a longitudinal or panel analysis—wherein the causally active variable is expected to produce an effect on an outcome variable after a suitable temporal lag (Heise 1970)—could be attempted and would provide substantial buttress to the validity of the model proposed.[16] It is clear, nonetheless, that Hechter's work is noteworthy for the application of the whole family of multiple regression techniques to regional data of great interest.

PROBLEMS OF APPLICATION OF MULTIVARIATE TECHNIQUES

Through a number of illustrations drawn chiefly from the field of political geography, I have attempted to establish that multivariate statistical analysis constitutes one promising strategy for regional analysis. There are, however, several specific problems I would like to raise with regard to the underlying purposes of using multivariate statistical analysis of areal data. These concern the derivation of descriptive regional clusters and boundaries from quantitative materials, the distinction between descriptive and explanatory use of multivariate techniques, the problem of the scope of the areal unit of analysis and its internal variation, and, finally, the treatment of space itself in analysis of areal distributions.

[15] Primarily that the data are for aggregated units, not points. Some sociologists (Hoiberg and Cloyd 1971) have advocated conversion of initially grouped data to point data by the assumption of continuous variation in space. As the discussion of religious versus social class homogeneity of French *départements* suggests, such an assumption would have to be justified in substantive or theoretical terms (see p. 44).

[16] Panel analysis applied to ecological units smaller than nation-states has been relatively rare (see Duncan *et al.* 1961:160–174). A very sophisticated project of considerable substantive as well as methodological interest is Hannan (1975).

Regionalization

When social or cultural phenomena are arrayed spatially, it will often be desirable to group the data into regions or areas that exhibit some kind of unity. Only by grouping can we eliminate relatively atypical local variation or provide the basis for cartographic representation; at the same time, systematic procedures can provide an empirical basis for the units and boundaries of comparative study. Identical procedures apply no matter what scale is involved—from areas of a city to regions of the world—and the term "regionalization" is usually applied to methods of delineating such homogeneous or otherwise unitary areas.

In human geography, regionalization is most often based on multiple criteria, most recently by an array of multivariate statistical procedures collectively labeled "numerical taxonomy" (Abler *et al.* 1971: Chapter 6; Berry 1966, 1967). Berry has outlined three steps in such a numerical analysis:

1. *Factor analysis* as a tool for systematically exploring the many relationships between the variables we use to characterize places, to determine the precise nature and bases of regional structure.
2. *Dimensional analysis,* to determine the degree of similarity of each pair of places studied in terms of regional economic structure.
3. *Grouping analysis,* to cluster into regions contiguous sets of similar places [1966:193].

These techniques are intimately related to one another and to others previously discussed in this paper, and it seems worthwhile making explicit just what it is they do.

Factor analysis or principal components analysis[17] applied to areal units is now usually termed "factorial ecology" (Berry 1971; Rees 1972). It begins with a matrix of correlation coefficients describing the pair-wise

---

[17] Principal components analysis is the more straightforward mathematical procedure of determining the latent roots of a matrix—in other words, hypothetical linear functions that successively approximate the correlations of the original data. Common factor analysis assumes that each variable of the matrix, in addition to being related to each of the other variables, carries with it its own degree of unique variance, often thought of as measurement error. This additional source of variance in the true factor analysis model requires that estimates be made of the "communality" of each variable with the others in the matrix. Common usage, however, does not distinguish these two models, and the term "factor analysis" is often applied to both. An additional complication that is somewhat controversial in the geographical literature is the subsequent imposition of simplicity constraints (e.g., minimizing the number of factors that are strongly related to any single variable). This is called "rotation," of which there are several varieties including some which allow correlation between *factors* (see Giggs and Mather 1975). Hunter (1972) discusses empirical criteria for choosing among the many options in factor analysis. Nie *et al.* (1975) provides a clear, nontechnical introduction and references for each of the programs in its widely used series of computer programs, including most of the procedures discussed in this paper.

association of spatially distributed characteristics, just as does regression analysis. Here, however, factor analysis parts company with regression techniques in that no variable or set of variables is singled out as criterion or predictor. Rather, the interrelations of all the variables entered and the way different subsets thereof "hang together" are used to construct a set of unmeasured variables (factors or components) that represent the simplest ways of reproducing the original matrix of correlations, within the restriction that the new variables are not correlated with one another.[18] The extent to which the original correlations can be reproduced and the number of factors required to do so (the factor structure) will vary depending on the nature of the data analyzed. From the original variables and their weights in deriving the factor (factor loadings), estimates can be made of where on the new variables a given unit falls (factor scores). Factor scores have the advantage of succinctly summarizing related variables, and the factor structure (number of factors) is a measure of the complexity of areal differentiation.

The recent efflorescence of ecological studies using factor analytic techniques has been made possible by the development of high-capacity computers and by the world-wide increase in governmental social accounting, particularly so-called "small-area statistics" (Brulard and Van der Haegen 1972). The scale of units subjected to factor analysis ranges from nation-states to wards or census tracts within cities (Rees 1971:223–224), with the preponderance being of the small statistical units that are available for most modern urban areas. This preponderance is largely due to the continuity of interest in urban subcommunities or "natural areas," as first stated by the Chicago group of urban sociologists (Rees 1972). An impressive degree of similarity or interpretable variance has appeared in the spatial structure of a wide range of modern cities, allowing the development of a rudimentary theory of resources, preferences, and subgroup residential location (Berry and Horton 1970: Chapter 10).

Of most direct interest to regional analysis are the smaller number of studies in which factor analysis has been applied to intermediate-scale units within nation-states (see bibliographic table, Berry 1971:223–224). Particularly interesting is Gould's (1970) investigation of the spread of

[18] Several multivariate procedures closely related to factor analysis do involve a theoretically determined ordering of the data, making them somewhat less purely formal. Canonical analysis computes linear functions of two sets of variables—as determined by the analyst—such that covariance among the sets is maximized. Ray (1971) used canonical analysis to investigate the relationship between economic variables, on the one hand, and ethnic culture variables, on the other, in Canadian national space. Discriminant analysis computes linear functions of a single set of variables, but in such a way that the functions best separate or order data units as specified by the analyst. In regional analysis, discriminant analysis can be used to isolate areas conforming more and less to a regional type (cf. Davies 1972). For general discussions, see Nie *et al.* (1975) and Cooley and Lohnes (1971).

indices of "modernization" across the national space of Tanzania at successive intervals from the 1920s to the early 1960s. In this case, factor analysis was applied to units in an areal grid[19] mapped from administrative-district social accounting data. The factor structure demonstrates the strong spatial association of virtually all the variables colonial and postcolonial governments have thought fit to report for subnational units of their territory. One may think of this as a "modernization" factor, although "administrative penetration" is closer to the content of most of the variables and is perhaps less ambiguous. Factor scores, representing the summary measure of "modernization" were mapped onto the grid units, and inspection of their spatial distribution suggested that "when we speak of modernization we are clearly discussing an emerging and strengthening urban system [Gould 1970:169]."

> What we have seen emerging in the space called Tanzania between 1920 and 1963, and underlying the very modernization process we have tried to measure and structure, are the dynamics of that most spatial of systems—the central-place structure; a *system* of *nodes* of various *sizes,* at differing *distances,* *linked* with varying intensities, influencing areas *contiguous* and *between,* structuring, focusing and serving their hinterlands, and acting as emergent poles of attraction for the surrounding population. For a crucial element in the development of central places is a rural-to-urban migration. In the African context this means the breaking of old allegiances to extended family, traditional authority, unquestioned belief, own people, and familiar place, and the forging of new alliances in the very process of questioning the old. And so, underlying any theory of modernization in space and time, there must be a deeper theory of the dynamics of central-place systems [Gould 1970:169; emphasis in original].[20]

Mapping of factor scores onto the original areal units is, in effect, a means of regionalization, especially where, as in Gould's modernization study, the factor structure is relatively simple. A more systematic procedure, capable of handling more complex, multifactor, areal differentiation, is suggested by Berry in the second and third steps of geographic numerical taxonomy. What he calls "dimensional analysis" (1966:193) involves calculation of the degree of similarity of each pair of

[19] Haggett (1966: Chapter 7) discusses various solutions to the problem of data collection units, including overlaying of regular grids on irregular administrative units. Markoff and Shapiro (1973) faced a similar problem in relating data obtained from overlapping reporting units in prerevolutionary France. Rather than assign all measures to a neutral grid, they chose to relate all their measures to the units for which primary dependent variables were available, and they developed methods for estimating variables across overlapping units. They also discuss the question of choice among competing units of analysis.

[20] From *Tanzania 1920–63: The Spatial Impress of the Modernization Process,* by Peter Gould, WORLD POLITICS, vol. XXII, no. 1 (copyright © 1970 by Princeton University Press. Reprinted by permission of Princeton University Press.

areal units on the major dimensions (factors) emerging from the factor analysis. This amounts to calculating distance between the units, not in two-dimensional physical space, but rather in n-dimensional factor space (Berry 1967).[21] In Berry's third step the similarity or distance matrix of all pairs of places is subjected to systematic grouping analysis, of which there are several varieties (Berry 1967:236-237). Grouping procedures are hierarchical, so that one can look for an optimum balance between the number of units grouped together and the amount of detail lost in the grouping process; if a still more objective determination of "natural" clusters is desired, Berry (1967:242-245) proposes a test based on the contiguity ratio (discussed later).

Either factor-score maps or grouping analysis applied to factor-similarity measures may produce physically dispersed but statistically similar "regional types" rather than regions as we usually think of them. Therefore, it is necessary to consider, and perhaps impose, a contiguity restraint on the grouping (cf. Abler et al. 1971:182-188). Berry (1966:198) also points out that unless one is willing to accept, for example, "a region comprising contiguous places that form a complete circle around some other region," one may also need to impose a physical compactness restraint on the grouping. All of this suggests that one needs to develop an explicit conception of the end purpose or purposes of regionalization. From our point of view, it seems necessary to develop a sociological conception of what a region or regional system is and what it does.

Most regional classification has been used with areal data of a structural nature—that is, data applying to each areal unit independently (Berry 1966:189; Rees 1972:267). This results in the production of formal or uniform regions (Haggett 1966:242). Another line of thinking has sought regional unity in the systematic organization of *dissimilar places* and their *relations*—that is, functional or nodal regions. Structural material is generally much more readily available than is dyadic or relational data, so it is often necessary to make inferences from the former to the latter, as Gould did in his discussion of the Tanzanian factor analysis, or, indeed, as was done by Christaller (1933) in his analysis of number of telephones as an indicator of the central-place system of southern Germany. Central-place theory, of course, implies a relationship between service facilities (a structural characteristic of each place) and transaction flows between places. Several recent studies have applied the procedures of numerical taxonomy to group central-place types (e.g., Smith, Chapter 8, Volume I) and thus, among other things, provide an objective regionalization based upon assumed flows.

[21] Dimensional analysis includes a whole family of specific techniques, including multidimensional scaling and smallest-space analysis. Explanation of these techniques and examples of their use are given in Laumann (1973), Young and Young (1973:91-93), and Smith (in Volume I).

In cases in which actual transactional flows can be measured, such as volume of trade or number of telephone calls, several quantitative methods have been proposed. Berry (1966) has argued that the same techniques of numerical taxonomy can be applied to transaction data and has done so for interregional trade in India. Factor analysis was applied to extract the main dimensions of the flow of trade, and these were in turn subjected to distance scaling and grouping. In a still further step, Berry made explicit the connection between formal (uniform) and functional (nodal) regionalizations. By means of canonical correlation (see footnote 18), he was able to demonstrate empirically a high relationship of the structural characteristics of various Indian regions and trade flows between them. However, factor analysis of flows between pairs of areal units does not seem particularly able to deal with the hierarchical relationships that characterize nodal regions. For such systems, it is necessary to take into account both direct and indirect connections. Although not yet extensively developed, graph theory may provide a means of doing so (Nystuen and Dacey 1961).

Description and Explanation in Areal Analysis

I have argued that a legitimate meaning of regional analysis is of a descriptive kind. Certainly part, perhaps the largest part, of what we mean by "regionalism" or "a regional effect" is a unique combination of values on a number of major variables. Even if we have "accounted for" a region's character in this way, it remains true that these features must be taken into account in investigations within the region. However, with the use of such complex statistical procedures, it is important to keep clear a distinction between descriptive and explanatory purposes to which the techniques may be put.

The statistical techniques described in the preceding section—factor analysis, dimensional analysis, and grouping analysis—are purely formal in the sense that they can be applied to any set of data. There is no assurance that the results will reflect the most important or theoretically relevant aspects of reality (Marchand 1975:118). In fact, these objective techniques pose a dilemma for the analyst. If one does not impose explicit theoretical constraints on acceptable solutions, then the results may prove uninterpretable or, worse, fallaciously interpretable in a causal sense (Armstrong 1967). If one does impose prior constraints on acceptable solutions, one runs the risk of ignoring what the data have to tell or of inadvertently constructing a tautology.[22] Thus, it appears most advisable

[22] If one assumes that an underlying dimension exists and that one's purpose is merely to provide an empirical measure thereof, then dropping measures that complicate the picture may be justified. However, if a scale construction technique—factor analysis, Guttman scale, or whatever—is used as empirical evidence of the existence of a unitary underlying process, then any screening, before or after the analysis, of potential measures is illegitimate.

to adopt the stance suggested by Janson (1969) concerning ecological factor analysis, that these are very useful *descriptive* techniques but ones that must be used in a tentative manner.

While careful work of a descriptive kind is necessary in any scholarly or scientific enterprise, the ultimate judge of any classificatory system is its usefulness in relation to other types of phenomena—that is, the part it plays in a system of explanation. Peter Gould, in characterizing as descriptive the results of his factor analysis of modernization in Tanzania, reminds us that "Description is not theory and only theory is explanation [1970:170]." The direction in which one proceeds, however, and the varia bles included in one's theory will depend upon discipline and interests.

I cannot prejudge where geographers will venture to provide the kind of theory Gould feels is needed (for previous theoretical directions, see Berry and Pred 1965). However, Gould has in fact pointed to many of the variables that interest sociologists and anthropologists: rural–urban migration, analysis of "traditional" social organization, and the emergence of new forms of social and political organization in the context of altered spatio-material conditions. Whether these variables will be entered as independent or dependent variables—while extremely important for the clarity of specific analyses—may not be important in the longer-run development of a system-oriented theory of social and economic organization in a spatial and temporal context. The contributions to the present volume are all aimed at partially redressing the imbalance created by the dramatic progress of geographers within recent years, clearly calling for parallel and, hopefully, contributing work by sociologists, anthropologists, political scientists, and others.

The Areal Unit of Analysis

I would like to turn now to problems concerning the scope of areal units used in either explanatory or descriptive statistical procedures. These problems have been raised in the context of the so-called "ecological fallacy" and in criticism of the descriptive utility of ecological statistics. Robinson (1950) pointed out that the size and sometimes even the direction of a "relationship" between two variables could be altered depending upon the amount of aggregation involved in the unit of analysis. He presumes that interest is always attached primarily to individuals and therefore that the lower the level of aggregation (preferably none) the better. More recently, however, sociologists have argued that interest may well attach to any of several levels of analysis (Dogan and Rokkan 1969) and that the effect of aggregation on relationships ought to be investigated empirically.

The matter may be grasped intuitively by thinking of maps shaded to indicate distribution of some property or variable. We feel uncomfortable with such maps when the scale of shaded units is so large as to obscure variability we know to exist within them or when conventional boundaries seem not to coincide with our understanding of the distribution of the phenomena. Maps of characteristics of U.S. states are an obvious example, but the same principle holds for units of any degree of aggregation, such as the census tracts upon which urban social-area analysis is usually based. The fact that a mean can be calculated and mapped for such a unit should not obscure the fact that similar means can be generated from radically different distributions and dissimilar means result from unequal groupings of similar subunits.

There seem to be two separable issues involved here, the *scale* of units and the *manner of aggregation* from points to areal units. Logically, the degree of spatial association between two variables is dependent on the extent to which the territorial unit has been subdivided; if there is only one unit, there is by definition complete association. Empirically, various authors have shown how scale can influence the strength and even direction of spatial associations. Collier's analysis of tree and house coverage in aerial photographs of highland Chiapas yielded different degrees of association when three different grid scales were used (Collier 1974:89–92). Lebart (1969), in a successive grouping of French *départements* based on graph theory, demonstrated that the tendency of socioeconomic variables to be similar in adjacent areas (spatial contiguity or autocorrelation) is so dependent on scale that a high contiguity ratio at one scale necessitates a reciprocally low measure at other scales. Collier somewhat pessimistically concludes that recognition of scale dependence of spatial relationships necessitates search of "each possible variable interrelation at every possible scale of analysis [1974:90]," but I would prefer to say that theoretical analysis of the units within which processes are thought to occur must accompany empirical search for relationships at different scales.

Turning to the problem of aggregation, the most sophisticated students (e.g., Hannan 1971; Hammond 1973) have realized that error due to aggregation comes about when the criteria by which units at one level are grouped together themselves vary across units. Very often, physical propinquity is a criterion by which units—say, households—are aggregated into larger units for which data may be available—census tracts, townships, or counties—but the way this criterion is applied may not be consistent across units, or even random, but systematically varying. When this is the case, some units may be appropriate descriptive units, corresponding to a "natural community," and others not. In the context of an explanatory model, the variable "grouping principle" may itself be related to one or more elements in the model being tested, and the error introduced is therefore correlated and confounding.

More concretely, the historical and social structural significance of the Anglo-American county and the French *département* clearly varies from national center to national periphery and from areas of early settlement to areas of later settlement (Stephan 1971). It seems quite possible, therefore, that descriptive statistics computed from data aggregated at the county or *département* level will be influenced by this differential significance and that several variables in a causal model based on such data might be influenced in common, distorting understanding of the causal processes involved.

While acknowledging that analysis must often proceed on the basis of "prepackaged" data, usually as grouped by the administrative apparatus collecting them, the type of regional analysis I have in mind would try to build up a picture of "effective units" using a variety of methods. Other papers in this volume are addressed to the question of how this might best be done. The researcher must take advantage of any knowledge he or she can obtain on the internal variation within administratively designated units in order to determine their degree of fit with "natural units."

Reed, for example, in his study of Southern regional identity in the United States, found it impossible to exploit the intraregional spatial variation that is apparent in his data on intensity of group identification and preference for Southern cultural traits (Reed 1972a:16–17). If these intraregional differences in "Southernness" merely reflect the spatial distribution of structural variables on which the South differs from the rest of the nation—if, for example, the most "Southern" places in the South are the rural and very small town areas with less well-educated populations— then that is important to know. However, Reed's discovery of a substantial residual when these variables are controlled suggests that this is probably not the case; other studies suggest the hypothesis that a reactive regional identity develops in the *centers* of the peripheral region, not in the periphery of that region (Aguirre Beltrán 1967; Collier 1975). These observations apply with equal force to Hechter's analysis of Celtic "peripheral sectionalism" in Britain. One could feel much more confidence in the accuracy of his interpretations if they were linked to the internal variations in reactive ethnic solidarity within the Celtic fringe (cf. Verdery, Chapter 7 in this volume). A periphery should also be seen as internally differentiated and organized.

Usually the analyst will have to be content with data felt to be complete enough at one level of aggregation but much more fragmentary at a lower level. It is important that this lower level of aggregation be exploited, no matter how limited, to come to some conception of internal variation within units of analysis. In some cases, however, relatively complete data from several levels may be available for analysis, and cross-level comparisons may hold interesting implications for the nature of the phenomena being studied.

Derivy and Dogan (1971), for example, were able to compare departmental electoral data, on which most of French political geography has been based, with data at the *canton* level for most of rural France; in other words, they could look at correlations derived from 87 *départements* and, at the same time, correlations over the 2477 *cantons* that make up those *départements*.

The Derivy and Dogan results are interesting because the association of religious affiliation and voting is virtually identical at departmental and cantonal levels, but the association of class structure–urbanization (that is, the proportion of workers in the population) with voting behavior is very much stronger at the lower level of aggregation. What this implies, of course, is that *départements* are more homogeneous with regard to religious practice than they are with regard to class structure–urbanization. In other words, *regions* of differential religious practice surround urban system *hierarchies,* and both are needed to understand the political orientation of different areas. Again, this illustrates the kind of perspective that regional analysis can bring to very diverse kinds of data.

Space in Regional Analysis

The final problem I wish to raise concerning multivariate analysis of spatially distributed data is the way in which space itself is treated in such analyses. As pointed out in connection with the cross-cultural survey tradition in American anthropology, physical propinquity has usually been regarded as a disturbing effect on functional associations of cultural traits, and techniques have been developed to rule out such an effect. Only a few methods allow the confrontation of a strict spatial effect (cultural diffusion, in this case) with the hypothesized functional associations, and the measures used in this type of endeavor are basically those developed by statistical geographers—in particular, Geary's (1954) contiguity ratio (For the most recent work in this field see Cliff and Ord 1973; Hepple 1974).

The contiguity ratio provides a test of the hypothesis that spatially contiguous units are more similar to each other than are all units or randomly selected units. This measure is meant to be used in conjunction with standard linear regression equations that attempt to explain variance in a criterion variable (such as voting behavior) by predictors of two sorts: spatial coordinates and more abstract variables, such as socioeconomic characteristics. When spatial coordinates are used, the effect is usually described as an "autocorrelation," analogous to the correlation of a variable with itself over time, or, in other words, relative stability. In econometric models, autocorrelation, often a large part of the variance of any given variable, is usually treated as a nuisance, necessarily eliminated before beginning serious analysis. Some students treat areal variation in the same way (Duncan *et al.* 1961:129).

Another approach, recalling the diffusionist school in cultural anthropology, would treat spatial coordinates as substantively interesting rather than as a disturbance to be removed; at the very least, spatial "effects" can act as clues to the kinds of organizational patterns of interest to sociologists and anthropologists. A recent geographical study of the diffusion of modernization in Sierra Leone may help to illustrate this.[23] Riddell (1970) presents an analysis that is in part similar to that of Gould (1970) discussed earlier. A principal-components analysis revealed a strong tendency for all aspects of "modernization" or "administrative penetration" to occur together temporally and spatially. Riddell takes the analysis one step further by applying "trend-surface analysis" (Haggett 1966:269–276), which is a cartographic representation of a regression analysis wherein the predictors are spatial coordinates. A number of separate analyses of this sort demonstrate that a large part of the spatiotemporal variance in modernization in Sierra Leone can be accounted for by distance from the coastal capital of Freetown. This is apparent in linear trend surfaces, derived from standard regression equations, but is more pronounced when higher-order equations and surfaces are generated.

> The first-order surface indicates a progression of modernization levels increasing inland from the coast, and subsequent higher-order surfaces indicate a warping of the east–west trend to incorporate the effects of the wedge of development associated with the rail line and to indicate the strong distance-decay function from Freetown inland [Riddell 1970:91–92].

In other words, distance from the source of modernization influences, Freetown, is a major explanatory factor, but the effects of distance are not necessarily monotonic in character; the effect of one unit of distance is greater close to Freetown than it is farther away.

Another result of Riddell's work is interesting because it shows that distance from a single center may have to be augmented or replaced by distance from a system of centers, usually a hierarchy of central places. In Riddell's analysis of Sierra Leone, distance from Freetown, even after higher-order effects are removed, does not eliminate the effect of modernization diffusion from the towns of the urban–administrative hierarchy. These areas show up as more modernized than would be predicted from distance alone, however weighted. This is not at all surprising, but it does point out how a second inherently spatial effect can enter into sociocultural systems. In the spatial diffusion literature these two ways have been referred to as "contagious" (single-centered) and "hierarchical," respectively (English and Mayfield 1972: Chapter 4). I assume

[23] Brown & Moore (1969) discuss the several traditions feeding into diffusion research, one closely akin to cultural anthropology, and the more geographical work pioneered by Hägerstrand (1953). Where the earlier work focused on *patterns* of diffusion, the work following from Hägerstrand has also attempted to specify the *processes* generating observed historical patterns.

that diffusion processes will always be important in regional analysis, especially since migration is recognized as following essentially similar patterns (Riddell 1970:95–127; Olsson 1965). I also assume, however, that other inherently spatial processes will be discovered—for example, the influence of a "heartland" and a "focus" city or a pilgrimage center in maintaining an ethnic or regional identity.[24] In these cases it would be wrong to "remove" the spatial autocorrelation term from an analysis; distance and relative location are part of the phenomenon under investigation.

The use of "regional differentiation" as an explanation of phenomena has been soundly criticized for its lack of specification of the operative processes (Duncan *et al.* 1961:129). In this view, "placing" of a phenomenon does nothing to explain it; saying that a place has a certain characteristic *because* it is in the South, for example, is either tautologous or unacceptably diffuse. Any one of the many characteristics of the region—what can be described as a "residua" of unspecified variables— may be the operative causal agent, and it is the analyst's responsibility to specify which one (cf. Przeworski and Teune 1970:24–30).

While agreeing with the thrust of this criticism, the response that regional analysis offers is four-fold. First, what are "residua" from the point of view of a comparative explanatory schema constitute the structure of the particular system when looking from the inside. This point was raised earlier in the discussion of studies of political geography. Second, distance and relative location are often powerful explanatory variables in the development of sociocultural systems. This is why I have argued for the substantive use of what would otherwise be treated as the nuisance of spatial autocorrelation. Third, regional analysis need not limit itself to such variables alone. While not stressed in this paper, environmental resource localization—ecological variables in a strict sense—must be an important part of a thoroughgoing regional analysis. Moreover, there appear to me to be important phenomena of an organizational kind (for example, Young's "reactive subsystem" hypothesis) or of an ecological *cum* organizational kind (for example, Aguirre Beltrán's "refuge region" hypothesis) that may be uncovered through analysis of spatial distributions. Naturally, one should strive for clarity concerning processes implied in any explanation. Specification of measures and possible sequences of causation are essential, whether they involve spatial, environmental, organizational, or cultural variables. Finally, while it should be the intent of the analyst to replace proper names with corresponding values of abstract

[24] Villeneuve and Dufournaud (1974) and Vallee (1969) have used distance from Montreal as a variable in explanation of the maintenance of French-Canadian ethnic identity outside of Quebec Province. The notion of the focus city and pilgrimage center is implicit in the "refuge region" hypothesis of Aguirre Beltrán (1967) and its specification with Zincanteco data by Collier (1975).

variables, this should not lead one to forget that those names generally are important to the people involved; they are symbols, potential bases for collective action, and probably much more. While little is known about how such symbols arise or function, it seems very dangerous to assume that they are always epiphenomenal, that they have no independent impact.

COMPARATIVE COMMUNITY STUDIES:
LINKING PRIMARY AND
SECONDARY DATA

As noted earlier, most community studies were intensive studies of single communities and, for the most part, reified community boundaries, making it impossible to treat them as part of larger systems. Furthermore, although many were conducted in the context of long-term traditions or by groups of field workers, comparison can hardly be said to have been among their goals. At best, they aimed for replication of what had been seen elsewhere or, more rarely, falsification of another's observations. Very rarely was variation treated as something to be expected and explained. To the extent that comparative community studies exist today, they arose from later scholars' picking up the pieces of diverse studies and only occasionally designing their own. In this final section I wish to raise some basic issues in designing such a study, some methods that suggest themselves, and some practical difficulties. While it may prove vacuous to raise such issues outside the context of a specific substantive problem, without such a discussion I fear that we will continue to have a dichotomy between community and system studies, with little to join them but after-the-fact comparative studies.

The discussion up to this point has assumed that data representing a spatial distribution were already available and did not have to be collected before analysis could begin. At this point it must be acknowledged that data of substantive interest to sociologists and anthropologists are often not conveniently packed away in statistical abstracts and ecological data banks. Even if relevant data are available, the data may not be available in a form that allows one to see the operation of living communities. The crucial problem an ethnographic field worker faces in dealing with distribution and explanation across space is getting enough cases to treat observations as characteristics of spatial units. For such data, it will often be necessary to conduct a new kind of field work, one whose intention is to establish a basis of comparison across communities within a context set by the analysis of a larger system or region. These two aspects of the same process I will call "comparative community studies" and "regional ethnography."

In intensive field work, whether in a small community or even in a household, the field worker becomes sensitive to the idea of stability amid variation. At each step in the writing of ethnography—from entries in a daily log to discussions of an individual, a family, an ecological setting, or a type of occurrence—the writer knows that he is generalizing, filtering, and extrapolating. All ethnographic statements are summaries over time, meaningful units built up over the long and often painful process of trying to make sense of what one sees and experiences. Perhaps this is one reason that ethnographic film making is so notoriously difficult; the camera records literally and indiscriminately the usual and the anomalous, the complete act and the behavior fragment, the significant and the insignificant.

When the field worker moves out of the particular household or community to which he has devoted so much time, he faces again the problem of unconstrained, "meaningless" variation. He can record impressions and observations, as a camera would, but he is acutely aware of the incompleteness of such observations. It has been typical for anthropologists to tour the general vicinity of their field sites, either before or after settling down to intensive work in a single community. By and large, material from such tours has been used, if at all, in a very fragmentary way. There seem to be two types of uses to which "data" obtained in such a way are typically put: (1) assurances to one's readers of the representativeness of the field site and the patterns seen "in microcosm" there and (2) documentation of the uniqueness of the field site, and, indeed, of every potential site. Until recently, the idea of systematic variation among communities of field sites appears to have been largely lacking.

The recognition of the significance of units larger than the village community and the importance of intercommunity variation has produced a number of useful but incomplete correctives in the writing of ethnography. One category of such correctives is the "village outward" approach (Fox, Chapter 4 in this volume)—investigations of the roles and practices visible in the local community that function to link the local community to larger systems. Studies of brokers and middlemen, of the process and functions of migration, and of marketing behavior of peasants are a few examples. Another reaction has been the town- and city-based ethnography that, together with rural–urban network studies, seems to constitute much of what is now called urban anthropology (see Southall 1973, especially the bibliography). Such studies are laudable, but their full development may be constrained by traditions and attitudes more appropriate to the intensive study of a single community. An explicitly comparative and systemic orientation is required in order to develop a vocabulary and a rhetoric that can deal with the organization of diversity that exists in a complex society.

It has been argued that comparison and explanation are not the job of the ethnographic field worker but of the specialized comparativist

(Goodenough 1956:37). In this view the field worker's responsibility is limited to making sense of life as he sees it in the local community and to making his materials available to those interested in comparison. The ideal is thus a plurality of meticulous ethnographies at the local level, ethnographic archives and data banks, and comparative studies derived from the latter. At the level of the community, a thriving field of "comparative community power structure" has developed on the borders of sociology and political science in just this fashion (Aiken 1970; Walton 1970).

Comparative studies based on previous individual community studies are necessary and worthwhile, but they inherently suffer from several related deficiencies. Just as a random sample of individuals in a community cannot raise relational issues effectively, so a sample of communities cannot deal with issues of boundaries, intercommunity relations, and so forth, unless a system of communities is investigated. The lack of such studies, except in the case of a few team projects, probably stems in large part from the traditions and professional strategies that militate against field workers' working in close proximity to one another. Another deficiency in after-the-fact comparative community studies concerns the range of community types that in fact have been studied and thus find their way into data archives; there seems no doubt that, even in the aggregate, these do not begin to constitute a representative selection of community types.

The groundwork for comparative community studies based on field work began to be laid when field workers started to map and describe not only the settlement that they knew most intimately, usually through residence, but also a group of related settlements. An interesting example in this respect is a comparison of the two books produced by Laurence Wylie on rural France, each labeled as a village study (Wylie 1957, 1966). *Village in the Vaucluse* is widely regarded as one of the liveliest of village ethnographies, but it gives a very limited picture of the relationships of the community to surrounding settlements or to the larger outside world. In retrospect, the picture it did give of village–nation relationships turned out to be misleading, and Wylie's subsequent publications on the village (Wylie 1963, 1957: epilogue to 3rd ed.) have stressed a more differentiated picture of response to change in rural France. In part because of this change of emphasis and because of collaboration with a number of student investigators, Wylie's second ethnography, *Chanzeaux: A Village in Anjou*, is much more than a village study. Although many find this study much less compelling reading than *Village in the Vaucluse*, there is no doubt that it provides a much more adequate view of differential response by structural and ecological sectors of the community to changes in the French national economy and polity. *Chanzeaux* is the study of a *commune*, the lowest-level political unit in France, but the *commune* as an

ecological unit is recognized as being composed of very different elements—the *bourg* (administrative center and largest settlement), farming
and wine villages (named places with varying populations and services),
hamlets, isolated farms, and chateaux. These ecological elements, together
with related structural categories, such as farm owner, farm tenant, farm
worker, bourgeois, and noble, are woven throughout the analysis. These
ecological and structural categories have very strong effects on such variables as religious orientation, political and other kinds of community participation, and adoption of newer farming techniques. They are also
important in the migration process as observed in Chanzeaux, which is
striking in its magnitude and shows a marked stepwise pattern (see Olsson
1965) through the "urban hierarchy."

Wylie's picture of the relation of the *commune* to the larger region is less
adequate, but nonetheless is significantly better than that in previous
studies. Chanzeaux is contrasted with its neighboring *commune*, St.
Lambert-du-Lattay. Compared to Chanzeaux, St. Lambert is more
integrated into a larger urban system by virtue of its dependence on wine
production and of its location, which is both on the national highway and
slightly closer to the regional city of Angers. It is difficult to tell from
Wylie's data what hierarchical relations exist between Chanzeaux and St.
Lambert (but see Wylie 1957: epilogue to 3rd ed.), although the greater
urban and secular orientation of the latter is apparent. A contemporary
replication of Tilly's justly famous analysis of the region (1964), especially
as it responds to stimuli originating at higher levels in the national system,
Nantes and Paris, and from the emerging multinational European system,
would more than repay the effort.

The prospect of regional ethnography is, of course, an ambitious
undertaking. Where basic "information field" studies—to choose the
broadest term possible—have not been developed by previous scholars or
organizations, then a fair amount of regional description or "region-build-
ing" work will have to be carried out to establish even minimal points of
reference. Fortunately, the general significance of retail and wholesale
marketing patterns and the techniques for studying them make this an
obvious starting place (cf. studies in Smith, Volume I). Without going into
more specific comments on the methodology of regional ethnography, I
would like to focus on the attitudes that are built into accepted
ethnographic field work techniques and point to ways in which these need
to be modified to permit more extensive studies.

A fundamental premise of the comparative method, whether in community studies or cross-cultural studies, is that error is significant only to
the extent that it is systematic and distorts the relationship between two or
more variables (Naroll 1970; Rummel 1970). This is an emphasis different
from that of the more general scholarly concern for accuracy of description. The difference of attitude becomes particularly important when the

field worker trained in the standards established for intensive field work in a single community imagines what can be done in the way of regional ethnography and comparative community study. Ideas for team research or collaborative work of various sorts emerge, of course, and in fact several such projects have contributed to our understanding of what it takes to grasp the reality of a large system (e.g., Vogt 1969; Wylie 1966). However, such arrangements are not often possible, and the individual field worker must be equipped with some alternative ideas for looking at larger systems and for generating data capable of supporting truly comparative studies at the community level. By concerning himself with error only insofar as it introduces systematic bias, the field worker will be open to considering data that have traditionally been disdained by anthropologists. Three categories suggest themselves, not necessarily exhausting the possibilities: government statistics, other kinds of available data, and key-informant interviewing.

The use of government statistics, using the term broadly enough to encompass any quantifiable information obtained from official sources, is not new to anthropologists. However, the emphasis in intensive field work on single communities has usually made this a minor source, relatively speaking. In addition, interaction with government officials is often difficult and may be dangerous for the continuance of one's project, if not for the safety of one's informants. In any case, anthropologists have tended to downplay the importance of governmental data sources and very often have regarded them as sour grapes not worth the effort needed to get at them. In the context of comparative and regional studies, such an attitude must be foregone. To this end, more attention may be needed than has been customary in the past to the questions of credentials, manner of entry into the field, and cooperative relationships with government agencies or local scholars.

More generally, field workers need to be acquainted with the range of possibly useful sources of "available data."[25] Christaller, for example, was able to develop ground breaking work on the empirical basis of German telephone directories (Christaller 1933: Appendix A). With cooperation from a telephone company or bureau, matrices of call density between places can provide an even more refined measurement of community centrality, regionalization, and so forth (Nystuen and Dacey 1961). Data gathered by commercial organizations, schools, churches, labor unions, and so forth may also be useful but may have to be accumulated from a number of dispersed administrative units. In this connection it is well to

---

[25] The term is Frank W. Young's, and I am indebted to him for his many novel suggestions regarding materials that may be useful in comparative community studies. The only published work that provides a similar kind of suggestiveness as to potentially useful available data, although not specifically directed to community-level phenomena, is Webb *et al.* (1966).

remember the laborious effort that went into the classic ecological studies prior to routine social accounting by governments (see Pfautz 1967, on Booth's study of poverty in London).

Some data sources may be exploited for purposes not usually recognized. Thus, remote sensing imagery (aerial and satellite photos) is recognized as an important resource for regional description and delineation (Peplies 1974), but its possible use for community comparison may be overlooked. Young and McCannell (1967) used low-level air photos to study community institutional complexity, and several anthropologists in Vogt (1974) describe the use of air photos to investigate settlement patterns and ecological relationships in such a way that not only allows comparison within their study areas but also makes replication on a broader scale clearly feasible. Depending, of course, on availability of coverage at an appropriate scale (see Stone 1974), remote sensing imagery can be used directly for analysis and for selection of communities with specified locational, ecological, and perhaps even institutional characteristics for comparative field work.

A third source of data for comparative community studies is that of one or a few informants in each of a number of selected places (Young and Young 1961). The idea of using informants is anything but new in anthropology, but its use has been somewhat eclipsed by the lengthening of the typical field work period, and consequently by greater reliance on participant observation, and by techniques that emphasize intracommunity variation (attitude surveys, for example). When the focus shifts to intercommunity variation and comparison, the use of one or a few key informants may be more justified, especially if informants are called upon to report relatively public or institutional features of the community itself (Zelditch 1962). Two research programs have been designed on such a basis, with varying success.

Campbell and LeVine (1961) proposed a cooperative project whereby comparative data on the antecedents of ethnocentrism could be generated relatively quickly by anthropologists engaged in other studies. Particularly important was the ability of informants to report on the traditional culture—"official or semiofficial trained custodians of the oral history," "old persons who once occupied central political positions in the community," and so on (LeVine and Campbell 1972: Appendix). However, this procedure was apparently successful only with respondents in the groups intensively studied for the field workers' main projects; the regional ethnographies designed to get at variation and at the complementarity of cross-community images did not materialize. The result is a body of data that is cross-culturally comparable, but one that does not allow analysis of any one system.

Sometime later, Young (1966) proposed similar cooperative work, but this time on "intervillage systems." By this he meant the investigation of specific phenomena of interest to the individual field worker within the comparative community context established by a relatively simple and standardized procedure. In fact, what he asked field workers to establish, through brief personal observation and informant interviewing, were a number of relatively public facts about places or communities and their relationship to surrounding communities. Young chooses to interpret these as measures of relative "differentiation," "solidarity," and "centrality," the major variables in what he calls "structural symbolic theory" (Young 1970; Young and Young 1973: Part I) They also happen to be approximately the same institutional features dealt with by classical central-place theory—that is, hierarchically distributed service functions—and Young and Young (1973) have begun an attempt to test the relative predictive power of these two theories in accounting for community structure and growth.

In the past 10 years an impressive array of comparative community studies has developed using Young's perspective and methodology, largely as graduate theses at Cornell University (see the bibliography in Young and Young 1973). Some are systemic in the sense that they analyze the full range of communities in a given system and thus can deal with reflexive phenomena such as intercommunity images, diffusion-like processes and community development as a systemic process. Others are comparisons of spatially dispersed samples of communities, either studied de novo or scored after the fact from previous studies.

Much of the work discussed in this paper has, in one way or another, addressed itself to the question of local response to macrosystem penetration. However, such work has very often had to rely on secondary materials of such a gross character (for example, on highly aggregated statistical bases) that the operative processes are obscure and the sense of the way communities actually react is missing, even if the available data extend over a considerable period of time. By the kind of extensive field work discussed, we can begin to fill the gap between the local community, so often and intensively studied from the inside, with only occasional sidelong glances "outward," and the statistical and administrative units with which the nation-state engulfs them.

The few examples that have been given do not constitute a fully worked-out strategy of the kind of comparative community studies that is needed, nor do the publications cited deal extensively with the enormous practical problems that must be surmounted in order to implement such studies. To avoid premature discouragement, it is important to remember that anthropologists and sociologists in the intensive field work tradition appear, in retrospect, to have been very reluctant to divulge their methods of procedure and inference, and, most especially, their difficulties. Only relatively recently have frank accounts of these difficulties begun to appear in print (Berreman 1962; bibliography in Jongmans and Gutkind 1967).

The kind of extensive field work necessary to develop regional ethnography and comparative community studies will certainly involve innovative solutions to problems of transportation, entrance, and rapport in communities, personal maintenance, and many other difficulties that by now have conventional solutions in the lore of intensive field work practice. So far, there are almost no published discussions of procedures and problems in extensive field work, Perlman (1970) being the single exception of which I am aware. The problems encountered and the solutions adopted in comparative surveys[26] may be of some use, but the community-level focus of this work and the necessity of handling sensitively such matters as boundaries and system interpretation will undoubtedly lead to other problems and other solutions.

The methods necessary for grasping large-scale social systems starting at the local level are not completely at hand. These will undoubtedly evolve as individual field workers try to describe and analyze the middle- and large-scale systems in which they find particular communities embedded. Until this exploratory effort *is* begun, however, we will still be left with only the "building bricks" of individual community studies. "Detailed community studies . . . leave us with only a pile of building bricks; we also need the mortar, the complex lattice of connections between countryside and village, village and village, village and town, town and city, city and nation [Casagrande 1959:6]." Regional analysis, as illustrated in this paper and in this volume, hopes to specify the nature of some of these connections by drawing on theoretical and methodological developments in geography and related fields. But without the efforts of individual field workers to apply these ideas and methods, the specifications will remain hypothetical and the "lattice of connections" little more than a metaphor.

ACKNOWLEDGMENTS

This paper does not report on results of my own research. However, much of the thinking behind the paper was developed as part of a project on community organization, ethnic identity, and social stratification in Taiwan, 1895 to the present. Identification and organization of relevant statistical and documentary materials available in American and Taiwanese libraries, and construction of a machine-readable ecological data file at the township level, based on both Japanese- and Chinese-period materials, were made possible by two grants from the Joint Committee on Contemporary China of the Social Science Research Council and the American Council of Learned Societies. Preliminary field work in northeastern Taiwan for a comparative community study linked to the historical–ecological analysis was supported by a supplemental grant from the Center for Research in International Studies, Stanford University. The preparation of this paper benefited from the editorial assistance of Nancy Olsen and the constructive criticisms of Brian Berry, Peter Gould, Michael Hechter, John Shelton Reed, and Frank Young.

[26] A comprehensive bibliography is provided in Rokkan *et al.* (1969). Illustrative problems are discussed and methods compared in the good selection of papers in Warwick and Osherson (1973: Part V). In general, community position has not been incorporated into individual or household surveys, although some of the Cornell studies do both (see Young and Young 1973).

REFERENCES

Abler, Ronald, John S. Adams, and Peter Gould
  1971 *Spatial organization: The geographer's view of the world.* Englewood Cliffs, N.J.:
         Prentice-Hall.
Aguirre Beltrán, Gonzalo
  1967 *Regiones de refugio: El desarrollo de la comunidad y el proceso dominical en
         mestizo America.* Mexico City: Instituto Indigenista Interamericano.
Aiken, Michael
  1970 The distribution of community power: Structural bases and social consequences. In
         The structure of community power, edited by Michael Aiken and Paul E. Mott.
         New York: Random House. Pp. 487-525.
Alihan, Milla A.
  1938 *Social ecology.* New York: Columbia Univ. Press.
Armstrong, J. Scott
  1967 Derivation of theory by means of factor analysis, or Tom Swift and his electric fac-
         tor analysis machine. *The American Statistician* **21:** 17-21.
Bell, Colin, and Howard Newby
  1972 *Community studies: An introduction to the sociology of the local community.* New
         York: Praeger.
Berreman, Gerald D.
  1962 *Behind many masks: Ethnography and impression management in a Himalayan
         village.* Ithaca, N.Y.: Society for Applied Anthropology.
Berry, Brian J. L.
  1966 *Essays on commodity flows and the spatial structure of the Indian economy.*
         Research Paper No. 111, Department of Geography, Univ. of Chicago.
  1967 Grouping and regionalizing: An approach to the problem using multivariate
         analysis. In *Quantitative geography. Part I: Economic and cultural topics.* Studies
         in Geography No. 13, Northwestern Univ. Pp. 219-251.
  1971 Comparative factorial ecology. *Economic Geography* **47:** Special supplement.
Berry, Brian J. L., and Frank E. Horton
  1970 *Geographic perspectives on urban systems.* Englewood Cliffs, N.J.: Prentice-Hall.
Berry, Brian J. L., and Duane F. Marble (Eds.)
  1968 *Spatial analysis: A reader in statistical geography.* Englewood Cliffs, N.J.: Prentice-
         Hall.
Berry, Brian J. L., and Allan Pred
  1965 *Central place studies: A bibliography of theory and applications.* (Expanded ed.)
         Philadelphia: Regional Science Research Institute.
Blalock, Hubert M., Jr.
  1964 *Causal inferences in non-experimental research.* Chapel Hill: Univ. of North
         Carolina Press.
  1967 *Toward a theory of minority-group relations.* New York: Wiley.
  1971 *Causal models in the social sciences,* edited by Hubert M. Blalock, Jr. Chicago:
         Aldine-Atherton.
Board, Christopher, Richard J. Chorley, Peter Haggett, and David R. Stoddard (Eds.)
  1969- *Progress in geography.* London: Arnold.
Brown, L. A., and E. G. Moore
  1969 Diffusion research in geography: A perspective. In *Progress in geography,* Volume I,
         edited by Christopher Board, Richard J. Chorley, Peter Haggett, and David R.
         Stoddard. London: Arnold. Pp. 119-157.
Brulard, Th., and H. Van der Haegen (Eds.)
  1972 *Small area statistics and their use for social geographical and planological research.*
         Acta Geographica Lovaniensia 10. Louvain, Belgium: Catholic Univ. of Leuven.

Burgess, Ernest W.
   1927   The determinants of gradients in the growth of the city. *Publications of the American Sociological Society* **21**: 178–184.
Campbell, Donald T., and Robert A. LeVine
   1961   A proposal for cooperative cross-cultural research on ethnocentrism. *Journal of Conflict Resolution* **5**: 82–108.
Casagrande, Joseph B.
   1959   Some observations on the study of intermediate societies. In *Intermediate societies, social mobility, and communication,* edited by Verne F. Ray. Proceedings of the American Ethnological Society. Pp. 1–10.
Christaller, Walter
   1933   *Die zentralen Orte in Suddeutschland.* Jena: Gustav Fischer Verlag. Translated by C. W. Baskin, 1966. *Central places in southern Germany.* Englewood Cliffs, N.J.: Prentice-Hall.
Cliff, A. D., and J. K. Ord
   1973   *Spatial autocorrelation.* Monographs in Spatial and Environmental Systems Analysis No. 5. New York: Academic Press.
Collier, George A.
   1974   The impact of air photo technology on the study of demography and ecology in highland Chiapas. In *Aerial photography in anthropological field research,* edited by Evon Z. Vogt. Cambridge, Mass.: Harvard Univ. Press. Pp. 78–93.
   1975   *Fields of the Tzotzil: The ecological bases of tradition in highland Chiapas.* Austin: Univ. of Texas Press.
Cooley, William W., and Paul R. Lohnes
   1971   *Multivariate data analysis.* New York: Wiley.
Davies, Christopher S.
   1972   A classification of Welsh regions. In *Man, space and environment: Concepts in contemporary human geography,* edited by Paul W. English and Robert C. Mayfield. New York: Oxford Univ. Press. Pp. 481–498.
Derivy, Daniel, and Mattei Dogan
   1971   Unité d'analyse et espace de référence en écologie politique: Le canton et le département Français. *Revue Française de Science Politique* **21**: 517–570.
Dogan, Mattei
   1969   A covariance analysis of French electoral data. In *Quantitative ecological analysis in the social sciences,* edited by Mattei Dogan and Stein Rokkan. Cambridge, Mass.: MIT Press. Pp. 285–298.
Dogan, Mattei, and Stein Rokkan (eds.)
   1969   *Quantitative ecological analysis in the social sciences.* Cambridge, Mass.: MIT Press. (Paperback edition published as *Social ecology,* 1974.)
Driver, Harold E.
   1966   Geographical–historical *versus* psycho-functional explanations of kin avoidances. *Current Anthropology* **7**: 131–148, 155–160.
   1970   Statistical studies of continuous geographical distributions. In *Handbook of method in cultural anthropology,* edited by Raoul Naroll and Ronald Cohen. Garden City, N.Y.: Natural History Press. Pp. 620–639.
Duncan, Otis D.
   1964   Social organization and the ecosystem. In *Handbook of modern sociology,* edited by Robert E. L. Faris. Chicago: Rand McNally. Pp. 37–82.
Duncan, Otis D., Ray P. Cuzzort, and Beverly Duncan
   1961   *Statistical geography: Problems in analyzing areal data.* Glencoe, Ill.: Free Press.
English, Paul W., and Robert C. Mayfield (Eds.)
   1972   *Man, space, and environment: Concepts in contemporary human geography.* New York: Oxford Univ. Press.

Galpin, Charles J.
1915   The social anatomy of an agricultural community. *Agricultural Experiment Station Research Bulletin No. 44.* Madison: Univ. of Wisconsin.

Gastil, Raymond D.
1971   Homocide and a regional culture of violence. *American Sociological Review* **36:** 412–427.

Geary, R. C.
1954   The contiguity ratio and statistical mapping. *The Incorporated Statistician* **5:** 115–145.

Geertz, Clifford
1963   *Agricultural involution: The process of ecological change in Indonesia.* Berkeley: Univ. of California Press.

Giggs, J. A., and P. M. Mather
1975   Factorial ecology and factor invariance: An investigation. *Economic Geography* **51:**366–382.

Goodenough, Ward H.
1956   Residence rules. *Southwestern Journal of Anthropology* **12:** 22–37.

Gould, Peter R.
1970   Tanzania 1920–63: The spatial impress of the modernization process. *World Politics* **22:** 144–170.

Hägerstrand, Torsten
1953   *Innovationsförloppet ur korologisk synpunkt.* Lund: Gleerup. Translated by Allan Pred, 1968. *Innovation Diffusion as a spatial process.* Chicago: Univ. of Chicago Press.

Haggett, Peter
1966   *Locational analysis in human geography.* New York: St. Martin's Press.

Hammond, John L., Jr.
1973   Two sources of error in ecological correlations. *American Sociological Review* **38:** 764–777.

Hannan, Michael T., Jr.
1971   Problems of aggregation. In *Causal models in the social sciences,* edited by Hubert M. Blalock, Jr. Chicago: Aldine-Atherton. Pp. 473–508.
1975   The dynamics of ethnic boundaries. Research proposal submitted to the National Science Foundation. Stanford, Calif.: Laboratory for Social Research.

Hartshorne, Richard
1959   *Perspective on the nature of geography.* Association of American Geographers Monograph No. 1 Chicago: Rand McNally.

Hawley, Amos
1950   *Human ecology: A theory of community structure.* New York: Ronald Press.

Hechter, Michael
1975   *Internal colonialism: The Celtic fringe in British national development, 1536–1966.* Berkeley: Univ. of California Press.

Heise, David R.
1970   Causal inference from panel data. In *Sociological methodology 1970,* edited by Edward F. Borgatta and George W. Bohrenstedt. San Francisco: Jossey-Bass. Pp. 3–27.

Hepple, Leslie W.
1974   The impact of stochastic process theory upon spatial analysis in human geography. In *Progress in geography,* Volume VI, edited by Christopher Board, Richard J. Chorley, Peter Haggett, and David R. Stoddart. London: Arnold. Pp. 89–142.

Hillery, George A.
1955   Definitions of community: Areas of agreement. *Rural Sociology* **20:** 111–123.

Hoiberg, Eric O., and Jerry S. Cloyd
    1971   Definition and measurement of continuous variation in ecological analysis. *American Sociological Review* **36**: 65–74.
Hunter, Alfred A.
    1972   Factorial ecology: A critique and some suggestions. *Demography* **9**: 107–118.
Janson, Carl-Gunnar
    1969   Some problems of ecological factor analysis. In *Quantitative ecological analysis in the social sciences,* edited by Mattei Dogan and Stein Rokkan. Cambridge, Mass.: MIT Press. Pp. 301–341.
Jongmans, D. G., and P. C. W. Gutkind (Eds.)
    1967   *Anthropologists in the field.* New York: Humanities Press.
Land, Kenneth C.
    1969   Principles of path analysis. In *Sociological methodology 1969,* edited by Edgar F. Borgatta. San Francisco: Jossey-Bass. Pp. 3–37.
Laumann, Edward O.
    1973   *Bonds of pluralism: The form and substance of urban social networks.* New York: Wiley.
Lebart, Judovic
    1969   Analyse statistique de la contiguité. *Publications de l'Institut de Statistique* **18**: 81–112. Univ. of Paris.
LeVine, Robert A., and Donald T. Campbell
    1972   *Ethnocentrism: Theories of conflict, ethnic attitudes, and group behavior.* New York: Wiley.
Lewis, Oscar
    1965   Further observations on the folk–urban continuum and urbanization, with special reference to Mexico City. In *The study of urbanization,* edited by Philip M. Hauser and Leo F. Schnore. New York: Wiley. Pp. 491–503.
Linz, Juan J.
    1969   Ecological analysis and survey research. In *Quantitative ecological analysis in the social sciences,* edited by Mattei Dogan and Stein Rokkan. Cambridge, Mass.: MIT Press. Pp. 91–132.
Loomis, Charles P., and J. Allan Beegle
    1950   *Rural social systems: A textbook in rural sociology and anthropology.* Englewood Cliffs, N.J.: Prentice-Hall.
Marchand, Bernard
    1975   On the information content of regional maps: The concept of geographical redundancy. *Economic Geography* **51**: 117–127.
Markoff, John, and Gilbert Shapiro
    1973   The linkage of data describing overlapping geographical units. *Historical Methods Newsletter* **7**: 34–46.
McKinney, John C., and Linda B. Bourque
    1971   The changing South: National incorporation of a region. *American Sociological Review* **36**: 399–412.
McRae, Duncan, Jr.
    1958   Religious and socioeconomic factors in the French vote, 1946–56. *American Journal of Sociology* **64**: 290–298.
Meyriat, Jean
    1960   Political science (1950–1958). *French Bibliographic Digest,* Series II, No. 32. New York: Cultural Center of the French Embassy.
Naroll, Raoul
    1970a Data quality control in cross-cultural surveys. In *Handbook of method in cultural anthropology,* edited by Raoul Naroll and Ronald Cohen. Garden City, N.Y.: Natural History Press. Pp. 927–945.

1970b Galton's problem. In *Handbook of method in cultural anthropology,* edited by Raoul Naroll and Ronald Cohen. Garden City, N.Y.: Natural History Press. Pp. 974–989.

Naroll, Raoul, and Ronald Cohen (Eds.)
1970 *Handbook of method in cultural anthropology.* Garden City, N.Y.: Natural History Press.

Nelson, Lowry
1969 *Rural sociology: Its origin and growth in the United States.* Minneapolis: Univ. of Minnesota Press.

Nie, Norman H. C. Hadlai Hull, Jean G. Jenkins, Karin Steinbrenner, and Dale H. Bent
1975 *SPSS: Statistical package for the social sciences.* New York. McGraw-Hill.

Nystuen, John D., and Michael F. Dacey
1961 A graph theory interpretation of nodal regions. *Papers and Proceedings of the Regional Science Association* **7:** 29–42.

Odum, Howard W., and Katherine Jocher (Eds.)
1945 *In search of the regional balance of America.* Chapel Hill: Univ. of North Carolina Press.

Odum, Howard W., and Harry E. Moore
1938 *American regionalism: A cultural–historical approach to national integration.* New York: Holt.

Olsson, Gunnar
1965 *Distance and human interaction.* Philadelphia: Regional Science Research Institute.

Park, Robert E.
1952 *Human communities: The city and human ecology.* Glencoe, Ill.: Free Press.

Park, Robert E., Ernest W. Burgess, and Roderick D. McKenzie
1925 *The city.* Chicago: Univ. of Chicago Press. (Reissued, 1967.)

Peplies, Melvin L.
1974 Regional analysis and remote sensing. In *Remote sensing: Techniques for environmental analysis,* edited by John E. Estes. New York: Wiley. Pp. 243–275.

Perlman, Melvin L.
1970 Intensive field work and scope sampling: Methods for studying the same problem at different levels. In *Marginal natives: Anthropologists at work,* edited by Morris Freilich. New York: Harper. Pp. 293–338.

Pfautz, Howard W. (Ed.)
1967 *Charles Booth on the city: Physical pattern and social structure.* Chicago: Univ. of Chicago Press.

Prescott, J. R. V.
1972 *Political geography.* London: Methuen.

Przeworski, Adam, and Henry Teune
1970 *The logic of comparative social inquiry.* New York: Wiley.

Ray, D. Michael
1971 From factorial to canonical ecology: The spatial interrelationships of economic and cultural differences in Canada. In Comparative factorial ecology, edited by Brian J. L. Berry. *Economic Geography* **47:** 344–355, special supplement.

Redfield, Robert
1955 *The little community: Viewpoints for the study of a human whole.* Chicago: Univ. of Chicago Press.

Reed, John S.
1972a *The enduring South: Subcultural persistence in mass society.* Lexington, Mass.: Heath.
1972b Whatever became of regional sociology? Unpublished manuscript, Univ. of North Carolina.

Rees, Philip H.
   1972   Problems of classifying subareas within cities. In *City classification handbook*, edited by Brian J. L. Berry. New York: Wiley. Pp. 265–330.
Riddell, J. Barry
   1970   *The spatial dynamics of modernization in Sierra Leone: Structure, diffusion, and response.* Evanston, Ill.: Northwestern Univ. Press.
Robinson, W. S.
   1950   Ecological correlations and the behavior of individuals. *American Sociological Review* 15: 351–357.
Rokkan, Stein, Sidney Verba, Jean Viet, and Elina Almasy
   1969   *Comparative survey analysis.* Paris: Mouton.
Rummel, Rudolph J.
   1970   Dimensions of error in cross-national data. In *Handbook of method in cultural anthropology*, edited by Raoul Naroll and Ronald Cohen. Garden City, N.Y.: Natural History Press. Pp. 946–961.
Short, James F. (Ed.)
   1971   *The social fabric of the metropolis: Contributions of the Chicago School of urban sociology.* Chicago: Univ. of Chicago Press.
Skinner, G. William
   1964–1965   Marketing and social structure in rural China. *Journal of Asian Studies* 24: 3–43, 195–228, 363–399.
Southall, Aidan (Ed.)
   1973   *Urban anthropology: cross-cultural studies of urbanization.* New York: Oxford Univ. Press.
Stephan, G. Edward
   1971   Variation in county size: A theory of segmental growth. *American Sociological Review* 36: 451–460.
Stone, Kirk H.
   1974   Developing geographical remote sensing. In *Remote sensing: Techniques for environmental analysis*, edited by John E. Estes. New York: Wiley. Pp. 1–15.
Suttles, Gerald D.
   1972   *The social construction of communities.* Chicago: Univ. of Chicago Press.
Taafe, Edward J. (Ed.)
   1970   *Geography: Behavioral and social science survey committee, geography panel report.* Englewood Cliffs, N.J.: Prentice-Hall.
Thernstrom, Stephan
   1964   Further reflections on the Yankee City series: The pitfalls of ahistorical social science. In *Poverty and progress: Social mobility in a nineteenth century city*, Appendix. Cambridge, Mass.: Harvard Univ. Press.
Thomas, Edwin N.
   1960   *Maps of residuals from regressions: Their characteristics and uses in geographic research.* Department of Geography Report No. 2. Iowa City: State Univ. of Iowa.
Tilly, Charles
   1964   *The Vendée: A sociological analysis of the counterrevolution of 1793.* Cambridge, Mass.: Harvard Univ. Press.
Trudgill, Peter
   1975   Linguistic geography and geographical linguistics. In *Progress in geography*, Volume VII, edited by Christopher Board, Richard J. Chorley, Peter Haggett, and David R. Stoddard. London: Arnold. Pp. 227–252.
Vallee, Frank G.
   1969   Regionalism and ethnicity: The French-Canadian case. In *Perspectives on regions and regionalism*, edited by B. Y. Card. Edmonton, Alberta, Canada: Western Association of Sociology and Anthropology. Pp. 19–25.

Villeneuve, Paul Y., and Christian Dufournaud
   1974   Facteurs écologiques et assimilation linguistique des Canadiens Français hors du
           Québec: Essai méthodologique. *The Canadian Geographer* **13**: 330-351.
Vogt, Evon Z.
   1969   *Zinacantan: A Maya community in the highlands of Chiapas.* Cambridge, Mass.:
           Harvard Univ. Press.
   1974   *Aerial photography in anthropological field research.* Cambridge, Mass.: Harvard
           Univ. Press.
Wagner, Philip L., and Marvin W. Mikesell (Eds.)
   1962   *Readings in cultural geography.* Chicago: Univ. of Chicago Press.
Walton, John
   1970   A systematic survey of community power research. In *The structure of community
           power,* edited by Michael Aiken and Paul E. Mott. New York: Random House. Pp.
           443-464.
Warner, W. Lloyd
   1949   *Democracy in Jonesville: A study in quality and inequality.* New York: Harper.
Warner, W. Lloyd, and Paul S. Lunt
   1941   *The social life of a modern community.* New Haven, Conn.: Yale Univ. Press.
Warwick, Donald P., and Samuel Osherson (Eds.)
   1973   *Comparative research methods.* Englewood Cliffs, N.J.: Prentice-Hall.
Webb, Eugene J., Donald T. Campbell, Richard D. Schwartz, and Lee Sechrest
   1966   *Unobtrusive measures: Nonreactive research in the social sciences.* Chicago: Rand
           McNally.
Weiss, Richard
   1962   Cultural boundaries and ethnographic maps. In *Readings in cultural geography,*
           edited by Philip L. Wagner and Marvin W. Mikesell. Chicago: Univ. of Chicago
           Press. Pp. 62-74.
Wylie, Laurence
   1957   *Village in the Vaucluse.* Cambridge, Mass.: Harvard Univ. Press. (3rd ed., 1974.)
   1963   Social change at the grass roots. In *In search of France,* edited by Stanley Hoffman.
           Cambridge, Mass.: Harvard Univ. Press. Pp. 159-234.
   1966   *Chanzeaux: A village in Anjou.* Cambridge, Mass.: Harvard Univ. Press.
Young, Frank W.
   1966   A proposal for cooperative cross-cultural research on intervillage systems. *Human
           Organization* **25:** 46-50.
   1970   Reactive subsystems. *American Sociological Review* **35:** 297-307.
Young, Frank W., and Dean McCannell
   1967   Structural differentiation of communities: An aerial photographic study. *Rural
           Sociology* **32:** 334-345.
Young, Frank W., and Ruth C. Young
   1961   Key informant reliability in rural Mexican villages. *Human Organization* **20:** 141-
           148.
   1973   *Comparative studies of community growth.* Rural Sociological Society Monograph
           No. 10. Morgantown: West Virginia Univ.
Zelditch, Morris, Jr.
   1962   Some methodological problems in field studies. *American Journal of Sociology* **67:**
           566-576.

Section B

MARRIAGE AND KINSHIP

In its treatment of marriage and kinship, two old warhorses of the intensive field work tradition, regional analysis develops some new problems and theories for those fields. Jean Jackson shows in Chapter 3 that the networks formed by kinship and marriage in a simple society provide vehicles by which such societies can be culturally organized in very complex ways. In the case she describes, the social units that contract marriages are also language groups who define the people they marry as "people who speak other languages." As a result, marriage networks organize a large regional system of considerable cultural diversity and provide the basis for social commonality among groups who would otherwise have little contact. Among the questions raised and addressed by this study are these: What are the boundaries and organizing features of network systems without nodal centers? What are the environmental characteristics or determinants of such network systems? How do they organize society?

In Chapter 4 Richard Fox argues that territorial kinship systems can define important political units in frontier areas of complex societies where administrative control is weak. In the two cases used, Scotland and northern India, lineages take on functions at the regional level quite different from their functions at the local level to provide the integrating mechanism for otherwise fragmented polities. Fox's study shows new properties of lineage organization and strikes a blow to the notion that kinship systems wither away with the development of the state.

Lawrence Crissman takes on, in Chapter 5, G. William Skinner's hypothesis that marketing communities define marriage communities in Chinese society. Since he uses data from Taiwan, where marketing has undergone considerable expansion and growth in the past century, Crissman redefines the hypothesis for modern marketing communities, broadening—and at the same time testing—the proposition that the economic institutions integrating complex societies have important effects on such basic local-level institutions as marriage.

Adams and Kasakoff, in Chapter 7, fit Crissman's study into a general framework by which endogamy can be understood in relation to central places in China. Their earlier paper, reprinted as Chapter 6, is concerned with the basic characteristics of endogamy everywhere, particularly the sizes of the groups involved, the distance from which spouses are sought, and the social composition of the various marriage groups found at different levels of the social system. Their findings indicate that marriage, besides providing an organizational system of its own, reflects other organizational systems in both simple and complex societies.

Chapter 3

Vaupés Marriage: A Network System in the Northwest Amazon[1]

Jean E. Jackson
Massachusetts Institute of Technology

INTRODUCTION

An analysis of the marriage system found in the Vaupés territory of southeastern Colombia demonstrates the utility of a regional approach to small-scale, kinship-based societies as well as to complex ones. The specific and at times unique characteristics of the Vaupés marriage system are discussed here, and consideration is given to the question of how much this marriage system can be seen as an adaptation to the particular ecosystem within which it operates. But the major intention is to demonstrate the advantages of taking the total regional ecosystem as the unit of analysis when doing research on any problem concerning social groupings in environments similar to the Vaupés: tropical forests where human populations have a hunting–fishing–gathering base with a substantial amount of horticulture. Because of this focus, conclusions relating to the specific ethnographic data and interpretation for the Vaupés are presented in a condensed form.

The format of the paper—a somewhat arbitrary one because there is no

[1] Data discussed in this paper were gathered during dissertation research in Colombia from October 1968 to November 1970 with support from the Danforth Foundation and the Stanford Committee for Research in International Studies. Eighteen months of this time were spent in the Vaupés territory with a longhouse group of Bará Indians on the Inambú River.

single point of entry into an integrated system (Haggett 1966:31)—is as
follows: (1) introduction to the Vaupés region, (2) regional aspects of social
structure, and (3) suggestions for a more formal regional analysis of
Vaupés marriage.

INTRODUCTION TO THE
VAUPÉS REGION

The Vaupés territory is the Colombian half of the area known as the
central Northwest Amazon, the other half being in adjacent Brazilian territory (Map 1). The central Northwest Amazon is characterized by multilingualism, language group exogamy, and the use of Tukano as a lingua
franca. The term "language group"[2] refers in this instance to exogamous

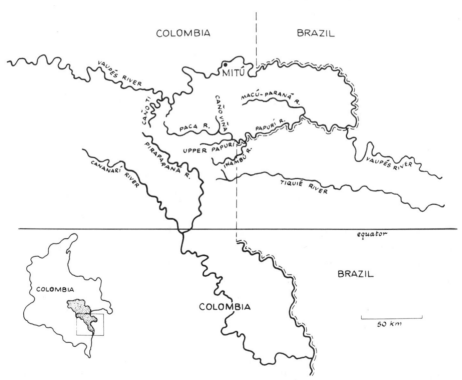

Map 1.   The eastern Colombian Vaupés. (After Jackson 1974, Figure 4.)

[2] The term "language group" is not entirely satisfactory, since it usually refers to a linguistic rather than a social unit. Use of terms specifically referring to marriage, such as
"exogamous group," has been avoided, since it has not been conclusively established that the
language-affiliated units are coterminous with the minimal exogamous units in the same
manner throughout the Vaupés region.

patrilineal descent units, each one of which is identified with a distinct language. Over 20 of these units are distributed throughout both Colombian and Brazilian sectors of the central Northwest Amazon. The central Northwest Amazon is also known linguistically as the area of the Eastern Tukanoan language family, and the Indians participating in language group exogamy are referred to as Tukanoans in this paper. However, some of the language groups in the marriage system speak Arawak, and possibly even Carib languages.

In terms of Colombian political boundaries, the Vaupés is the eastern part of the Comisaría del Vaupés. Although generalizations in this paper probably apply to the entire central Northwest Amazon region, the term "Vaupés" is used throughout because most of the field work was carried out in Colombia. The Vaupés lies approximately between the equator and 1° north latitude and between 69° and 71° west longitude. The entire Comisaría del Vaupés has a territory of 90,625 square kilometers,[3] and the most recent census gives a figure of approximately 14,000 for the total population, including non-Indians. Population density is roughly .2 inhabitants per square kilometer (Atlas de Colombia 1969:xiii).

The entire Vaupés is characterized by humid, tropical rain forest. Geologically, the region is an extension of the westernmost Guiana Shield (Moser and Tayler 1963:440). In appearance it is an undifferentiated stretch of forest, streams, and rivers, with some permanent swamps dominated by the mirití palm. Interfluvial areas can be quite hilly, so that abundant land exists for settlements and horticulture even when much of the region is flooded during high water. Limestone outcrops (cerros), visible from far away, are important landmarks for Indians, as are some of the mirití swamps.

The Vaupés is one of the headwater regions of the Northwest Amazon river drainage, most of its rivers eventually emptying into the Rio Negro in Brazil. The rivers of the region are known for their inky black color and relatively acidic water resulting from their crystalline beds (Bates 1965:178). Most rivers have a strong flow and numerous rapids, which are also important landmarks. All travel of any duration or with any sizable cargo is by river, using dugout canoes.

With the exception perhaps of the interfluvial areas between the main river basins, the Vaupés has no natural barriers dividing its territory. For the most part, materials needed for manufacturing artifacts and the foods gathered in the forests and rivers are found in all parts of the region. A trade network facilitates distribution of the few localized items, both raw materials and manufactured objects. Resource homogeneity is characteristic of the region, however, and probably limits the amount of trade.

---

[3] Sorensen (1967:670) gives a population of about 10,000 for the central Northwest Amazon, comparing the size of its territory to New England.

Because the rivers of the region flow east and south into Brazil, access by river is from distant Amazon river ports. As a result, the central Northwest Amazon has had little contact with the population centers of either Colombia or Brazil. Isolation of the Vaupés has been strengthened by the fact that it offers relatively poor resources for national exploitation. No oil, minerals, or gems have been discovered, and no exploitation of forest products has been attempted except for the rubber-gathering industry. Although rubber-gathering has made an important impact on the Vaupés region and continues, in a muted way, to affect the Indians of the region, factors such as poor accessibility, flooding, insects, and the like have prevented any large-scale colonization of the area for farming or animal husbandry. Thus, while some areas of the region are significantly altered due to the effects of rubber gathers and missionaries, the region is relatively unacculturated.

Tukanoan Indians traditionally live in multifamily longhouses, one per settlement, on or near rivers. Longhouses, as well as the more recent settlement pattern of nucleated villages of one to four small houses, are separated from one another by 2 to 10 hours of canoe travel. At present four to eight nuclear families inhabit a longhouse. The men of a settlement hunt, fish, and clear swidden fields in which the women grow bitter manioc and other crops. Change of longhouse site occurs approximately every 8 to 12 years, rarely because available or suitable land is exhausted. Women must be able to walk to their fields, but this would permit a longhouse unit to stay at one site much longer than it actually does.[4] Rights to territory surrounding a longhouse site are best considered usufruct rights.

It is important to note that land use is similar throughout the region. Several factors contribute to this, one being the similarity of terrain and the general availability of many resources throughout the region. Tukanoans have almost identical methods of subsistence technology, material inventories, and so forth, if we disregard the differential effects of acculturation. Moreover, one does not find, in the rather egalitarian society that characterizes the Vaupés today, a significant amount of exclusive control of scarce resources by different social units; that is, no discernible social units occupy distinct economic niches or locate their settlements at particular strategic points of the landscape. [A somewhat different situation may have existed in the past, however (Goldman 1963; Koch-Grünberg 1909–1910).] A somewhat artificially maintained system of specialization in the manufacture of certain artifacts, mainly of a cere-

---

[4] It is definitely the case that a scarcity of land exists in and near mission towns, but at present nowhere else. Goldman describes a somewhat different situation for the Cubeo in 1939–1940, where available land for manioc plantations was a decisive factor in choosing a longhouse site, because sibs had to retain their traditional boundaries. However, he notes that "from terrain alone there is no doubt that the Vaupés could have supported far greater Indian populations than it did at the time of first contact [1963:36]."

monial nature, does exist in the Vaupés. The specialization is organized along the lines of language group boundaries and sib rank within a specific language group.[5]

A final point regarding land use is that Tukanoans can and frequently do move about the region. The fact that longhouses hold only from four to eight nuclear families and that they are separated by anywhere from 2 hours' to a day's canoe travel means that traveling and visiting are extremely important activities.[6] Visits are made for various reasons, such as trade, ceremonies, and courtship. Travel, whether by trail or canoe, is difficult and time consuming. A trip will involve much preparation and will last at least a few days. This can be seen as a contributing factor to the well-established rules of hospitality for which the Northwest Amazon is famous: One can find overnight lodging almost anywhere, and Indians will usually elect to spend the night in a longhouse rather than make camp in the forest. Another contributing factor to the hospitality pattern is that, in situations of short-term visiting, excessive demands are rarely made on the hosts. En route Indians carry their own food, and a family visiting another settlement helps to support itself the man will hunt and fish, and the woman will help in processing manioc from another woman's garden. Visiting among settlements has probably increased in recent times because of the cessation of raids and feuds, making travel easier and reducing the need to live with one's closest agnates in well-fortified longhouses.

The frequency of movement of this sort undoubtedly influences variables related to systemic movement, such as produced by the marriage system, and influences the native cognitive view of the Vaupés. Evidence exists that Indians feel themselves to be part of a pan-Vaupés system. The native model appears to encompass a large geographical area wherein live people basically similar to "us." Distance and differentiation are conceptualized in terms of degrees, not in terms of categorical limits beyond which "we" and "our territory" end. Even beyond the Vaupés region, the conceptualization seems to involve an ever increasing geographical area with ever increasing social and cultural differentiation. There are no generally recognized natural or artificial boundaries beyond which live people who are definitely enemies or strangers. Bará Indians will describe "enemy" Indians who live in the east as cannibals who wear distinctive

---

[5] See Jackson (1972b); Chagnon (1968:100) discusses a similar situation among the Yąnomamö.

[6] This is readily apparent to an anthropologist attempting the Herculean task of conducting a household census. Although the patrilocal rule states that one should live with one's closest agnates, adjusting this rule to reality frequently involves arbitrary decisions on the part of the ethnographer. Indians travel a great deal, sometimes staying in other settlements for prolonged periods of time, even several months. Quarrels sometimes result in the permanent dissolution of a residence group, who will go to "visit" other kinsmen, eventually taking up residence with them. Thus, at any point in time a significant proportion of Indians are not living where they are "supposed" to.

clothing and ornaments, but will describe Carihona Indians, equally distant in geographical terms, as "our brothers." Criteria that exclude whites, Makú,[7] and Cubeo[8] are readily offered by Papurí Tukanoans when discussing how "real people" ought to live. On the other hand, it is obvious that Cubeo, at least, are included in conceptualizations of "us," or "people." Goldman (personal communication) indicates that the Cubeo, although they conceive of themselves as a tribal entity, also see themselves as only part of a larger entity. C. Hugh-Jones has stated that "Indians conceive of themselves as part of a social system which theoretically has no social, geographical, or linguistic limits [1971:10]."

Culturally homogeneous regional systems occur in many areas of low-land South America, involving networks of trade and economic exchange (both intratribal and intertribal), marriage exchange, feasting, and military alliances, or interaction between culturally distinct groups who occupy different niches within a single ecosystem. But the Vaupés appears to be culturally integrated by regional network relationships to a very marked degree. Answers to questions of why this is so, as well as to what was the nature of the Vaupés system in previous periods, cannot be com-pletely answered at present, although some reasonable hypotheses can be offered.

Undoubtedly, a crucial factor in the evolution of the Vaupés system is population density. It is almost certain that at earlier periods the Vaupés had a higher population density, a more territorially based control over scarce resources, and more stratification among the groups exploiting those resources. Goldman's (1963) description of the Cubeo of the period of 1939–1940 certainly indicates this, as do writings from earlier travelers. At that time, groups with higher rank and more allies—and more numbers among themselves—apparently occupied the larger rivers, particularly sites on river mouths. Such locations had military advantages and confer-red higher status. Control over groups such as Makú and lower-ranking sibs seems to have been a major consideration, its present unimportance probably due to decline in population and to the disappearance of active raiding and feuding.

The higher population density Goldman reports for the Cubeo in 1939 probably also lies behind their greater use of the landscape to mirror social arrangements. Cubeo phratric organization and sib rank are expressed

[7] In a comprehensive study of the Vaupés regional system, it would be essential to discuss the trading and servant–master relationships between Makú and Tukanoans (Jackson 1973; Silverwood-Cope 1972). Makú are small groups of Indians who are more forest than river oriented, who speak non-Tukanoan languages, and who do not have rules of marriage relating to linguistic exogamy. Since this paper is limited to the Vaupés marriage system, it does not include Makú.

[8] Cubeo do not marry out of their linguistic unit either. For fuller discussions on non-Indians, Makú, and the Vaupés in general, see Goldman (1948, 1963), Reichel-Dolmatoff (1971), and Sorensen (1967).

quite clearly by the location of settlements. Whether the present situation among Tukanoans (who are located to the south of the Cubeo) represents a simple breakdown in the system, after falling below a critical minimum population density, or a more creative process of adaptation to the changing demographic situation is an open question. Factors leading to lowered population density in the Vaupés may have been increasing scarcity of game and aquatic life,[9] inroads of white-introduced disease, effects of the rubber-gathering industry and mission towns, and out-migration.

It seems evident that changing population density and population migrations were also important factors in the evolution of the present Vaupés (Tukanoan) marriage system. Two kinds of explanations have been offered (Sorensen 1967) to account for the way in which demographic and spatial factors might give rise to a system involving linguistic exogamy. The first, a fusion model, suggests that a cul-de-sac situation arose due to pressure from missions, rubber gatherers, and other agents of the national economies of either Brazil or Colombia. The resulting squeeze of territory necessitated more interaction among distinct cultural groups, a necessity increased by declines in population from disease. Various mechanisms arose that facilitated interaction among the previously separated or hostile groups. One of these mechanisms was intermarriage, and the heretofore truly distinct tribal-like groups assimilated to the point of sharing a common culture and a rule of exogamy applied to what originally were endogamous units. Language came to be the main marker distinguishing these exogamous units, whereas originally it was but one of many cultural differences separating them.

The second type of explanation, a fission model, postulates an original situation characterized by endogamous (again, probably tribal-like) units with exogamous moieties within each one. Of the various markers distinguishing one moiety from the other, speech differences came to be the most crucial, until ultimately what was once a single protolanguage spoken by the entire endogamous unit divided into two languages along the lines of the moiety division. The rule of marriage came to be expressed as "We marry people who speak a different language" [see Jackson (1972b, 1974) and Sorensen (1967) for further discussion].

These two models probably describe how different segments of the Vaupés population simultaneously evolved into the present Tukanoan

---

[9] Statements about a relative scarcity of game and fish are impressionistic, based on conversations with colleagues and some of the literature on the Amazon basin (e.g., Bates 1965:178). Hunting does not seem as productive in the Vaupés as it is for the Amahuaca (Carneiro 1970:333), or even perhaps the "starving" Sirionó (Holmberg 1969:74), who are able to live in bands of up to 50 adults. The Kuikuru, according to Oberg, have fishing that compares favorably to that along the Northwest Coast (Carneiro 1970:247), certainly not the case in the Vaupés. Whether the Vaupés environment at present is capable of sustaining the large populations reported by such writers as Orellana for the flood plains at the time of the first contact (see Goldman 1963:2) is an open question.

marriage system. While outsider groups were increasingly being incorporated through intermarriage, the idea concerning marriage to a person
affiliated with a different language was becoming the most important rule
of marriage. It diffused into the moiety-based groups, increasing the stress
on speech differences in these groups as the most significant marker distinguishing each exogamous unit.

REGIONAL ASPECTS OF VAUPÉS
SOCIAL ORGANIZATION

When applied to the Vaupés, the term "tribe" so easily leads to confusion and incorrect assumptions that I have insisted on using other terms,
although all of them to date ("language aggregate," "language group") are
awkward and not entirely free of confusion themselves. No single generally
accepted definition of "tribe" exists in anthropology (Helm 1968), but
those most frequently offered are concerned with the presence of one or
more of the following traits: (1) contiguous "tribal" territory; (2)
integrated political, ceremonial, or warrior "tribal" roles; (3) greater
intratribal than intertribal interaction; (4) more intratribal than inter-
tribal marriage; and (5) significant cultural differences separating neighboring "tribal" groups. A final criterion is distinct language. But none of
the definitions that utilize any or all of the other traits permits calling the
Vaupés language groups tribes. Yet the ethnographic literature refers to
Vaupés language groups as tribes, although some authors note difficulties
with this usage (Fulop 1955; Reichel-Dolmatoff 1971:4; Sorensen 1967).

The tribal concept is certainly a hindrance to understanding the marriage system. For instance, a priest who spoke Tukano and who was quite
familiar with Vaupés marriage patterns once speculated for my benefit
about the genetic differences among the "tribes" of the Vaupés. (He was
reminded by an Indian that everyone's mother was from a different
"tribe.") More important, the cultural integration of the Vaupés has
generally been obscured by the use of the term "tribe" for the exogamous
language groups of the region. Thus, while most anthropologists notice the
broad territorial reach and integrating features of the Vaupés cultural
"system," most have been concerned with describing a single "tribe" (language group). As a result, none has taken the full-fledged regional
approach in research—either in conceptualization or methodology—that is
necessary for understanding Vaupés social organization. I was certainly no
exception when I began my research. A brief description of how my
research orientation evolved may illustrate the importance of a regional
concept of the Vaupés.

I arrived in the Vaupés with a research proposal about the beliefs and
practices related to disease and curing in a lowland tribe with a minimum

of contact with modern medicine. I planned to work in a single or at most a few settlements. I realized that it would be impossible to carry out my planned project after finding myself in a settlement with four languages where the rule of exogamy required all in-marrying women to come from another language group and where every Indian was at least trilingual. Children began acquiring two languages almost from the beginning of language learning. Where I had assumed that there would be a reasonably large homogeneous population accessible to me, I found that the long-houses of the region, each holding fewer than 30 individuals, were at least half an hour by river from one another and that frequently the nearest neighboring longhouses belonged to different language groups (Map 2). (The longhouses nearest to the Bará longhouse where I spent most of my time were Tuyuka, Tukano, and Desana.) Eventually I became interested in studying the multilingual situation itself, particularly the way it related to marriage and social structure.

I began to record marriage and census data, both at the longhouse where I was living and during my travels. My interest grew as I realized the extent to which the marriage system involved a rather large amount of territory. Some of the marriages in a given settlement always involved partners from quite distant natal settlements. Also impressive was the extensive knowledge almost all Indians had of the Vaupés region. Tukanoans display a great interest in the physical and social geography of

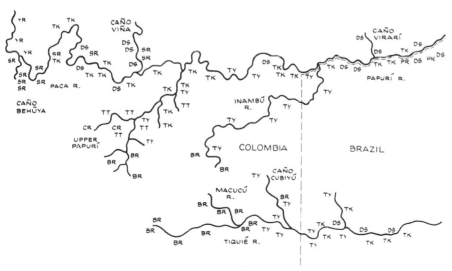

Map 2. Language group distribution of settlements on a section of the Vaupés. The language groups represented are indicated as follows: BR = Bará; TY = Tuyuka; TK = Tukano; DS = Desana; TT = Tatuyo; SR = Siriano; YR = Yurutí; CR = Carapana; and PR = Piratapuya. Each pair of letters represents a settlement (a longhouse or small village). (After Jackson 1974, Figure 6.)

the Vaupés, although those of the Papurí drainage are not as curious about Cubeo territory to the north of the Vaupés River. They acquire information by travel and sometimes by living in different sections of the region, but they also learn much of what they know from conversations, through committing facts about settlements and topography to memory. I became convinced that theirs was the proper perspective to take regarding Vaupés social organization.

I eventually tried to study as broad a population as possible, with the goal of a complete census for marriages of living individuals of the upper and middle Papurí river and its tributaries. I traveled on this river during my canoe trips in and out of the region every 2 or 3 months, and also traveled with the members of the longhouse with whom I stayed. During these trips I gathered and cross-checked information. I always traveled with a different crew of boatmen, usually changing crews at least once during the 6-to-10-day one-way trip. Nights were spent at Indian settlements, and I would gather genealogies at these times, using a boatman as an interpreter. Map making was similarly accomplished, resulting in crude maps that nonetheless demonstrate, along with the accompanying genealogical data, the extent to which marriages unify subsections of the region and, to a lesser extent, the entire Vaupés region. A preliminary description of the social units of the Vaupés, together with a tentative analysis of their interrelationships in the region, follows.

We can characterize language groups as named patrilineal descent units identified with a specific language (their *father language*; Sorensen 1967), the members of which (1) observe a rule of exogamy, (2) terminologically distinguish at this level agnates from other kinsmen, and (3) identify with co-members as "brother people," using a distinct name, language, and certain other differences as boundary-defining markers. These other differences consist of (a) separate semimythical founding ancestors, (b) the right to ancestral power through the use of certain linguistic property, such as sacred chants, and (c) the right to manufacture certain ceremonial objects. Membership in these groups is permanent and public; the one fact that will be known about an Indian before anything else is his or her language group membership.

Vaupés social structure is segmentary and follows a rule of patrilineal descent. Its units, in ascending order of inclusion, are the *local descent group*, the *sib*, the *language group*, and a possible more inclusive exogamic unit, here called the *phratry*. (See Figure 1.)

Certain structural principles operate in Vaupés marriages, and these can be verbalized by Tukanoans. Vaupés Indians have a prescriptive marriage system—that is, one in which the category of marriageable people for any given ego is covered by a single kinship term. Marriage rules also incorporate a rule of direct, or sister, exchange, the ideal case being one in which a man obtains a wife by exchanging his real sister for another man's

Level	1			2		3
I						
II	Bará	Tukano	Yurutí	Tuyuka	etc.	etc.
III	waí mahá · waíñakoroa · wamútañara	(approximately 30 sibs)	etc.		etc.	etc.
IV	A B C D · M N O · Z Y X					

Levels: I = Phratry. (An unnamed unit composed of various language groups. Members of a phratry do not intermarry and state that a sibling relationship exists between co-members.) II = Language group. (What is commonly referred to as "tribe." Membership is determined by a rule of patrilineal descent, and members share a father language.) III = Sib. (Named groups occupying one or more longhouses along a stretch of river. Sibs are ranked, and membership is determined by patrilineal descent.) IV = Local descent group. (Co-agnates who are one another's closest agnatic kin who share the same settlement, usually a longhouse. Can be coterminous with the sib.)

The letters represent current locations of local descent groups who are known by their settlement name. The sib name is permanent, but the settlement name changes when the local descent group moves its longhouse site. For example, A = pĩmanaka buro in 1970.

Figure 1. A visual outline of Vaupés social structure. (After Jackson 1974, Figure 5.)

real sister. This principle, combined with the basically Dravidian type of
kinship terminology, means that the category of potential marriage
partners includes ego's bilateral cross-cousins (for further discussion, see
Jackson 1972a). Two more principles are the previously mentioned one of
linguistic exogamy, and residential exogamy. The latter is the result of the
operation of patrilocality and language group exogamy rules; but it is a
cognitive principle in its own right. Finally, a principle of marriage
alliance operates, which means that two affinally related kin groups will
consider it advantageous to continue to exchange women over time. These
marriage principles are not to be seen as rigidly enforced rules; the degree
to which they actually determine marriage decisions is, in fact, the focus
of investigation. They are principles in the sense that they are the
culturally approved patterns of marriage for Tukanoans and in general
represent the ideal type of marriage from the point of view of any given
individual.

The *settlement* occupies a position of extreme importance in Vaupés
social structure. It is, with very few exceptions, the maximal unit of food
production and consumption. Each settlement is quite isolated and, as a
consequence, autonomous in many respects. Its membership is a tightly
knit group of people who see one another constantly and see other people
infrequently. Children are reared in this setting, developing affective ties
far closer with settlement members than with outsiders. Settlement
members always represent at least three language groups, and among the
members several languages are intermittently spoken. Children spend
most of their time with their mothers and in-married aunts, who by definition are affiliated with father languages other than the child's own; these
women frequently speak their own father languages among themselves.
Cross-cutting linguistic and descent group membership within all settlements gives considerable saliency to these divisions at the most local level
of the region.

Strictly speaking, two units should be distinguished when considering
local-level social organization. "Settlement" (a longhouse or small village)
is a cover term here for *residential group* and *local descent group*, which
are analytically distinct concepts and which never completely overlap in
membership. If all the inhabitants of a settlement are being discussed, one
is speaking of the residential group. The local descent group at a settlement, on the other hand, is composed of only those people who belong to it
as co-agnates. In-married women, for instance, are members in absentia of
the local descent groups of their natal longhouses; they never lose these
ties.[10] Differences between these two types of local groups affect the roles

---

[10] The differences between residence and local descent group are not only analytically
necessary but have meaning to Tukanoans as well. The fact that the in-married women of a
settlement do not belong to the same residential and local descent groups gives them a pivotal
and at times equivocal position in some situations (see Jackson 1972b).

assumed by the members of each and influence the way in which each type of unit relates to equivalent other local units.

The settlement is, then, the most important unit in the Vaupés social system; it is the intersection of the residential group and the local descent group, and it is an isolated and autonomous unit in many economic, political, interactional, and psychological respects. It is almost certain that more inclusive units are not as cognitively important for Tukanoan Indians. More inclusive nonarbitrarily defined *territorial* groupings cannot be totally specified at present, given the necessity of delineating both their general defining features and their applicability to all geographical subsections of the Vaupés.

It is apparent, however, that settlements in the Vaupés are not autonomous to the degree that they are in some other lowland South American societies. Vaupés settlements are exogamous, to begin with, and marital interaction is not necessarily limited to a narrow range of choice from among a few close neighboring settlements affiliated with one or two affinal language groups. Additionally, settlements having only 30 or so members must at times interact with people from other settlements to accomplish the economic exchanges and ceremonial activities that still characterize the region. In the past, military considerations also produced intersettlement interaction, through the creation of alliances and enemy groups.

The *sib* is a local group that is named, has members descended from a common mythical ancestor, and occupies a fixed position in the set of ranked sibs comprising a language group. In cognitive terms, the sib is seen as a group whose members share common residence and close agnatic kinship. In actual terms, where the members of a given sib reside varies greatly.[11] A sib can be a single longhouse or village, excluding, of course, the in-married women (ideally, in other words, the sib is coterminous with the local descent group at a single longhouse). Occasionally two sibs are represented in a single longhouse. Sometimes members of a sib live in several dispersed settlements. Or a sib will be represented by two or more settlements with contiguous territory, usually along a continuous stretch of river. In sum, the constituency of a sib in spatial terms is variable; it may or may not be the local descent group or even a descent group formed by several neighboring settlements. Although probably always a somewhat fluid unit—expectable in areas of low population density and frequent shifts in residence site—recent changes have undoubtedly resulted in the declining viability of the sib as a localized unit of social organization.

A more inclusive territorial unit than either the settlement or most sibs

[11] While the traditional pattern was a 6- to 12-family patrilocal longhouse, at present some villages have a much larger number of people (the largest, Acaricuara mission, has 30 houses), with more than one language group represented. This has necessitated some adjustments in coding some of the information in the marriage sample.

can be termed the *neighborhood,* a group of settlements along a stretch of river or on two rivers with well-traveled trails connecting them. Criteria for inclusion would be territorial continuity and frequency of interaction. When the settlements of a neighborhood are found to be identified with more than one language group, then the affinal relationships among them must be analyzed. When they are found to belong to a single language group, other kinds of relationships have produced enough interaction to warrant considering them a neighborhood. Normally a neighborhood would include a single sib or two sibs sharing a similar position in rank. An anthropologist who studied a single settlement would undoubtedly become well acquainted with not only his or her own settlement but also the neighborhood it was in. However, an ethnography about a single neighborhood would not be adequate for most topics of study in the Vaupés, just as one confined to a single settlement would not be. In the first place, neighborhoods are quite variable and remain to be defined more precisely; generalizations about them would require studies in several parts of the Vaupés. Also, all settlements are oriented in very important ways to settlements outside their own neighborhoods.

Units more inclusive than the local descent group and sib and, like them, based on patrilineal descent principles that, unlike them, not nearly so territorially circumscribed are the *language group* and the *phratry* (cf. Figure 1). It should be noted that at present the language group is considered a nonterritorial group only in the sense that it does not occupy continuous or almost continuous territory. The degree of language group interspersion varies subregionally, but all language groups are located in easily discernible sections of the Vaupés (cf. Map 2). It is equally true that all language groups have some of their member settlements interspersed with settlements belonging to other language groups.

The phratry is an exogamic level more inclusive than that of the language group. A quick scanning of Table 1, based on a sample of 534 marriages, demonstrates that the exchange of marriage partners between language groups is patterned. It can be seen that some language groups do not intermarry at all (for example, Bará–Tukano, Tuyuka–Desana), while others intermarry regularly. This is statistical evidence supporting native statements about a more inclusive phratric level. The sample of 534 marriages is not representative of the total Vaupés marriage population, including only 8 of the 20 or more language groups in the Vaupés and focusing mainly on the middle and upper Papurí drainage. Hence, insofar as these language groups have members residing elsewhere, the sample does not accurately represent their total marriage pattern; nor does it take into account marriages made between members of these 8 language groups and the language groups not included in this sample. But it does give a fairly complete picture of marriages made among 8 language groups dur-

TABLE 1

Marriage between Selected Language Groups in the Vaupés

Husband's Language Group		Wife's Language Group								Row Total	% Column
		Bará	Tuyuka	Tukano	Desana	Carapana	Tatuyo	Siriano	Yurutí		
Bará	N	0	55	0	7	2	12	1	0	77	
	%	0.0	71.4	0.0	9.1	2.6	15.6	1.3	0.0	100.0	(14.4)
Tuyuka	N	58	0	71	3	0	6	7	0	145	
	%	40.0	0.0	49.0	2.1	0.0	4.1	4.8	0.0	100.0	(27.2)
Tukano	N	0	47	1	45	4	5	20	5	127	
	%	0.0	37.0	0.8	35.4	3.1	3.9	15.7	3.9	100.0	(27.2)
Desana	N	5	2	36	0	2	0	10	0	55	
	%	9.1	3.6	65.5	0.0	3.6	0.0	18.2	0.0	100.0	(10.3)
Carapana	N	3	0	6	4	0	10	2	2	27	
	%	11.1	0.0	22.2	14.8	0.0	37.0	7.4	7.4	100.0	(5.1)
Tatuyo	N	10	0	5	1	2	0	0	2	20	
	%	50.0	0.0	25.0	5.0	10.0	0.0	0.0	10.0	100.0	(3.7)
Siriano	N	2	8	27	14	5	1	0	14	71	
	%	2.8	11.3	38.0	19.7	7.0	1.4	0.0	19.7	100.0	(13.3)
Yurutí	N	2	0	2	0	1	1	6	0	12	
	%	16.7	0.0	16.7	0.0	8.3	8.3	50.0	0.0	100.0	(2.2)
Column N		80	112	148	74	16	35	46	23	534	
Column %		15.0	21.0	27.7	13.9	3.0	6.6	8.6	4.3	100.0	(100.0)

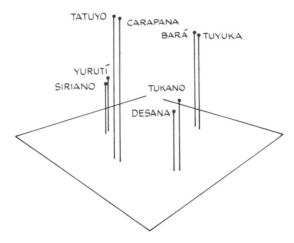

Figure 2. Marital distance between language groups. This figure is a three-dimensional spatial representation of marriage preferences among eight language groups (data from Table 1). (After Jackson and Romney 1973.)

ing the last 30 years in the settlements along the middle and upper Papurí and its tributaries.

Figure 2, using the data in Table 1, shows the pattern of marriage preferences in terms of Euclidian space, through the use of three-dimensional scaling techniques (Jackson 1972b; Jackson and Romney 1973). [These are marriage preferences as they appear after removing the effects of the size of the groups involved, using a technique developed by Romney (1971:191–213).] The resulting illustration shows quite clearly that the eight groups form four pairs, each of which has a high frequency of intermarriage. The next highest frequency of intermarriage occurs between groups that are adjacent in adjoining pairs.[12]

Table 1 and Figure 2 vividly demonstrate the existence of a broad regional network in Vaupés marriage. Such patterning in marriage preferences would not have been apparent had data gathering been limited to a few neighboring settlements. Native informants do mention this kind of marriage preference (cf. Figure 1), and therefore some of the ethnographic literature on the Vaupés briefly discusses phratric organization (Fulop 1955; Sorensen 1967). But without data on a relatively large subsystem of the Vaupés, the actual degree to which phratric organization was important could not be assessed.

Moreover, Indians make other statements about how they marry that contradict the statistical data. For example, an informant might very well state that people always try to make marriages between bilateral cross-cousins, preferably first cousins, who live in neighboring longhouses. But

[12] A. Kimball Romney analyzed this marriage data and derived the model in Figure 2. I gratefully acknowledge his interest and contributions.

only some marriages follow this rule, and not all the exceptions can be explained by demographic impossibility or "breakdown of tradition." Generally, such statements can be interpreted as normative rules about the most advantageous marriage to make in the abstract. Often, these generalizations include the ideal of marrying close—genealogically *and* geographically. Other normative generalizations, however, are based on quite different considerations. Hence, statistical analysis must be used to corroborate and interpret informants' views.

Even the large sample used here is not fully adequate for understanding Vaupés marriage patterns. It is known that Bará of one river tend to marry Paneroa and Tatuyo, while Bará of another river tend to marry Tuyuka and Desana; that is, the location of a settlement affiliated with a given language group influences its marriage strategy and thus the general or regional pattern of marriage. Hence, to discover the total picture regarding marriage preferences in a region such as the Vaupés, a large sample must be taken that includes the marriages made by members of many language groups in several different parts of the region. (See Adams and Kasakoff, Chapter 6, this volume, for a general discussion of regional marriage data.)

In conclusion, it can be seen that structural principles (such as a prescriptive kinship terminology) only set constraints to marriage in the Vaupés, so that in reality no one particular principle determines group interaction. In this regard, the Vaupés marriage system contrasts with Australian or Gê systems in which group membership determines affinal relations more completely. An acceptable model of marriage in the Vaupés, therefore, is one based on network formation as the outcome of at least three sets of factors: (1) environmental constraints, (2) a set of social structural principles, and (3) a set of shared decision-making rules for choosing among the alternatives offered by the first two sets of factors. Such a network formation model would describe general patterns of marital interaction derived from observed relationships between units (of whatever level of inclusiveness, both territorial and nonterritorial) in which marriage has been one type of interaction. An adequate model necessarily includes spatial considerations, for the entire region is the field of action.

TOWARD A MORE FORMAL REGIONAL ANALYSIS OF VAUPÉS MARRIAGE

Marriage is to be seen as a kind of movement between pairs of the various types of units already described and involves movement of people, goods, and intangible commodities, such as prestige. This movement takes place over *routes,* and the sum of these routes forms the marriage network organization of the Vaupés. Basically, routes can be either *physical* or *social*. Social routes can be seen as either *kinship* routes (ascriptive) or *contractual* routes (involving friendship and other nonascriptive relationships). Understanding a given marital relationship between two units (two settlements, two language groups, or the like) requires knowledge of the influences of these kinds of routes upon each other. Obviously, a marriage has both kinship and contractual elements, these in turn being influenced by the geographical routes between the units undertaking the marriage.

Measuring the distance and determining the probability of utilization of a given route between two intermarrying settlements is a complex matter. For example, if a marriage has not occurred for many years between two distant but contiguous settlements, the "route" has altered considerably, for the trail connecting the settlements can virtually disappear. Informants know of many trails that have become overgrown because of shifts in alliance formation. Or, as happened in the recent past, if a pair of affinally related settlements started feuding, booby traps might be placed along the trail, effectively ending its utilization by anyone.

Kinship routes are the paths between interacting components (individuals or kinship-based groups) in the system. Kinship routes are defined in both genealogical and categorical ("relational") terms.[13] Of course, in a system like the Vaupés, actual individuals are often related to each other through several kinship routes, because many marriages take place between their relatives. Sometimes the kin term an ego uses to an alter would be different if another route were used to trace the relationship. Which route is actually employed and how the terminological system is manipulated by people with vested interests in particular marriage alliances are important areas of inquiry. The kinds of units connected by kinship routes can be individuals or large units such as local descent groups or even entire language groups. Table 2 illustrates how certain terms of the zero generation (ego's own) in the Bará language are used to express relationships between units at three levels. Note that spatial location is incorporated into this usage as well.

Roughly speaking, contractual routes are those formed along lines other than propinquity or kinship. These would include trading relationships,[14] friendships formed during sojourns at rubber camps, or relationships made by individuals at remote settlements in order to avail themselves of

[13] The distinction between genealogically and categorically defined paths between kinsmen is an ongoing debate in kinship semantics analysis that has important implications for Vaupés ethnography. Basically the question is whether a given ego and alter who refer to each other with kin terms are kinsmen because of the one or more parent–child links that connect them or because they are members of certain social categories (Jackson 1972a).

[14] Some trading relationships, such as the "ceremonial brother-in-law" (*he-tenü*) mentioned by C. Hugh-Jones (n.d.), are routes built on preexisting kinship routes.

TABLE 2
Zero Generation Terminology at Three Levels of Inclusion[a]

	Ego to Alter	Longhouse to Longhouse Local Descent Group to Local Descent Group	Language Group to Language Group
First group (e.g., Inambú Bará)	"my siblings" agnates	"our brothers" "our real brothers" agnates	"our brothers" "brothers-people" "we speak one language" agnates
Second group (e.g., Inambú Tuyuka)	"my cross-cousins" "my mother's people" father's sisters' children	"our cross-cousins" "our affines/brothers-in-law" pairs of longhouses which have exchanged women	"our cross-cousins" "our menkó-mahkára" "father's sister people" "where we exchange women" potential affines
Third group (e.g., Pirata-puya of waíoperi (Piracuara))	"my mother's children" uterine half-sibling matrilateral parallel cousin	"longhouses far away" "distant kinsmen" "our mothers are sisters; our fathers aren't brothers"	"our mothers are sisters to each other" "mother's children from the waking-up times"[b] "pahkó-mahkára": "mother's children people" affines of affines

a. Quotes around statements indicate how Indians talk about relationships.
b. Information from C. Hugh-Jones.

the information and influence of individuals in mission towns. Marriages do result from contact along such routes. In fact, when contractual relationships become firmly established, they gradually move into the idiom of kinship, since in the widest sense an Indian is a kinsman of all semisedentary Indians in the Vaupés region. Although no general statements of principles can be formulated at present regarding this type of route, contractual relationships are quite important as routes along which interaction affecting marital alliance occurs.

Distance of routes is important to any analysis of the Vaupés marriage system. One can measure distance within various dimensions; it is possible to think of geographical, kinship, marital, social–interactional, and linguistic distance, all of which have regional parameters. Distance is a feature of meaning in the terms of Table 2. The relationship of an ego to an alter or one entire language group to another can be stated using Bará terms that describe relative marital and geographical distance. Figure 3 illustrates the native assumption of a correlation existing between linguistic and marital distance (that is, "people we marry" are more distant than "people we don't marry—our brothers"). This has resulted in a native classification of distance among the languages (obtained from Bará informants of the Papurí drainage) that is strongly influenced by actual marriage patterns in specific geographical areas of the Vaupés.

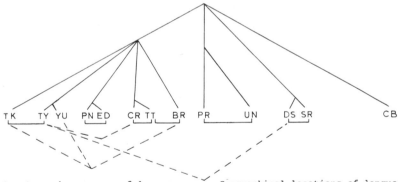

Tree structure above names of languages represents Sorensen's reconstruction of the Eastern Tukanoan family.

Brackets under two language names represent language groups which intermarry in at least one region of the Vaupés.

Tree structure under names of languages represents the Bará model of relative language distance: connecting dashed lines show languages which are said to be more similar than the languages of intermarrying language groups.

Geographical locations of language groups represented by brackets showing inter-marriage:

Tukano and Tuyuka: middle Papurí
Paneroa and Edulia: Piraparaná
Carapana and Tatuyo: upper Papurí
Tatuyo and Bará: upper Papurí
Piratapuya and Uanano: lower Papurí
Desana and Siriano: Caño Viña

Names of languages, from left to right: Tukano, Tuyuka, Yurutí, Paneroa, Edulia, Carapana, Tatuyo, Bará, Piratapuya, Uanano, Desana, Siriano, and Cubeo.

Figure 3. Two conflicting models of language distance.

The significance of the distance between the natal settlements of a particular couple contemplating marriage cannot be interpreted as a simple direct correlation between increasing distance (geographical, kinship, or whatever) and increasing undesirability of a prospective marriage alliance. For example, given that a specific settlement has married several of its women into one or two nearby settlements, it may be more advantageous from its point of view to make the next marriages with settlements relatively far away. This may have been particularly important in times of raiding and feuding, when hostilities were often between settlements having affinal relationships (see Chagnon 1968 for a comparable situation).

Nonetheless, distance does structure marriages so that fewer marriages occur across great distances. Figure 4 shows geographical distance between marriage partners' natal settlements at the time of marriage (based on the map in Appendix II, Jackson 1972b), graphing the linear distance between spouses' settlements for a sample of 635 marriages.

Figure 4 can be interpreted as follows. The horizontal axis represents distance measured in inches on a map; 1 inch is roughly equivalent to 3.1 miles. The mean linear distance for the sample is 7.57 (with a standard

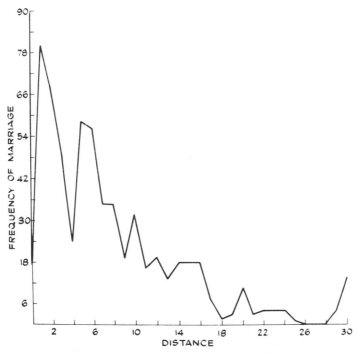

Figure 4. Linear distance between spouses' natal settlements. Horizontal axis: distance (as-the-crow-flies distance measured in inches on Appendix II map in Jackson 1972b) between spouses' settlements. Vertical axis: frequency of marriages (sample size of 635 marriages).

deviation of 6.60), or very roughly 22 miles. Distances were rounded off to
the nearest inch, and settlements are neither randomly nor continuously
placed on the Vaupés landscape—hence the jagged line, especially the
jumps between 3 inches (49 marriages), 4 inches (24 marriages), and 5
inches (58 marriages). Such jumps are not ethnographically meaningful
and would disappear with a larger sample. No marriages were assigned a
value of zero unless the man and woman were from the same settlement; if
they were from different settlements, they were always assigned a number
of 1 even though rounding off would have assigned them zero. This was
done to highlight residential endogamy, a very recent occurrence. (All
residentially endogamous marriages in the sample involved individuals living in mission towns.) Any marriage that involved a distance of 30 or more
inches on the map, 93 miles as the crow flies, was assigned a value of 30—
hence the marked increase in the number of marriages with that value.
(Most of these cases were anomalous, involving a non-Indian partner or
taking place during a man's residence in a rubber camp.) Some of these
marriages involved distances extending beyond the boundaries of the map.

    Figure 4 basically shows that the majority of marriages in this sample
did not occur between settlements that are geographically closest to each
other. The degree to which this sample shows a real preference for marriages between settlements that are not contiguous is not known. And the
proportion of marriages that occur between settlements that are not
contiguous (first eliminating settlements that are prohibited as affines by
the social structural principles discussed earlier) has yet to be worked out
in quantitative terms. Such a statement about marriage preferences would
have to eliminate the effects of differential settlement size and
geographical constraints. It does seem to be the case, however, that, having
removed these constraints on spouse selection, a significant proportion of
marriages does not occur between settlements that are nearest neighbors.
Figure 5 and Map 3 illustrate, for a single settlement, marriages between it
and certain other settlements over three generations. They show a marked
tendency toward alliance making—expectable, given other sources of
information, such as informant discussions and the implications of the
kinship terminologies of the various Vaupés languages. Clearly, the settlement *púmanaka buro* does not marry only into neighboring settlements
(Figure 5).

    Obviously, however, as-the-crow-flies distance between two settlements
is not the most accurate measurement of the distance between them for
understanding native decision making based on that distance. Just as
physical distance can be affected by the state of the trail between two settlements and how frequently it is traveled, what we might call social
distance is a function of (1) linear distance, (2) travel distance (making
adjustments on a linear distance value in terms of the actual distance
covered when traveling between two settlements), and (3) the degree to

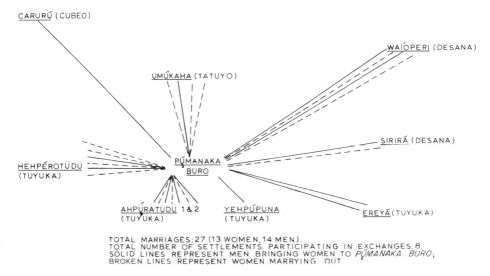

TOTAL MARRIAGES: 27 (13 WOMEN, 14 MEN).
TOTAL NUMBER OF SETTLEMENTS PARTICIPATING IN EXCHANGES: 8.
SOLID LINES REPRESENT MEN BRINGING WOMEN TO *PÚMANAKA BURO*;
BROKEN LINES REPRESENT WOMEN MARRYING OUT

Figure 5.   Marriages during three generations at *púmanaka buro.*

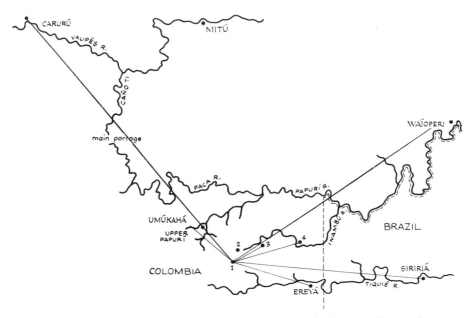

Map 3.   Locations of settlements intermarrying with *púmanaka buro.* The Bará settlement of *púmanaka buro* is located at 1, and the Tuyuka settlements of *yehpúpuna, ahpúratüdü,* and *hehpérotüdü* are located at 2, 3, and 4, respectively. The map is not to scale.

which interaction exists between two settlements. Marriage making, or the
lack of it, between two settlements will produce a change in social distance
between two settlements. A new marriage can decrease the distance
between two settlements by further cementing a well-established alliance.
Or the distance can be increased by one settlement's not completing its
part of an exchange marriage and the other settlement's considering itself
cheated of a woman to which it is entitled. On the other hand, literal
physical distance between the two settlements in this type of situation is
important. If a settlement considers itself owed a woman, its demands will
have far less impact if it is located far away from the debtor settlement. In
turn, the debtor settlement may have decided not to honor the original
contract in part because the claims of the other settlement could be easily
disregarded.

Figures 4 and 5 and Map 3 illustrate the importance of seeing marriage
in terms of *movement*. Movement involves many individuals and is an
exchange of people, goods, and such intangibles as prestige or, in the past,
military security. To a certain degree it occurs not only between two individuals and their families but is also an activity that occurs between settlements, sibs, language groups, and phratries. Marriage making is not a
single event but an ongoing process, initiated long before a woman moves
to her husband's settlement, continuing long after the couple is perceived
to have a stable marriage. To the degree that a marriage establishes or
continues an alliance, the movement between settlements resulting from it
is a permanent process. Indeed, marriage as an organizing principle
behind much interaction in the Vaupés is apparent to Vaupés natives and
readily acknowledged by them.

The concept *field of movement* used in regional studies has several useful applications to the Vaupés situation. Although, as Figures 4 and 5 and
Map 3 indicate, settlements do not marry within a tightly constricted area,
it is also the case that some marriages *are* statistically improbable and are
seen by the Indians as anomalous. A model of Vaupés marriage with
regard to distance between settlements might resemble what Haggett calls
a "mean field" (1966:41). This model would specify the point at which
marriage between two settlements at given distances from each other is
extremely unlikely. A particular settlement would not necessarily occupy
the center of its mean field due to several types of possible distortions; for
instance, it might tend to marry farther in the downstream direction or
toward a mission town. The international boundary between Colombia
and Brazil might cause some skewing in the patterns of some settlements,
due to the fact that many Indian children now go to school in mission
towns and are supposed to attend a school in the same country as their settlement.

Research objectives related to the concept of field of movement might
be (1) how and why a settlement's mean field changes over time; (2) why

certain settlements within a given settlement's mean field are not actually related through affinal exchanges, even though principles of social structure make them potential affines; and (3) how marriage patterns vary from subregion to subregion in the Vaupés. I expect that certain regions, such as the Piraparaná River basin (isolated from acculturative influences and located on the periphery of the regional system), would have settlements characterized by a smaller average mean field, both in terms of the territory included within their mean fields and in terms of the number of language groups and sibs represented by the settlements within their mean fields.

I feel that nonarbitrary subregions, defined by amount of marital interaction, exist and can be discovered. There will be problems of overlap and of peripheral settlements (or sibs) having more interaction outside their subregional boundaries. But, given the geographical setting with its river networks, which greatly influence communication frequencies, it is hoped that such subregions can be successfully delineated.

CONCLUSIONS

Most of the ethnographers who have written recently on the Vaupés have commented on the degree of homogeneity found throughout the region. They note that this is so despite no or sporadic contact between many of its inhabitants (see Goldman 1948:763–764; Reichel-Dolmatoff 1971:16[15]; Sorensen 1967:673–674). The cultural homogeneity is readily apparent even to a nonanthropologist, regardless of how one defines "culture." The similarity of observable phenomena throughout the region is indisputable, and similarities in the cognitive orientation of Vaupés natives, their "models for perceiving, relating, and interpreting [Goodenough 1964:36]" their world, can be demonstrated as well. Tukanoans, for instance, assume that Vaupés rules of marriage apply throughout the region, and people who do not observe these rules—whites, Makú, and Cubeo—are criticized and ridiculed for their inappropriate behavior. The origin myths of the various language groups, although occurring in more than 20 languages, share many basic similarities, use the entire region as their setting, and contain plots involving many of the present-day language groups.

Linguistic evidence also shows that the discrete languages of the Vaupés are by no means indications of similarity discrete cultures. Semantic cate-

[15] Reichel-Dolmatoff argues that an economic diversification along the lines of language group boundaries exists in native cognitive orientation that, he admits, "does not correspond entirely to economic reality [1971:17]," based on distinctions between hunting, fishing, and horticultural groups. His evidence for this is not convincing, and it would be surprising to find such an arrangement among groups with a direct exchange marriage system.

gories in many of the languages appear to be similar if not identical. This is not surprising given that Tukanoans everywhere behave very similarly and must deal with the same landscape, physical and social, regardless of formal identification with specific father languages (see Jackson 1974).

The degree to which the differences that are found in the Vaupés—particularly linguistic ones—*are* cultural differences rather than significant distinctions within a single culture is an important question. Perhaps most of the heterogeneity that exists should be considered an aid in the organization of interaction among the various social units within the region in much the same way as highly visible differences in uniforms aid in the organization and playing of a football game. The fact that it is language that serves as the emblem of distinct units, which must remain distinct for the system to work, has undoubtedly obscured the underlying similarities. Few anthropologists have encountered such widespread multilingualism in either their own society or the anthropological literature. Multilingualism is assumed to be characteristic only of complex societies. Thus, differences separating the language groups of the Vaupés tend to be overemphasized (exacerbated by calling the language groups tribes), despite the fact that differences in language do not, a priori, indicate deep cultural divisions. Hence, the essentially homogeneous and regionally integrated characteristics of the Vaupés are only briefly considered in the ethnographic literature. [Sorensen (1967) is an exception with regard to linguistically related concerns.]

Various anthropological biases work against viewing the Vaupés and similar societies as unified systems. It is far more convenient to conclude that a smaller unit of study is ethnographically justified, particularly in tropical forest research, which is so frequently characterized by dispersed settlements and absence of roads or other efficient transportation. However, all "simple" societies are structured by more than face-to-face interaction. The most dispersed populations of the world (hunter–gatherers, such as the Shoshone, Montagnais–Naskapi, Bushmen, and aboriginal Australians[16]) are ipso facto regional systems because local groups exploit large geographical areas, coming into frequent though sporadic contact with other local groups. Local group interdependence, fluidity in territorial boundaries, and fluctuation in the membership of the local group—all characteristic of such regional systems—suggest how we might understand the organization of a system such as the Vaupés. For while there is greater rigidity of affiliation to social groups and categories in the Vaupés than in most hunter–gatherer populations, local groups in the Vaupés *do* have flexibility and choice of action within the structural framework of their institutions, as well as considerable local group contact,

[16] See Leacock (1955:31–47), Lee and DeVore (1968:150–157), and Yengoyan (1970:256–260).

exchange, and movement within the region. Indeed, the type of regional system discussed here fits most societies of the Amazon and Orinoco basin to some extent.[17] This suggests that the ecological setting will determine the kind of regional organization that a system will have.

In brief, the environmental features of the Vaupés that render it unlike most other regional systems considered in this volume are precisely those that provide the key to its comprehension:

1. *Demography.* Low population density, dispersed population, and infrequent local group contact lead to regional systems without nodes or hierarchies in any significant sense. Societies with these demographic characteristics exploit ecosystems similar to that of the Vaupés territory more efficiently than would central-place-organized populations. Hence, certain environmental variables give rise to local systems based on network rather than central-place formation.

2. *Subsistence patterns.* Under the particular subsistence arrangements of swidden agriculture, which requires access to extensive lands not recently cultivated, and given the need for extensive territory for hunting and collecting practices, demand for nonlocal goods and services is best met through network formation rather than hierarchical redistribution. In other words, economic organization is most efficient when distributing various resources (also dispersed throughout the landscape) through a system that is even-handed, that requires little capital or storage, and that maximizes the social benefits of generalized reciprocity. Undoubtedly the patterns of raiding and feuding characterizing the Vaupés until recently have played an important role in the evolution of a system such as is found at present—these patterns themselves having been influenced by certain ecological inputs. Indeed, the economic fragility of swidden systems requires a self-reinforcing exchange system in which economic support is maintained not so much by exchanges of goods as by the kinds of social relationships that allow potential changes of personnel.

3. *Sociological factors.* The settlement pattern, multifamily longhouse arrangements, patrilineal sibs, and the like can all be seen as adaptations to a tropical rain forest environment, given a certain technology. These institutions, in turn, lead to a regional system organized through marriage exchanges rather than commodity exchanges, wherein regional organization is perpetuated by exchange of personnel rather than of goods.

[17] Analogies to even the linguistic–marriage system found in the Vaupés do exist elsewhere (see Bright and Bright 1965; Owen 1965; Tindale 1953). Examples of regional orientation in lowland interior South American societies are discussed in Jackson (1975).

REFERENCES

Atlas de Colombia
  1969 Bogotá:Instituto Geográfico "Agustín Codazzi."
Bates, Marston
  1965 *The land and wildlife of South America.* Amsterdam: Time-Life.
Bright, J. O., and W. Bright
  1965 Semantic structures in northwestern California and the Sapir–Whorf hypothesis. *American Anthropologist* **67:** 249–258.
Carneiro, Robert
  1970 The transition from hunting to horticulture in the Amazon basin. *Proceedings of the Eighth International Congress of Anthropological and Ethnological Sciences,* Tokyo, **III:** 244–248.
Chagnon, Napoleon A.
  1968 *Yǫnomamö: The fierce people.* New York: Holt.
  1974 *Studying the Yǫnomamö.* New York: Holt.
Fulop, Marcos
  1955 Notas sobre los términos y el sistema de parentesco de los Tukano. *Revista Colombiana de Antropología* **4:** 123–164.
Goldman, Irving
  1948 Tribes of the Uaupés–Caquetá region. *Bureau of American Ethnology Bulletin* **143:** 763–798.
  1963 *The Cubeo: Indians of the Northwest Amazon.* Urbana: Univ. of Illinois Press.
Goodenough, Ward H.
  1964 Cultural anthropology and linguistics. In *Language in culture and society,* edited by Dell Hymes. New York: Harper. Pp. 36–39.
Haggett, Peter
  1966 *Locational analysis in human geography.* New York: St. Martin's Press.
Helm, June (Ed.)
  1968 *Essays on the problem of tribe.* Seattle: Univ. of Washington Press.
Holmberg, Allan R.
  1969 *Nomads of the long bow: The Sirionó of eastern Bolivia.* New York: Natural History Press.
Hugh-Jones, Christine
  1971 Untitled manuscript on Piraparaná social structure.
Jackson, Jean E.
  1972a Bará zero generation terminology and marriage. Paper presented at the MSSB Conference on Formal Methods in Kinship Semantics, Riverside.
  1972b Marriage and linguistic identity among the Bará Indians of the Vaupés, Colombia. Unpublished Ph.D. dissertation, Stanford Univ.
  1973 Relations between semi-sedentary and nomadic Indians of the Vaupés, Colombia. Paper presented at the annual meeting of the Southwestern Anthropological Association, San Francisco.
  1974 Language identity of the Colombian Vaupés Indians. In *Explorations in the ethnography of speaking,* edited by R. Bauman and J. Sherzer. New York: Cambridge Univ. Press. Pp. 50–64.
  1975 Recent ethnography of indigenous northern lowland South America. In Volume IV of *Annual review of anthropology,* edited by B. Siegel. Palo Alto, Calif.: Annual Reviews. Pp. 307–340.
Jackson, Jean E., and A. Kimball Romney
  1973 A note on Bará exogamy. Unpublished manuscript.
Koch-Grünberg, Theodor
  1909–1910 *Zwei Jahre unter den Indianern. Reisen in Nordwest-Brasilien* 1903/1905. 2 vols. Berlin: Ernst Wasmuth.

Leacock, Eleanor B.
  1955 Matrilocality in a simple hunting economy (Montagnais Naskapi). *Southwestern Journal of Anthropology* **11**: 31–47.
Lee, Richard B., and Irven DeVore
  1968 *Man the hunter*. Chicago: Aldine.
Moser, Brian, and Donald Tayler
  1963 Tribes of the Piraparaná. *The Geographical Journal* **129**: 437–449.
Owen, Roger
  1965 Patrilocal band: A linguistic and cultural heterogeneous unit. *American Anthropologist* **67**: 675–690.
Reichel-Dolmatoff, Gerardo
  1971 *Amazonian cosmos: The sexual and religious symbolism of the Tukano Indians.* Chicago Univ. of Chicago Press.
Romney, A. Kimball
  1971 Measuring endogamy. In *Explorations in mathematical anthropology,* edited by Paul Kay. Cambridge, Mass.: MIT Press. Pp. 191–213.
Silverwood-Cope, Peter
  1972 A contribution to the ethnography of the Colombian Makú. Unpublished Ph.D. dissertation, Univ. of Cambridge.
Sorensen, Arthur P., Jr.
  1967 Multilingualism in the Northwest Amazon. *American Anthropologist* **69**: 670–682.
Tindale, Norman B.
  1953 Tribal and inter-tribal marriage among the Australian aborigines. *Human Biology* **25**: 169–190.
Yengoyan, Aram A.
  1970 Australian section systems—Demographic components and interactional similarities with the !Kung Bushmen. *Proceedings of the Eighth International Congress of Anthropological and Ethnological Sciences,* Tokyo, **III**: 256–260.

Chapter 4

Lineage Cells and Regional Definition in Complex Societies

Richard G. Fox
Duke University

Recent studies of the traditional complex societies of India, the Near East, and Latin America—and even of the Mediterranean and northern Europe, where supposedly no "natives" live—have brought anthropology closer to fulfillment as a science of *all* mankind and further from an often paternalistic and narrow scholarly involvement with the primitive world. Unlike the anthropologist's experience in the primitive world, however, no longer does the microcosm studied by anthropology replicate in large degree the entire society (Manners 1965:179–195). Instead, the village, caste group, city ward, or other local segment intensively studied by the anthropologist reflects only the endpoints in an inclusive web of social relations binding localities with national political, economic, and cultural institutions.

How, then, does the anthropologist see the nation from his village, comprehend the elite from knowing the peasant, analyze the urban Great Tradition from understanding village folk traditions? Recent studies of traditional complex societies espouse two distinctive approaches to the ties linking local communities with national society. One solution has been the "village-outward" perspective, in which the local community's links to the outside are charted through brokers, patron clientage, and other mediating institutions. The other solution defines regional marketing areas or corporate kin webs which constitute the cellular structure of the complex society, the many local parts which comprise the national whole.

This paper explores the validity and usefulness of the latter cellular approach through comparison of localized unilineal kin groups and their relationship to national polity in traditional northern India and the Scottish Highlands. The first part of this paper briefly reviews the two viewpoints which have emerged in the anthropology of complex societies. It argues that concern with the political anthropology of complex societies leads to both a study of regions in relation to the national political order and a focus on the interplay of state power with regional community organization. The second part illustrates how this approach helps analyze the nature of state–locality interrelations in traditional northern India. The third part charts a similar pattern of state–locality linkage through localized kin groups from the presently limited and retrospectively romantic literature on the Scottish Highlands in the two centuries before the 1745 rebellion. A concluding statement utilizes the northern Indian and Scottish material for generalizations about state–locality relations in traditional societies and as illustrations of a cellular approach to the anthropology of complex societies.

COMPLEX SOCIETIES

The anthropology of complex societies began with self-contained community studies in peasant Latin America, village India, and other rural components of Third World nations. As anthropologists became more attuned to the complexity of these societies and as they increasingly threw off the methodological baggage brought from the primitive world, they soon recognized that these communities could not be treated as isolates and could only be comprehended in their many stranded links with the larger society.

Anthropologists began to pursue both methodologies and theoretical directions which promised to bring the complex society down to the scholar in his mud hut village. Techniques such as network and situational analysis (Barnes 1954; Mitchell 1969) and perspectives such as "village outward" and "quasi-groups" (Mayer 1966) have made the anthropological observer more sensitive to the impact of the larger society upon his local community and to the dependency of the village and its inhabitants on the nation. Such "village-outward" investigations (this term will be used as generic for all such studies) emphasize the "interstitial, supplementary, and parallel" social institutions which bind local communities to "major, over-arching institutions [Wolf 1966a:2]." Kinship links, patron-client ties, broker and middleman relations, and voluntary associations (Anderson and Anderson 1966; Silverman 1967; Weingrod 1968; Wolf

1966a, 1966b) all form major axes leading up from village community to national society. Silverman's conclusion about mediators in central Italy is an excellent statement of this approach:

> *Looking outward from the community,* the mediators' relationships with the national system were of two kinds. First, the local patrons had extensive ties with near and distant kinsmen, friends, and business associates . . . in other village centers, in towns, and in cities of the region. . . . Second, the . . . patrons, as well as their equal numbers in other communities, were themselves clients to more powerful, higher status patrons. . . . Thus through a hierarchy of patronage . . . this community was linked to the higher units of organization within the nation [1967:290; emphasis added].

In the "village-outward" perspective, therefore, anthropologists generate the complex society from perceiving its impact on local communities. In a scholarly sense, the larger society appears as an extension of the local community; we begin at the village bottom of patron–client ties in Italy, and only as we ascend the ladder of locality–nation relations does the Italian nation appear. Such studies provide important insights into the *processes* of state–locality linkage, into the individual manipulative channels from village to nation for power, glory, or social repute.

In its emphasis on the processes and channels linking locality and nation, the "village-outward" approach says little about the *structure* of complex societies or about the manner in which village communities compose and are situated within the organization of the larger society. Two assumptions implicit in the "village-outward" perspective may actually impede investigation of the social components of complex societies: (1) The village or local community is often taken as the locus of state–locality relations; the nation exists in a sociological sense only to the extent that it is coalesced by the many strands of patron clientage, friendships, quasi-groups, and other "interstitial and supplementary" relationships. (2) These networks of relations may tell us how the boundaries of village community life are abridged and penetrated by national institutions; they say a good deal less about the social composition of complex societies as wholes and the manner in which their constituent local communities adhere to form them.

A variant method of conceptualizing the relations between locality and nation is through a "cellular" model [to use Lattimore's (1960) term] of complex societies. Traditional complex societies were characterized by the presence of many autonomous, often self-sufficient political, economic, or kinship regions which in varying degree were tied together by national institutions and a centralized state. The organization of such regions coupled with the extent and method of their adherence to more encompassing economic, political, or genealogical institutions can be used to define the complex society anthropologically. This approach does not take the village as a necessary starting point for investigation, nor does it necessarily emphasize the processes of patron clientage, kinship, or friendship which channel locality–nation relations. The important avenues of inquiry become the composition of the constituent cells in a particular complex society, the extent and adaptability of these cellular regions, the fashion in which these regions are linked to the nation and state, and the extent to which they are so linked.

Several recent studies focus on the cellular or regional constituents of particular complex societies and on their historical or contemporary pattern of segmentation and integration with the larger society. Traditional Chinese marketing communities, according to G. William Skinner, were self-contained economic and distributive cells which also set informal boundaries for regional politics, state administration, peasant marriages and extended kin groups, voluntary associations, and patron–client ties. Variant patterns of religious traditions and language usage also had their major focus and institutionalization at the level of the market region (Skinner 1964, 1971). To recognize the primacy of such Chinese market cells is to undercut basic assumptions hitherto accepted in the anthropology of complex societies. Skinner writes:

> Anthropological work on Chinese society, by focusing attention almost exclusively on the village, has with few exceptions distorted the reality of rural social structure. Insofar as the Chinese peasant can be said to live in a self-contained world, that world is not the village but the standard marketing community [1964:32].

Is the cellular analysis of Chinese market regions applicable to other complex societies? Although such marketing deployment undoubtedly exists in any preindustrial complex society (as Skinner notes), other bases of regional organization may prove of greater structural importance in specific complex societies. Alternative cellular models may achieve "greater structural importance" by emically reflecting indigenous beliefs about the cellular pattern and/or by etically analyzing the efficient cellular composition of a specific complex society. Recent work on northern India suggests that the ideology and activity of unilineal kin groups formed the important building blocks of traditional society (Fox 1971a, 1971b; Pradhan 1966; Singh 1968; Stein in press). This paper suggests that such cellular kinship groups also organized local regions in premodern Highland Scotland. These localized and politically dominant "clans," or, more correctly, lineages, were territorially recognized and utilized by central state power at the lowest level of its bureaucratic administration. These two cases duplicate Skinner's Chinese analysis in the importance accorded a regional approach; they depart from his analysis by specifying a different organization for such regions and, consequently, a different pattern of state–locality relations. The presentation of the Indian and Scottish material differs from Skinner's work on China in still another respect. Rather than the mapping and modeling of regional cells, my emphasis is on the ebb and flow of (political) relations between national institutions or authorities and the regional cell. Like the "village-outward" approach, state–locality relations remain the prime focus. But the cellular approach delineates the regional organization of a complex society through which such relations necessarily flow. My own research on northern India probed the nature of corporate kinship cells, and I now turn to a brief recapitulation of this material before discussing the Scottish data.

THE CASE OF NORTHERN INDIA

The basic building block of northern Indian society was a territorially nucleated stratified lineage belonging to a locally dominant caste.[1] Even though the ethnographic and historical literature from Uttar Pradesh, Rajasthan, Punjab, and Bihar label these corporate kin bodies clans or tribes, the term "stratified lineage" more aptly specifies two important qualities of these groups: Wide differences in wealth and power existed within the kin group, and exact genealogical connections between the brethren were traced and were important in the determination of power and wealth. A typical stratified lineage consisted of at least six to eight generations of patrilineal kin descended from the lineage founder. The lineage brethren occupied a contiguous territory over which they ruled and within which remnants of conquered and subordinated lineages might continue to exist in the capacity of tenants to the dominant stratified lineage. Stratified lineages owed their origins variously to adventurers and freebooters, court favorites, or tax collectors who through guile, military prowess, or imperial favor gained control over a region, subdued its indigenes, constructed a central mud fortress with defensive walls, and settled nearby villages with close kinsmen. Over several generations the lineage population proliferated and became a substantial percentage of the local village population, the lineage militia drawn from among this population grew more potent, and the wealth and power differential between direct descendants of the lineage founder (generally reckoned by primogeniture) and cadet lines grew apace.

Although the stratifed lineage was the most inclusive kin body of corporate political, military, and administrative behavior at the regional level, claims to a common patrilineal descent often linked it with other nearby

[1] For greater detail on the stratified lineage and unilineal kin groups in northern India, see Fox (1971a, 1971b).

stratified lineages. Genealogical connections, usually of the most spurious sort, often linked stratified lineages into all-India status categories which served prestige and ideological functions and had little local behavioral significance. Most stratified lineages thus claimed "membership" in status categories such as Rajput, Bhuinhar, Jat, or other locally dominant castes.

The corporateness of a stratified lineage did not solely reside in its genealogical constitution or its occupation of a contiguous territory. The stratified lineage was the widest kin body recognized within the administrative and revenue organization of the northern Indian state, whoever its rulers and whatever its de jure bureaucratic organization. Such political recognition by central authority was primarily concerned with the collection of government land revenue through the hereditary elite of the stratified lineage. Political recognition buttressed the self-definition, cohesion, and corporate activities of such lineages and tended to make them behaviorally, economically, and politically significant to their kin membership. This significance explains why the boundaries of corporate economic and political behavior between kinsmen were generally smaller than the extent of recognized genealogical connection; the mandate of government is also the mandate for corporate kin activity.

The administrative recognition and duties appended to the stratified lineage often meant that lineage territories corresponded to the boundaries of low-level state administrative or revenue divisions such as the *pargana, tappa,* or *taluka* wherein the state abrogated its right to direct taxation in favor of the lineage elite (the state's internal weakness often gave little choice to central authorities in this matter). The extent to which the state administratively recognized lineage boundaries varied with its own power and with the internal cohesion of the lineage; that is, it varied with the power of the state to circumvent the lineage organization and with the power of the lineage to resist state intervention. A puissant state imposed its own administrative boundaries on the kin locality or recognized only the territories of the most genealogically shallow kin groups, with little local influence. A weak polity perforce accepted a low-level administrative territory whose extent faithfully mirrored the regional lineage situation.

The lineage elite acted as hinge figures or brokers linking the lineage territory to state authority. Variously called *rajas, chaudharis, talukdars,* or *babus,* the lineage elite usually inherited their prerogatives of power and influence, either as autocratic leaders or republican representatives of their kin groups. The state used them to collect the land revenue due in the lineage territory, a privilege which conferred upon the lineage elite great autonomy and power. The lineage elite held proprietary title to only a small fraction of the lineage territory, but their managerial rights in the collection of state land revenue gave them important executive powers. Their lower-ranking kin brethren viewed them as paramount in rank and wealth within the lineage and provided the substance of their military following. At times, both the kin body and the state attempted to circumvent the elite and replace them with a more direct channel between local community and state power. In turn, the lineage elite manipulated both their kin obligations and following as well as their state duties in order to cement their superiority over their kinsmen and to maintain local autonomy from the state. For example, the elite commonly settled foreign families, kin groups, and Brahmans on their kin lands in order to establish a loyal class of retainers apart from the kin order. When the raja in his role of revenue payer was strong, he would commonly try to strip his lineage mates of their proprietary rights and reduce them to undertenants. Conversely, when the state was strong, it would attempt to dispossess the lineage elite of its superior powers and to deal directly with the lineage brethren.

The relationship between the state and its lineage cells was not static in northern India (as Skinner also notes for China). The interplay between state power, the lineage elite, and the lineage brethren led to a developmental cycle in which a succession of stages in the birth, maturity, and demise of the stratified lineage depended on an interrelated set of factors including the power of the state, the power of the lineage elite, the land available for lineage expansion, and the size of the lineage population. Briefly summarized, the developmental cycle indicates that lineage strength and regional influence increase as state power weakens, while the reverse process obtains when the state gains power. The apex of lineage strength allows the kin elite to become regional autocrats, whereas under conditions of state prowess their status is much reduced until they may lose all political and economic precedence within their stratified lineage. At all times, the state at the national level and the stratified lineage at the regional level are linked in a constant interplay of power which binds them inextricably together.

The following section explores the analogues of the northern Indian situation to be found in the Scottish Highlands between the seventeenth and nineteenth centuries.

THE CASE OF HIGHLAND SCOTLAND

Shorn of their Victorian romantic overlay of tartan setts, bagpipe rants, and claymore honor, the clans, or traditional unilineal kin groups of Highland Scotland, bear marked resemblance to northern Indian stratified lineages. The Scottish Highlands comprise the rugged and infertile mainland country north and west of the Firths of Forth and Clyde as well as the islands of Skye, the Outer Hebrides, the Uists, and so on lying off the western coast of the Scottish land mass. In these "regions, mountainous and wild," are found the various clans associated with Scotland (such as

Macgregor, Grant, Campbell, MacLeod, Macpherson), their traditional
pastoral economy, and the "clannish" feeling which made this region a
constant paramilitary threat to lowland Scot and English monarch alike
until after "the '45." In this uprising (1745–1746), the Stuart Pretender
and his Highland legions were defeated at Culloden by the forces of the
Hanover King of England, and the Highlands underwent a military
subjugation and social destruction which, however, did not fully extirpate
the kin basis of society until midway in the nineteenth century
(Macpherson 1967:149–192).

Highland Clans: Origin and Constitution

Scottish clans, like their northern Indian counterparts, arose and pros-
pered during periods of political decentralization or state weakness.
Conversely, they were only subdued and then neutralized when state
power was sufficently strong to penetrate their mountain and island fast-
nesses. The clans therefore existed in a complex and ever changing interaction with central authorities wherein ascendancy of the one reflected or
generated decreasing power in the other. Scholars generally trace the
origins of the Highland kin regime to the political and territorial fragmentation of Celtic tribes under pressure from feudal institutions
introduced by Scottish rulers from the eleventh century onward [Skene
1971 (1880) III:287]. Evidence suggests, however, that clan origins may be
as diverse (and nontribal) as those encountered for northern Indian
stratified lineages. Some Highland clans have an antiquity of pedigree
which may revert to the Celts; others originate from the military strength
and opportunism of their founders quite apart from any elevated
genealogy; still others arise from the ramifying descendants of lowlanders
and English interlopers appointed as feudal overlords by the Scottish
Crown (Grant 1930:479–481, 496). What sets these diverse clan origins
into a common mold is that they all result in a system of territorial dominance and social stratification based on agnatic principles. The links
between clan chief and commoner, proprietor and tenant, or elite and
peasant are phrased in terms of kinship.

The highly ramified and widely dispersed Macdonald clan will serve as
an exemplar throughout this exposition of Highland kinship and region.[2]
Other than the Campbells, their inveterate enemies, no other Highland kin

---

[2] Clan Donald's traditional genealogy descends from an illustrious Irish ancestry many
hundreds of years before Christ. The first quasi-historical figure in Scotland is Somerled,
self-proclaimed Thane or Regulus of Argyll. Somerled is said to have evicted Norse power
from the Western Isles in the twelfth century and to have carved out what later became the
territories comprising the Lordship of the Isles. The Macdonalds, the Macdougalls, the
Macintyres, and other Highlanders trace descent (or some other connection) to Somerled. See
Anonymous (n.d.), Macdonald and Macdonald (1896–1904), and Macintyre (1901).

group has had so profound an impact on Scottish history and national development as Clan Donald. In the Highland uprisings of the eighteenth century, Macdonalds generally mustered out for the Jacobite resistance to the Hanover kings. Yet over the previous 500 years they had spilled great amounts of their own and others' blood, forfeited great tracts of land to the Crown, and expended great sums of treasure in evading the royal authorities of Scotland and in creating their own military and administrative preserve in the western reaches of the Highlands and Islands (see Map 1). Macdonalds had successfully pursued so independent a policy that throughout the thirteenth and fourteenth centuries—and until their ultimate forfeiture to the Scottish Crown in 1494—the Macdonald Lords of the Isles ruled virtually as de facto potentates in the western Highlands (Grant 1930: 484–485; Macdonald and Macdonald 1896–1904 I:120ff).

Macdonald independence from Scottish royal authority waned significantly from the fifteenth century onward, at least in the form of a separate polity contained within the Scottish realm. Forfeiture of the Lordship of the Isles did not, however, weaken the importance of various Macdonald

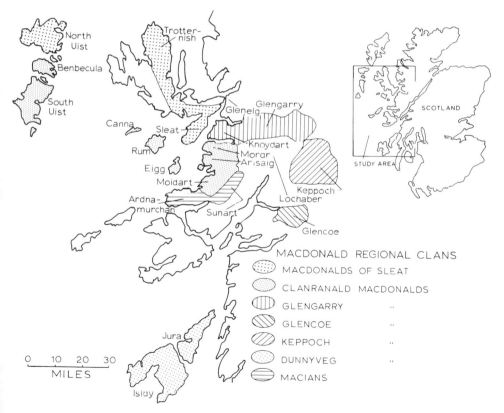

Map 1.   Location of Macdonald regional clans.

kin groups as regionally dominant elites bearing at times only nominal allegiance to the Scottish ruler. This more localized political self-sufficiency partially depended on the remoteness of Macdonald lands from the seat of power in the Scottish lowlands. More significantly, it rested on a skillful manipulation of Scottish and English interests by the Macdonalds, who switched allegiances from one national power to the other depending on the vagaries of the political situation and potential rewards (Gregory 1881:23). With the union of the Scottish and English Crowns under James I (James VI of Scotland), this source of political freedom was lost, and Macdonald independence, lands, and local influence increasingly gave way in the seventeenth century to the Campbell Dukes of Argyll and Earls of Breadalbane, empowered by Scottish kings to tame the "wild clans" of the northwest (Cregeen 1968:155–157). For the Macdonalds, the 1715 and 1745 Highland uprisings were not assertions of Stuart legitimacy over the Hanover usurpers so much as last-ditch efforts to resurrect their eroded powers and to contravene the "rapacity" of the Campbells (Prebble 1966). Ultimately, when Clan Donald's power is broken, its chiefs destitute or London-based absentees, its population emigrant to Nova Scotia and North Carolina in the eighteenth century or migrant to Glasgow and other industrial cities in the nineteenth, so too do the Highlands cease to be an independent political and cultural region within the Scottish nation.

Like northern Indian unilineal kin reckoning in its most inclusive forms, Scottish clans taken in their widest and popular designation were dispersed over a wide countryside. As in northern India, the boundaries of genealogical reckoning greatly exceeded the limits of the kin groups that were most significant for land ownership, military undertaking, marital arrangements, and political maneuvering. Inclusive categories of kinship such as the Macdonalds, Macdougalls, or MacLeods will be termed "clans of recognition" because they performed primarily ideological rather than behavioral functions. These agnatic categories did not undertake concerted military, economic, or political activities because they were territorially dispersed and because they lacked state recognition in matters of land tenure and local administration. Their behavioral reality was greatest when royal power was ineffective and when ties of marriage and land grants between their constituent kin groups forged links through stratification and clientage. In some cases such clans of recognition reflected the historical pedigree of formerly unified and corporate clans that had dispersed and fractionated. In other situations the clan of recognition represented only a common status designation adopted by formerly distinct regional kin groups who promoted such genealogical ties for increased status and prestige throughout the Highlands (Grant 1930:508–509, 511; Skene 1971 III:315).

The Macdonald genealogical web thus subsumed a number of corporate kin groups, each with independent chiefs, political policies, landholdings, and even different reconstructions of their common Macdonald pedigree. Neither warfare, cattle raiding, nor intermarriage was interdicted these several Macdonalds. Their claim to common membership in the category of Clan Donald at times led to concerted military action against common enemies and in general accorded them an ancestry recognized throughout the Highlands as prestigious. The several "spurious" or dubious Macdonald kin groups mentioned in contemporary Macdonald genealogies and those "Macdonalds" who existed in a genealogical vacuum indicate how frequently the status was assumed for prestige enhancement rather than gained by birthright.[3] The genealogical material on the Macdonald clan of recognition contained in this paper is undoubtedly the result of centuries of fabrication, interpolation, and rationalization. It is presented not as a "true" and proper guide to Macdonald pedigrees but as an index of the important levels of agnatic kinship found in the Highlands and their relationship to regional political dominance and territories.

Within the Macdonald clan of recognition, at least five politically independent kin groups are recognized in present-day clan annals or by the Clan Donald Society. Because these kin groups—to be referred to as "regional clans" hereafter—exercised political dominance over specific territories which were recognized in the Scottish feudal state, they are the political, military, and economic analogues of stratified lineages in northern India. The Macdonalds of Sleat, the Clanranald Macdonalds, the Glencoe Macdonalds, the Glengarry Macdonalds, and the Macdonalds of Keppoch (the latter two clans assumed the spelling "Macdonnell" in the seventeenth century) represent regional clans which successfully dominated large territories in the western Highlands and Islands over several centuries. All but the Glengarry Macdonalds existed as separate entities by the middle of the fourteenth century (Macdonald and Macdonald 1896–1904 I:203). Other Macdonald kin groups of equally long pedigree are generally accorded an inferior place in clan annals because their territorial control was short-lived or because they never achieved a dominant and independent political identity within a region. The Macian Macdonalds, the Clan Godfrey, and the Macdonalds of Dunnyveg represent such aborted regional clans. Figure 1 indicates the descent of these Macdonald regional clans, along with several regionally unsuccessful kin groups and other Macdonald and non-Macdonald offshoots. Map 1 represents the location and approximate territorial boundaries of the major successful and aborted regional clans of Macdonalds.

The terms "aborted" and "successful" indicate only the opposite poles

<hr />

[3] Thus the Maclavertys, the Darrochs, the Martins of Bealloch and Duntulm, the Siolachadh Mhurchaid, and others mentioned in Macdonald and Macdonald (1896–1904, Vol. III, genealogical section).

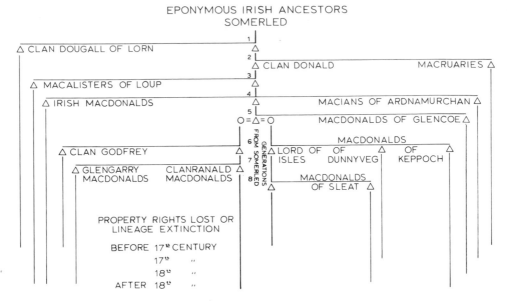

Figure 1.   The descent of Clan Donald.

in a continuum of dominance which characterized regional clans. A major factor in the relative strength of a regional clan, incipient or developed, was its ability to carve out a dependent territory (the boundaries of which are considered later) and to maintain it under pressure of incursions from neighboring clans, from fragmentation within the regional clan, and, most important, from the intervention of Scottish royal authority, which continually attempted to subvert its independence. However, in the last case, the weakly centralized Scottish feudal state often was forced to empower certain clans and their chiefs in order to undercut the powers of others. Thus, the successful Macdonald chiefs of Sleat were for most of the sixteenth century without state-recognized proprietary title to their lands (Macdonald and Macdonald 1896–1904 III:105). Their rise to prominence and a leading status among Macdonalds in the century before "the '45" (they are now considered the most direct descendants of the Lords of the Isles) evolved only after their relations with the Scottish Crown became amicable. Similarly, the Glengarry Macdonalds did not break away from Clanranald until the middle of the sixteenth century, when they received a royal grant to their lands and when they came under the protection of the powerful Grant family (Macdonald and Macdonald 1896–1904 II:372, 401).

Among the oldest Macdonald regional clans, the Keppoch and Glencoe Macdonalds were nevertheless continually threatened with loss of their territorial possessions and dominance. They depended heavily on marital alliances and land grants from Clanranald and entered into political alliances with neighbor clans to maintain a quasi-independence. These regional clans practiced the most extensive raiding of their neighbors, again an outcome of their unfavorable position with respect to power and landholding (Macdonald and Macdonald 1896–1904 II:617; Prebble 1966).

The aborted or short-lived regional clans generally fell before more aggressive neighboring clans, some of whom were other Macdonald regional clans and others of whom (such as the Campbells) were subsidized in their incursions by Scottish royal authority. The Macian Macdonalds inhabited Ardnamurchan, an area which passed at an early date into the Campbell orbit. At first, the Macians remained in situ as feudal inferiors of the Campbells, but later they were dispossessed, forced to migrate elsewhere (often becoming underlings of other Macdonald regional clan chiefs), and their lands settled with Hendersons, MacPhees, Maclachlans, Macphersons, and others (Macdonald 1889:6). The Clan Godfrey originally inhabited North Uist, but when the Lord of the Isles resumed their land grant in favor of one of his sons, they became the tenants of other Macdonalds or scattered throughout the western Highlands (Macdonald and Macdonald 1896–1904 III: genealogical section, Macgorraidh). The Macdonalds of Knoydart ceased to be an independent political and territorial entity when, in 1613, the Glengarry Macdonalds, armed with a royal commission to expunge them, conquered their territory (Macdonald and Macdonald 1896–1904 II:413).

Regional Clans and Territorial Dominance

In popular and some scholarly opinion (such as the numerous clan maps with each Highland district color-coded to a specific clan), Scottish clans occupied mutually exclusive territories in the Highlands and were bound together in a strict patrilineal brotherhood of military enterprise, social prestige, and genealogical connection. The foregoing material on regional clans gives the lie to the latter assumption. This section will set to rest the former assertion by indicating the numerous clans within any single regional clan's territory and their complex interrelations.

Within a specific locale, the territorial boundaries of which were generally recognized by the Scottish Crown in its feudal grants to regional clan chiefs, several dozen clans might be found represented (Macpherson 1966:1–43, 1968:81–111). In such locales a single *dominant clan* existed which was superior to all others in terms of landholding and often population and which was the agent through which central authorities channeled their relations with the locale.[4] This dominant clan was one of the constituent regional clans of a larger clan of recognition—thus, the Macdonalds of Sleat were dominant in the Trotternish and Sleat localities on the Isle of Skye, and the Macians had once been dominant in the Ardnamurchan area. Other clans resident in a locale were subordinate in terms of land tenure and political relations with the state. Such subordinate clans might include segments of regional clans which were dominant in other locales. Tables 1 and 2 indicate the distribution of such clan segments in two contiguous areas of the western Highlands: Knoydart and North Morar, the orbit of the Glengarry Macdonalds; and South Morar, Arisaig, and Moidart, the mainland possessions of the Clanranald Macdonalds.[5] Thus, Macdonald populations were found throughout the Highlands under the rule and as tenants of Macintoshes, Campbells, and others. Even a locale dominated by a specific Macdonald regional clan might contain other Macdonalds living in a subservient condition, as when the Macdonalds of Knoydart were overrun by Glengarry or when Clan Godfrey sunk to the condition of tenants under the Macdonald Lord of the Isles. In 1784 the Macdonalds or Macdonnells of Scotus (Scothouse) in Knoydart, a lineage within the Glengarry regional clan, had the following distribution of tenants by clan (Fraser-Macintosh 1889–1890:88):

Macdonnell	12
Macdougall	3
Mackay	3
Campbell	2

[4] Robin Fox (1967) has suggested that Highland clans were cognatic in nature rather than agnatic. A similar criticism is made by Stern (in press) for the use of unilineal principles to explain regionally dominant kin groups in northern India. Since unilineal kin groups form political entities in both Highland Scotland and northern India, it must be understood that agnation organizes the dominant elements in the regional kin cells whereas affinality and cognation may characterize the manner in which co-resident but politically subordinate kin groups are attached to the elite agnatic line. The situation in the Scottish Highlands and northern India appears comparable to the condition of the acephalous Nuer, as reinterpreted by Kathleen Gough (1971). After criticizing Evans-Pritchard's original formulation of the agnatic principle as "overhomogenized," she writes that there is an "unevenness in the operation of the agnatic principle among different layers of the population . . . agnation has become (at least fictionally) a *more* pervasive principle of *political* organization [among the eastern Nuer] for the conquering aristocrats than it is for the more homogeneous and longer-established western Nuer and Dinka . . . agnation seems to have become a *less* constant and pervasive principle of organization for the conquered, captured, immigrant, or otherwise absorbed Dinka and for the many Nuer who do not belong to the dominant clan in each tribe. In the case of such persons, who 'greatly outnumber the dominant clanspeople,' residential ties, which are based on cognatic or affinal ties to segments of the dominant clan, far outweigh agnatic ties in the establishment of day-to-day obligations and loyalties [1971:90]."

[5] These figures are derived from the Census of Scotland for 1841, which, although a rather late date for finding Highland social institutions intact, is nevertheless the first reliable enumeration.

Kennedy	2
Macpherson	2
Others (5)	5

Subordinate clans were allied to the dominant kin group by marital connections and matrilocal residence, by "fictitious" ties of brotherhood (wherein the dominant clan name might be assumed), or by less personal ties of tenancy (wherein lands were held by so-called "native" men) (Macpherson 1967:149-192; Robertson 1862 II:262). Dominant clans seem to have adopted the political strategy of male exogamy to forge strong links with their subordinate clans, although they also utilized the alternative strategy of female endogamy to maintain close relations within their clan group (Macpherson 1968:81-111). A strong impetus for affinal ties between dominant and subordinate clans came from the dangers of divided allegiance among subordinate clans. When the latter were linked to a dominant clan only in the capacity of tenants, or "native" men, they often looked beyond the locally dominant clan for leadership and political support, and their loyalties based on clan allegiance to a nonresident chief

TABLE 1
Distribution of Clans in Knoydart and North Morar as of 1841

	Enumeration Districts			
Clan	#5	#6	#7	Total
Macdonald	245	40	144	429
Macvarish	1		12	13
Macissac	12			12
Other Macdonald Septs (4)	4	3	3	10
Gilles	7		143	150
Maclellan	23	11	72	106
Cameron	26	20	30	76
Mackinnon	72	3	1	76
Macpherson	35	8	14	57
Macdougall	42		15	57
Kennedy	46			46
Macmillan	18	1		19
Macphail	18			18
Robertson	15	1		16
Stewart	9	7		16
Nicolson	7	7		14
Macinnes	8	4		12
Others (28)	58	11	87	156
Total (49)	646	116	521	1,283

TABLE 2
Distribution of Clans in South Morar, Arisaig and Moidart as of 1841

Clan	Enumeration Districts																	Total
	#8	#9	#10	#11	#12	#13	#27	#28	#29	#30	#31	#32	#33	#34	#35	#36	#37	
Macdonald	94	50	69	55	96	100	4	22	99	58	36	42	32	53	51	15	2	878
Macissac	56	36	8	16	1	6				1			1	1			5	131
Macvarish	29	14	8	19		1		2	1	9	4			1	1	9		98
Macgill			6						1	7	7		16	12				49
Other Macdonald Septs (3)	1	14	6	8										5			7	41
Gilles							5	29	20	10	10	6	7	4	16			107
Macinnes			3	15	2	1		7	1	13	9	8	9		1	3	9	81
Macpherson			2	13	22	2	4	1			1	1	1		1			59
Macdougall	11					6	2	2	12	1	2	7		7	6	4	8	57
Cameron						7	17	14		1	1			1			8	49
Smith				7		1		9		3	9	3	1	16				49
Maclean	10			1	1	1			1	1	13	9	7		2			46
Mackinnon						2			3	1	7	25	1					39
Macneil	1		8	8		9			6							1		32
Maclellan	1							2	23	1				1	1			30
Macmaster			1		13	11		4										29
Others (66)	4	41	60	51	25	52	5	50	34	108	126	34	55	36	31	22	47	781
Total (84)	207	155	171	193	161	199	37	142	201	213	225	134	130	137	110	55	86	2,556

conflicted with their obligations to the dominant kin group arising from their tenant status (Collier 1953:39).

In some Highland locales no single dominant clan held sway, and congeries of smaller kin groups existed which were subordinate to a powerful feudal lord (who may, however, have been the chief of a clan dominant in another Highland region). The absence of a dominant clan generally betokened the strength of the feudal proprietor (as, for example, the Campbell Duke of Argyll who replaced Macians with many new clans in Ardnamurchan) and his ability to strip away all elite social classes standing between the tenant and himself. Another element which complicated the Highland situation was the many "broken men" who roamed the countryside unattached to any kin group. Having been driven from their natal clan region or having voluntarily forsworn their brethren, broken men were a large mobile population allied with any dominant clan or chief who would guarantee them safety and land (Grant 1930:513). In spite of the increasing interpolation of such feudal usages and the growing power of Scottish central authority and its feudal minions during the several centuries before "the '45," most of Highland Scotland generally remained divided into territories under the dominance of regional clans.

The many clan segments and broken men which clustered around the agnatic nucleus of a dominant clan in a single locale constituted the cellular unit of Highland society as late as a century after Bonnie Prince Charlie's defeat at Culloden (Macpherson 1967, 1968). As in northern India, the boundaries of this kin body (with its satellite kin groups and dependent broken men) formed a unit for territorial leadership, military defense through kin militias, social status, intermarriage, and property holdings which seemingly was mechanically duplicated throughout the Scottish Highlands and Islands.

Two matters have yet to be considered: What was the formal organization of government through which these kin territories were linked to and incorporated within Scottish royal administration, and how did these kin territories originate and what was the nature of their boundaries? Both questions require a short digression into Scottish land tenures in their relationship to the internal stratification of a regional clan.

Land Tenure and the Regional Clan Elite

The internal social hierarchy of a Highland regional clan bore many resemblances to its counterpart, the stratified lineage, in northern India. One minimal lineage (*clann*)[6] provided the chief who was nominally given jurisdiction over all lands and kin brethren within the regional clan's terri-

---

[6] This terminology follows Macpherson (1966), wherein the *clann* is defined as a minimal lineage and the *sliochd* (pl. *sliochdan*) is defined as a maximal lineage within a regional clan.

tory, even though he may have shared actual proprietary title with his high-ranking kinsmen and the leading families of subordinate clans. His high status, ancient pedigree, and noble bearing earned the chief the respect of his kin following, various customary payments from the clan population, and the role of regional spokesman to the Scottish Crown. The history of Scotland is replete with royal summonses to Clanranald, Glengarry, Sleat, Keppoch, and Glencoe (the chiefs of these regional clans are referred to in this manner) to account for the actions of their subordinates, to put to the horn a specific *clann,* to assemble in Edinburgh, or to produce a military force.[7] Clan chiefs enjoyed jural authority delegated from the state—the power of "pit and gallows"—and often executed punitive measures against neighboring regional clans (for the chief's own aggrandizement) under commissions of "fire and sword" authorized to them by the Scottish Crown.

Below the chief came men of high rank, his close or distant agnates who represented cadet lines which occupied smaller areas within the regional clan territory as "tacksmen," or tenants of the chief. Under certain conditions, tacksmen were granted only life interests in their lands; they were replaced with other, closer cadets when a new chief succeeded or after several (customarily, three) generations. They thereafter sank to an undistinguished status within the regional clan. In other situations, tacksmen enjoyed a hereditary tenancy in their lands which allowed them some degree of autonomy from the regional clan chief (Robertson 1862:262). In the latter case, tacksmen came to head cadet lines of some generational depth—usually *sliochdan,* or maximal lineages (although the boundary between *clann* and *sliochd* is a fluid one)—which often served as the genealogical base for the formation of a new regional clan under opportune political conditions (compare Glengarry Macdonalds discussed earlier). Figures 2 and 3 indicate the various *clanns* and *sliochdan* within the Clanranald and Glencoe Macdonald regional clans which achieved proprietary, although not political independence, from their regional clan chiefs. However, not all tacksmen were agnates of the chief. A powerful kin head might make land grants to subordinate clans related through marriage or claiming a common clan of recognition with the chief. Such tacksmen rarely achieved the independence and longevity of the tacksmen who were agnates of the regional clan chief. In general, tacksmen acted as political and economic intermediaries between the chief and the commoner population (including the chief's lower-ranking clan mates) within the regional

---

[7] Such royal summonses were often not honored by Macdonald chiefs, especially when they were called to appear before the Crown to answer for their behavior or that of their clan brethren. Scottish kings also utilized these audiences in an opportunistic manner, as in 1540, when the monarch assembled the Highland chiefs and then imprisoned them (Macdonald and Macdonald 1896–1904 II:258).

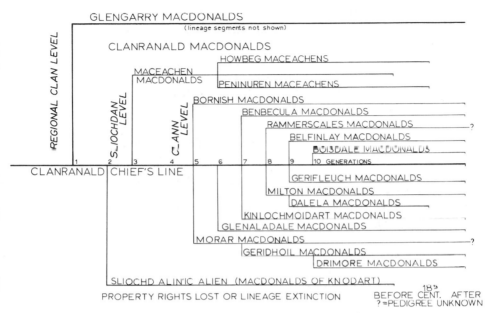

Figure 2.   The Clanranald Macdonalds.

clan territory and also served as line officers in the kin militia (Gray 1957:23).

At the bottom of the regional clan hierarchy came the many undistinguished members of *clanns*—either related agnatically or through marriage with chief and tacksmen or merely native men   who represented the workers in the fields, the drovers of cattle, the body of the regional clan militia, and the followers of chief and tacksmen. It has been said that the chief and the clan system in general cultivated people, not crops. A large body of armed retainers, or "tail," guaranteed the prestige and power of chief and tacksmen alike, no matter the consequences of overpopulation and constant land division for the Highlands. Only after the military and political disaster of Culloden do many tacksmen emigrate to America, and only then do chiefs turn from cultivating men to raising sheep on lands newly cleared of their former kin and nonkin dependents.

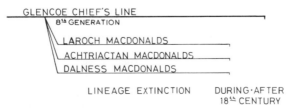

Figure 3.   The Macdonalds of Glencoe.

As in northern India, the system of land tenures provided the major articulation between Scottish royal authority and the regional clan territories. However, the model of polity in northern India was a highly centralized bureaucratic state; in Scotland the model was a decentralized, feudal regime. Highland lands were given out by royal authority in a succession of feus and subinfeudations which reached from the noble magnate with fortified castle down to the lowly clansman herding his cattle as tenant of the great. Feudal lords who held proprietary rights over Highland lands were in some cases Crown appointees having no hereditary connection with the underholders, in other cases alien regional clan chiefs who had gained control over new territories through marriage, conquest, or state favoritism, and in most cases indigenous regional clan chiefs who were further set above their tacksmen and kin brethren by this state imprimatur. The chief as well as his tacksmen defended the usufructory and occupancy rights of their lower-ranking kinsmen who held land under a hereditary agnatic tenure called *duthchas* (Eyre-Todd 1923:5; Gray 1957:12–13; Macpherson 1966:7; Robertson 1862:262).

Crown appointees granted superior land rights over a territory with a strong dominant clan generally found them worthless because the clan chief and his tacksmen and brethren would physically oppose his possession and occupancy. Throughout most of the sixteenth century, neither Clanranald nor Sleat held formal titles to their lands, but the support of their clan brethren prevented any de facto alteration in their proprietary rights (Macdonald and Macdonald 1896–1904 II:258–294, III:105). Therefore, until successful and expansive clans of recognition like the Campbells and Grants appeared, most feudal dispositions recognized the existent regional clan chiefs as superior holders or at most attempted to play one powerful regional clan off against another. Over the course of several centuries before "the '45," the tenurial system was further complicated by a progressive interpolation of feudal rights at the local level, an index of the increasing authority of the Scottish Crown. For example, the tacksmen heading *sliochdan* and *clanns* increasingly achieved greater permanency and proprietary independence from their regional clan chief by obtaining royal charters confirming them in their patrimonial lands.[8] Most of the Clanranald and Glencoe *clanns* and *sliochdan* noted in Figures 2 and 3 were successful in obtaining such royal grants.

Regional Clans and Territorial Boundaries

The system of feudal tenures discussed in the previous section recognized no social institutions at the regional or local level other than

[8] Compare the situation of Clanranald in the 1530s noted in Macdonald and Macdonald (1896–1904 II:256) and the general description given earlier (I:414); see also Lang (1929 I:138).

clan chiefs or, at times, their tacksmen. Such men were chartered in landed possessions by the royal power as individuals, not as representatives of regional kin bodies (Grant 1930:487). What, then, is the territorial reality of regional clans? Is their regional dominance merely an epiphenomenon of their chief's feudal position, and if regional clans were "real," how were they recognized in state administration?

Royal charters did not grant chiefs or tacksmen random chunks of land. Under the Anglo-Norman kings of Scotland, feudalism was introduced atop a preexisting land tenure system based on a core of agnatic inheritance that often carried down from regional clan chief to tacksmen to clan brethren. The boundaries of land control and political power that the early feudal state found in the Highlands were kin boundaries, and it incorporated such boundaries into its feudal system.

Most commentators on Scottish history have insisted that prefeudal clan (or "tribal") territories became the later baronies of the feudal system and that clan chiefs were transformed from heads of kin to feudal lords of various degree (Lang 1929 I:133–134; Robertson 1862 II:262; Skene 1902:113ff; and the most recent discussion, Barrow 1973). Lang believed that the creation of feudal rights beginning in the twelfth century under King David and pursued by his successors rarely displaced the original clan population. When clan chiefs were co-opted into the feudal system, they became barons or other royal officials who performed duties for the Crown and who possessed their lands at the behest of the king rather than as a legacy of their descent (Lang 1929:136–138). The links between central authority and regional clans thus came in the form of royal administrators who were clan chiefs or tacksmen supervising their dependent territories as both agnatic head of the kin group and feudal subordinate of the king.

The assertion that clan chiefs became barons, or feudal lords, is buttressed by good historical evidence. However, the evidence for regional clan territories' being coterminous with the boundaries of such feudal estates is scant. No data exist to allow mapping of regional clans before the imposition of the feudal system. Furthermore, the demographic, proprietary, and political alterations of the last several centuries make projections from the recent past to the medieval period dubious. Nevertheless, even as late as the mid-nineteenth century, a striking conformity existed between the boundaries of regions formerly held in feudal title by Macdonald regional clan chiefs and a high incidence of Macdonald population. Contiguous regions which were not under Macdonald hegemony have a much lower incidence of Macdonald population. Thus, in Knoydart and North Morar, the homeland of the Macdonalds of Knoydart later absorbed by Glengarry, the percentage of Macdonalds in the 1841 total population was over 30 percent, whereas the adjacent district of Glenelg contained less than 8 percent. In the old Clanranald territories of South Morar, Arisaig, and Moidart, the percentage of Macdonalds exceeded 34 percent, while the contiguous territory of Ardnamurchan from which the Macian Macdonalds were expelled by Campbell dominance had only 3.5 percent Macdonalds. The divergence is not so great on the Isle of Skye, perhaps because the political prominence of Sleat was more recent. The Macdonald territories of Trotternish and Sleat contained 14.9 percent and 15.2 percent Macdonalds, respectively, whereas non-Macdonald Steinscholl contained 10.4 percent. Although thoroughly inadequate for a valid quantitative assessment, these data do imply that the territorial limits of clan population coincide with the boundaries assigned by the Crown to feudal estates. In all those territories traditionally incorporated into Macdonald regional clans, Macdonalds represented either the largest single clan or a major proportion of the population (ranging from a sixth to a third).

As in northern India, so too in Highland Scotland was the relationship of state administrative locale to clan region undoubtedly variable and ever changing. Even an observer miraculously set down amidst the big-kilted Macdonalds of the sixteenth century could only have mapped the pattern by stereotyping it at a single moment in time. Perhaps it is enough to know that royal authority considered clan distributions in their allocations of feudal grants, if no more than in judging the military potential of the chiefs' kin militias. The alternative is to accept an old-fashioned unilineal evolutionism which conceives of Highland society as having changed irrevocably from an ancient "tribalism" to a medieval feudalism. The fallacy of the unilineal "tribal" approach is that it portrays the state as solely a passive recipient of inviolable and unitary kin territories and ignores the continuing interplay between Crown and clan at the regional level. Undoubtedly the state attempted to weaken regional clan leaders by favoring the proprietary independence of lineage segments within the regional clan. As in the case of the Glengarry separation from Clanranald, state imprimatur or feudal grant is to some extent a charter of legitimacy for the formation of new kin territorial units. To see the continuing interplay of regional clans and state policy avoids a portrayal of all feudal territories in the Highlands as survivals of an *uralt* Celtic tribal condition and more accurately conceives the wax and wane of kin territories, without denying that such territories formed the basis for feudal domains.

This constant interplay is in fact an index of the vital role such kin groups played throughout the history of pre-nineteenth century Scotland in linking locality with nation, realm with region. Unlike traditional China, where it is possible to map and model an invariable territorial network of regional marketing cells, the cellular unit of the Highlands had changeable and irregular boundaries, and its genealogical depth also fluctuated. The elements of commodity flow and of spatial efficiency in marketing that necessarily defined Chinese cells territorially were absent in Highland Scotland. Instead, the invariable element consisted of the ideology and corporate behavior associated with genealogical reckoning, as confirmed by royal land grants—the former mapped and modeled only in the minds of kinsmen, the latter charted only in the registers of the state. If premodern China is a construction of equivalent (hexagonal) building blocks, Highland Scotland before "the '45" and pre-British northern India form jigsaw puzzles of odd-shaped pieces and nonequivalent boundaries.

CONCLUSIONS

Although the cellular character of Highland Scotland and northern India cannot be encompassed within a generative model of the same power and scope as Christaller's and Skinner's (because it cannot be modeled territorially), nevertheless some important variables underlying the potency of corporate kin groups can be adduced. Such kin-defined regions appear and play an exceptional role in state–locality interrelations when:

1. Corporate kin groups exist which are internally ranked on the basis of kinship and where such rank determines access to political power, economic wealth, and military personnel. Variations in the kin cohesiveness, military participation ratio, and ecological circumstances of such kin groups will influence their size, political autonomy, and internal stratification.
2. Central political authorities and state institutions are impotent and must rule through local surrogates, generally drawn from such regionally dominant kin bodies. The degree of state incapacity explains in part the variation in the power and autonomy of such regional kin cells.
3. Marketing or commodity flows between regions or even within regions are not a major factor in the disposition of settlement, and a high degree of local economic autonomy obtains.[9] Decreasing economic autonomy would accentuate the role of marketing systems in defining regional cells.

While the foregoing list of variables is admittedly inductive and extrapolated from only two cases, data on lineage organization (in relation to state power) from the Scottish Border country and from traditional

---

[9] The relative unimportance of commodity flows in the determination of regional cells has a different basis in Highland Scotland and northern India. In northern India the caste order and widespread *jajmani* system lodged occupational and craft specialization of a high order in a village community or contiguous group of communities. In the Scottish Highlands the economic autonomy of individual settlements was also well developed, but in the absence of a highly elaborate division of labor at the local level. Apart from the occasional punitive raid to the lowlands or the sale of Highland cattle, a very simple living standard (in English eyes) was maintained by use of home-made plaids, weapons, and most other commodities.

China provide some confirmation. This material also indicates that greatest explanatory weight must be given the political variable of state power in the determination of regional kin cells.

Before the unification of the Scottish and English Crowns under James I (James VI of Scotland), the Border country was a hilly no man's land lying on the international frontier of the two realms. State power, whether from Edinburgh or London, intervened here as haltingly and inconclusively as it did in the Highlands because internal control was continually counteracted by external dissidence between Scotland and England. Large kin bodies (which also contained nonkinsmen, broken men, and feudal dependents) called "surnames," each led by chiefs who may also have been feudal lords and officers of the state, organized these march regions politically and militarily. Such were the Halls, Robsons, Ainslies, Bells, Grahams, and Littles; the Armstrongs and Elliots, even more complex, contained several separate kin groups, each with two or more leaders. Smout writes, "Highland life was actually very similar to Border life in the sixteenth century, and for the same reason that the land was hilly and the king remote [1969:47]." However, when James VI of Scotland ascended the English throne, the international frontier and its political marginality disappeared, and the many autonomous surname kin groups were ruthlessly suppressed to the extent that the region eventually became administered by Crown appointees.

A similar importance is accorded political marginality and state incompetence in studies of Chinese lineage organization. Jack Potter focuses on the variable size and ramification of lineages in traditional China rather than on their regional political functions. He identifies four factors underlying strong lineage development: productive agriculture, frontier location, weak central power, and commercial wealth. Among these factors frontier location and state impotence (in reality, the same political condition)[10] led to the assumption of political, military, and administrative functions by Chinese lineages, much as they did in Highland Scotland and northern India. The role of central authority in curtailing such lineage developments is also very clear: "the imperial government only tolerated a lineage organization strong enough to maintain effective control over its members. When lineages grew too large and powerful, the government saw this as a direct threat to its power and authority and exerted every effort to limit lineage strength [Potter 1970:135–136]."

Whereas in traditional China the state was evidently able to subdue such lineage efflorescence in most regions and epochs, the less puissant central authorities in pre-British northern India and Highland Scotland

[10] That the important variable is state competency rather than frontier location per se is suggested by Burton Pasternak's (1969) criticism of Freedman's (1970) notion that strong lineages necessarily exist in frontier locations.

before "the '45" were often forced to co-opt regional kin cells into their administrative hierarchy and therefore into the overall design of the complex society. The historical process by which such kin regions arose and were nominally incorporated into state machinery and then, with increased state power, forcibly effaced is well illustrated by the Scottish Border country in the fifteenth through seventeenth centuries.

Highland Scotland and northern India represent complex societies in which unilineal kin groups were encapsulated in the administrative machinery of the state. This common condition in two distinctive world regions gives the lie to the many grand theories which envision state societies as territorially organized and inimical to the continuation of kin groups. What is often viewed as a direct conflict between opposing social institutions—state versus kinship—can become under certain conditions a symbiosis wherein kinship organizes the lowest level of the state order, while territory pertains to superior echelons. A contest of power ensues between these two different orders wherein the state intervenes, suppresses, and hopes to extirpate the local kin group (even while co-opting it administratively), an extermination that the latter resists by becoming internally more cohesive, by posing a greater military threat, and by organizing regions at a still greater tangent to state structure. For very long periods in precolonial societies, the state is not able to suppress fully such local or regional kin groups, and, as in northern India and the Scottish Highlands, central authorities accept a modus vivendi which incorporates these lineages and clans as active institutions in the political process.

REFERENCES

Anderson, Robert, and Barbara Anderson
    1966   *Bus stop for Paris.* Garden City, N.Y.: Doubleday.
Anonymous
    n.d.   Dunollie Castle and the chiefs of the Clan Macdougall. Unpublished manuscript, Edinburgh Public Library.
Barnes, J.
    1954   Class and communities in a Norwegian island parish. *Human Relations* **7**: 39–58.
Barrow, G. W. S.
    1973   *The kingdom of the Scots.* London: Arnold.
Collier, Adam
    1953   *The crofting problem.* New York: Cambridge Univ. Press.
Cregeen, Eric R.
    1968   The changing role of the House of Argyll in the Scottish Highlands. In *History and social anthropology,* edited by I. M. Lewis. London: Tavistock. Pp. 153–192.
Eyre-Todd, George
    1923   *Highland clans of Scotland.* London: Heath, Cranton.
Fox, Richard G.
    1971a *Kin, clan, raja and rule: State–hinterland relations in pre-industrial northern India.* Berkeley: Univ. of California Press.

1971b Rurban settlements and Rajput clans in northern India. In *Urban India: Society, space and image,* edited by Richard G. Fox. Durham, N.C.: Program in Comparative Studies on Southern Asia, Duke Univ. Pp. 167–185.

Fox, Robin
1967 *Kinship and marriage.* London: Penguin Books.

Fraser-Macintosh, Charles
1889–1890 Minor Highland families, No. 3: The Macdonnells of Scotus. *Transactions of the Gaelic Society of Inverness* **XVI.**

Freedman, Maurice
1970 Introduction in *Family and kinship in Chinese society.* Stanford, Calif.: Stanford Univ. Press. Pp. 121–138.

Gough, Kathleen
1971 Nuer kinship: A re-examination. In *The translation of culture,* edited by T. O. Beidelman. London: Tavistock. Pp. 79–122.

Grant, I. F.
1930 *Social and economic development of Scotland before 1603.* Edinburgh: Oliver and Boyd.

Gray, Malcolm
1957 *The Highland economy, 1750–1850.* Edinburgh: Oliver and Boyd.

Gregory, Donald
1881 *The history of the western Highlands and the Isles of Scotland.* (2nd ed.) London: Hamilton, Adams.

Lang, Andrew
1929 *A history of Scotland from the Roman occupation.* (5th ed.) Edinburgh: Blackwood.

Lattimore, Owen
1960 *Inner Asian frontiers of China.* Boston: Beacon Press.

Macdonald, Angus, and Archibald Macdonald
1896–1904 *The Clan Donald.* (3 volumes) Inverness: Northern Counties, Pub.

Macdonald, Charles
1889 *Moidart, or among the Clanranalds.* Oban: Cameron.

Macintyre, Duncan
1901 *The Macintyres of Glenoe and Camus-na-H-Erie.* Edinburgh: Oliver and Boyd.

Macpherson, Alan G.
1966 An old Highland genealogy and the evolution of a Scottish clan. *Scottish Studies* **10:** 1–43.
1967 An old Highland register: Survivals of clanship and social change in Laggan, Inverness-Shire, 1775–1854: Part I. *Scottish Studies* **11:** 149–192.
1968 An old Highland register: Survivals of clanship and social change in Laggan, Inverness-Shire, 1775–1854: Part II. *Scottish Studies* **12:** 81–111.

Manners, Robert
1965 Remittances and the unit of analysis in anthropological research. *Southwestern Journal of Anthropology* **21:** 179–195.

Mayer, Adrian
1966 The significance of quasi-groups in the study of complex societies. In *The social anthropology of complex societies,* edited by M. Banton. New York: Praeger. Pp. 97–122.

Mitchell, J. Clyde (Ed.)
1969 *Social networks in urban situations.* Manchester: Manchester Univ. Press.

Pasternak, Burton
1969 The role of the frontier in Chinese lineage development. *Journal of Asian Studies* **28:** 551–561.

Potter, Jack
   1970   Land and lineage in traditional China. In *Family and kinship in Chinese society,* edited by M. Freedman. Stanford, Calif.: Stanford Univ. Press. Pp. 121–138.
Pradhan, M. C.
   1966   *The political system of the Jats of northern India.* New York: Oxford Univ. Press.
Prebble, John
   1966   *Glencoe.* London: Penguin Books.
Robertson, E. William
   1862   *Scotland under her early kings: A history of the kingdom to the close of the thirteenth century.* (2 volumes) Edinburgh: Edmonston and Douglas.
Silverman, Sydel
   1967   The community–nation mediator in traditional central Italy. In *Peasant society: A reader,* edited by J. Potter, M. Diaz, and G. Foster. Boston: Little, Brown. Pp. 279–293.
Singh, Kashi Nath
   1968   The territorial basis of medieval town and village in eastern Uttar Pradesh. *Annals of the Association of American Geographers* **58:** 203–213.
Skene, William F.
   1902   *The Highlanders of Scotland,* edited by A. Macbain. Stirling: Mackay.
   1971   *Celtic Scotland: A history of ancient Alban. Vol. III: Land and people.* Freeport,
   (1880)   N.Y.: Books for Libraries Press.
Skinner, G. William
   1964   Marketing and social structure in rural China: Part I. *Journal of Asian Studies* **24:** 3–43.
   1971   Chinese peasants and the closed community: An open and shut case. *Comparative Studies in Society and History* **13:** 301–324.
Smout, T. C.
   1969   *A history of the Scottish people, 1560–1830.* New York: Scribners.
Stein, Burton
   In press   The segmentary state in south India. In *Realm and region in traditional India,* edited by Richard G. Fox. Durham, N.C.: Program in Comparative Studies on Southern Asia, Duke Univ.
Stern, Henri
   In press   Power in traditional India: Territory, caste, and kinship. In *Realm and region in traditional India,* edited by Richard G. Fox. Durham, N.C.: Program in Comparative Studies on Southern Asia, Duke Univ.
Weingrod, Alex
   1968   Patrons, patronage, and political parties. *Comparative Studies in Society and History* **10:** 377–401.
Wolf, Eric R.
   1966a   Kinship, friendship and patron–client relations in complex societies. In *The social anthropology of complex societies,* edited by M. Banton. New York: Praeger. Pp. 1–22.
   1966b   *Peasants.* Englewood Cliffs, N.J.: Prentice-Hall.

Chapter 5

Spatial Aspects of Marriage Patterns as Influenced by Marketing Behavior in West Central Taiwan

Lawrence W. Crissman
University of Illinois at Urbana-Champaign

THE RATIONALE

Perhaps the most important aspect of the first of G. William Skinner's series of articles entitled "Marketing and Social Structure in Rural China" was the hypothesis he presented in the concluding section, "Marketing Structures as Social Systems" (1964:32–43). The essential idea is that marketing communities—the social expressions of standard (and higher-level) marketing areas—were highly significant units of traditional Chinese rural social organization. It was they, not villages, that provided primary extrafamilial (or extralineage) identity; it was they that were the loci of peasant cultural traditions; and it was they that set the limits of peasant horizons in that social knowledge of others was limited to members of families that attended the same standard market. Such social knowledge not only derived from social interaction but was itself a prime determinant of social relationships. Given the importance in Chinese society of basing interpersonal relationships whenever possible on preexisting knowledge of, or culturally defined commonality with, other persons it is indeed to be expected that the common identity and mutual knowledge of one another's affairs that people acquired by attending the same periodic market every few days over a lifetime would provide very strong foundations for relationships of all kinds. Marriage, and the affinal relationships it creates, is especially dependent upon prior acquaintance (or awareness), due to its great significance to corporate domestic units.

Skinner adduces considerable evidence to support his hypotheses taken from his aborted field work and from the literature on traditional China. Other substantiating facts can be brought forward. A Chinaman's native place, which is an inherited attribute like a surname, is commonly referred to by naming a market town even though the place is a village in the town's hinterland. Religious beliefs and practices, standards of weights and measures, styles in items of material culture, and dialect differences are all known to have been associated with marketing systems, at least in some instances. Localized corporate patrilineages, rotating credit clubs, religious organizations, secret society lodges, and gentry–peasant patron–client relationships that gave rise to an essential, if informal, component of imperial administration were all limited to specific marketing communities.

There is good evidence for these cultural and social aspects of traditional Chinese marketing communities, even though no one has ever explicitly studied them in the field. No one ever will conduct such research since traditional China no longer exists, but there still remain many ways to investigate the social and cultural concomitants of traditional Chinese marketing structures. They range from reading the classical literature with new understanding to doing documentary research in local gazetteers and published genealogies. The latter are of particular significance with regard to the notion that standard marketing communities set limits on intermarriage for the peasantry, since they usually list the origins of incoming brides. Such research has not yet been done, however, and Skinner's statement that "there is, in short, a distinct tendency for the standard marketing community to be endogamous for the peasantry [1964:36]" must be considered as a hypothesis only.

It is a compelling hypothesis, nonetheless. The reasonableness of supposing that peasants contracted for daughters-in-law with others who attended the same standard market derives from their known preference for previously unmarried, unrelated girls from "good" families—that is, those on or slightly below their own socioeconomic level. Parents' funerals and sons' marriages were the largest investments that peasant families ordinarily made, and the families from which daughters-in-law were taken were usually investigated with great care. Although go-betweens were employed in order to get leads on prospective candidates and to help in the negotiations over bride-price and dowry, it was not wise to trust any third party completely, since the professional or semiprofessional go-betweens to be found working the crowds at every market were known occasionally to misrepresent sickly hags as strong and fecund lasses. A girl's family also required assurance that their daughter would not be abnormally mistreated by the strange family she would enter on marriage. It therefore behooved each party to an engagement to have personal knowledge of the other. This would normally already be the case if the families had been attending the same market and hearing gossip about each other for years, but even if they were not initially acquainted, they could easily find out about each other if they participated in the same marketing community. On the other hand, peasants had no resources for investigating a family that marketed elsewhere.

Although the opportunity to do field research in traditional China in order to test the hypotheses that marketing areas set limits to connubium for peasants is gone forever, it is possible to test the hypotheses on Taiwan—the only Chinese territory with a large, settled rural population where it is presently possible to do research.[1] The Hong Kong New Territories are not nearly so suitable, since at the present time they are little more than suburbs of the city and, in addition, contain a large number of refugees who in fact do most of the farming (gardening, actually). It is of course the case that rural marketing on Taiwan is thoroughly modernized in terms of a very high level of commercialization and ubiquitous motorized transport. However, if an association between marketing habits and marriage patterns can be established for contemporary Taiwan, there should be no difficulty in arguing backward to traditional Chinese settings, where the relationship can be expected to have been even stronger.

Skinner hypothesizes that in modernized trading systems, peasants' (or postpeasants') sense of community retracts to their villages while their social horizons expand to include members of the trading areas centered on erstwhile intermediate and central towns. It is claimed that marriage areas are likely to grow accordingly (1965:221). Under both traditional and modern conditions, therefore, marketing is presumed to have a causative effect on marriages. Since the reasoning underlying the supposed relationship is the same in both cases, there is good justification for considering proof of a positive correlation in modernized marketing systems to be a powerful indication of the existence of an equivalent cause-and-effect relation in traditional marketing communities, given the persistence of cultural rules regarding marriage choices. On the other hand, the absence of any demonstrable connection on Taiwan would not necessarily prove anything at all about the traditional mainland because the thoroughgoing changes in government, the economy, and technology could conceivably have disrupted traditional Chinese patterns beyond recognition.

THE TAIWANESE CASE

Field work was conducted in Changhua Hsien, Taiwan, in 1967–1968.[2] Changhua County is located approximately halfway between the northern

[1] William Parish, Jr., and Martin Whyte have independently gathered some useful information on marriages within and between communes on the basis of interviews with refugees in Hong Kong.

[2] I am grateful to the London-Cornell Project for East and Southeast Asian Societies, Cornell University, for the grant that supported my research.

and southern extremities of the island on the populous west coast, occupying the northernmost part of the coastal plain that continues on to the
south of Tainan City. The Changhua Plain is roughly triangular, measuring 45 kilometers north to south and 40 kilometers east to west along its
southern base. Due to the relative abundance of water and the good soil in
the eastern half, Changhua produces a large rice surplus and has an
overall population density of nearly 1000 people per square kilometer
(2800 per square mile), although the local density varies greatly.

The southwestern third of the plain, where the field work was
concentrated, has poorer soils and is less well watered than most other portions of the plain, especially along the coastline. As a result, sweet
potatoes, peanuts, sugar cane, and, lately, asparagus are grown instead of
rice in approximately half of the fields. The population of the field area
totals around 185,000 at an average density of only 565 persons per square
kilometer (1580 per square mile). It encompasses the five sub-Hsien
administrative districts, or townships, of Erhlin Chen, Fang-yuan Hsiang,
Ta-ch'eng Hsiang, Chu-t'ang Hsiang, and P'i-t'ou Hsiang (see Map 1).
Following local custom, the field area minus P'i-t'ou Township will be
referred to as the "four Hsiang-Chen." Each township is divided into 15 to
30 districts containing from 700 to 2000 persons. There are exactly 100 of
these subtownship districts in the field area, some of which are divisions
of large villages or towns while others include a number of smaller
settlements.

The first part of the research investigated the local marketing system.
On the basis of a complete business census conducted in every settlement
in the field area and some surrounding large towns, a Guttman Scalogram
was constructed that ranked all 207 of the sample settlements along a
dimension of commercial complexity defined by the 156 business activities
that occurred in three or more of the cases. (Complete details are to be
found in Crissman 1972 or 1973.) The scale clearly segregates three levels
of market towns termed central, intermediate, and standard towns on
analogy with Skinner's terminology for traditional markets on the mainland. They are basically different from traditional mainland marketing
towns, however, since marketing activity on Taiwan is not periodic (and
never has been, at least not in Changhua). Rural towns in contemporary
Taiwan are equivalent in some respects to the modernized trading centers
that evolved under the influence of mechanized transport in mainland
China (Skinner 1965). On Taiwan, however, marketing systems continually intensified as they modernized due to the simultaneous growth of
mechanized transport, population, commercialization, and per capita
incomes. As a result, and in contrast to the mainland where modernization led to the demise of standard markets, postwar Taiwan has seen the
emergence of standard trading systems, producing a three-level hierarchy
of relatively modernized rural towns.

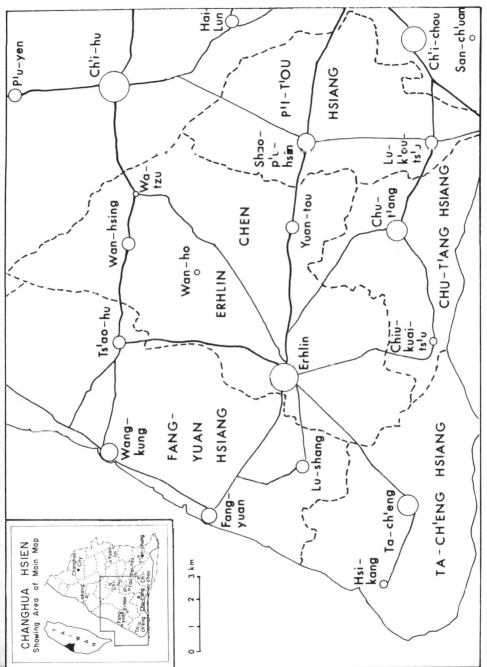

Map 1. Towns in the field area. Township boundaries are indicated by dashed lines and major roads by solid lines. The circles representing market towns are roughly proportional to commercial complexity, not population.

There is only one central town in the field area, although there are others just outside it. The town of Erhlin, in which the study was based, has a population of approximately 10,000 people and has 850 businesses of over 150 different kinds, ranging from fish stalls in the market to prosperous construction contractors. There are four intermediate towns: Ta-ch'eng, Chu-t'ang, Shao-p'u-hsin, and Wang-kung. They have an average of about 4500 people and 200 businesses distributed among nearly 80 varieties. The field area contains six standard towns: Fang-yuan, Lu-k'ou-ts'u, Wan-hsing, Ts'ao-hu, Lu-shang, and Yuan-tou. They have 4300 people on the average (the range is from 2000 to 6500) and have an average of under 80 businesses of just on 40 kinds. There are a few smaller business centers, termed minor towns, that have around 25 businesses and greatly varying populations.

There are just about 200 settlements in the field area that do not have an appreciable variety or number of businesses. Such villages range in size from hamlets containing only a few families to giant aggregations with more than 3000 people. The average village size is around 100 households (500–600 persons), but the mean size is 70 households, while the mode is between 30 and 40, reflecting the fact that there are many small villages but that those with over 2000 people are not at all uncommon either. Villages are located about 1 kilometer from one another on the average. Where there are no real roads, they are linked by networks of footpaths and oxcart trails that are also suitable for use by bicycles and motorcycles.

After establishing the hierarchy of local market towns, information on marketing behavior was gathered through questionnaires administered in every village in the field area with more than 10 households. Given the approximately 35,000 households that participate in marketing at the 11 towns in the field area, some sampling procedure had to be employed, and it was decided that a stratified sample rather than a random sample was desirable in order to produce equivalent information on every settlement. It was also assumed that all the people living in a single village would, on the average, shop in the same towns at approximately the same frequencies as their fellow villagers. That assumption is supported by the fact that all people living in a given village are about the same distance from surrounding towns and have available to them the same general means of transportation. They would, despite some differences in wealth, have need of the same basic sorts of goods and services, at least on a daily or weekly basis. Their preferences for market towns should therefore be roughly the same.

On the basis of such reasoning, it was decided that one or perhaps two questionnaires per village would be adequate, although in an attempt to ensure representative information, the questions about marketing places were phrased so as to ask about all people living in a village rather than about the specific household being interviewed. The questions were designed to be asked orally in Taiwanese Hokkien or Hakka by untrained local assistants who had contacts throughout the areas in which they worked. Questions were asked about prewar marketing habits as well as current practices.[3] There were usually a number of villagers present when the questionnaires were administered, and the responses typically represent a consensus. The results of the survey of marketing patterns are presented subsequently and, in somewhat different form, in Crissman (1972, 1973).

The data on marriages presented in this paper were acquired from the official Household Registration Records.[4] Since 1905 or 1906, every individual on Taiwan has by law been registered, and detailed records have been kept of the composition of every household on the island. These records were begun as an aid to the Japanese police force in keeping track of the population of the first Japanese colony but are now maintained by the township governments. Every birth, death, marriage, or other change in household composition must be reported. The Household Registration Records are in fact quite accurate—if they are not perfect, they are certainly 90 to 95 percent correct. Data in statistically useful quantities can be taken from them within a reasonable period of time with limited resources. In addition, 60 years of historical depth can be acquired without trusting fallible human memory concerning somebody's deceased grandmother's natal village. Clerks who normally keep the records were hired, at reasonably handsome hourly rates, to record the origin and destination of all women married into or out of a large sample of districts strategically located with regard to the towns in the field area. This information was obtained for three 10-year periods, beginning in 1910, and altogether includes information on many thousands of marriages.

Marriage is an appropriate subject with which to investigate the effects of marketing on other aspects of Chinese social organization because it creates so many other kinds of important relationships. Mother's brothers have important ritual roles and can be trusted friends and advisers. Brothers-in-law are expected to be friends and often engage in business ventures together, partly because one's wife's brother is a potential ally not shared with one's brothers. Marriage can, in addition to creating certain relationships, reflect a number of others. Friends, acquaintances, and associates of all kinds are apt, if they like and respect each other, to agree to marriage between their children. This not only assures a known

[3] People were asked to remember which towns people from their villages had patronized "under the Japanese." Trusting memory for information 25 years old is a risky business, and it is very likely that the data for prewar marketing are somewhat distorted by present habits, but to the extent that different estimates were given, they should be an indication of what went on before or during the war.

[4] I am particularly thankful to the Joint Commission on Rural Reconstruction for their invaluable aid in my quest for access to the Household Registration Records. Provincial officials were helpful as well.

quantity as an affine but also tends to cement valuable relationships with a tie that is difficult to sever. Therefore, an association of marketing with marriage is indicative of an association with other kinds of social relationships as well, even though the reasons may be too variable and murky to fathom.

Marriage data had to be utilized if the social and cultural concomitants of marketing were to be investigated at all in the field. This is so because many other behaviors clearly were not closely related to marketing habits, perhaps because of the modern conditions that prevail. No evidence for the association of cultural differences with marketing areas belonging to different towns could be discerned. The very minor dialect differences that exist derive from different ancestral origins in Fukien Province. Architectural styles in brick farmhouses vary slightly from one very small locality (a handful of villages, perhaps) to another and are sometimes observable on opposite sides of the same towns (Chu-t'ang, for instance). There are some religious peculiarities with regard to rare or even unique deities, but they are the property of single villages or of people with the same surname.

People do not identify with market towns, at least not with standard towns. The townships are usually invoked when someone is asked his native place, although someone living in Fang-yuan Hsiang, for instance, might claim to be from Erhlin were he asked where he was from while on the streets of a distant city. Nonlocals are not expected to know where remote Hsiang are located, but they usually have an idea about the location of large towns. Identification with Erhlin could also be the result of the fact that the four Hsiang-Chen are a county election district and an administrative unit with regard to certain specialized functions. Modern trading systems were not hypothesized by Skinner as constituting communities, and they were not discovered to be such.

Marketing areas, not being communities, are not a locus for political activity except insofar as they are coincident with township boundaries or election districts. The near identity of the townships of Ta-ch'eng and Chu-t'ang with the primary marketing areas centered on the respective township seats is no mystery. In the course of experimenting with local administrative organization during the early years of their rule, the Japanese *sometimes* established administrative boundaries on the basis of existing social features, such as fields owned or worked by residents of particular villages or towns habitually patronized.

There is some evidence that at an earlier time religious organization was related to at least Erhlin's marketing area. The names and villages (or districts, during the Japanese period) of contributors to a series of renovations of Erhlin Town's Ma-tsu Temple, going back to the nineteenth century, are carved on stone inlays in the walls of the temple courtyard. The homes of contributors are scattered throughout what are now the four

Hsiang-Chen, although most are relatively close to town. At the present time, however, participation in religious affairs centered on the temples in Erhlin Town is determined more by political factionalism than by anything else.

Since the end of World War II, if not before, each of the temples in Erhlin Town has had as its major contributors and officers members of only one of two "factions" that have been in competition for elective positions since such were first created by the Japanese. When a very large and important nonrecurring religious festival was held in the winter of 1967, in which literally every family in town participated with public displays of foodstuffs and banquets for guests from throughout the county and beyond, the only surrounding villages that participated, either in the closed temple ceremonies or with public displays of pig carcasses cut in half and decorated to resemble mythological beasts, were those dominated by the same political faction that controls the temples.

In conclusion, most of the social and cultural concomitants of marketing communities suggested for the mainland were found to be absent in the field area. This is in part a consequence of the existence of modern trading systems on Taiwan but also reflects the efficient sub-Hsien administrative system inherited from the Japanese as well as the island's history as a recent frontier area. Marriages, however, still occur for the same reasons and in much the same way as they did on the mainland. Not only are marriage patterns indicative of other patterns of social relationships, but they are hypothesized to be dependent on marketing under both traditional and modern conditions so that the demonstration of a causative relationship in the field area can be taken as strong support for the same relationship on the mainland.

MARRIAGE AND MARKETING DATA

The Household Registration Records are now kept, by each township office, on the basis of subtownship districts, or *li* and *ts'un*. During the period of Japanese colonial administration, they were kept on the basis of the equivalent *pao,* also referred to as *buraku* (*ho*). There have been some changes in the details of the information recorded for each household, but the general format is the same, and the records are essentially continuous from the early 1900s up to the present. In some cases the officials and clerks who worked for the Japanese police when they had responsibility for the records are still keeping the same records for the present township governments. However, around 1950 the 62 districts then in the field area were divided into 100 new districts with high-sounding Mandarin names instead of the traditional and more earthy Hokkien appellations such as "Nine Devil Spot" and "Fish Shack." As a result of this subtownship reor-

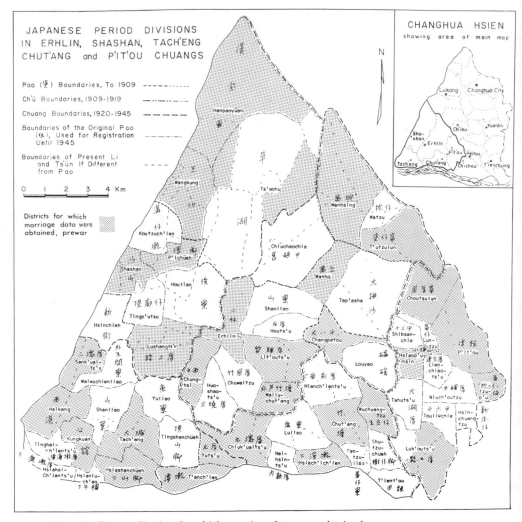

Map 2. Prewar districts for which marriage data were obtained.

ganization, some of the postwar marriage data were not drawn from exactly the same units as was the prewar information.

Maps 2 and 3 display prewar and postwar subtownship districts in the field area and indicate the ones for which marriage data were obtained. It was judged economically unfeasible and scientifically unnecessary to include them all. However, all of the towns in the field area were included (usually only samples from them in the postwar period). In addition, representative districts throughout the marketing areas of Erhlin, each of the intermediate towns, and some of the standard towns were selected. Preference was given to those located near the boundarics between mar-

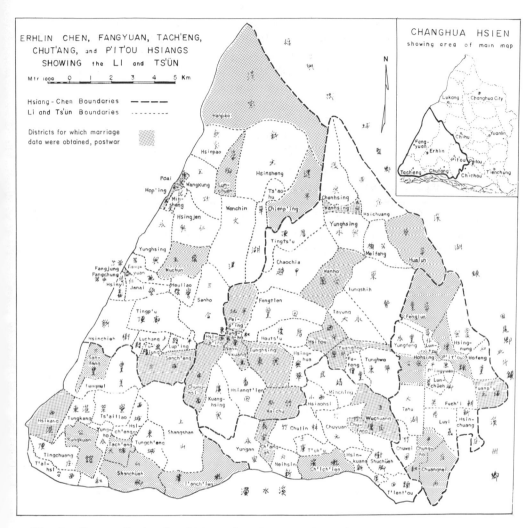

Map 3. Postwar districts for which marriage data were obtained.

keting areas belonging to towns at the same and different levels, since it was assumed that they would provide the harshest test for the hypothesis that marketing areas influence marriage patterns. Altogether, data were collected for 30 of the 62 prewar districts and for 37 of the 100 postwar districts.

It was not judged necessary or economically feasible to gather information on the entire time period for which the records exist either. Consequently, only three 10-year periods were examined, demographic calculations having shown that 10 years would encompass enough marriages to provide adequate statistics.

Data for the period immediately preceding the field research were of course desired, so the decade from 1958 to 1967 was selected. It also made sense to get as early a view of marriage patterns as possible, as long as it was based on accurate data. Since the records were begun in about 1905–1906, it was decided to gather information for the decade between 1910 and 1919, by which time there is every reason to believe that accuracy had been achieved by the highly efficient Japanese police force. The 1910–1919 decade was also early enough to avoid strong influences from commercialization of the economy and the creation of the transport infrastructure by the Japanese. In addition, it was a decade during which the then-equivalents of townships did not change, although the present township boundaries were not established until 1920. The decade from 1935 to 1944 was the third one selected. It comes almost exactly midway between the other two and represents the full fruition of Japanese colonial policies, but not the postwar conditions that brought about the appearance of standard trading systems. World War II did not cause extensive social disruption on Taiwan.

The data obtained concern women's change of residence at marriage. It is of course normal on Taiwan, as elsewhere in China, for a bride to take up residence in her husband's domestic corporation upon her marriage. The transfer is recorded in the Household Registration Records twice: once to sign her out of her parents' household, notation being made of the address of the family she is marrying into, and once to sign her into her new family, notation being made of her place of origin. It is thus possible to discover, from the records for a single district, where all the women from that district went when they got married and also where all the women came from who married into that district. Thus, although the data were collected for only a sample of districts, they *concern* all the districts in the field area (as well as other localities throughout the county and even the island). Each of the 100 districts involved can be assigned a rank with respect to each of the sample districts on the basis of the number of inter-marriages between the two of them.

The information on marketing patterns, described earlier, was gathered on the basis of villages, but averaging figures for districts containing multiple settlements caused only a minimal loss of information. When expressed in terms of units of 10 percent of marketing done at various centers, the marketing data also allow all the districts in the field are to be assigned a rank with respect to the amount of marketing their residents do at any one of the towns.

Inhabitants of most of the districts in the field area were reported to do some of their marketing at Erhlin, the central town. Exceptions were the northernmost district in Fang-yuan Hsiang, districts in central and southeastern Chu-t'ang Hsiang, and all of those in P'i-t'ou Hsiang. Districts within approximately 3 or 4 kilometers of Erhlin rank in the ninth or tenth deciles (80 to 100 percent of marketing done at Erhlin). Those in a more distant ring out to about 6 or 7 kilometers rank in the fifth to the eighth deciles, while the remainder are in the first to the fourth deciles (primarily the first and second).

Taking the locations and levels of surrounding towns into consideration, it is apparent that Ehrlin provides standard, intermediate, and central marketing functions for immediately surrounding districts. Somewhat more distant areas are served by their own standard towns, which supply 50 to 70 percent of the needs of inhabitants of immediately adjacent districts. Those surrounding more distant intermediate towns do 80 to 90 percent of their marketing at those centers, since they provide both standard and intermediate functions, and people must go to the central town of Erhlin for only 10 to 20 percent of their needs. Some districts are so situated with respect to towns that their residents split their custom three ways, 50 to 60 percent going to their nearby standard town, 20 to 30 percent to the nearest intermediate town, and the remaining 10 to 20 percent to a central town.

As a convention, districts ranking in the sixth decile and above with respect to a particular town (that is, 50 percent or more of marketing done at that town) will be said to belong to the town's *primary* marketing area, while a *secondary* marketing area consists of districts in the first through fifth deciles. Each district belongs to one, and only one, primary marketing area. Districts immediately around Erhlin do not belong to any secondary area because all levels of marketing are done at the central town. Other districts belong to one or two secondary areas of towns at different levels from their primary town.

Difficult as the foregoing patterns are to visualize or to map in any simple manner (see Crissman 1973 for a series of maps), they correspond nicely to the predictions of central-place models that specify just such divisions of custom and overlaps of marketing hinterlands belonging to centers at different levels. In the present context the figures on percentage of marketing done at various towns are significant because the rank orders they establish can be compared with ranks in terms of intermarriages in order to test the hypothesis that a causal relation exists between the two variables. To the extent that marketing habits induce marriage patterns (the reverse being improbable), two districts that both rank high with respect to marketing at a particular town should also have a high ranking with regard to intermarriages, while districts on the periphery of a marketing hinterland (and that do not also rank high in terms of marketing at another town) should have a low ranking in terms of intermarriage.[5] When marketing habits change, as they do when new towns emerge and develop,

[5] The relative sizes of the populations of different districts, which vary from 700 or 800 to over 2000, of course enter into the number of intermarriages that occur. Fortunately, on the basis of a trial computer run in which population differences among districts were evened out by a complicated procedure, it could be concluded that differences in district populations have no appreciable effect on the ultimate statistical measures that were sought.

marriage patterns should eventually become realigned after a lag for new social relationships to become well established.

STATISTICAL CORRELATIONS

Kendall's *Tau* (see Siegal 1956 for a mathematical description) is a non-parametric correlation coefficient that is capable of assessing the correspondence between such sets of rank orders, and it was employed in the generation of the statistics in Table 1.[6] It is particularly suitable because radically different kinds of data can be compared once they have been reduced to rank orders.

When two sets of ranks match perfectly, *Tau* is ± 1. If they are perfect mirror inversions, *Tau* is -1. If the relation between them is perfectly random, *Tau* is 0, while if it is more than random but less than perfect, *Tau* ranges between ± 1 and -1. Tests of significance are available to establish confidence levels, but judgment is required to decide the importance of a *Tau* of $\pm .2$ as opposed to one of $\pm .8$. In general, people accustomed to the statistic begin to show interest when it rises above $\pm .3$ or so. However, when dealing with a data structure such as the one in question, in which a large number of cases have ranks of 0 in one or both orders being compared, certain anomalies can occur. For instance, positive correlations can be muted if the number of cases with ranks above 0 in one order is every much fewer than in the other. This occurs because a high degree of correspondence with respect to higher ranks may be overwhelmed by lack of correspondence at lower ranks. This can happen, for instance, when small standard marketing areas are compared to appreciably larger marriage networks. Nonetheless, *Tau* is an appropriate statistic for this task, and some interesting and useful measures were generated from the marriage and marketing data.

The statistic was also used to test a variety of other possible influences on marriage patterns, including surname distributions, the existence of a Hakka enclave, relative prosperity, and political factionalism (which has a geographical basis, at least in part). For the postwar period, 24 potentially contributing variables were compared separately to number of in-marrying women, out-marrying women, and total intermarriages (as well as other changes in residence). For the prewar period, only 10 variables were included but were compared for both of the sample decades.

The interpretation of all the correlation coefficients produced in the hours of computer time consumed was a lengthy task that yielded information mostly of interest only to a student of the southwestern corner of the Changhua Plain. Some of it is discussed briefly in Crissman (1973).

[6] I am indebted to the London-Cornell Project for East and Southeast Asian Societies, Cornell University, for a grant that allowed me to engage a programmer and the computer.

Of somewhat more general interest is the corroboration of hypergamous tendencies in Chinese marriage arrangements. Women tend to marry away from the impoverished coastal area (often via the Hakkas) and up the central-place hierarchy (and ultimately out of the field area). The expected absence of any tendency for marriage alliances among surname groups can also be demonstrated. Political factionalism did not generate significant statistics, although this is almost certainly an artifact of the data base and structure.[7]

The only factors that consistently produced meaningfully high correlations with marriage patterns were marketing habits and simple propinquity. A rank order of all districts in terms of distance from each of the sample districts was created by measuring the length of the most likely routes between them, which were usually assumed to be the ones that incorporated improved roads and that passed through towns. In light of the known significance of propinquity in influencing marriage patterns in the United States and elsewhere, it was not surprising to discover that distance between the residences of brides' and grooms' families produced very strong negative correlations on Taiwan as well.

Table 1 presents statistics measuring correlations between marriage patterns and marketing behavior, as well as some that show the effects of propinquity. Each of the sample districts is listed, under all the towns at which its people do any of their marketing, in order of decreasing percentages of postwar marketing done at the town. (The statistics for districts listed under more than one town are of course those that pertain to marketing at the town under which the district is listed each time.)

Figures marked with an asterisk are not significant at the .05 level, while almost all of the others are significant above .005. The statistics enclosed in parentheses are unreliable for one reason or another, or they have very idiosyncratic explanations (see Crissman 1973 for details). Districts marked with an asterisk are divisions of prewar districts. Since their populations are only a sample of the populations of the prewar districts, the *Tau*'s generated by the marriages of those different sets of people are not precisely equivalent, and some of the differences between 1935–1944 and 1958–1967 statistics could be due to such differences in the two populations.

All of the prewar statistics on marketing at towns other than Erhlin, Ta-ch'eng, and Chu't'ang had to be computed on the basis of postwar marketing data, since none of the other towns (except for Fang-yuan) was in existence as anything but a village or perhaps a minor town before the war. The 1935–1944 statistics under those three towns were generated on the basis of reports of marketing behavior "in Japanese times." Corresponding figures for 1910–1919 also used the same, circa World War II, information, since no useful data on very early marketing behavior could

---

[7] For some detailed information on the factions, see Crissman (1969:1–67).

TABLE 1

Kendall's Rank Order Correlation Coefficient Tau *Measuring the Relationship between Marriage Patterns and Marketing Behavior for Three Ten-Year Periods*

Postwar District Name[a]	Distance	% M[b]	Marketing			% M[b]
	1958-67	1967	1958-67	1935-44	1910-19	Prewar
Erhlin Town						
*Tung-ho	-.367	10	.344			
*Hsi-p'ing	-.572	10	.512	(.096*[c])	(-.155)[d]	10
*Pei-p'ing	-.472	10	.584			
*Nan-kuang	-.437	10	.359			
Chung-hsi	-.500	10	.356	.329	.174	10
*Tung-hsing	-.384	10	.308	(-.187)	(.348)	10
Wai-chu	-.479	9	.190	.211	(.324)	10
Wu-chun	-.498	8	.289	.404	.359	8
Wan-ho	-.464	8	(.073*)	.287	(.274)	10
*Hsi-tou	-.499	7	.188	.344	(.238)	9
*Yuan-tou	-.375	2	(.033*)			
*T'an-ch'ien	-.573	5	.193	-.024*	.078*	2
				-.145	.087*	2
Lun-chüeh	-.505	4	.222	-.145	.087*	7
Chien-p'ing	-.532	4	.171	.389	.382	7
San-feng	-.383	4	.074	.149	.162	6
*Ch'ang-an	-.510	4	.018	.039	-.059	4
*Fu-jung	-.475	4	.304	.407	.406	9
*Fang-chung	-.514	3	.180	.339	.326	5
*Fang-jung	-.362	3	.063*			
*Ho-p'ing	-.538	1	.127	.387	.431	7
*Po-ai	-.625	1	.183			
*Wan-hsing	-.432	1	.057*	.180	(.288)	9
*Hua-lun	-.550	1	-.092	.211	(.316)	0
*Hsi-kang	-.638	1	.177	.072*	.159	1
Kung-kuan	-.592	1	.188	.134	.075*	1
Shan-chüeh	-.581	1	.182	.080*	.181	1
Wu-chuang	-.445	1	-.049	-.074	-.087	3

continued on next page

TABLE 1 (continued)

Postwar District Name[a]	Distance 1958-67	% M^b 1967	Marketing			% M^b Prewar
			1958-67	1935-44	1910-19	
Ta-ch'eng Town						
*Ta-ch'eng	-.495	9	.463	.282	.437	9
Shan-chüeh	-.581	9	.370	.629	.612	9
Kung-kuan	-.592	9	.362	.516	.558	9
*Hsi-kang	-.638	5	.231	.740	.464	9
San-feng	-.383	5	.301	.409	.455	4
*T'an-ch'ien	-.573	3	.161	.559 .428	.612 .545	8 8
Chu-t'ang Town						
*Chu-t'ang	-.445	10	.589	.674	.450	10
Ch'i-ch'ien	-.531	9	.760	.803	.163	9
Wu-chuang	-.445	6	.334	.610	.316	7
*Ch'ang-an	-.510	(1)	.506	.449	.214	6
Shao-p'u-hsin Town						
Ho-hsing	-.537	8	.711	.570	.472	—
Feng-lun	-.677	5	.154	.698	.483	—
*P'i-t'ou	-.600	4	.298	.343	.343	—
Yuan-p'u	-.564	11		.534	.481	—
Wang-kung Town						
*Ho-p'ing	-.538	8	.054*	.133*	.262	—
*Po-ai	-.625	8	.040*			
Lun-chüeh	-.505	2	-.198	.406	.454	—
*Han-pao	-.346	2	-.150	.570	.722	—
Fang-yuan Town						
*Fang-chung	-.514	7	.118	.543	.157	—
*Fang-jung	-.362	7	.213			
Wu-chun	-.498	2	.073*	.581	.609	—
*Fu-jung	-.475	1	-.184	.225	.484	—

continued on next page

TABLE 1 (continued)

Postwar District Name[a]	Distance	% M^b	Marketing			% M^b
	1958-67	1967	1958-67	1935-44	1910-19	Prewar
Lu-k'ou-ts'u Town						
Chung-ho	-.451	8	.528	.121	.068*	—
Chuang-nei	-.504	8	.493	.136	.137	—
Wu-chuang	-.445	2	.234	nd[e]	nd	—
Yuan-tou Town						
*Yuan-tou	-.375	8	(.258)	.964	.550	—
*Hsi-tou	-.499	3	-.467			
Wan-hsing Town						
*Wan-hsing	-.432	7	.133	.977	.573	—
Wan-ho	-.464	2	.082	nd	nd	—
Ts'ao-hu Town						
Chien-p'ing	-.532	6	-.974	nd	nd	—
Lun-chüeh	-.505	1	-.780	nd	nd	—

a. Divisions of prewar districts are asterisked.
b. Market dependence on place (in 10 percents).
c. Statistics with asterisks are not significant at the .05 level.
d. Statistics in parentheses are unreliable for one reason or another (see text).
e. No data.
f. Town did not exist prewar.

be obtained. However, marketing hinterlands in the field area appear not to have changed much over time except for the creation and promotion of lower-level towns around the periphery of Erhlin's once giant marketing area, and the comparison of marriage patterns to asynchronous marketing patterns for lower-level towns is not, therefore, a critical distortion. In fact, it serves to heighten any temporal changes in marriage patterns because the marketing patterns to which they are being compared are, in effect, held constant.

Due to space limitations, Table 1 contains *Tau*'s measuring the correlation between distance and number of marriages for the 1958-1967 decade only. They range into the high $-.600$s in all three time periods, but the mean changes, being $-.44$ in the 1910s, $-.55$ just before and during the war, and $-.50$ in the recent period. This is a reflection of the fact, quite noticeable on mapped distributions, that marriage areas were considerably larger in the 1935–1944 decade than they are at present. The postwar concentration of marriages in more limited areas results in only slightly lower correlations because the effects of propinquity are still strong within the reduced range. In only 6 percent of all cases do Tau's for distance fall below $-.25$. The majority of those cases are for the earliest decade, when numbers of marriages were small and the records perhaps not as comprehensive as they later became. Erhlin Town accounts for two of the low Tau's, a result of the fact that before the war marriages in and out of Erhlin were scattered throughout the entire area.

In 25 percent of all cases, some statistic for marketing shows a higher correlation than distance, but distance is usually considerably higher and is far more consistently high. Partial correlations worked on a small sample of districts indicate that correlations between marriages and marketing, on the one hand, and marriage and distance, on the other, are mutually independent. This finding must, however, be tempered by the realization that distance tends to set the limits within which the effects of marketing behavior are manifested. That this is so can be perceived on mapped distributions of marriages, which can often be interpreted as spatially constricted marriage areas modified by marketing areas.

Although simple propinquity consistently produces the best correlations with marriage patterns, the marketing data generate statistics high enough to prove interesting. The mean of *all* correlations between marketing and marriage was .36 in the 1910–1919 decade, went up to .41 for 1935–1944, and then declined to .30 for the postwar decade. These figures compare fairly well with the average Tau's for distance quoted earlier ($-.44$, $-.55$, and $-.50$).

Some highly significant averages appear when districts in primary areas are segregated from those in secondary areas and levels of the central-place hierarchy are distinguished. For the postwar decade the average correlation for districts within Erhlin's primary area is .332. For districts in intermediate-town primary areas, the average is .416, excluding Wang-kung. That perennial exception to almost everything produces nonsignificant, nearly random Tau's even for districts within the town itself. If Ts'ao-hu's aberrant figure is excluded, the average for standard-town primary districts is .295. For the 1935–1944 decade, considering only correlations produced by contemporaneous data, the average for districts in Erhlin's primary area (which was far larger at that time) is .228, while districts in the primary areas of Ta-ch'eng and Chu-t'ang average .526 and .634, respectively.

For the present period, marketing at Chu-t'ang produces by far the best set of correlations of any town in the field area. Its primary districts average .561, which is higher than any Tau's for distance among the same districts. The other long-established intermediate towns produce decent, if not outstanding, correlations between marketing and marriage: For primary districts, again, Ta-ch'eng averages .345 and Shao-p'u-hsin averages .388.

Among standard towns, marketing done at Lu-k'ou-tsu produces far higher correlations (.538, .493, and .234) than that done at any of the others. Lu-k'ou-ts'u has been a standard town at least since the military road from Ch'i-hu to Hsi-lo was built during the war and has therefore had time to establish itself as a local institution. The statistics for marketing and marriage for all other standard towns, and for Wang-kung as well (which in all characteristics other than commercial complexity is similar to standard towns rather than to other intermediate towns), are either very low or highly irregular. This is a result of the manner in which the statistics were generated. Standard-town marketing areas are very small; their primary areas average only 4.5 districts (about half of which are in the towns themselves), and their secondary areas add only another 2.5 districts on the average. Since marriage areas normally extend over 30 or 40 districts, the number for which information on both marketing and marriage can be directly compared by the statistical program is only a small proportion of the total number of districts for which marriage data are present. Therefore, either random or meaningless figures are bound to be produced. As a result, according to Table 1, marketing done at standard towns that have developed since the war is not related to marriage patterns. Given the consideration that the length of time a town has been established should have a strong bearing on the social field surrounding it, the statistics may well be telling the truth, albeit perhaps coincidentally.

INTERPRETATIONS

The hypothesis that frequency of marketing is related to amount of intermarriage is supported by the figures in Table 1. An inspection will show that there is clearly an association between decile rankings in terms of marketing at particular towns and the strength of the correlation coefficients measuring the correspondence of marriage and marketing patterns. The relation can be most clearly perceived for the districts listed under Ta-ch'eng Town. It can also be readily discerned with regard to Chu-t'ang and Lu-k'ou-ts'u.[8] The association is present for Erhlin as well, but the number of sample districts that do some of their marketing there is so large that simple displays are necessary to bring it out clearly.

By dichotomizing primary and secondary marketing areas and likewise segregating *Tau*'s above and below .200 (reliable ones only), the fourfold matrices shown in Tables 2 and 3 were created. Table 2, for the postwar decade, has 28 percent of the 25 districts with good statistics listed under Erhlin in the upper left-hand corner—they are in Erhlin's primary mar-

---

[8] In the case of Chu-t'ang, it should be noted that Chang-an District's frequency of marketing at that town has probably been seriously underrepresented.

TABLE 2
Dichotomization of Correlation Coefficients Tau Above and Below
.200 with Respect to Erhlin's Primary and Secondary Marketing
Areas, 1958-1967

	Primary Marketing Area	Secondary Marketing Area	Total
Tau above .200	7 (28%)	2 (8%)	9 (36%)
Tau below .200	3 (12%)	13 (52%)	16 (64%)
Total	10 (40%)	15 (60%)	25 (100%)

keting area and have *Tau*'s for marriage and marketing above .200. The
opposite corner contains 52 percent of the districts, those in Erhlin's secondary area with *Tau*'s of less than .200. Only 20 percent of the districts
are inappropriately distributed, split 2 to 3 between the other two corners.
When the same procedure is performed for the 1935-1944 decade, as
shown in Table 3 (reliable statistics only, again), 45 percent of the districts
manifest both a high degree of marketing and high correlation between
marketing and marriage, while 35 percent are low in marketing and low in
correlation with marriage. Again, only 20 percent do not support the
association, being split 1 to 3, with the majority being in Erhlin's primary
area but having low correlation coefficients.

Two general temporal changes in marriage patterns have occurred since
the war. The most important is the increase of intermarriages with areas
outside the field area. In particular, local women have married men living
in distant parts of the island. Many of these marriages are contracted with
young men from the region who have gone to the eastern coast or to towns
or cities all over Taiwan to work but who still marry local girls—either
those chosen by their parents or those with whom liaison has been main-

TABLE 3
Dichotomization of Correlation Coefficients Tau Above and Below
.200 with Respect to Erhlin's Primary and Secondary Marketing
Areas, 1935-1944

	Primary Marketing Area	Secondary Marketing Area	Total
Tau above .200	9 (45%)	1 (5%)	10 (50%)
Tau below .200	3 (15%)	7 (35%)	10 (50%)
Total	12 (60%)	8 (40%)	20 (100%)

tained. Girls as well as youths leave home for work, however. If their marriages occur outside the field area after they have officially changed their residences, which must be done for any stay longer than a few months, then the marriages do not appear in the local Household Registration Records. As a result, overall numbers of marriages recorded for the 1958–1967 period are not as large as postwar population growth would lead one to expect.

The other general trend, which is perhaps only a minor aspect of the first one, is the postwar increase in the movement of women from west to east away from the coastal area. This tendency has become more noticeable because countermovement of women toward the coast from Erhlin Chen and Chu-t'ang Hsiang has almost ceased. In addition, absolutely greater numbers of brides are now being exported from Fang-yuan and Ta-ch'eng Townships, and they are going somewhat further afield. It is unlikely that this is the result of marketing patterns, however, since Chu-t'ang Hsiang receives many women from Ta-ch'eng Hsiang, yet neither area participates in marketing at Erhlin to any appreciable extent.

Most of the districts sampled in Fang-yuan Hsiang also send women east to Erhlin Chen, but it is very difficult to interpret the effect of this move ment on the statistics, since for the most part there has been a significa drop in correlations with marketing at Erhlin between 1935–1944 ar 1958–1967. The explanation for the lower postwar correlations must sure' be sought in the postwar emergence of three new towns in Fang-yu Hsiang: Ts'ao-hu, Wang-kung, and Lu-shang.[9] They have significan lowered the amount of marketing done at Erhlin by people living in Fa yuan Township.

This is direct evidence for the effect of marketing on marriage. Grant it is a disruptive effect, since marketing at the new towns has not (at lea as yet) produced any positive change in marriage patterns that can b measured by the statistical program employed. Yet all of the new towns that have emerged in the last decade or so around the periphery of Erhlin's marketing area, not just those in Fang-yuan Hsiang but near Wan-hsing and Yuan-tou as well, are associated with a marked decline in the correlation of marriages in their immediate surroundings with marketing at Erhlin. The cause of this can be assigned to the patronage they have drawn away from Erhlin, since their situations have nothing else in common.

The same effect is present with regard to T'an-ch'ien District under Ta-ch'eng Town. Owing to the inauguration some years ago of hourly bus service directly to Erhlin (but not to Ta-ch'eng Town), people in T'an-ch'ien now do most of their marketing at Erhlin. Their marriages are not,

[9] Further description of changes in the marketing system on the Changhua Plain over time appears in Crissman (1972, 1973) and in Volume I, Chapter 6.

as yet at least, any more highly correlated with marketing at Erhlin than are those of other women-exporting districts in Ta-ch'eng Hsiang that do only central marketing there. However, T'an-ch'ien's new marketing habits have disrupted the earlier quite strong correlation of its marriages with marketing at Ta-ch'eng Town, so that it is now on the average less than half that of the other districts in the same marketing area.

A precisely analogous situation has occurred with regard to Feng-lun District under Shao-p'u-hsin Town. Before the war its marriages were highly correlated with marketing there, but in the postwar period the association has fallen off drastically. The principal difference between the two time periods is the existence of the broad military road constructed during the war. It passes along the boundary of Feng-lun District and provides a direct route to Ch'i-hu across a river that cannot be forded easily. Parts of the district are closer to Ch'i-hu than they are to Shao-p'u-hsin, and the northern part is now actually in Ch'i-hu's primary area, while all of it is in the secondary area of that central town. At present, four-tenths of all the marketing of the whole district is done at Ch'i-hu. While the marriage correlations with marketing at Shao-p'u-hsin fell from .398 to .154 between 1944 and the 1958–1967 decade, correlations with marketing at Ch'i-hu (that done by districts in the field area only) rose from .024 to .329. The road to Ch'i-hu from Feng-lun has been in existence longer than bus service to Erhlin has been available for people in T'an-ch'ien. With time, the relation between T'an-ch'ien's marriages and marketing at Erhlin may be expected to improve as much as has the relation between Feng-lun's marriages and marketing at Ch'i-hu Town.

It is not difficult to account for the fact that the first effect of changed marketing patterns, whether due to new standard towns or to new roads and transport services, is the disruption of old patterns without a concomitant creation of new patterns. The latter take time to emerge, while the lapse of relationships that results from changing marketing habits can have a far more immediate effect. Whether or not, in 10 years' time, the inhabitants of standard-town primary areas will have begun to select brides from other families they become acquainted with while buying daily necessities cannot be predicted with any certainty. The populations involved are large enough to make it possible (6000 to 10,000), but still other factors may preclude it. Good correlations between marriage patterns and new marketing habits have, however, emerged in the past after enough time has elapsed. This tendency can be clearly discerned by viewing certain sequences of correlations in the light of the historical development of particular towns.

Chu-t'ang Town grew from virtually nothing after having been designated as an administrative center during early Japanese experiments in local administrative organization. By 1910 it had begun to acquire commercial functions; by 1920 it was a stop on the narrow-gauge rail line between Erhlin and Pei-tou and had become enough of a local center to be established as the seat of a township that was largely delimited on the basis of local marketing patterns. Marriage correlations for the 1910–1919 decade (computed on the basis of later, circa 1940, marketing habits) are not outstanding. However, those for the 1935–1944 decade, when Chu-t'ang was an established and thriving standard town, are among the best for any town at any time. The prewar marketing information with which prewar marriage data were compared defines a fairly large and coherent primary marketing area with approximately 70 percent of all marketing done at Chu-t'ang. Postwar correlations have remained generally high.

The same dramatic rise in correlations can be seen with regard to Lu-k'ou-ts'u, but it comes between the 1935–1944 and 1958–1967 decades after Lu-k'ou-ts'u had become a standard town. It was only a minor town in 1930, but sometime during the war it reached standard town status and was firmly established by 1950. This was early enough for patterns of local marriages in the 1960s to have become adjusted to the marketing being done there; even Wu-chang, with only 20 percent participation in the Lu-k'ou-ts'u market, shows a fair marriage correlation.

The positive effects of marketing habits on marriage patterns can also be seen with regard to the northeastern sector of Erhlin Chen, which is actually closer to Ch'i-hu. Like Chu-t'ang, Ch'i-hu Town arose from humble beginnings during the Japanese colonial period, but it grew faster than Chu-t'ang because it was a major transport nexus and the site of a sugar mill. It was a standard town by 1910 and had caught up to Erhlin's intermediate status by 1930; it has kept pace since, both towns having become central towns by the 1940s. The growth of Ch'i-hu as a central place is reflected in progressively lower correlations of marriage with marketing at Erhlin Town for districts near Ch'i-hu Town (Wan-hsing and Hua-lun). Erhlin Town now serves that northeastern part of the township as an administrative center only, although before Ch'i-hu Town grew commercially, it was a marketing center as well.

Correlations with marriage for marketing at Ch'i-hu Town (field area districts only) with respect to Hua-lun District are as follows: 1910–1919, .352; 1935–1944, .519; and 1958–1967, .353. The prewar sequence shows a trend opposite to that for marketing at Erhlin as presented in Table 1. The lower postwar figures for both towns may be the result of the rise of Wan-hsing as a standard town. Figures for marriages and field area marketing at Ch'i-hu Town for Wan-hsing District, which now contains only the town itself but which extended appreciably to both the north and the south before the war, are 1910–1919, .407; 1935–1944, .536; and 1958–1967, .389. The same prewar trend as for Hua-lun is evident, and the same lower postwar figures appear with regard to both Ch'i-hu's and Erhlin's marketing areas.

CONCLUSION

The findings discussed in this paper are somewhat equivocal. It is clear that mere propinquity is the single most powerful correlative of marriage patterns. However, it is also evident that of the other variables investigated (including commercial complexity, wealth of districts, distance from the unpleasant coastal region, distribution of the most prevalent surnames, and allegiance to political "factions"), the percentage of marketing done at various towns produced the second best set of correlations. Some coefficients for marketing are in fact higher than corresponding ones for distance.

It is certain that the postwar emergence of new standard towns has had the effect of disrupting existing marriage patterns as well as previous marketing areas. Evidence for the creation of new marriage patterns as a result of changing marketing habits was found with respect to Ch'u-t'ang, Lu-k'ou-ts'u, and Ch'i-hu, all towns that became well established under the Japanese colonial administration. It would appear that the relationship between marketing and marriage is a fragile one—a change in towns patronized has the immediate effect of throwing prior marriage patterns into disarray, and it takes a much longer time for new marriage patterns based on the new marketing habits to emerge. Nonetheless, the evidence that has been presented is sufficient to demonstrate that marketing has a causative effect on marriages in the field area.

The fact that good evidence for this relationship could be found in Changhua Hsien, Taiwan, which has had a history different from any part of mainland China—differences including some basic changes in demography, transport facilities, local administration, and all aspects of the economy under 50 years of Japanese rule and 25 postwar years as a part of the Republic of China—is powerful support indeed for G. William Skinner's hypothesis that marketing is a basic determinant of other aspects of rural Chinese social organization. Since the marketing system in contemporary Changhua is a hypertrophied example of the kinds of systems that Skinner describes as resulting from the introduction of modernized transport, there should be no difficulty in extending the findings of this study to modernized trading systems on the Chinese mainland. Further, since the causation invoked to account for the effects of marketing on marriage is the same for both traditional Chinese marketing systems and modernized Chinese trading systems, the field study in Changhua also strongly supports the hypothesis that standard marketing communities set limits to connubia for the traditional Chinese peasantry. The degree of intermarriage should, in fact, have been much higher on the mainland, since many of the intrusive factors that negatively affect the relationship on Taiwan were absent from the traditional Chinese milieu.

REFERENCES

Crissman, Lawrence W.
  1969 Each for his own: The Taiwanese response to K. M. T. local administration. Paper
       delivered at the London–Cornell Project Conference on Modernized and Moderniz-
       ing Governments in East and Southeast Asia, Ste-Adèle-en-Haut, Provence de
       Québec, Canada.
  1972 Marketing on the Changua Plain, Taiwan. In *Economic organization in Chinese
       society,* edited by W. E. Willmott. Stanford, Calif.: Stanford Univ. Press.
  1973 Town and country: Central place theory and Chinese marketing systems, with
       particular reference to southwestern Changhua Hsien, Taiwan. Unpublished Ph.D.
       dissertation, Cornell Univ.
Siegal, Sidney
  1956 *Nonparametric statistics for the behavioral sciences.* New York: McGraw-Hill.
Skinner, G. William
  1964 Marketing and social structure in rural China: Part I. *Journal of Asian Studies* **24:**
       3–43.
  1965 Marketing and social structure in rural China: Part II. *Journal of Asian Studies* **24:**
       195–228.

Chapter 6

Factors Underlying Endogamous Group Size[1]

John W. Adams
University of South Carolina

Alice Bee Kasakoff
University of South Carolina

Endogamy is the tendency of people to mate within their own group. Endogamous groups are important as a social universe in which all sorts of basic interaction go on; the study of endogamy is therefore the study of social communication in the broadest sense. This article describes the range of sizes of endogamous groups and some of the reasons for variations that exist within this range. It discusses to what extent and by what forces the social horizon of man is confined; for confined it is, and our evidence indicates that even modern society, with its sophisticated means of transport and communication, fits quite nicely into the set of conclusions we have reached for primitive groups.

What we are able to present here are no more than first approximations; the statistical information about marriage upon which we have had to depend is not available for most societies of the world and what is avail-

[1] Editor's note: This paper was originally given at the Ninth International Congress of Anthropological and Ethnological Sciences in Chicago in 1973 and is published in *Population and Social Organization,* edited by Moni Nag (The Hague: Mouton, 1975). It is reprinted here in its original form except that the tables and figures have been redone. (The authors would like to thank Darby Erd of the Institute of Archaeology and Ethnology, University of South Carolina, for redrawing the figures.) The following paper, "Central-Place Theory and Endogamy in China" (Chapter 7), relates this paper to studies that have utilized central-place theory in China.

able is limited. But more important are the many methodological and conceptual problems that exist and that are partly responsible for deficiencies in the data. The purpose here is as much to explore these with a hope of guiding further work as it is to present a broad outline of the nature and sizes of the groups within which endogamy occurs.

We came to this topic from an attempt to describe the marriage patterns of the Gitksan, a group on the Northwest Coast among whom we had done field work. We were interested in whether any of the models Lévi-Strauss had discussed applied; that is, if there were marriage to particular kinds of relatives. But we soon found that to determine this statistically we had to delineate a marriage universe for our sample. There were strong preferences to marry within the same village and within a set of villages which formed a dialect group. Yet there were also flows of people both between villages in the same dialect group and between the two different (minor) dialect groups we had studied.

We discovered, however, that the marriage universe of most individuals was very small. Because of this, many of the statistical techniques that had been developed for demonstrating marriage patterns were difficult to apply (see Kasakoff 1974). The size of the marriage universe, the endogamous group, limited the number and type of marriage patterns that could be found within it, and thus our attention turned to the problems of delineating marriage universes themselves.

PROCEDURES

It was important to know how the Gitksan compared with other societies but we found that little work had been done on this topic. Limited as we were by the way other ethnographers had tabulated their data, we began with the simplest and most obvious ways of describing marriage universes. We plotted the sizes of endogamous groups reported by ethnographers against the percentages of endogamy they reported for these groups. Next, we plotted the percentages of endogamy against the distances traveled for spouses. We made no attempt to draw a systematic sample—this would have been difficult in any case because only half the ethnographies we consulted had any information on endogamy at all, and only about half of those had information that could actually be used—but we used 21 societies of a variety of economic types from all over the world. (See Figures 1 and 1a.)

We were interested in answering the question, "Of the people who belonged to a group before marriage, how many subsequently married someone who also belonged to that group before marriage?" The relevant information was reported quite differently by different ethnographers and it was not always easy to get an accurate answer from the data provided.

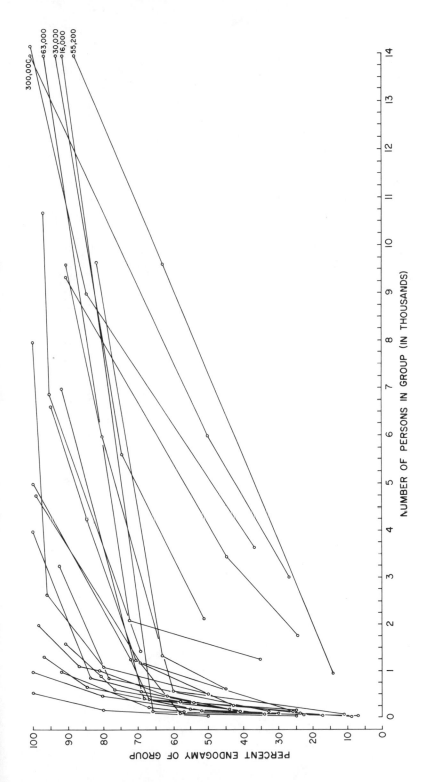

Figure 1. The sizes of endogamous groups. In all figures, lines connect endogamous groups from the same society.

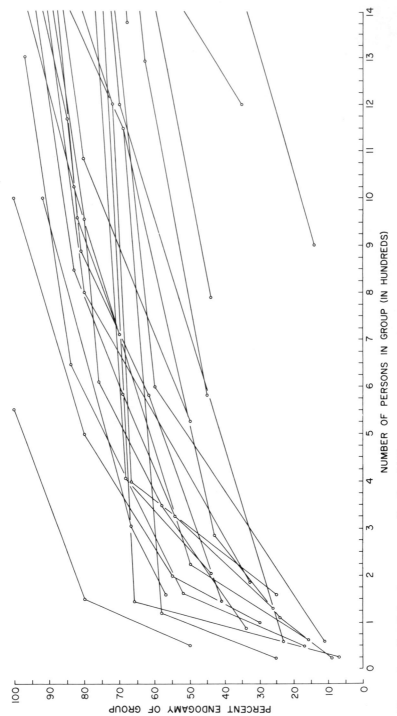

Figure 1a. Detail showing groups smaller than 1400.

NUMBER OF PERSONS IN GROUP (IN HUNDREDS)

PERCENT ENDOGAMY OF GROUP

Usually ethnographies contain statistics compiled from a census made when the field work was done, giving the origin of the spouses living in a local group at that time. The most obvious way to compute an endogamy rate from such data would be to take the percentage of the total that were endogamous.

But there are problems with this method. Because the local group described was rarely a closed marriage universe, individuals who were in it before marriage have left it to marry elsewhere; their marriages were not included in the figures. If one uses a percentage of extant marriages as the endogamy rate, one is, in effect, substituting the choices of people who moved to the group upon marriage for those of people who left it. This rate does not give a true picture of the choices of people from the local group.

It would be acceptable if one could assume that all the similar local groups in the region had the same endogamy rates and that the people coming in were in fact balanced by those going out, but this is surely never the case. For example, the different barrios of Tepoztlan (Lewis 1951) have different endogamy rates. They range from 14–42 percent (computed by the method to be described below) for the outlying barrios. This might be supposed to be the result of the small size of these barrios (the average is 186 persons), but the central barrios which average 793 persons also have varying rates (from 34–50 percent).

Rather than combine information on members of different local groups, we decided to use information only on individuals who had been part of the group before marriage. Each marriage was considered *two* marriage choices and we counted only the choices of individuals from the local groups for which complete information was provided. For example, Leach's information on Pul Eliya (1961:82) states that there were 39 "extant marriages of living residents of Pul Eliya (including latest marriages of widows, widowers, and divorced males)." The totals appear in Table 1.

There is information about the marriage choices of 18 (5 + 8 + 5) women and 31 (21 + 5 + 5) men originally from Pul Eliya. The denominator is the sum, 49. The numerator is 20, since there are 10 endogamous

TABLE 1
Extant Marriages of Living Residents of Pul Eliya[a]
==

Diga marriages, wife from another village	21
Diga marriages, wife from Pul Eliya	5
Binna marriages, husband from another village	8
Binna marriages, husband from Pul Eliya	5
Total	39

a. Diga *marriages are virilocal,* binna *marriages uxorilocal.*

marriages, each of which involves two choices. The percentage of endogamous marriage choices for Pul Eliya is 20 out of 49, or 41 percent. We
used this method to arrive at all the figures quoted in the article and
entered on the charts.

If we had taken the endogamy rate to be a percentage of extant marriages it would have been 10 out of 39, or 26 percent, for Pul Eliya.
However, this is no more accurate than our method because Pul Eliya has
not engaged in a balanced exchange of spouses with other villages. This
can be demonstrated by a second set of figures where Leach has tabulated
the marriages "extant at various dates between 1850 and 1954 of which at
least one partner was born in Pul Eliya [1961:83]." Here he has followed
people who left Pul Eliya at marriage and we have the information we
need to answer the question we posed; the endogamy rate from these
figures is 34 percent. Our method, therefore, slightly *overestimates*
endogamy. This is because the people who left the village at marriage are
left out of our count. Endogamous marriages are counted twice, as it were,
while exogamous marriages are counted only for the partner who remains
in the village.

This type of distortion was minimal for societies where data for a relatively closed marriage universe were provided because very few people left
the sphere of reporting and almost everyone could be "followed" from his
original local group to the group into which he had married. This sort of
information was available for Tikopia (Firth 1959), Tiwi (Goodale 1971;
Hart and Piling 1962), San Bernadino Contla (Nutini 1968), and
Tepoztlan (Lewis 1951); for all of these societies full information was provided on the marriages of a group with over 90 percent endogamy. Distortion was a little greater for two societies for which information on groups
with 67 and 69 percent endogamy was given: Telefolmin (Craig 1969) and
the Negev (Marx 1967). In all these societies we averaged the rates for
groups of the same type: for example, we averaged the rates for the barrios
of Tepoztlan and used the average on our charts.

The information for the rest of the societies came from tabulations of
the marriages in communities that had lower rates of endogamy. If figures
which followed people who left those communities were provided, as was
the case if marriage information came from genealogies rather than
censuses, we used such figures for our estimates and the rates are an
accurate answer to our question, with no distortion, for the community
that was the focus of the study. (But such a rate is probably not
representative of similar communities in the region.) The societies for
which such "following" figures were available were Turkey (Stirling 1965),
Pul Eliya, Round Lake Ojibwa (Rodgers 1968), Enga (Meggitt 1965),
Daribi (Wagner 1969), and Maring (Rappaport 1969).

But for the remaining nine communities in our sample, we did not have
information on the people who had left at marriage, and our method of
counting overestimated endogamy. The difference of 7 percentage points

between the two estimates for Pul Eliya is probably characteristic of the magnitude of the overestimate for groups of about 30 percent endogamy in these societies. For the larger groups in those societies, the more inclusive groups with higher endogamy rates, the overestimate is probably smaller.

It might have been possible to compensate for the different types of ethnographic reports and use different ways of counting for each one, but rather than expend this effort on information that was so obviously faulty in other ways, we decided to go ahead with the method we have described—a method that kept information from different local groups separate unless it was possible to have virtually complete information on the choices of several comparable groups in a region. Our goal was simply to get some rough estimates of basic parameters rather than to arrive at final conclusions.

SEMICLOSED GROUPS

The concept of a 100-percent endogamous group did not prove to be very fruitful in our research. Such groups are extremely rare and when they do occur they break down into smaller semiclosed groups. We came to refer to these as "80-percent groups" because usually the rate of endogamy for such groups is about 80 percent though it can range from 70 to 90 percent. When ethnographers report higher rates of endogamy these rates usually refer to very large groups, such as an entire ethnic group or a nation. The 80-percent group we are speaking of here can be recognized by the fact that after the rate of endogamy that defines this group is reached, group sizes increase almost astronomically for very small increases in rates of endogamy. The 80-percent groups typically range from several hundred to 10,000 individuals.

We found such groups in all the societies we had information about. Even isolated island societies like the Tiwi and Tikopia have *two* 80-percent groups, clearly separated geographically. This is all the more remarkable because travel to all points in their social space is not difficult and the overall population of these societies is quite small. It is almost as though a society has to have another one, very similar to it, nearby.

In effect, 80-percent groups are semiautonomous social microcosms within which a large proportion of daily interaction occurs. They are always local groups of some kind: the Tiwi occupy two islands, each of which is an 80-percent group, and the Tikopia have two districts on different sides of the island. For pastoralists, the 80-percent group is typically the "tribe" the ethnographer studied. In the New Guinea highlands it is a valley, while in peasant societies it is either a set of small villages near each other or a neighborhood within a large settlement. For the Gitksan it was a set of three (or four) villages which were also a subdialect group.

Marriages outside of this group are made either by high-status individuals who "represent" their locality in some larger system or by persons who live close to other 80-percent groups. But villages on the border between two 80-percent groups confine most of their marriages to one of them, even though the rate may be slightly lower than it is for localities which are near the centers. The 80-percent groups, therefore, appear to be discrete, although the degree of discreteness may depend on geographical barriers.

ENDOGAMOUS GROUP SIZE

When we plot percentages of endogamy on a vertical axis against size of group on the horizontal we find that (1) the majority of societies are bunched together, but (2) a few bunch closer to the vertical, i.e., high endogamy in small groups, and (3) a few closer to the horizontal, i.e., low endogamy in large groups.

Those nearer the vertical in our sample are the Ojibwa, Tiwi, Basseri (Barth 1961), and peasants of the Negev; those nearer the horizontal are villages in China (Baker 1968; Diamond 1969) and Japan (Nakane 1967) and densely populated societies in the highlands of New Guinea (see Table 2 and Figures 1 and 1a).

The societies near the vertical furnish some information on the limits of endogamy in human beings. Due to the difficulty of finding spouses of suitable age in small groups, there is a lower limit on the sizes of groups that can have certain percentages of endogamy. The most endogamous society we have record of is the Round Lake Ojibwa in which 50 percent of the marriage choices were reportedly made within a group of 50 individuals and 80 percent within a group of 150.

While this sounds extreme (and, quite frankly, we question whether it is indeed possible to keep this rate up for a long period of time), the existence of societies which come close to these figures in other parts of the world does seem to lend them some credence. For example, among the Basseri 68 percent of the marriage choices are made within a group a little smaller than 150, and among both peasants in the Negev and the Telefolmin, approximately 60 percent of the marriage choices fall within a similar-sized group. The figures on Tiwi and Tikopia are not very different: 52 percent in a group of 180 (Tikopia) and 55 percent in a group of 200 (Tiwi).

The Round Lake Ojibwa do seem to be exceptional in the small size of their 80-percent group, however, since there is no other society that comes even close to making this percentage of their marriage choices in such a small group (150 people). The next largest group we have for this percentage is among the Tiwi who make 80 percent of their marriage choices within a group of 500. This latter figure compares quite well with

TABLE 2
Data for Figures 1, 1a

Societies	(Percent Endogamy/Group Population)
1. Basseri	(7/25) (66/143) (91/16000)
2. Chimbu	(24/1700) (44/3400) (90/9350)
3. Daribi	(26/130) (54/325) (69/585) (83/845) (100/4000)
4. Enga	(51/2100) (75/5600) (92/30000)
5. Hal-Farrug	(45/580) (63/1290) (82/9800)
6. Japan (rural)	(14/900) (63/9600) (88/55200)
7. Konda Valley	
. Dani	(25/160) (67/400) (72/1200) (100/5000)
8. K'un Shen	(25/3000) (50/6000) (100/300000)
9. Maring	(44/204) (68/408) (92/7000)
10. Melpa	(35/1200) (73/1960) (96/63000)
11. Negev	
(a) Bedouins	(9/23) (24/109) (43/285) (69/1150) (99/4830)
(b) Peasants	(25/23) (58/121) continue with (69/1150)
12. Pul Eliya	
(a) 1931	(34/87) (58/348) (76/609) (80/957) (91/1566)
(b) 1954	(41/146) (62/584) (81/884) (85/1168) (98/1898)
13. Round Lake	
Ojibwa	(50/50) (80/150) (100/550)
14. Contla	
(a) Central	(68/1373) (95/6863) (97/10699)
(b) Outlying	(70/714) (82/959) (94/3836) (97/10699)
15. Sheung Shui	(37/3600) (86/9000) (100/14080)
16. Telefolmin	(57/160) (67/312) (92/1000)
17. Tepoztlan	
(a) Central	(44/790) (80/2300) (93/3200)
(b) Outlying	(33/186) (80/800) (93/3200)
18. Tikopia	
(a) 1929	(17/49) (52/165) (84/645) (97/1300)
(b) 1952	(16/65) (50/227) (83/1026) (98/1750)
19. Tiwi	(30/100) (55/200) (80/500) (100/1000)
20. Turkish Villages	
(a) Sakaltutan	(11/60) (60/600) (80/6000) (90/9600)
(b) Elbasi	(23/60) (70/1200) (84/4200) (94/6600)
21. Zinacantan	(50/523) (80/1086) (96/2583) (100/8000)

the physical anthropologists' notion of size of the isolate in hunting societies, which Birdsell (1968) has suggested was 500 for aboriginal Australia. But in the majority of societies the 80-percent group is much larger than this and ranges from 850 to 55,000.

In fact, the estimate of a physical anthropologist (Bunak, quoted in Spuhler 1967:251) that "many contemporary rural populations of Europe, North America, and Negro Africa are composed of demes numbering 1500 to 4000 individuals, with about 80-percent endogamy" is borne out by our work. And, if we amend this statement to say the demes range from 850 to 10,000 individuals, we shall include every society in our sample except the Ojibwa, the Tiwi, Tikopia of 1929, some sparsely populated societies in New Guinea, but also rural Japan, which is unique in having an 80-percent group of approximately 55,000 people (but see below).

Thus, there appears to be an upper as well as a lower limit on endogamous group size. Even in societies where it is possible to come in contact with a very large number of people, as is the case in the more densely populated areas in our sample, and even where such contact is actually maintained through markets and the like, the marriage universe is probably limited to groups of 10,000 at the most.

THE EFFECT OF POPULATION DENSITY

The size of endogamous groups is related to population density, which in turn is related to the type of subsistence economy. Societies with the smallest 80-percent groups are those with the lowest population densities: hunters and gatherers, pastoralists, and sparsely populated horticultural societies in the New Guinea highlands. The largest 80-percent groups are found in peasant societies and in the most densely populated societies in the New Guinea highlands, all societies whose livelihood is based on farming. There are exceptions to this relationship: Tikopia, for example, has a very high population density but quite small 80-percent groups, doubtless due to its island situation. Also, the Mexican cultures, Tepoztlan, San Bernadino Contla, and Zinacantan (Vogt 1970), have smaller 80-percent groups than other societies with similar population densities. But in general the relationship holds and suggests that the size of the 80-percent group is the outcome of the opportunity to travel. And, indeed, we find that when we plot the percentages of endogamy against the radii of circles within which each percentage of marriage choices is made, the differences between most of the cultures disappear: in societies with large and small endogamous groups people seem to go the same distance for their spouses; 80–100 percent of spouses are found within a day's journey, that is, 7 miles, and usually the distance is under 4 miles (see Table 3 and Figures 2 and 2a).

The only exceptions are the Ojibwa, the Basseri, and Bedouins of the Negev, and the Tiwi, who are very sparsely settled. These people have to travel much farther for their spouses (25 to 30 miles) than those in the majority of societies. But, even though nomadic pastoralists do travel farther, this is compensated for by their means of transport, horse or camel rather than on foot, and so for them the spouses are also within a day's travel. It is only the hunting and gathering populations that are very

TABLE 3
Data for Figures 2, 2a
===

Societies	(Percent Endogamy/Distance)
1. Basseri	(7/0) (66/0) (91/25)
2. Chimbu	(24/1.18) (44/1.84) (90/3.08)
3. Daribi	(26/0) (54/2.32) (69/3) (83/3.75)
4. Enga	(51/2.35) (75/3.85) (92/8.95)
5. Hal-Farrug	(45/0) (63/0) (82/2)
6. Japan (rural)	(14/0) (63/3.1) (88/7.4)
7. Konda Valley Dani	(25/1.30) (67/2.32) (72/3.52) (100/7.3)
8. K'un Shen	(25/0) (50/1) (100/10)
9. Maring	(44/1) (68/1.41) (92/5.84)
10. Melpa	(35/2.64) (73/3.08) (96/17.83)
11. Negev	
(a) Bedouins	(9/0) (24/0) (43/4.36) (69/8.95) (99/17)
(b) Peasants	(25/0) (58/0) continue with (43/4.36)
12. Pul Eliya	
(a) 1931	(34/0) (58/1.5) (76/3) (80/6) (91/10)
(b) 1954	(41/0) (62/1.5) (81/3) (85/6) (98/10)
13. Round Lake Ojibwa	(50/17.9) (80/30.9) (100/59.2)
14. Contla	
(a) Central	(68/.375) (95/1.5) (97/3.56)
(b) Outlying	(70/0) (82/.75) (94/2.25) (97/3.56)
15. Sheung Shui	(37/6) (86/6) (100/6)
16. Telefolmin	(57/0) (67/.75) (92/10)
17. Tepoztlan	
(a) Central	(44/0) (93/1)
(b) Outlying	(33/0) (93/1)
18. Tikopia	
(a) 1929	(17/0) (52/.125) (84/.875) (97/1)
(b) 1952	(16/0) (50/.125) (83/.875) (98/1)
19. Tiwi	(30/8) (55/12) (80/17) (100/31)
20. Turkish Villages	
(a) Sakaltutan	(11/0) (60/0) (80/3.5) (90/7.7)
(b) Elbasi	(23/0) (70/0) (84/5) (94/8)
21. Zinacantan	(50/0) (80/.5) (96/1) (100/3.6)

sparsely settled, e.g., the Tiwi and the Ojibwa, for whom it often takes longer than a day to go and return from relatives by marriage.

Incidentally, the societies we have studied are not very different from urban populations of today. The results of eight propinquity studies made in a variety of American cities at different dates show that over half the people found their marriage partners within 21 city blocks, that is, roughly 2½ miles (Katz and Hill 1963:43). This is true of all of the societies we

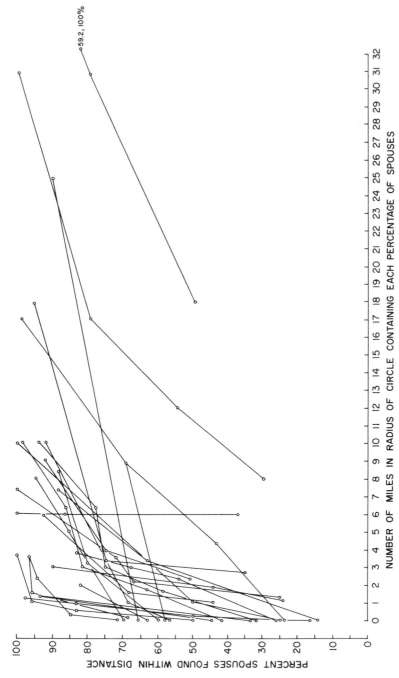

Figure 2. The distance traveled for spouses. Where there was no direct information given on the distance traveled for spouses, the entries for Figure 2 were calculated from population density and the sizes of groups in Figure 1.

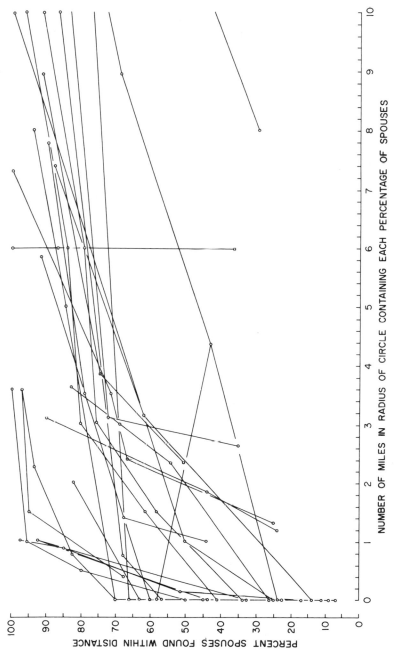

Figure 2a. Detail for distance under 10 miles.

studied as well, except for the nomadic pastoralists and hunters and gatherers. Thus, in societies quite different in scale and population density, and even in those like our own, with sophisticated means of transport, most marriages are made within a small geographical area of about the same size.

There are, then, three important "constants" that appear to determine the sizes of endogamous groups, each important for societies with different population densities. In those with very low densities the important factor is the minimum size for a viable human population. In these societies people will have to travel far to make contact with another community. In most such societies people don't have to go all the way to their spouse's abode; instead, the mating process is facilitated by periodic meetings at a convenient place either for reasons of subsistence or for ceremonials.

But for societies with higher densities, in which the minimum number of people live close by, the important constant would seem to be the distance traveled easily in a day. There the minimum population is always exceeded and the size of the 80-percent group depends almost entirely on population density. It is as though a grid determined by the daily walking distance were laid down and the sizes of 80-percent groups resulted from the number of persons in each space on the grid.

The tribes discussed in *Pigs, Pearlshells, and Women* (Glasse and Meggitt 1969) illustrate this dramatically. They have quite different endogamous group sizes. But this is due almost entirely to their different population densities. When that is held constant, which occurs when the percentages of endogamy within particular groups are plotted against the land area those groups occupy, the societies fall neatly into a straight line. What is more, the number of clans in groups at each percentage of endogamy is nearly the same in all the societies.

And for societies with very high population densities, the important constant is the upper limit on the sizes of 80-percent groups. Theoretically, this suggests that at very high densities people travel even less than they could in a day to find their spouses. Actually, however, in societies of high density travel patterns no longer seem to limit the sizes of endogamous groups. Instead, social class restrictions take over. This may explain why Mexican villages do not have as large endogamous groups as one would expect from their population densities (although this may also be due to their being located in valleys).

REGIONAL PATTERNS

From this it might seem as though propinquity were a prime determinant of endogamous group sizes, but this is in part due to the lack of other data. Most anthropologists start with a single community as the focus of study and move outward from there. The result is a set of concentric circles centered on the community: higher and higher percentages of endogamy occurring within circles with larger and larger radii. For the first few societies we looked at, the rates of endogamy were 30 percent for the local group, 50 percent for the immediate neighborhood of the local group, and 80 percent for the geographical region. (These were Tiwi, who had 30–50–80; Gitksan and Zinacantan, both of whom had 50- and 80-percent groups; and Tikopia, who had 27–50–80. These figures are not arcane, however. They simply represent the likely rates if there really were endogamy; for 30 percent is more than half of 50 percent, which is more than half of 80 percent. Moreover, not all societies report these particular rates.)

The concentric circle approach seems to be the most readily available way of ordering marriage data when the ethnographer has nothing "interesting" to report by way of kinship preferences. Indeed it is almost an anthropological folk model of endogamy. The result is almost certainly a very partial view of endogamy. Often ethnographies mention social groups which, on reading between the lines, appear to structure marriage, but the endogamy rates are not reported in those terms. For example, in Mexican societies bride and groom must often contribute equally to marriage payments (Lewis 1951; Nutini 1968). This should foster marriages of economic equals, yet figures on social class are lacking; we have endogamy rates for the barrios instead. In other societies, data on disputes indicate the existence of factions which have as cores what appear to be endogamous kindreds. Yet because these groups are relatively amorphous, and, indeed, may perhaps be defined better by marriage than by any other criterion, they are usually not explicitly described, let alone used as the basis for the tabulation of marriage choices. The fact is that ethnographers do not set out to describe marriage choice and groups based on it; therefore, they mention it only when it coincides with groups formed on other bases.

And rarely do ethnographers report rates of endogamy for the entire set of subgroups that constitute a semiclosed region. But in the studies that do give more details, we can see that the marriage patterns cannot be characterized by concentric circles. Factors other than propinquity come into play. The "circles" are different for different subgroups.

We will illustrate the sorts of regional patterns that one finds by describing three societies in detail: the Ojibwa, a hunting and gathering group of low population density (data are from Dunning 1959); Bedouins of the Negev (Marx 1967), a pastoralist society also with low population density; and Hal-Farrug (Boissevain 1969a, 1969b), a village in Malta where the population density is very high.

The Ojibwa

Among the Ojibwa, marriage choices are motivated largely by manpower requirements. Traplines must be worked by at least 2 adult males (and the upper limit seems to be about 11). Normally a father and son or two brothers provide the men needed but due to demographic accidents, etc., some men may have no sons to pass their line to. If they have daughters the men who work the line will usually be sons-in-law. Thus, within the band, choices are not made at random but from economic considerations. Families with large numbers of brothers send some of them to live uxorilocally while families with few brothers or with all young children may have to rely on men from other families for their trapping manpower. Marriages between sibling groups with complementary characteristics seem to be preferred, and in each generation sexually skewed sibling groups seem to have a tendency to form endogamous enclaves.

Some marriages between bands are caused by pressure on resources. Men who marry into other bands for this reason reside uxorilocally. The result is that sibling groups consisting largely of women are more exogamous than those that are more evenly balanced. Other marriages between bands are caused simply by the shortage of women of appropriate ages.

In sum, even in a small society like the Ojibwa, marriages at certain distances are not simply the result of casual social encounter. How far away one marries depends, in part at least, on the minimum number of people needed to make this particular system work. Here there are so few encounters outside the band, and the band is so small, that one suspects that one creates many encounters in order to be able to make marriages. Unlike the situation on our frontier, there were no mail-order brides. One used one's relatives in other bands instead of the advertisements, and these people also could vouch for a bride's suitability: If one comes from outside there is always the danger of getting a leftover from the local marriage market, someone left over for good reason. Thus, marriage choices did not result solely from proximity, and proximity, together with the social encounters that went on with neighboring bands, was kept up at least partly to provide marriage partners.

Moreover, even in this situation economic needs divide the people in one local settlement into endogamous enclaves which, though dependent on demographic accidents and thus constantly shifting from generation to generation, are nevertheless real. And these needs also result in some types of people—those in sexually skewed sibling groups—marrying farther out than others.

Bedouins of the Negev

Bedouins marry either very close by or very far away, skipping over their middle-distance neighbors in a checkerboard pattern. The marriages close by are largely political, to link the smallest units of the society together into larger groups, often incorporating peoples who originated from quite far away, several generations back. The result is a subtribe knitted together by marriage ties which are carefully allotted to keep all of the segments united, usually through marriages to the group of the chief, which is the largest in size. Furthermore, the subtribe belongs to a tribe whose territory extends in a band across two major ecological zones, hilly country and plains. In dry years one might have to move one's flocks into the hilly country because the wells in the plains dry up. Therefore, subtribes that own land predominantly in the plains marry into subtribes in the hilly area, often into the zone of a different tribe. These are the only marriages that occur outside of the subtribe, except for a few far-flung marriages of polygynous chiefs. Thus, one will have relatives in the other subtribes of one's own zone only at two generations removed or through the polygynous chief of one's subtribe. Here is a case, then, where proximity is avoided in order to take out a certain type of ecological insurance and complex marriage rules thus force people out of their local groups, often quite far away, to find wives.

A different form of uncertainty prevails in Greece. The Sarakatsani (Campbell 1964) were the only society examined that could not be put on our charts because the only statistic reported on them was that virtually all marriages took place with other Sarakatsani. There were no "circles of endogamy." A closer look revealed that there were no local groups because shepherds had to make new leases for pasture every year. Pasture land was scarce and the best strategy seemed to be for a family to marry spouses from as many areas as possible so as to be able to get the best pasture arrangement. This would also help in marketing produce, getting favors from the settled people, etc. Here the uncertainty is not in the natural environment, but in the human one: the situation of being a landless group in a complex, economically differentiated, modern society.

All of these societies would fall outside of the proximity range talked about above: They go more than a day's journey for their spouses. Among the Ojibwa this seems to be due simply to very low population density and the need to find a minimum group, but in the other societies there is also a conscious desire to marry people from far away and people close to home are "turned down." Even in the Ojibwa case there are people living in one's own band whom one could marry if there were not extensive, quasi-moiety rules of exogamy to follow. That two of these societies should be mobile pastoralists and the other mobile hunters and gatherers suggests that the need to avoid proximity may be limited to certain types of economies. On the other hand, the case of the Sarakatsani shows that ethnic enclaves of quite different economies might have to follow this strategy in order to cope with the dominant society.

Hal-Farrug

A third example, Malta, is a society in which the local group is divided into classes that are more or less endogamous. Here, then, physical proximity gives way to social proximity in making marriage choices. Not only is this society densely populated in the extreme but communication by bus with other parts of the island is frequent. In fact, many work outside their village, commuting every day to another community. Nevertheless, marriage ties are separate from work ties and it seems to be the girl of one's own locality whom one marries. Casual encounters occur all the time with a huge number of people, but spouses are chosen from the local community only. Thus, marriages do not come automatically from a certain *amount* of social mixing. There are different *kinds* of social mixing and marriages result from only one kind.

There are four occupational classes: farmers, manual laborers, skilled laborers, and a bourgeoisie of architects, doctors, teachers. These four groups are more or less endogamous. Furthermore, there are also factions which are even more endogamous than the classes. One faction is made up of more people from higher classes than others, but there are people from all four classes in every faction. Paradoxically, breaking down the population to such an extent results in the same problem we saw among the Ojibwa: In the smallest class, the bourgeoisie, people have trouble finding spouses close to home and must move far away to find them. These people have the money and power to get the ban on first-cousin marriages lifted by the church, so their strategy is either to marry more closely than the other classes or to go farther afield to find suitable partners. Not only is their marriage universe smaller than those of the other classes, but due to their low population density they must also go farther afield.

The middle groups are larger than the higher (and lower) classes. But even though they seem to be able to find spouses in their village and faction, the group is larger than the minimums we have from the Ojibwa and many other societies, and they seem to want to marry into the six closest neighboring villages even though they could probably find spouses in their natal villages. The reason for this is far from clear.

On the other hand, the lowest group, the farmers, is again small, though not so small as the highest class. They, too, appear to marry into the neighboring six villages but in their case it might well be a question of simply finding enough available people of the proper social category and faction. (Note: the factions are found only within the community, and there is no data on whether they structure marriage outside of it, but it seems that one might avoid marrying into a family into which a member of the opposing faction of one's own community had married.)

In Malta, therefore, not only is the local group broken down into endogamous enclaves, both classes and factions, but this results in different pressures on different classes to marry out. The highest and lowest classes are too small to be endogamous within a single village, even though the highest group has changed the kinship rules to permit them to have a larger endogamous group. The middle groups appear to marry into a larger endogamous group than they have to. They marry out presumably for quite different reasons than the other classes, though the ethnographer does not tell us why.

BEYOND PROPINQUITY

These case studies indicate that there is probably no society in which proximity alone determines marriage choice. For within local groups different segments make different choices and thus belong to different endogamous enclaves; moreover, in some societies there is a conscious attempt to avoid making choices on the basis of proximity in order to spread marriage ties more evenly throughout a larger area (see Yengoyan 1968).

The *actual* group from which a person selects his mate is probably quite a bit smaller than those we have discussed in the first part of this article. Those figures probably represent simply the outer limits on marriage choice, the largest number of people from whom a spouse is chosen. The percentages express the chance that a person picked at random from a local group finds his spouse within that group. Actually, however, to take the extreme case, no one in Japan actually chooses from 55,000 people. Since the groups are inclusive, that segment of the 55,000 who are in an individual's 30-percent group are the ones most likely to be chosen. Of the rest, many are slated to marry into their own 30-percent and 50-percent groups. More important, people are not picked at random to marry. Many factors narrow down choice, a selection of which we have tried to provide in the preceding case descriptions.

We doubt if we will actually find that the small group of possible mates is always the same size, but the few studies which have made estimates of this (Dyke 1971; Goldberg 1967; and our own unpublished materials on the Gitksan) have come up with strikingly similar results. This is all the more suggestive since each society had different criteria for choosing mates, most of which were used by the researchers in making up their lists of potential spouses. It is difficult to make the figures exactly comparable, but 15 to 30 would probably encompass all three estimates. (This is the number of *unmarried* individuals who meet various age and relationship criteria.) And if allowances were made for enclaves that might exist within the local groups which were the bases for these studies, the number might be even lower. Lest it be thought that the similarity is the result of these all being "small-scale" societies, the following quotation from a study of marriage in present-day Seattle is well taken:

American students taking a course in marriage and the family sometimes react ethnocentrically when they learn of such exotic mate selection practices as go-betweens, family-arranged marriages, etc. On the other hand, the sociologist may sometimes overemphasize the cultural relativity of marriage norms by exaggerating the extent of cultural variability. Taking arranged marriage as one extreme and the American image of unrestricted individualism and romantic love as the other extreme, the range of variation in degrees of freedom in mate selection appears to be from one to infinity. The propinquity studies suggest that the actual range from one cultural extreme to the other may be only from one to about half a dozen or so [Catton and Smitcich 1964:529].

CONCLUSIONS

To review what we have said briefly:

1. Endogamous groups are semiclosed, not completely closed.
2. This means that there are always at least two marriage patterns in every society: marriage within the group and marriage outside of it. To understand endogamy, then, we have to take account of the variety of rules that characterizes a society rather than assigning only one marriage pattern to each.
3. Endogamous groups form systems of interlocking subgroups which extend over regions.
4. Their sizes are closely tied to population density; but there are also upper and lower limits which set sizes at high and low densities, respectively.

Most anthropologists see marriage in terms of *rules* that guide behavior. They have implicitly followed Lowie (1961:17) in seeing the tendency to marry people nearby as universal; thus, they consign it to the realm of "natural" tendencies that are not properly the study of anthropologists. Only if the rule is as extreme as the caste system found in India or other places is it worthy of study.

Another common view is to speak of endogamy in terms of marriage to relatives. Here again anthropology stresses rules that vary between cultures and that in some sense go against nature. The work of Lévi-Strauss (1953), of course, comes to mind here. From our point of view, his distinctions seem quite arbitrary. The different elementary structures produce marriage universes of the same size. And father's brother's daughter marriage, which he excludes from his typology, can result in marriage universes that are similar in size to those of societies where marriage is an exchange between different unilineal groups. Furthermore, his distinction between elementary and complex structures is not the result of a difference in scale as he suggested. In both types of societies actual marriage choices are made within a relatively small group of people. We find that the groups that are most highly endogamous—which are also those with the lowest population densities—are the ones most likely to have preferences for kin (see Cavalli-Sforza 1958:401). It is a moot point, therefore, whether they are small because of the preference, or have preferences for kin because they are so small. In any case, there is no correlation found so far between type of preference and degree of endogamy.

Romney (1971) has discussed the requirements of a mathematically satisfying proof of marriage preferences. But, as he himself has pointed out, anthropologists have rarely collected the data necessary to carry out such proofs. Because of their focus on a single community, they do not have the information on intermarriage between a set of communities that would be needed to demonstrate mathematically that their community is endogamous. We are trying to develop a new set of hypotheses about what natural marriage systems look like. After we do so, if the data are available, we would like to test mathematically whether, for example, the villages in a region are endogamous and arrive at a notion of the actual percentage that characterizes them—probably using Romney's method.

It would be important to find out what effect the existence of semi-closed groups would have on the algorithm. But at this point the application of his method would be premature: we must instead take the hints available in ethnographies and synthesize from them a new set of models of marriage systems based on endogamy rather than exogamy. If marriage systems are communication systems, as Lévi-Strauss has pointed out (1953:536), we ought to know more about their boundaries.

Geographers and physical anthropologists have already devoted a great deal of effort to the mapping of marriage over distance. And curves we obtained resemble curves of phenomena involving interaction over distance these other disciplines have examined. They are all highly leptokurtic, that is, very peaked: Studies of migration distances, distances separating spouses before marriage, distances separating the birthplace of the parents and that of the child, number of phone calls between two places—all have shown this form. (For a sampling of such findings see Cavalli-Sforza and Bodmer 1971; Morrill and Pitts 1967; Stewart 1947; Sutter 1963; Zipf 1949.)

The same sorts of distributions characterize gene dispersal in species other than man (Bateman 1963) and, interestingly, it has been shown mathematically that the leptokurtosis results from different rates of dispersal for different individuals, the same phenomenon as the different marriage patterns within the same society that we have stressed. Geographers interested in diffusion of inventions have used measures such as these to create a "mean information field," a set of probabilities that a person will learn about a certain invention from people at varying distances from himself (Hägerstrand 1965).

We would like to underscore the finding of these researchers that, despite the simplicity of the fact that interaction is very intense nearby and falls off rapidly the farther one gets from an individual, the underlying mechanisms that produce such curves are quite complex (Cavalli-Sforza and Bodmer 1971). Certainly the attitude among anthropologists such as Lowie that these things are the same the world over and can be factored out of cultural descriptions is not correct.

Different researchers have found that their data fit different theoretical distributions (see Sutter 1963). Some have had to combine two distributions to account for their findings (Morrill and Pitts 1967; Thanh and Sutter 1963). We have shown that the scale of distances for these curves varies from society to society depending on travel opportunity and population density. Moreover, there are always subgroups in society whose boundaries are not set by proximity. And in the same society existing under identical technological restrictions different subgroups marry different distances from home. The data we have had to work with are too crude to tell whether the *forms* of the curves differ from society to society (and from subgroup to subgroup) but this does seem to be the case. The size of a village and its distance from others do affect the shape of the curves.

The explanations that have been given for these different curves are circular. Sometimes they are little more than descriptions of a behavioral regularity (Harvey 1969:110–111, 159). They result from an insularity of approach in the different fields, so that one field explains the curve with concepts central to a second field, while that field, in turn, is found to have explained it with concepts central to the first. Thus, geneticists explain their curves of marriage distances as having to do with the probability of interaction at various distances, but the sociologists and geographers base their formulations of the "laws" of interaction on the very same data that the geneticists use.

In reality, then, all that any of the disciplines have are a variety of sets of data showing that interaction, a frequent example of which is marriage, decreases sharply with distance. Most often the theory advanced is an economic one, that the time and resources invested are less if interaction is nearby rather than far away: To stay put is cheaper.

A more sophisticated idea, Stouffer's theory of intervening opportunity (1940), which states that besides the sizes of places and the distance one must take into account the number of opportunities between two places that would deflect interaction away from the more distant points, has recently been shown to be inadequate to account for the data on marriage distances (Catton and Smitcich 1964), though it is useful in other applications.

In order to break out of this circularity we ought to abandon the egocentric point of view of the geographers and physical anthropologists and the community-centered point of view of the social anthropologist and adopt a regional approach. Our remarks here are intended to give some idea of the kind of regional organization one finds in marriage systems. We need a theory complementary to central-place theory for marriage choice. Only then will we be able to see how different subgroups intermarry to create a regional marriage pool; in effect we will be able to see how semiclosed groups arise and what factors lead them to be only semiclosed: why some people go farther than others. Only with such an approach, we feel, can we arrive at a more precise idea of the sizes of endogamous groups than we have been able to outline here.

REFERENCES

Baker, Hugh
    1968   *A Chinese lineage village.* Stanford, Calif.: Univ. Press.

Barth, F.
    1961   *Nomads of south Persia.* Boston: Little, Brown.

Bateman, A. J.
    1963   Data from plants and animals. In *Les déplacements humains,* edited by Jean Sutter. Paris: Hachette. Pp. 85-91.

Birdsell, Joseph B.
    1968   Some predictions for the Pleistocene based on equilibrium systems among recent hunter-gatherers. In *Man the hunter,* edited by Richard B. Lee and Irven DeVore. Chicago: Aldine. Pp. 229-240.

Boissevain, J.
    1969a *Hal-Farrug: A village in Malta.* New York: Holt.
    1969b *Saints and fireworks.* London School of Economics Monographs on Social Anthropology 30. London: Althone.

Brown, Paula
    1969   Marriage in Chimbu. In *Pigs, pearlshells, and women: Marriage in the New Guinea highlands,* edited by R. M. Glasse and M. J. Meggitt. Englewood Cliffs, N.J.: Prentice-Hall. Pp. 77-95.

Campbell, J. K.
    1964   *Honour, family, and patronage.* Oxford: Clarendon Press.

Catton, William R., and R. J. Smitcich
    1964   A comparison of mathematical models for the effect of residential propinquity on mate selection. *American Sociological Review* **29:** 522-529.

Cavalli-Sforza, L. L.
    1958   Some data on the genetic structure of human populations. In *Proceedings of the Tenth International Congress of Genetics,* 390-407.

Cavalli-Sforza, L. L., and W. F. Bodmer
    1971   *The genetics of human populations.* San Francisco: Freeman.

Craig, Ruth
    1969   Marriage among the Telefolmin In *Pigs, pearlshells, and women: Marriage in the New Guinea highlands,* edited by R. M. Glasse and M. J. Meggitt. Englewood Cliffs, N.J.: Prentice-Hall. Pp. 176-197.

Diamond, Norma
    1969   *K'un Shen: A Taiwan village.* New York: Holt.

Dunning, R. W.
    1959   *Social and economic change among the northern Ojibwa.* Toronto: Univ. of Toronto.

Dyke, Bennett
    1971   Potential mates in a small human population. *Social Biology* **18:** 28-39.

Firth, Raymond
  1959   *Social change in Tikopia.* London: Allen and Unwin.
Glasse, R. M., and M. J. Meggitt (Eds.)
  1969   *Pigs, pearlshells, and women: Marriage in the New Guinea highlands.* Englewood
         Cliffs N.J.: Prentice-Hall.
Goldberg, Harvey
  1967   FBD marriage and demography among Tripolitanian Jews in Israel. *Southwestern
         Journal of Anthropology* **23:** 176–191.
Goodale, Jane
  1971   *Tiwi wives.* American Ethnological Society Monograph 51. Seattle: Univ. of
         Washington.
Hägerstrand, Torsten
  1965   Aspects of the spatial structure of social communication and the diffusion of
         information. *Regional Science Association, Papers and Proceedings* **16.**
Hart, C. W. M., and Arnold R. Piling
  1962   *The Tiwi of north Australia.* New York: Holt.
Harvey, David
  1969   *Explanation in geography.* New York: St. Martin's Press.
Kasakoff, Alice
  1974   Lévi-Strauss' idea of the social unconscious: The problem of elementary and complex
         structures in Gitksan marriage choice. In *The unconscious in culture: The structu-
         ralism of Lévi-Strauss in perspective,* edited by Ino Rossi. New York: Dutton.
         Pp. 143–170.
Katz, A. M., and R. Hill
  1963   Residential propinquity and marital selection: A review of theory, method and fact.
         In *Les déplacements humains,* edited by Jean Sutter. Paris: Hachette. Pp. 41–61.
Leach, E. R.
  1961   *Pul Eliya: A village in Ceylon.* New York: Cambridge Univ. Press.
Lévi-Strauss, Claude
  1953   Social structure. In *Anthropology today,* edited by A. L. Kroeber. Chicago: Univ. of
         Chicago Press. Pp. 524–553.
Lewis, Oscar
  1951   *Life in a Mexican village.* Urbana: Univ. of Illinois Press.
Lowie, Robert H.
  1961   *Primitive society.* New York: Harper.
Marx, Emanuel
  1967   *Bedouin of the Negev.* New York: Praeger.
Meggitt, M.
  1965   *The lineage system of the Mae-Engae of New Guinea.* Edinburgh: Oliver and Boyd.
Morrill, Richard L., and Forrest R. Pitts
  1967   Marriage migration and the mean information field: A study in uniqueness and
         generality. *Annals of the Association of American Geographers* **57:** 401–422.
Nakane, Chie
  1967   *Kinship and economic organization in rural Japan. London* School of Economics
         Monographs on Social Anthropology 32. London: Althone.
Nutini, Hugo
  1968   *San Bernadino Contla: Marriage and family structure in a Tlaxcalan municipio.*
         Pittsburgh: Univ. of Pittsburgh Press.
O'Brien, Denise
  1969   Marriage among the Konda Valley Dani. In *Pigs, pearlshells, and women: Marriage
         in the New Guinea highlands,* edited by R. M. Glasse and M. J. Meggitt. Englewood
         Cliffs, N.J.: Prentice-Hall. Pp. 159–175.

Rappaport, Roy
   1969   Marriage among the Maring. In *Pigs, pearlshells, and women: Marriage in the New Guinea highlands*, edited by R. M. Glasse and M. J. Meggitt. Englewood Cliffs, N.J.: Prentice-Hall. Pp. 117–137.
Rodgers, Edward S.
   1968   Band organization among the Indians of the Eastern subarctic Canada. In *Contributions of anthropology: Band societies*, edited by David Damas. National Museums of Canada Bulletin No. 228. Ottawa: Queen's Printer. Pp. 21–50.
Romney, A. K.
   1971   Measuring endogamy. In *Explorations in mathematical anthropology*, edited by Paul Kay. Cambridge, Mass.: MIT Press. Pp. 191–213.
Spuhler, J. N.
   1967   Behavior and mating patterns in human populations. In *Genetic diversity and human behavior*, edited by J. N. Spuhler. Chicago: Aldine. Pp. 241–268.
Stewart, John Q.
   1947   Empirical mathematical rules concerning the distribution and equilibrium of population. *Geographical Review* **37**: 461–485.
Stirling, Paul
   1965   *Turkish village*. New York: Wiley.
Stouffer, Samuel A.
   1940   Intervening opportunities: A theory relating mobility and distance. *American Sociological Review* **5**: 845–867.
Strathern, Andrew, and Marilyn Strathern
   1969   Marriage in Melpa. In *Pigs, pearlshells, and women: Marriage in the New Guinea highlands*, edited by R. M. Glasse and M. J. Meggitt, Englewood Cliffs, N.J.: Prentice-Hall. Pp. 137–158.
Sutter, Jean (Ed.)
   1963   *Les déplacements humains*. Paris: Hachette.
Thanh, Luu-Mau, and Jean Sutter
   1963   Contribution à l'étude de la répartition des distances séparant les domiciles des épous dans un département Français: Influence de la consanguinité. In *Les déplacements humains*, edited by Jean Sutter. Paris: Hachette. Pp. 123–139.
Vogt, Evon Z.
   1970   *The Zinacantecos of Mexico*. New York: Holt.
Wagner, R.
   1969   Marriage among the Daribi. In *Pigs, pearlshells, and women: Marriage in the New Guinea highlands*, edited by R. M. Glasse and M. J. Meggitt. Englewood Cliffs, N.J.: Prentice-Hall. Pp. 56–76.
Yengoyan, Aram
   1968   Demographic and ecological influences on aboriginal Australian marriage sections. In *Man the hunter*, edited by Richard B. Lee and Irven DeVore. Chicago: Aldine. Pp. 185–199.
Zipf, G. K.
   1949   *Human behavior and the principle of least effort*. Reading, Mass.: Addison-Wesley.

Chapter 7

Central-Place Theory and Endogamy in China

John W. Adams
University of South Carolina

Alice Bee Kasakoff
University of South Carolina

Our paper "Factors Underlying Endogamous Group Size" (1975) (Chapter 6 in this volume) concluded with the remark that some theory analogous to central-place theory was necessary for further work on the problem of regional interrelationships between marriage groups. What we had in mind was a theory that would enable us to reconstruct the regional data from the fragmentary hints supplied by ethnologists of single villages, a theory that, by extrapolation, would facilitate the computation of missing information. We also wanted a theory that would account for interlocking semiautonomous units at different hierarchical levels. Carol Smith has since drawn our attention to research that has utilized central-place theory to describe marriage patterns: that of G. William Skinner (1964, 1965) on mainland China; and the attempts by Crissman (1972, 1973, Chapter 5 in this volume) and Knapp (1971) to verify his results on Taiwan. Since this is the only body of research that has used central-place theory in an effort to describe marriage patterns, an examination of it should be helpful to any further effort to conceptualize endogamy as a regional process. We wish to comment briefly on it in the light of the findings reported in our original paper.

Skinner proposed (1964) that the standard marketing community of traditional China was almost completely endogamous and that it was

175

TABLE 1
Stages of Marriage and Market Communities in China: Verified
Endogamous Groups

Endogamous Groups	Stage One Skinner's Traditional System	Stage Two Skinner's Modernized System	Stage Three Modern Taiwan
"30% group"		Village	Village (26.5%)
"50% group"			Intermediate market (62%)
"80% group"	Standard market community (92%)	Intermediate market area (80% ?)	Central market area (80%)

isomorphic with the Chinese peasants' social horizons. His thesis is very difficult to test, given the social changes that have occurred in China since 1949. However, Crissman and Knapp decided to test it by doing field work in Taiwan, where the social and economic situations still bear strong resemblances to the situation described by Skinner.

A problem with comparing the three studies, however, is that the sets of data describe situations of differing degrees of socioeconomic complexity. Both Knapp and Crissman find strong confirmation for Skinner's principal hypothesis of a correlation between marketing areas and endogamy, but their field work was done in regions in which greater modernization had occurred, in which the population densities were greater, and in which higher-order central places had become important to peasants. The situations are summarized in Table 1, which fits their respective findings within our generalized schema of groups within which 30, 50, and 80 percent of marriages occur. The table represents at best a rough approximation of the three sets of findings and requires some technical justification, which we present in the following section. Readers may therefore wish to skip to the subsequent section.

AMBIGUITIES AND PROBLEMS
IN THE DATA

Anyone who tries to put the information from the three researchers into a common framework immediately faces several problems. The first, and perhaps the most crucial, is that Crissman does not report his data in the same form as the others did, nor as we did in our original paper. He reports correlations between marriage and marketing instead of giving rates of endogamy as such. The only way to utilize his work is to attempt to amalgamate his study with Knapp's. This seems justified because Crissman's and Knapp's marketing systems seem so similar. But it must be pointed out that to assume that the marriages are therefore similar assumes exactly what the authors have set out to prove and what we have decided to examine, in part, in this chapter.

This raises a second problem, which, though not so crucial, still deserves mention: fitting Knapp's and Crissman's data into the same set of marketing categories. Both studied settlements situated around a large town, and the population sizes of the areas they studied were similar. Both also distinguish three levels in a hierarchy of settlements. For Knapp, these are Chung-li (the major town he studied), "town," and "village center." For Crissman, they are "central market town" (Ehrlin), "intermediate town," and "standard town." (We will adopt his terminology because of its similarity to Skinner's.) The highest and middle levels appear to refer to the same kinds of places in both studies, but the lowest level does not. Only a few of the "village centers" in Knapp's study can be equated with Crissman's standard towns. This is because only six of them (plus the two intermediate towns) sell cloth, which was a defining attribute of such towns for Crissman (1972:223).

A further problem arises, moreover, in comparing Knapp with Crissman. Although Knapp's aim was to study the relationship between marriage and marketing, he does not report his marriage data in terms of the marketing units. Instead, he uses the administrative units of the area. He provides rates of village endogamy (*ts'un* and *li*), *hsiang-chen* endogamy (administrative districts, four of which were included in his study), and *hsien* endogamy. (The *hsien* is a unit that includes, besides the four *hsiang-chen* he studied, five others, three of which probably contain central market towns on the same hierarchical level as Chung-li.)

Although the rates of endogamy for these units fall rather neatly into the 30–50–80 schema we outlined in our original paper (26.5 percent *ts'un-li* endogamy; 54.7 percent *hsiang-chen* endogamy; 85.3 percent *hsien* endogamy), it is important to bear in mind that these are administrative and not marketing units. That this is the case does not seem, however, to indicate that administrative units structure marriage rather than marketing activities. Instead, it seems to result from a considerable overlap betweeen the two hierarchies, which also requires some discussion. The reasoning is somewhat complex, and we include it only to make clear exactly what the limitations of the data are, limitations we will comment upon later.

To take the smallest units first, the villages, or *ts'un-li*, are not the same as the lowest level in Crissman's study, the area patronizing a standard town. Such towns would be frequented by persons from several villages. Such a town does not have a parallel in the administrative hierarchy

Knapp uses to report his marriage findings. The only bit of hard data that shows that villages patronizing a standard town form an endogamous unit is that one can see some faint clusters around such towns in the map Knapp provides. This map shows lines that link the natal household of the bride with the household she married into. But since such units consist of several villages, the endogamy rate would have to be greater than the rate of village endogamy Knapp reports. We estimate that the rate would be 45 percent.

The second level of endogamy Knapp reports, *hsiang-chen* endogamy, corresponds roughly with the intermediate market area. In one case this is clear: Lung-t'an is both a *hsiang* and an intermediate market area. Its endogamy rate is 62 percent, the rate we chose for this level in our table. The reason the average rate for *hsiang-chen* is only 54.8 percent is that the other *hsiang-chen* have lower rates of endogamy. This appears to reflect the fact that they do not correspond with market areas. Two of them form a single market area, while the third markets in another central town on the same level as Chung-li, but outside the study area.

The largest unit for which Knapp provides endogamy rates is the *hsien.* Since it is more inclusive than the study area, the rate of endogamy probably includes marriages into areas that do not market at Chung-li, Knapp's central market town. This does not mean that the central market area is not about 80 percent endogamous. The unit he studied was not on the coast, as Crissman's was. Therefore, hypergamy of women from the west who marry to the east (and into the area Knapp studied) seems to be a movement from outside the market area of Chung-li. Yet it might well be that these western areas do market there. These could counterbalance the marriages of others into different central market areas. But, because Knapp delineated his area by administrative and not marketing criteria, we do not know whether or not this is the case. Without further information, however, 80 percent seemed to us to be a good estimate of endogamy for central market areas.

Another problem we encountered was simply the lack of data on marriage for either of the two types of marketing systems Skinner described, the traditional and the modern. The only information on the traditional system was his comment in a footnote to his original article that 95 percent of the households contained only people born within the standard marketing community, except for one corner where the figure was 80 percent. Since that corner was one fifth of the area, the overall rate becomes 92 percent, which we have used as a crude indicator of the rate of endogamy for the standard marketing community in the traditional system. But there is no information on marriage whatsoever for Skinner's modern marketing system.

It probably is obvious at this point in our discussion that more data are needed even in an area of the world in which two studies have focused on marriage in detail. It is unfortunate that there are no agreed-upon categories or formulas for describing endogamy so that it would be easier to compare systems than it has been for us. It is even more unfortunate that Knapp reported rates by administrative rather than marketing units. If it is so difficult to fit these studies into one set of categories, how can we hope to compare systems from different parts of the world?

STAGES OF DEVELOPMENT

When we began this research, we expected that Crissman and Knapp would find a system like the one Skinner hypothesized for modernized China (Stage Two in Table 1). In this, the standard markets have died out, and the intermediate markets have become the most important to the peasant. His social horizons, however, shrink to the village level. Since Skinner stressed the importance of the intermediate markets, we felt that these would be the 80-percent groups. Even though the intermediate markets overlap in his model and therefore should not be 100 percent endogamous, they would be about 80 percent endogamous if the rate were figured on the basis of the proportion of villages that are on the border between two areas, versus the proportion that are clearly in one or the other area. It was because Knapp reported only 60 percent endogamy for this unit that we hypothesized that the Taiwanese had reached a further stage of modernization, a stage in which the central as well as intermediate towns were important economically, and for marriage as well.

Such a stage seems to be a logical one to follow the modernization Skinner notes. In his reasoning the peasants' shift from standard to intermediate market towns is the result of improvement in transportation. If transportation further improves, people will eventually turn from the intermediate towns and begin to patronize central ones. When this is coupled with the enlargement of the hinterland of the intermediate market that is also a central market town, which Crissman has described (1972:244), a very small improvement in transportation could lead to a refocusing on the higher-level central place. Perhaps in Taiwan this development was also related to the railroad network that links the central market towns but that seems to have developed before the roads linking intermediate market towns.[1]

[1] There are some tantalizing suggestions in Crissman's article from which it is possible to infer that his system is intermediate between Stage Two and Stage Three in our tables. First, he mentions marriage areas of 30 to 40 districts; these may be 80-percent groups, in which case they would be subdivisions of the 100-district area he studied. If the percentage of marketing is at all indicative of the percentage of marriage, then intermediate marketing areas should be 80 percent endogamous and standard areas 50 percent to 70 percent endogamous (no information is provided on the percentage of marketing done in the central area, but it must be close to 100 percent). The contraction of marriage areas since the war that Crissman notes also suggests that intermediate market areas may be more endogamous than Knapp found them to be in his area. We will have to wait for actual rates of endogamy to be reported to settle this issue, however.

What kind of a community is this new 80-percent group centered around a central market town? It is quite large, probably about 150,000 persons, and Crissman says that for marketing purposes it is discrete. Crissman feels that it is not a true community, but we do not agree. While people may not know one another by sight, as they did in Stage One, the central town nevertheless seems important socially and politically. Crissman describes a festival in which persons came to the central town from all over its market area. But because the festival involved only one of the two political factions in the area, he felt that a true sense of community was lacking. This seems to us to be idealizing the nature of the community in human affairs. Certainly, if people care enough to be polarized into factions, a community must exist. Although Ehrlin's central market area is not a formal political unit, it does seem to be a focus of local politics. The officers of the Farmer's Association, which operates the salt monopoly for the area, are all "active in local politics," for example (Crissman 1973:134).

Will the intermediate market towns suffer the fate that Skinner hypothesized that the standard market towns suffered in the transition from the first to the second stage? In Taiwan this does not seem to have happened. In fact, intermediate market towns are still quite important in both Knapp's and Crissman's areas and are growing. The reason may be that the 80-percent groups formed around the central market town are so large that they are unwieldy for many social purposes. If the intermediate market area maintains a rate of 60 percent endogamy, this means that a majority of the marriages that occur are still within a local framework.

We should also mention two levels below that of the standard market town that appear to be important in Taiwan. The village is one. While Skinner felt that the social horizons of the peasant shrank to the level of the village in the modernized system, the intermediate town being important only economically, we were still unprepared for the relatively high rate of village endogamy on Taiwan. It is puzzling because, while each has a cluster of shops, peasants told Knapp that they shopped for "daily needs" in only a few centers (not all of them standard market towns, however). Here, then, is a clear case of marriage *not* being caused by marketing activity. Rather, such shops appear to serve social, not economic, functions.

A second level that may be important for endogamy seems to exist between the village and the standard town. Knapp describes two kinds of places that may possibly be the same: places where people shop for "daily needs" and temple sites. Both occur in more places than standard towns as we have defined them. Moreover, Knapp gives nonoverlapping schedules for temple festivities reminiscent of market schedules in traditional mainland China.

But while our three stages differ in the number of levels important for endogamy, the difference is probably not as extreme as its appears from Table 1. If units that are not defined by marketing can structure marriage in the third stage, this could have happened before as well. And, in fact, the first and second stages in our first table, which we took from Skinner's models, appeared oversimplified when compared with societies in other parts of the world. We have found no societies where there were not at least two levels of endogamous groups, and in most cases we found three such levels.[2] For this reason we have hypothesized that villages with about 30 percent endogamy occurred in all three stages and suggest intermediate units as well. Table 2 shows the complete systems we hypothesize for all three stages.

To summarize, then, we postulate a three-stage movement. In the first, the 80-percent groups are standard marketing areas. In the second, the intermediate marketing areas are the 80-percent groups. In the third, the 80-percent groups are central marketing areas; these areas are, however, divided into intermediate areas that are 60 percent endogamous and thus not discrete. Underlying all three are villages with about 30 percent endogamy. Two basic changes occur over time. First, the 50-percent and

TABLE 2
Stages of Marriage and Market Communities in China: Hypothetical
Complete Systems

Endogamous Groups	Stage One Skinner's Traditional System	Stage Two Skinner's Modernized System	Stage Three Modern Taiwan
"30% group"	Village (26.5%)	Village (26.5%)	Village (26.5%) Temple sites or daily needs (35%) Standard market community (45%)
"50% group"	Minor market area (60%)	Standard market community (60%)	Intermediate market area (62%)
"80% group"	Standard market community (92%)	Intermediate market area (80%)	Central market area (80%)

[2] The only exception was the Sarakatsani (Campbell 1964), among whom the largest endogamous group was the entire ethnic group and for whom no other endogamous group was reported. This seemed to be the result of their moving from year to year for pasturage in no fixed cycle.

80-percent groups become larger; several 80-percent groups during the preceding stage form one such group in the next. Second, more levels are added to the hierarchy of groups. These new levels are groups that are larger than villages but smaller than standard marketing communities. Only some of them appear to be market areas. They may serve further to anchor peasant interaction to their localities. Thus, the peasant can retain his local identification while at the same time being integrated, economically and politically, into a larger unit.

INTERLOCKING UNITS

Since none of the endogamous groups we have discussed is completely discrete, each one overlaps in some way with other groups. Unfortunately, none of the studies mentioned shows *exactly* how the semiautonomous marriage communities depicted interlock. However, examples of several processes that would result in interlocking can be taken from the data, and a closer examination of them should at least highlight the issues that need to be explored in more detail in the future.

If the standard marketing communities still maintain their endogamy with rates of about 45 percent in the last stage, as we have indicated in Table 2, the result would be an interesting set of interlocking marriage areas. Since the intermediate market areas bisect or trisect some of the old standard marketing communities, the maintenance of endogamy on the level of the standard marketing community could result in a lack of correlation between marriage and marketing in intermediate market towns. This could explain Crissman's correlations between marriage and distance, as well. The endogamy of the standard marketing communities, then, could be maintained by marriages between people who market at different intermediate towns but who share the same standard market town (or religious duties, if a level of endogamy corresponding with temple sites also exists). This type of pattern could contribute to the 80 percent endogamy of the larger central market areas. It would also mean that the 80-percent groups would be relatively localized and smaller in population than they might appear to be at first glance. Instead of marrying a woman from the opposite side of the central market town, a person would simply marry a girl from his standard marketing community, one living near, but not in, the hinterland of his intermediate market town.

Marriage on a class basis is another process that deserves detailed study, since it is undoubtedly responsible for the lack of complete endogamy of at least some, if not all, the endogamous groups we have discussed. In Skinner's original formulation each of the three types of markets, standard, intermediate, and central, served the needs of a different social stratum. The isomorphism between the number of levels and the number of strata raises the question of whether in his modern stage, in which the standard markets have died, there is also a blurring of the distinction between peasants and local elite. What type of class system is implied in our third stage? Are there now more strata to correspond to the increased number of levels in the hierarchy? How have the relative numbers of persons in different classes changed through time? The reduction in the rate of endogamy of intermediate market areas from 80 percent in Stage Two to 60 percent in Stage Three could simply be the result of there being more local elite in Stage Three than there were in Stage Two, for example.

Analogous to the elite marriages that Skinner postulated linked standard marketing communities in the traditional system is the hypergamy of persons living in the more urbanized parts of the towns Crissman described. For example, Crissman's data indicate that people in the more rural parts of such towns marry others who market in the town, but that people in the commercial parts of the same towns marry people from other intermediate towns who market in the central market town. The marriage strategies of the farmers, craftsmen, and laborers living in the more rural part of town seem to differ from those of the shopkeepers and businessmen in the commercial part (Crissman 1973:277). The former might make nearly all of their marriages (except for the west-to-east hypergamy discussed earlier) within the hinterland of the intermediate market town, or perhaps within that of surrounding intermediate towns. The shopkeepers and businessmen, however, might make few marriages in that area. The endogamy rates of businessmen in intermediate towns could well be below 60 percent; for the farmers, craftsmen, and laborers, however, it might be close to 80 percent.

The same type of process is occurring within the central market town. Crissman has noted that the correlations between marriage and both distance and marketing are lower for the central parts of Ehrlin than they are for the outlying parts of the town (1973:276–277). These people must be marrying outside the study area altogether. It would be important to see exactly how these outside marriages are distributed. Is there yet another level in the hierarchy above that of the central market area that is important for the marriages of such elites? It is interesting that both Crissman and Knapp (and Skinner too, for that matter) followed the anthropological penchant for studying a smaller, less complex part of the total system; they studied an area around a central market town that was not, however, the administrative seat of the *hsien* in which it was located. There may be important marriages between the elites of the areas they studied and persons in the administrative seat that they have therefore missed. Analogous to this sort of hypergamy is the movement of poorer women from west to east within the peasant class.

MECHANISMS AND EXPLANATIONS

A basic question raised by these studies is why a marketing system should affect a system of marriage in the first place. A ready answer to this question might be that marketing, by virtue of its frequency, will tend to establish the spatial parameters for all sorts of interactions, such as marriage, that are less frequent. At the same time, however, brides as a form of "commodity" are in general unspecialized and hence can be more readily acquired at shorter distances than those manufactured or exotic goods that are most economically distributed through a network of specialized regional centers. This would explain, for instance, Crissman's finding that propinquity influences marriage more than marketing, though marketing is nonetheless influential. With the development of a marketing system, however, there is also a development of social and economic stratification, with a concomitant specialization in the kinds and varieties of brides. We may assume that the more prestigious matches are to be made with or among the wealthier and more sophisticated townsmen rather than among the peasantry. But it should also be borne in mind that there is a continuum of sorts in the amount of wealth that rural and urban people possess. Hence, even when searching for a bride from a wealthy family, the gentry need not necessarily go to a center of economic specialization to find one. This would explain why some groups that are not centered around markets nevertheless have high endogamy rates.

Villages may not be important for marketing, but they still foster frequent interaction between residents due to children's play groups, limited sources of water, and the like. Thus it is important to isolate exactly which kinds of frequent interaction foster marriage and which do not, especially in view of the idea that familiarity breeds contempt. It is clear that marketing together does seem to be important in fostering marriage, but why is this so? Our view of regional marriage systems could differ depending on the answer. If, for example, the crucial thing is that the marriage market is operated by brokers operating out of towns that are the foci of endogamous groups, would it be better for each broker to have a monopoly of a particular area or for the broker to share information about borderline areas with a counterpart in another town on the same level? If the crucial matter is for a person to be able to check independently the match arranged by the broker through his own personal network (Crissman, Chapter 5 in this volume), then perhaps the marriage areas should be relatively discrete, so that one's own network has a better chance of overlapping with one's spouse's.

Both Crissman's and Knapp's data show that the increase in importance of higher-level central places does *not* lead to a decrease in the importance of the lower-level ones, as Skinner hypothesized in his modernized stage.

The marketing functions of such places have been demonstrated, but the other social functions that they have are only suggested. Until more attention is paid to them, we will know very little about the other kinds of interaction, if any, that foster marriage.

CONCLUSIONS

Clearly, profound changes in the nature and composition of endogamous groups occur during periods of economic development, but what those changes are beyond the undoubted internal differentiation of the groups, and addition of more levels to the hierarchy, we do not know (return migration, brides from the Old Country, and so forth). There is a redundancy of social communication that fosters multiplex relationships among people, and there is also a redundancy of background that furthers understanding. Endogamy as a topic is ambiguous for many reasons, not least because it operates to reduce the strangeness and discontinuities produced by exogamy.

In general, Skinner's original hypothesis of the identity of marketing and marriage communities is reasonable in the light of our findings on endogamous groups (Adams and Kasakoff 1975). Both Crissman's and Knapp's findings are also congruent with ours—and, we believe, with Skinner's. To return to the conclusions we drew in our original article (Chapter 6, this volume), all of these studies have found semiclosed, not completely closed, groups. In fact, Skinner has pointed out (1971) that in China, at least, and probably in other places as well, the degree of openness of communities was cyclical, reaching a peak during periods of economic prosperity. This may explain the variation in the rates of endogamy of the 80-percent groups in our tables; modern Taiwan, in a state of economic expansion, should have lower rates of endogamy in its 80-percent groups, perhaps, than Skinner's rural Szechwan, his example of traditional China. In addition, all of the studies describe several different marriage patterns corresponding to tendencies of different strata to marry in different ways.

Our findings about the sizes of endogamous groups and their relationship to population density are amply confirmed by Skinner's discussion of the sizes of standard marketing communities in traditional China (1964: Table 1); he even finds an upper limit on the sizes of such groups (8870), which is surprisingly close to our figure of 10,000. The extremely large 80-percent groups in modern Taiwan were prefigured in our paper by the situation in rural Japan, though they exceed those in size. The relationship between population density and the sizes of 80-percent groups at very high population densities, such as those in Taiwan, is not a simple one and is the subject of future research. Nevertheless, we have tried to suggest that in Taiwan, as in Japan, the actual 80-percent groups of particular strata are probably not as large as would appear from the figure for the entire region, and Knapp and Crissman have furnished us with some useful data that allow us to visualize exactly how this might occur.

Through their use of central-place theory, these studies have demonstrated the existence of systems of interlocking groups above the village level, groups that are significant for marriages as well as for marketing. However, the situation is more complex than any of these authors has portrayed it. Not only are there endogamous units that do not appear to result from marketing, but the units interlock in several different ways that have yet to be fully elucidated.

The failure of these authors to portray the complexity of these systems arises, we feel, from their attempt to view marriage solely from the perspective of marketing. The question to be asked is not "Does marketing structure marriage?" but rather "What does an entire social system, including marketing and marriage, not to mention politics, classes, and religious organizations, look like as a *regional* system?" We have tried to make observations about the kinds of inquiry that might be pursued in future field studies, so that some of the processes underlying such regional social systems might be more completely understood. It seems to us that central-place theory is useful not because it allows us to predict the sizes and interrelationships of marriage communities solely from data on marketing—the studies on Taiwan show that this is not possible—but because it provides us with a set of possibilities, almost a language, with which we can conceptualize the organization of any kind of social system in which distance is important.

REFERENCES

Adams, John W., and Alice Bee Kasakoff
   1975   Factors underlying endogamous group size. In *Population and social organization,* edited by Moni Nag. The Hague: Mouton. (Reprinted as Chapter 6 in this volume.)
Campbell, J. K.
   1964   *Honour, family and patronage.* Oxford: Clarendon Press.
Crissman, Lawrence W.
   1972   Marketing on the Changhua Plain, Taiwan. In *Economic organization in Chinese society,* edited by W. E. Willmott. Stanford, Calif.: Stanford Univ. Press. Pp. 212–259.
   1973   Town and country: Central place theory and Chinese marketing systems, with particular reference to southwestern Changhua Hsien, Taiwan. Unpublished Ph.D. dissertation, Cornell Univ.
Knapp, Ronald
   1971   Marketing and social patterns in rural Taiwan. *Annals of the Association of American Geographers* **61:** 131–155.

Skinner, G. William
  1964 Marketing and social structure in rural China: part I. *Journal of Asian Studies* **24:** 3–43.
  1965 Marketing and social structure in rural China: part II. *Journal of Asian Studies* **24:** 195–228.
  1971 Chinese peasants and the closed community: An open and shut case. *Comparative Studies in Society and History* **13:** 270–281.

Section C

RELIGION, POLITICS, AND STRATIFICATION

Religion, politics, and stratification are basic organizing systems of complex societies. By looking at them in regional perspective, Verdery, Howell, and Beck show how they relate to environmental constraints on the one hand and to cultural identities on the other hand. Katherine Verdery asks the question "What articulates Welsh ethnic identity?" and places it in the context of the regional system and subsystems of Wales as they are physiologically defined. Taking off from Hechter's study of Wales as an internal colony of England, Verdery finds that local-level systems of organization, particularly that of religious sectarianism, are critical to understanding the process by which some people in Wales define themselves as a group distinct from the dominant colonizers. She makes her case by a careful examination of religious affiliation through time and space in relation to other markers of specifically Welsh ethnic identity. From this she is able to explain not only who define themselves as Welsh, and where, but also why the political organization of Welsh ethnic identity has taken its present and distinctive form.

Julia Howell looks at a similar process in a very distant and different society, an interior administrative region of Java. Using 1971 electoral results, she examines both cultural identity (*abangan* versus *santri*) and less stable political orientations. By placing politics and cultural identity in the context of an ecologically and administratively defined regional system, Howell determines the complex processes by which people in that system have aligned themselves as both cultural and political actors—processes begun at different periods of history and utilizing various mechanisms to mobilize support.

Brenda Beck also works within the framework of a physiologically defined regional system, asking both how the region has shaped social organization and reciprocally how social organization has shaped the region. The region, Koṅku, is a naturally bounded one in southern India over which many different political and cultural groups have held power, influencing but not destroying local-level organization. What has given Koṅku integrity over time is one dominant caste, based in the core area of the region. Beck is specifically concerned with how and why caste organization differs in the areas away from the core, and she uses data from sample points in the region on caste groups, numbers, settlement organization, and food transaction patterns to develop an explanation. The model she constructs not only addresses the determinants and consequences of regionally dominant castes in India but also suggests the processes by which any culturally defined group can become dominant in a regional system.

Chapter 8

Ethnicity and Local Systems: The Religious Organization of Welshness

Katherine Verdery
Stanford University

The trouble in Northern Ireland has had a place in the headlines for so long that knowledge of the conflict there is almost universal. It is less widely known that the situation in Belfast is but the most troubling manifestation of growing nationalist sentiments throughout the Celtic fringe; and if one has heard at all of Welsh or Scottish nationalism, it is unlikely that Cornish or Manx nationalism strikes an equally familiar note. The publicity fetched by the Celtic movements is proportional to their strength and organization, and it testifies to internal variety in the ethnic mobilization of the regions that comprise Britain.

Similarly, any traveler to Scotland learns that the Highlands and Islands are more Scottish than Glasgow or Fife, and anyone who has talked with a Welshman—particularly one from the northwest—will know that the heartland of Welsh ethnicity is in the north and west, while parts of the south barely qualify as Welsh and the eastern border does not even merit consideration. One glance at a map showing the distribution of one or another Welsh trait—language retention, voting patterns on the serving of liquor on Sundays, Welsh Nonconformity—confirms the notion that Welshness, whatever it may be, is not uniformly spread across the landscape of Wales. The purpose of the following analysis is to pursue these several streams of thought—ethnic variation, regional differences, and degrees of mobilized ethnicity—toward a confluence. Because the data necessitate a historical treatment, the flow of the discussion will be shaped by variations in the temporal substrate.

INTRODUCTION: VIEWS OF ETHNICITY

The traditional sociological view of ethnicity as a primordial sentiment destined to dissolve as industrialization progresses has recently given way to the idea that ethnicity is actively generated. It involves the creation and maintenance of boundaries that structure relations among divergent groups within a region and that may, in fact, be *brought about* by inequities intrinsic to the spread of industrialism. Leach's (1954) treatment of interethnic relations in highland Burma contained the germ of the present viewpoint, but credit for current thinking along these lines goes to Fredrik Barth and his colleagues (Barth 1969). They analyzed ecological variation and the consequent complementarity of or competition for resources among adjacent groups, to argue that ecologically grounded interactions set the stage for social differentiation and for the manipulation of status. Such cultural attributes as language, religion, dress, or customs are not, they believe, primordial and ascribed qualities of groups but symbolic statements of social position, used to structure interaction or to dramatize the crossing of a social boundary.

The work of Hechter combines Barth's ideas with earlier-developed notions of internal colonialism (Gonzalez Casanova 1965; Stavenhagen 1965) in order to counter the functionalist argument that industrialism inevitably entails the integration of ethnic minorities within a national industrial culture (Hechter 1971, 1973, 1974, 1975). Hechter claims that the model of internal colonialism, with its focus on the chance progression of industrialization across space and its analogies between interethnic and imperial–colonial relations, both illuminates the persistence of ethnic identifications in as highly industrialized a society as Great Britain and also serves as a better guide for public policy. The argument states that spatial discrepancies in the progress of industrialism produce relatively more- and less-advantaged groups, the former gaining a disproportionate share of resources and power. This "core" then attempts to withhold its resource advantage from the "peripheral" groups by institutionalizing the existing inequality. It defines eligibility for high status in terms of its own membership, which it makes more visible by accentuating cultural differences between itself and the peripheries. The internal colonialism model of national development predicts, therefore, that far from gradually submerging cultural differences in the sea of a mass industrial culture, unequal industrialization and the salience of culturally based discriminations within it will provoke "peripheral sectionalism," as peripheral groups react to the situation by politicizing their ethnicity.

This paper attempts to build on Hechter's work in two ways, by applying his own logic at another spatial level—within a peripheral region—and by inquiring into the specific mechanisms through which "peripheral sectionalism" is generated. Hechter's publications to date leave room for both these refinements. First, his interest in Celtic ethnicity as a whole leads him to gloss over discernible variations in ethnic identity in each portion of the Celtic fringe. Within any one part—that is, within Scotland, Ireland, or Wales—an extension of Hechter's model would predict variations in peripheral sectionalism based on unequal distributions of resources and capital investments, with consequent internal discrepancies in economic development and differentiation. Second, because Hechter's aim is to establish the validity of the reactive argument as against the functionalist one, his analysis slights the actual mechanisms through which reactive solidarity develops. My discussion orients toward these two unexploited niches by asking about the systemic patterning of resources and economic structures within which ethnic groups interact and about the dynamics of activating latent primordial attachments.

Because I regard politicization as the most important facet of ethnicity, my analysis focuses on the *mobilization* of ethnic identity and its political articulation. Several assumptions underlie my argument. First, I regard the capacity to organize as a crucial resource generally monopolized and effectively wielded by superordinate powers; successful reaction by peripheral groups often involves their acquiring their own organizational resources for competing in the political arena. Although organizing power may first develop in only one segment of the periphery, it then becomes a resource that can be used throughout. Second, I view ethnic "groups" as categories constituting fields of recruitment for the mobilization of political groups defined in ethnic terms. It is probable that rudimentary ethnic awareness already exists—most Welsh have never considered themselves English—but this ascriptive identification is *not* a sufficient condition for producing goal-directed group action. Third, I assume that such organization hinges upon the presence or the appearance of social institutions that provide a communicative focus, either explicitly or through periodic centralization of population flow; that specifically *ethnic* mobilization hinges upon the ethnic group's having a considerable monopoly of these social institutions; and that ethnic mobilization may emerge even through an institution which does not initially state its goals in ethnic terms. Organization is assumed to be more effective when it involves the superimposition of several social cleavages—religious, ethnic, rural-urban, social—or when several different institutions draw together essentially the same population for different functions. Conversely, where social cleavages cross-cut one another or where the boundaries of different institutional hinterlands are not coterminous, effective organization will be weakened. Finally, I hold that all of the above varies systematically within spatially structured regions.[1]

[1] Many of these assumptions derive from the work of Breton (1964) and its adaptation by Vallee (1969), and from Charsley (1974). Although there is not space in the text to discuss their work, it supported my way of shaping the argument.

These notions are explored through an illustrative example drawn from a portion of the Celtic fringe, Wales. I argue that the Welsh were effectively mobilized by Nonconformist religious institutions, which organized the population on the basis of religious issues that later took on anti-English significance. I do not contend that ideas of "Welshness" or "Englishness" had not previously existed but only that they had not been institutionally articulated until the advent of Nonconformity. I then argue that where the population was spread among several competing sects, ethnic mobilization was less efficient than where people were concentrated in one or two denominations. Insufficient data preclude convincing proof of this thesis, which was first suggested by a close reading of anthropological monographs on Wales.[2] But the existence of complete census data in fairly small geographic units, although they are for three different time periods, makes the case a good one for illustrating regional analysis of the problem.

The visual part of the argument consists of mapped distributions of religious affiliation for 1851, language for 1891, and language and voting behavior (the only real index of ethnic mobilization) for 1970–1971. Before introducing these maps, I sketch the historical background and set forth the rationale for regarding religion as the basis of ethnic organization. I then elaborate each of the themes I have touched upon, as follows: After describing the regional structure and the variation of ethnicity within it, I map 1851 religious affiliation within this structure and explain the distribution that is seen. Finally, I explain how political mobilization fits into the regional and religious contexts.

SOCIAL AND ECONOMIC BACKGROUND

"Wales," said the Bishop of St. David's in 1886, "is at present nothing more than the Highlands of England without a Highland Line; it is a geographical expression [cited in Coupland 1954:217]." The boundary between England and Wales has been relatively stable for over 400 years. Administrative rearrangements pared off a slice here or added one there, but the border is reasonably congruent with Offa's Dyke, the wall of demarcation erected in the eighth century between Welsh principalities and the Anglo-Saxon kingdom of Mercia. From the times of Saxon and Norman advances that drove the indigenous Celts up into the forests and high ground to the west, until the stabilization of the boundary in 1536 by the union of England and Wales, the border consisted of a fluctuating line slowly graphing the equation between topography and the force of the invaders' offensive. Both Anglo-Saxons and Normans turned the region of

[2] See Emmett (1964), Frankenberg (1957), Hughes (1960), Jenkins (1960, 1971), Jones (1960), Owen (1960), and Rees (1950).

greatest contact into a buffer zone by farming out the border territories to independent lords, who had considerable autonomy.

Topography is the chief determinant of the boundary, but additional features show marked discontinuity on either side of the border (see Sylvester 1969). Across the line of demarcation, there are abrupt shifts in the density of settlement, predominance of one or another settlement type (nucleated or seminucleated versus dispersed), soil types (sandstones giving way eastward to brown earths) and natural forestation, and proportions of rough grazing to arable land. The border also corresponds closely with the boundary between two- and three-field systems of agriculture. In short, the political and ethnic border has many ecological correlates. Map 1 shows Wales and eastern England, with some of the major settlements. The dashed gray line shows the approximate location of the border; the dashed black lines showing physiographic regions will be explained later.[3]

Throughout the Middle Ages, Wales had consisted of independent principalities; the southern and eastern portions were gradually absorbed into the manorial organization of the Norman lordships, a process that was well advanced when Henry Tudor became King Henry VII of England in 1485. The Norman administration provoked differentiation on all possible fronts: Heightened commerce and a quasi-servile organization differentiated the entire buffer zone from the rest of Wales; divergent administrative and legal systems distinguished each separate lordship from the others; and within each lordship the explicit division of domains into "Welshries" and "Englishries" (upland and lowland distinctions, the lowland ones being further differentiated by their relative proximity to towns or to the manor) contributed diversity to the internal structure and integration of every domain.

The coronation of Henry Tudor, descended of a union between Welsh and English royal blood, was seen by the Welsh as the repossession of their liberty (Williams 1950:18), and his accession did, in fact, mark the beginning of privileges and minor offices for Welshmen. When Parliament under Henry VIII passed the Acts of Union between England and Wales in 1536 and 1542, the expressed aims were judicial and administrative uniformity and an end to legal discrimination against the Welsh "allies," by extending the English system throughout. The union caused no immediate disruption of Welsh affairs. Because of the greater social mobility encouraged by political integration, Welsh gentry began rapidly adopting

---

[3] Settlements shown are those that have been important in both the nineteenth and twentieth centuries. Names of the most important settlements are printed in large letters, intermediate settlements are in medium-sized letters, and minor ones are in small letters.

The gray line marking the Welsh–English border does not correspond to any real historical boundary but approximates where the border lay. Since each of my three time periods has a slightly different boundary, I prefer to show only the general location of the line.

Map 1. Wales and western English midlands, showing major settlements, river systems, and regional boundaries.

the language and customs of their English counterparts (Pool 1971:44), but otherwise the quiet co-optation of the sociopolitical structure offered no clear threat to Welsh cultural identity, well ensconced in its geographic fortress.

After two centuries in which the Welsh economy remained relatively unchanged from its traditional reliance on subsistence agriculture with some exporting of produce to England,[4] shifts in the export market began

---

[4] Jones Pierce (1972:339) has convincingly argued against the customary view that Wales had a pastoral economy until English market demands altered the pattern; he claims that Norman influence in the twelfth through fourteenth centuries revolutionized the pre-

to push toward specialization in animal husbandry. This specialization was encouraged both by the generally abysmal state of roads in Wales, which made transport of anything that could not move itself very costly, and increasingly by food demands of the populations of industrializing English centers. The Napoleonic Wars and the ensuing agricultural inflation made even the remotest parts of Wales economically viable. At the same time, industrialization was slowly beginning to creep into Wales. From minimal development in the late eighteenth century, industry took off in the nineteenth, spurred by English military necessities for the war in America and the discovery of the wealth of mineral resources in South Wales. Ironworks sprang into existence, financed by English capitalists, and transport improvements undergirded a mammoth coal boom that centered in the narrow valleys and coastal ports of the south. Industrial development in South Wales was so extensive that it siphoned off the surplus rural population created by the agricultural depression after the Napoleonic Wars. This produced massive centers in South Wales, unparalleled elsewhere in the country, and the imbalance persists into the present.

The economic stance of English capitalists was rapacious rather than developmental. Investments were made only for clear profit and without concern for fostering the growth of the local economy. With time, Wales took on an unambiguously tributary status, as failure to diversify local industry led to a near-total dependence on outside markets. The pattern of central places was more suited to demands of the English than to those of the Welsh—until 1954, the capital of Wales was, in fact, London. As can be seen in Map 2, the major transport routes that had been laid down by 1850 served to channel traffic toward England rather than to integrate the countryside of Wales. "Internal colonialism" increasingly characterized the situation of the Welsh as the nineteenth century wore on. All elements of the model are present: English monopoly of credit, capital, commerce, and entrepreneurial activity; the progressive specialization of the economy toward one or two exports, and its orientation largely to external markets; the exogenous determination of labor and other social movements; and the allocation of social roles in accordance with ethnic distinctions (cf. Hechter 1971:36).

Divergent social statuses came to be reinforced by another distinction, that between Anglican and Nonconformist. The earliest forms of Protestant dissent were introduced from England in the late 1600s, were largely anglicizing in their goals, and began to make real progress only after evangelization was started in Welsh. Through itinerant preaching, Puritans and Quakers gained small numbers of adherents in nearly all parts of Wales; Baptists and Independents, beginning at about the same

---

dominantly pastoral economy, transforming it into one of mixed subsistence agriculture throughout the country, though pastoralism continued to predominate in the uplands.

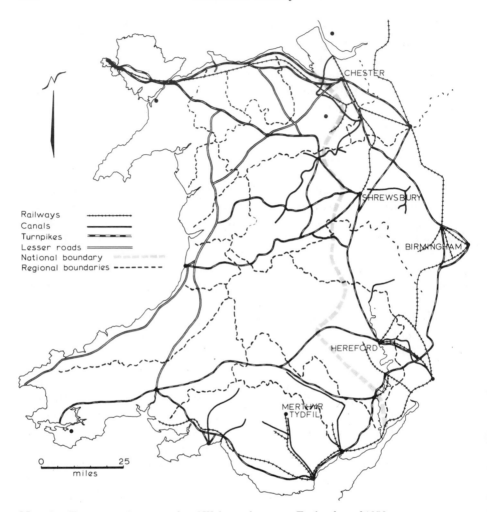

Map 2.   Transportation networks of Wales and western England as of 1850.

time as the others, gained larger followings. All of the sects started their efforts in the south of Wales and had greater initial success there than in the north, and all made greater inroads along the borders where contact with England was greatest.

The 1700s saw further religious revivals, culminating in the rapid spread of Calvinistic Methodism. Like other dissenters, the early Calvinistic Methodist leaders were inspired from England, but theological disagreements soon led them to shape the movement in a peculiarly Welsh way. This movement originated in the south, as had the others, but by the late 1700s it had a powerful organizing center in the north, in Merionethshire. The last denomination to begin active recruiting was Wesleyan Methodism, which entered Wales from the northeast and spread especially through the northern and eastern areas. While its success was less than that of Calvinistic Methodism,[5] it contributed to the takeover of the countryside by Nonconformity and, as with all the revivals, aided the expansion of other sects.

By 1850, three-fourths of the population of Wales was Nonconformist; another revival in 1859 made the proportion even higher. Religious distinctions compounded the differences and tensions between gentry and tenant, ironmaster and laborer. Landlords clung as a body to Anglicanism, and English industrialists, many of them English Nonconformists when they arrived in Wales, returned to Anglicanism as an affirmation of their elite status. But while Nonconformity exacerbated these class differences, its superimposition on rural and industrial areas alike provided the one link to unite the socially and economically divergent parts of Wales. Among the Welsh there had grown up a national religion that contributed, perhaps in the idea of the equality of all men before God, a sense of resistance (Williams 1950:156–157).

The period after 1850 was marked by increasingly frequent manifestations of what Welsh historians refer to as a "national awakening" (Morgan 1963; Williams 1950) and what I interpret as increasing politicization of issues centering around ethnic status. Country-wide voting habits evidence the change most clearly: More and more of the seats long held by gentry were successfully challenged by local farmers, and the age-old hegemony of the Conservative Party was lost to the Liberals. Significant extensions of the franchise in 1867 made the election of 1868 a critical test. Several candidates campaigned on explicitly nationalistic lines, affirming the right of the Welsh to say to their English propertied class, "We are the Welsh people and not you. This country is ours and not yours, and therefore we claim to have our own principles and sentiments and feelings represented in the Commons' House of Parliament [reported in Morgan 1963:v]." The speaker of these lines was among those elected, and from this time on, political developments had increasingly nationalistic overtones.[6]

By 1900, however, this movement was beginning to lose momentum, and by World War I its force seemed fully spent. The sputtering out of ethnic politics is partially explained by its loss of impetus when Nonconformity

[5] Welsh Methodism or Calvinistic Methodism, now called the Presbyterian Church of Wales, differs from Wesleyan Methodism both organizationally and theologically. Although the differences between Welsh and English variants of the other sects were not as great as the differences that gave rise to the Calvinistic Methodist variant, I should note that all the sects took on special characteristics in their Welsh environment and became distinct from their English counterparts. All of them also championed the Welsh language and common people.

[6] Other events support the idea of a national awakening in the latter 1800s: the inflamed local response to the damning report of an 1847 Parliamentary Commission on the state of education in Wales; the first calls for Home Rule, culminating in the formation of a Young Wales movement; the election of several advocates of Home Rule to Parliament; a cultural renaissance similar to those occurring in continental Europe; tithe riots in the 1880s; and the battle for mandatory closing of public houses on Sundays.

won the issue of disestablishment in 1914; by the co-optation of Welsh political leaders (Lloyd George is the best example); and by the development of strong labor movements in the south, which split rural and industrial Wales. Why, then, should ethnic politics suddenly rebound in the 1960s—with gratifying repetition of its spatial pattern—after being moribund for over 50 years? Hechter suggests that the answer lies in national-level party politics. Both the Liberal and Labour parties had drawn continual support from Wales by incorporating Welsh issues into their political platforms—particularly when they were not in office. Ethnic sentiments thus defused were revived, however, when the Labour Party was elected to office and failed to deliver on the idea of Welsh self-government (Hechter 1973:338). The ranks of Plaid Cymru, the Welsh Nationalist Party, then began to swell.

Ethnic mobilization in Wales currently takes the form of votes for candidates from the Welsh Nationalist Party; while still numerically small, the proportion of the vote for this party has doubled in each election.[7] The more moderate nationalists devote themselves to promoting the Welsh language [Evans and Rhys (1968:249) report that even some monoglot English parents send their children to Welsh-language schools] or perhaps to arguing against Sunday pub openings or debating the form that Welsh autonomy should take. Earlier goals that have been won consisted of establishing a national capital in Cardiff, gaining official status for the Welsh language in the school system, and creating a Secretary of State for Wales.

If the evidence I have summarized justifies an assertion that the latter half of the nineteenth century was the focal period of ethnic politicization, then the central question of this analysis—how the variables connected with ethnic mobilization and its spatial pattern are interrelated— necessitates historical evidence. It is unfortunate that although there are good historical data for my independent variable, religious affiliation, there is nothing but the already cited impressionistic evidence for my dependent variable, ethnic mobilization, until the Welsh Nationalist voting statistics of the 1960s. The 1891 linguistic census can serve as an index of Welsh *cultural* distribution, but no active behavior can be extrapolated from it. The voting statistics that Hechter successfully uses in his analysis are not discriminating enough for my purposes, for they provide no way of distinguishing *ethnically* motivated from *class*-based non-Conservative voting. Since the internal variations in ethnicity are crucial to my point of view, aggregated voting statistics are not a satisfactory index. I have been

[7] In a 1966 by-election the first Welsh Nationalist candidate was elected to Parliament, from Carmarthenshire. No other Nationalist candidate was successful until 1974, when two were elected; but the percentage of the vote grew in each election. In 1966 about 2.8 percent of the electorate voted Welsh Nationalist, about 5 percent in 1970, and about 11 percent in 1974.

unable to uncover any that are, and it is for this reason that my argument proceeds deductively: I first discuss alternative mobilizing institutions, then present evidence to clarify the logic behind an organizational role for Nonconformity, and finally examine the regional distributions of religion and ethnicity.

MOBILIZING INSTITUTIONS:
ALLIANCE AND DISSENT

Given my postulate that ethnic mobilization cannot occur in the absence of centralizing institutions, it is appropriate to ask what were some of the institutions of mid-nineteenth century Wales that were limited primarily to members of the ethnic minority, could unite the populace and enhance internal communication, and served to focus activity. The question is especially apt in view of the often advanced claim that Wales had a peculiarly centerless social tradition:

> It is clear that the clustered village is not a feature of Welsh traditional life, for where villages are found in Wales they are either widely spaced or in areas of strong English contact [Sylvester 1969:203].

> Visitors to Wales in all ages have been impressed by the lack of visible signs of community life.... But there exists in upland Wales a diffused form of society which is not only able to function without a unifying social centre but seems opposed to all forms of centralization.... Until comparatively recently, everything which normally makes a village seems to have been scattered [Rees 1950:100, 103].

Rees further suggests (p. 108) that the distinction between town and country became largely an English Welsh distinction, for towns were alien structures imposed by the English on a rural culture that had already crystallized around unnucleated settlements and services.

Centralized marketing, usually associated with nucleated centers, has been shown to be a classic mechanism for consolidating local populations (Skinner 1964), but there is little to indicate that it was significant in Wales. A few indigenous Welsh boroughs existed in premodern times, largely in coastal locations. Most centers resulted from English influence, especially the boroughs and markets that grew up around Norman manors and the later centers created by industrialism and overall commercialization. But these were imposed on the "centerless" Welsh landscape, where itinerant peddlers and craftsmen had for centuries mediated the distribution of goods and the provision of services. Marketing systems in Wales developed in tandem with the expansion of the British economy from the eighteenth century on, reaching full centralization after the mid-nineteenth century (Jones 1973:113); but even then the systems were unstable, as changes in the technology and location of transport by-passed some developing centers and nourished the growth of others.

The most important point, however, is that even where marketing was well established, markets were not frequented exclusively by Welshmen. On the contrary: For centuries, English was the customary language of the markets, even those with predominantly Welsh-speaking hinterlands, and English merchants had long had either exclusive or monopolistic trading privileges. The towns created by the English "remained alien to the Welsh countryside and were regarded by the Welsh people with unconcealed dislike [Williams 1950:11]."

At the same time, the fact that many of these towns constituted centers of an alien administration precluded the success of a second potential centralizing agent: the flow of populations through administrative centers. Courts served as the administrative seats that determined where one had to go to settle disputes and manage one's affairs, but the use of English in the courts and the non-Welsh law they administered merely accentuated the foreign nature of the administrative apparatus and reduced Welsh orientation to those centers. In addition, incongruities between English administrative divisions and the older Welsh ones, plus the recalcitrancies of dispersed settlement and extensive common pastures, entailed frequent reshuffling of the boundaries and made the administrative map of Wales impossibly complex (Sylvester 1969:131).

The organizational capacities of another centralizing function, work, may have borne some fruit in Welsh industrial areas through the gradual development of trade unions, which by the end of the nineteenth century had produced a solid working-class organization. But union membership was not based on appeals to ethnicity and included many ethnic groups besides the Welsh. Work arrangements in other areas of Wales were not a unifying force, since they consisted largely of dyadic labor exchanges among farmers.

The neat parish boundaries of the Anglican Church bore no relationship to patterns of movement among the Welsh, whose participation in the Church had always been marginal. Educational institutions were similarly colonizing in their effects and did not provide suitable rallying points. Among native institutions, the flow-inducing activities that existed were too infrequent to generate an enduring organization; periodic fairs, annual sheep-dog trials, intervillage competitions of various kinds—all occurred too seldom to sustain an effective mobilization of the hinterlands. Nor were the more constant ties of kinship and neighborhood, which loom so large in monographs on Welsh rural life, sufficiently organized to serve as focal points for political mobilization.

The one institution that could serve such a purpose was the Nonconformist chapel. Nonconformist churchgoing included two services plus Sunday school on Sundays and two or three additional week-night meetings. The chapels themselves were scattered about the countryside, and they further maximized contact with people and minimized the adverse effects of distance by holding their evening meetings in different houses throughout the area. Moreover, they developed an extensive recreational life to supplant traditional activities that had been outlawed by Nonconformist beliefs: They held singing festivals, musical and literary events, debates, popular lectures, and other gatherings—something the Anglican Church had never done with such vigor. In comparison with the chapels, all other social occasions, such as fairs, were of minor weight. Even in the twentieth century, Davies finds that religious participation constitutes the *only* organized social contact for one-third of the families in his study area; his conclusion that "the closely integrated community ties based on religion have broken down [1970:187]" strongly implies that a century ago they were of far greater importance. Special support for the power of Nonconformity comes from Hughes's description of a northwest Welsh farming region. This area has molded scattered farmsteads into a self-conscious Welsh community "without the simultaneous appearance of a cluster of settlement which would serve as a focus of interest. . . . It is useful to examine the nature of this exclusiveness . . . and to indicate how, in its present form, it is to be attributed above all to the presence of Nonconformist chapels [Hughes 1960:167.]."

The chapel monopoly on Welsh life has several significant aspects. (1) Chapels had a specifically Welsh linguistic identification and membership. Recruitment in Welsh simultaneously increased internal communications—while clarifying the networks along which conversion would proceed—and created a barrier to outsiders. Nonfoncormist-generated Sunday schools and circulating schools made Welsh the language of education as well as of religion, and the importance of both in people's lives served to legitimize the language in unprecedented fashion. Thus, religious institutions sharpened the clarity and superimposition of social, religious, and linguistic cleavages, especially in those areas where the main social cleavage was between landlord and tenant. (2) Not only was Nonconformity positively tied to Welshness, but it harbored some subtle anti-English elements, most notably its refusal to be confined to towns and parish centers. As Rees observes, "The growth of the hamlet as a center is only now recovering from the reverse suffered through the revitalisation of the countryside by Nonconformity [1950:104]." (3) Solidarity based on chapel membership was rendered absolute by the excessive particularism of chapel affiliation. One was not just a Nonconformist, or just a Baptist, but a member of a *particular* chapel, an exclusive congregation that always came together for worship and developed a firm solidary bond.

The negative argument that chapels were the only possible institution with organizational force must be supplemented by showing a positive link between this organizing potential and ethnic politics. The existence of such a connection is amply attested in histories of Wales.

An association between religion (and language) and nationalism appears often in the literature. Parts of the connection are the anti-English and anti-Anglican symbolism of Nonconformity; its legitimation of the language and its invigoration of "national pride"; its massive public-education efforts; its alliance with an ethnic sensibility through alleged discrimination directed expressly at Nonconformist laborers by their English employers. This identification of Nonconformity with Welsh self-respect was cemented when the 1847 Parliamentary Commission on education laid much of the ignorance, backwardness, and general moral turpitude they found in Wales at the doors of Nonconformist influence and the persistence of the Welsh language.

Aside from these symbolic associations, however, Nonconformity served more actively to articulate the ethnic dimension alongside reinforced differences in social class, in two ways. First, conversion became a social statement for dissociating oneself from the gentry and from anglicization in general (this will be further discussed below). Second, Nonconformity provided an alternative and particularly Welsh system of prestige, based on the values of religious dissent rather than on English values and English-defined mobility. For the Welsh, the status system had long been truncated and had involved shedding one's Welshness in order to move up the ladder. Nonconformist orthodoxy now supplied new social sanctions; important social distinctions, as well as evaluations of individual merit, were mirrored in the elected hierarchy of authority within the chapels, which naturally did not include the gentry (see Jenkins 1960:53, 1971:189). The proliferation of offices within chapels, combined with the proliferation of chapels themselves, multiplied status positions and made mobility aspirations feasible in a society where such positions had always been scarce (Harris 1963:19) and where upward mobility had required resources beyond the reach of most Welshmen. With the spread of Nonconformity, there grew up a conflicting definition of the resources legitimate to the pursuit of status, which, while it probably meant little to those with great social ambitions, was of strong appeal to those further down the ladder. When the Nonconformist leaders officially split off from Anglicanism by beginning to ordain their own ministers in 1811, the implications for the Welsh prestige system were as if they had begun to mint money.

But the strongest link of all between Nonconformity and emergent politicization was the gradual forging of a radical political movement based on religious issues, despite the rampant fragmentation and internal quarrels of the different sects. As Nonconformity came to encompass most of the Welsh, Nonconformist influence began to be directed, irrespective of doctrinal disputes, toward Welsh issues and the struggle for Welsh equality. The Baptists were more politically active than the Independents and both more so than the Methodists, but in the latter part of the nineteenth century the Methodists were radicalized and joined with the others to create a strong political force. Their leaders exhorted the populace to vote against local gentry in the crucial 1868 election. Chapels were willingly turned over to political meetings of the Liberal Party. It was suspected that Nonconformist ministers had influenced workers in the 1831 workers' riots, and it was clear that the ministers encouraged among their working-class congregations antipathy to the Anglican Church and the aristocracy (Jones 1973:154, 194). Nonconformists were further involved in the tithe wars of the 1880s, when large numbers of farmers (spurred, no doubt, by an agrarian crisis) began to refuse to tithe to the Anglican Church.[8]

The issue that clinched it all and makes comprehensible the otherwise bewildering unity among bickering denominations was disestablishment, which emerged as the paramount national question after the 1868 elections. Cries for religious equality were now uttered as demands for removal of "the alien church." This issue more than any other was "worked intensively by journalists, preachers, and politicians (often the same people) [Dunbabin 1974:211]," and a full national program emerged from initially vague Welsh aspirations. Disestablishment came to symbolize a rejection of all anglicizing influences within Wales and to unify the people as never before. "There were no real politics at all in Wales till the sixties, no national politics till the eighties.... the distinctive, the dominant feature of Welsh politics was not the class-conflict, agrarian or industrial; it was their association with religion [Coupland 1954:214, 216]."

It is ironic that this torrent of religious-based organizational fervor probably had an English source. Pierce declares that one of the most decisive developments in the new politics was "the introduction of the conception of political strategy and organization . . . into the Welsh constituencies [1960:175]." In 1862 the English-born Society for the Liberation of Religion from State Patronage and Control convened a conference in South Wales, where they set out to teach politics to the Welsh dissenters, to disseminate information, to encourage discussion, and to "transmute the incipient radicalism of the sects into a purposeful, properly organized political activity [Pierce 1960:175]." The 1868 election was the Nonconformists' first test of their organizational powers. Pierce's analysis (also

---

[8] This is not to imply that there had never been agitation before the Nonconformists' involvement or that earlier unrest was totally devoid of ethnic content. But the accounts of episodes of rural discontent (see Jones 1973) and riots among coal workers give the impression that these events were reactions to social conditions that were not defined in strictly—or even primarily—ethnic terms.

found in Morgan 1963:17) is independently supported by the information
that only in 1864 did the Calvinistic Methodists' two separate northern
and southern branches combine into one country-wide organization; in
1868 the loose Baptist Union was formed, and the Independents followed
suit in 1871 (Rees 1883:456).

I interpret the connection between Nonconformity and ethnic political
action in terms of the emergence of a new elite in Welsh society, the
Nonconformist leaders. The traditional gentry had climbed completely out
of the system; having adopted the life-style and resources of the English,
they had *become* English and lost any claim to leadership of the Welsh.
The growth of Nonconformity threw up a new group of leaders to replace
these, a group whose intimate association with Welshness gave them
cultural hegemony both in local communities and throughout Wales. Their
united attack on the established church constituted an assault on the main
institution that circumscribed their authority and blocked their acquisi-
tion of further resources. By identifying their own struggle with that of the
Welsh as a disadvantaged group, they capitalized upon the congruence of
social cleavages and ethnic discrimination, and they banked this capital to
finance the elimination of their principal competitor, the Anglican
Church.

Despite the organizational assets of the Nonconformist chapels, the
Welsh Nationalist movement appears feeble when compared with other
Celtic movements such as the IRA. There is one easy answer to the question of why unifying capacity far outstrips any observable ethnic unity:
Welsh Nonconformity was homogeneous only in its opposition to Anglicanism and the presence of the English. Given the rampant denomina-
tionalism that littered the countryside with myriad chapels, as it still does,
it is a wonder that the denominations managed to unite at all. Throughout
the nineteenth century, lack of centralization plus internal politicking
fostered the continual hiving off of members to form new congregations, if
not entire new sects. Chapels competed sharply with one another in
various events (from theological debates to singing competitions) and carried their interdenominational partisanships into local political elections,
as still happens today. But they also sustained many theological and personal animosities, whose acerbity often gave rise to censure on cross-
denominational marriages (Davies 1965:51). The distinction between
member and adherent (one who attends services but does not receive com-
munion and cannot hold church office) further divided congregations
internally, and fierce particularistic loyalties exacerbated many quarrels
both between and among sects. Examples of all these phenomena abound
in the monographic literature, revealing the great significance of sectarianism in social organization, for it affected both local and supralocal
alliances (Rees 1950:114–115).

Rampant sectarianism had several consequences. First, the endless
repetition of the same kinds of activity and organization within a small

space precluded the emergence of a larger organic unity. Second, the independent operation of hundreds of chapels not only made internal communication far from perfect but also confined the influence of any one leader largely within his own sect, at most (Pool 1971:20); thus, it was only if *all* leaders were exercising the same kind of influence that a movement was likely to emerge. This contrasts with the internal discipline and near-perfect communications of the Irish national party, whose cell-like organization based on Roman Catholic parishes made for a very effective formal structure (Pool 1971:62). The divided Welsh congregations could never have produced so structured a grass-roots organization.

Further impediments lay in the varieties of organization to be found among the denominations. Nonconformity is on the whole decentralized, but each group has its own system of decentralization and range of territorial coverage. Quakers had a well-organized hierarchy of meetings culminating in an annual session in London. For Baptists and Independents, autonomy of the local congregation is a doctrinal cornerstone, and they do not invest their larger unions with hierarchical authority, nor do they regularize formal associations of chapels at lower levels. Wesleyan Methodism has conferences and societies encompassing all of Britain. Calvinistic Methodism has a presbyterian structure confined to Wales, with several well-defined levels hierarchically ranked in authority.

But as if this fragmentation and organizational chaos were not enough, the sects go even further: Each has events that bring together more than one local congregation (circuit meetings, the Sunday school system, preaching contests, singing festivals, and the like), but not one of them has its supralocal units congruent with those of another. Thus, as in the regional organizations surrounding Rees's parish of Llanfihangel yng Ngwynfa, Calvinistic Methodists are grouped with localities to the south and west for their periodic events, and Independents orient to the east, while for Wesleyan Methodists the parish is divided in half (Rees 1950:116–117). Because few other social boundaries in Wales seem to coincide—parishes are not coterminous with chapel districts, nor these with socially defined neighborhoods, and marketing hinterlands contain no important social grouping in addition to themselves—such solidarity as may have developed in the hinterlands of any of these institutions was not reinforced anywhere else.

TESTING THE MODEL:
REGIONS, RELIGION, AND
POLITICIZATION

The preceding historical outline has pointed up the status of Wales as an internal colony of England and has elucidated the religious basis of the

Welsh political movement; it is now necessary to specify the interrelations of these variables. The degree of internal colonialism varied throughout Wales according to variations in regional economic structure, which in turn affected both the distribution of *cultural* features and the spread of *social* phenomena—in particular, religious conversion. Regional structuring of denominational recruitment consequently shaped the form that religious-based politicization would take. Each of these ideas will be discussed in turn.

Regions and the Distribution of Ethnic Inducements

To examine the covariation of manifest ethnicity and degrees of internal colonialization, one must have a systematic framework for looking at both variables. I employ a framework based on physiographically defined regions, which I prefer to alternative possible regionalizations[9] because it is prior to, rather than emergent from, the social and cultural events that play upon it. Altitude contours constituting the watersheds of rivers and tributaries were traced to provide the outlines of natural systems, whose implications for social phenomena consist in their significance for population movement. As Map 2 has shown, the skeletal transport system implicit in these regions was not fully adopted by the English, though the Welsh used it extensively. The physiographic regions of Wales are shown bounded by dashed black lines on Maps 1, 2, 3, 4, and 7 and by solid lines on Map 6. The maps show 13 regions (numbered outside their margins on Maps 3, 4, and 7); lighter dashed lines indicate some watersheds that, while they are sometimes reflected in the data, do not separate full-fledged regions. The regions outlined are not all of equal weight, for the more rugged landscape of the north makes for a larger number of minor river systems; but the altitudes defining them are no less than those encircling the southern regions. Variations in altitude are shown by the varying width of the watershed lines on Map 6.

For ease of exposition, I have collapsed the 13 regions into five larger units. Each of these differs as a whole from the others, although all of them contain the same sort of internal structure in that each one consists of an agricultural rural upland climaxing on a zone of higher urbanization and industrialism in the coastal lowlands (the center for region 1 is the

---

[9] The best of the proposed regionalizations is the multivariate factor analysis suggested by Davies (1972). Nonetheless, I prefer an a priori division, even though some parts of the discussion I present could be made in terms of his three regions. Other possible ways of regionalizing, such as defining nodal regions on the basis of settlement hierarchies with stepwise scaling of functions, are inappropriate for the English-dominated Welsh central-place system.

English city of Birmingham). The five larger regions are numbered and the subregions lettered within their respective regions. Region 1, the east, consists of subregions 1a and 1b; region 2, the south, contains subregions 2a and 2b; subregions 3a, 3b, 3c, and 3d make up region 3, the west; region 4, the northwest, contains 4a and 4b; and 5a, 5b, and 5c comprise region 5, the northeast.[10]

I will illustrate the utility of this regional division first in a general way, by discussing how it shaped spatial differences in the manifestation of ethnic traits. If one assumes that regionally structured contrasts in the internal colonialization of Wales provided Welshmen differentially with incentives for a favorable or even an imitative stance toward the English, then one can examine differences in the strength of ethnicity by looking at social positions across space in terms of their inherent vulnerability to anglicization. The consequences of anglicization for later mappings of ethnic identity are obvious, but many Welshmen seem not to have perceived these consequences in specifically *ethnic,* as opposed to socioeconomic, terms until fairly late in the game. They saw the learning of English, for example, as necessary to their economic advancement and as in no way a threat to their Welshness (Evans and Rhys 1968:246).

Vulnerability to anglicization is best analyzed through its variation temporally and spatially and by social class. Of all the Welsh regions, region 1 (the east) would historically have been the first victim to surrender to the lure of anglicization, through most time periods and for most of its population. Its terrain is mountainous, but several river valleys make it readily penetrable, 1b and southern 1a in particular. Although this area received fewer developmental investments than anywhere else in Wales, its easy access to English markets commercialized its agriculture earlier and more fully than elsewhere. Its relatively undifferentiated population circulated through English markets, mixed with English people (far more than with Welsh), oriented its economic structure to English demand and its values to English values, migrated seasonally for work in the English lowlands, and even moved there permanently. Moreover, although most of the land was rented, English markets induced agricultural specialization that proved a more prosperous livelihood than the mixed subsistence agricul-

[10] There are anomalies in this regionalization, which could no doubt be improved upon (see Olsen, Chapter 2, this volume, for a discussion of problems in regional identification). Some of the anomalies, such as subregions 3c and 3d, are discussed in the text. My decision to give them full subregional status entailed that I do the same with all the small coastal regions, for the sake of consistency. The grouping of subregions into larger regions could also have been done in more than one way. Pembrokeshire is difficult to place—as it seems to be in any discussion—for its English population and industrial development put it with region 2, but its agrarian northern and eastern portions place it with region 3. By grouping 3a and 3b and then treating Pembroke as the lowland urbanized center of region 3, I maintain consistency with my other groupings.

ture of the north and west. The people of region 1 thus benefited from the advantages of colonial peripherality without suffering the overt consequences of ethnic discrimination. While many retained Welsh features, they were among the least likely to participate in a Welsh reaction, and the region was in fact among the last to have Welsh Nationalist candidates stand for election in its counties (in 1962 and 1964).

Within region 1, 1b was the more advantaged subregion, having never experienced the investment and subsequent withdrawal of industrial inputs. But in 1a, early development of the wool industry gave way to neglect as the serendipitous construction of railways by-passed the area and killed off the nascent industry. This exposure to the spatial inequities of industrialism, plus the rougher terrain and more costly transport that reduced the profitability of commercialized agriculture, helps to account for the differences displayed by regions 1a (Montgomeryshire) and 1b (Radnorshire) on the ethnic maps.

Most of region 2 (except for its uppermost reaches) and the lowlands of region 5c followed region 1 in their vulnerability to English ways. The internal–colonial logic applied uniformly would predict greater co-optation here than in the remaining regions, but the internal diversity of population necessitates a more discriminating analysis. Industry was more advanced in region 2 than in any other part of Wales, as was population admixture with the English. The sectors of the Welsh populace most susceptible to anglicization were those who profited within the industrial system— through well-paid employment in industry or through well-situated farms that could provision urban markets. Spatially, these groups were probably concentrated in the agricultural lowlands, along the coasts, or in the mining centers. Temporally, their advantage crested in the mid-nineteeth century, at the height of industrial and population growth; after this, gradual cutbacks reduced many of them to more marginal positions, and continued changes in the transport networks altered the locational advantages of some farmers. Their allegiance to the English system would thus have begun to diminish.

Those least susceptible to anglicization in region 2 were the most disadvantaged within these same groups, living in upland valleys and regional peripheries: colliers and unskilled workers (often subject to ethnic or religious discrimination and always subject to layoffs) and, to a lesser extent, small farmers on marginal land, whose volatility would have been raised by any decline in market demand or any rerouting of transport. These groups were—and have remained—among the most unmoved by anglicization and most prone to reaction. The largest percentages of Welsh Nationalist voting ever recorded were in Glamorganshire in the upland coal-mining areas of Caerffili (40.4 percent in 1968) and West Rhondda (39.9 percent in 1967). Progressive social differentiation through time and the continual slowing of economic growth have increased the radicalization of these groups, many of whom responded through labor union activity. In any case, their interspersal in a varied population obscures their ethnic clout just as it buries their Welsh-speaking numbers (in 1971 Glamorgan contained 83,900 persons literate in Welsh, almost as many as the combined total—84,300—for the three counties with the highest rates, Anglesey, Merioneth, and Cardigan). Thus, although the weight of numbers puts region 2, with lowland 5c close behind it, squarely in the anglicizing camp through time, there have been and remain pockets of Welshmen highly predisposed toward ethnic reaction.

Region 3 (excepting Pembroke, whose large English population exempts it from much of what follows) contained somewhat greater homogeneity than region 2, and tendencies to "pass" into the English system existed mainly among the Welsh gentry and the more well-to-do farmers located in lowland valleys. Subregion 3a was notably more advantaged than 3b; although both had richer land than regions 4 and 5, 3a's proximity to industrializing centers gave it the benefits of provisioning urban markets, and its own coastal portion was moderately industrialized as well. The lowland parts of 3b had some provisioning functions, but more prevalent were subsistence agriculture and stock raising for export. Transport deficiencies and early withdrawal of investments from the small industries of 3b (primarily textiles with some mineral extraction and shipping) provided a basis for resistance to anglicization.

Throughout region 3, susceptibility was lower in the uplands among tenants and small independent farmers, whose landholdings dwindled as the wealthier consolidated ever larger estates; whose inferior social status was increasingly emphasized by the richer farmers as well as the gentry; and whose distance from transportation minimized the benefits of integration into urban-centered markets. Seasonal migration to southern industrial centers kept these uplanders well aware of the "uneven spread of industrialization through territorial space" (Hechter 1971:41) within their own peripheral system. Reaction among these less favored groups probably solidified by the early nineteenth century, when the investment pattern changed, and their divergence from the more favored groups widened steadily as southern growth augmented the opportunities for the latter while doing nothing for the former. Religious data underscore the existence of incentives toward anglicization for advantaged sectors: The religious population in all but two districts of the counties of Pembroke, Carmarthen, and Cardigan was over 19 percent Anglican; in seven of these districts (three in Carmarthen, four in Cardigan), 98.5 percent or more of the population is Welsh-born, indicating that Anglicanism was indeed an option taken by Welshmen.

The anomalous regions 3c and 3d were very peripheral to region 3. In

3c, the urban center of Aberystwyth, with its sizable English population and greater occupational differentiation than subregions south of it, introduced English influence atypical for the region's location. The dominant size of the town itself within the regional statistics has the effect of obscuring the Welshness of its regional hinterlands. Subregion 3d is unusual among western coastal regions because it opens into anglicized subregion 1a through a low pass, and in addition it was long administered as the westernmost extension of the county of Montgomery (one of the Norman lordships). Thus, it too exhibits Englishness atypical for its position.

Least vulnerable to anglicizing tendencies were region 4 and the uplands of 5. North Wales had industrial promise nearly equal to that of the south, and exploitation of mineral deposits had begun in parts of regions 4 and 5, financed almost exclusively by English capital. But the terrain was rough and transport costly; investments for improvement were stalled because the area was a dead end; increasingly, capital began to be diverted to the more accessible and profitable regions of the south. In the coastal lowlands of region 4, especially in minor port towns, there were a few positive incentives toward Englishness, with anglicization having maximum appeal in the English-centered lowlands of 5c. For most of regions 4 and 5, however, English penetration had few effects that were not short-lived, the "uneven spread of industrialization through territorial space" appeared more capricious and exploitative than anywhere else, and anglicization had, if anything, negative appeal. Westward and inland, region 4 and the uplands of 5 lapsed into subsistence agriculture, marginal to English markets or major urban centers, and nursing—in the view of some commentators—a special sense of injustice and violation (Emmett 1964; Williams 1950).

Long before the 1850s the roots of anti-English sentiment in this area had been sunk, and they had been nourished by perennial agricultural crises. But in these regions as in no others, there were pressures of a different sort that tended to inhibit the expression of anti-English feeling. In nineteenth-century Wales agricultural tenancy was widespread. I speculate, however, that the degree of control that the gentry exercised over their tenants varied in inverse relation to quality of the land, proximity to other means of securing a livelihood, and proximity to commercial centers for agricultural markets—in short, their control varied with economic structure both within and across regions. Where alternative employment existed, as in the lowlands of regions 5 and 2, threats of eviction were far less effective than where such alternatives were minimal (regions 4 and upland 5). Where successful export specialization (region 1) or the provisioning of urban centers (parts of region 3) made agriculture more viable than elsewhere, landlords were not pushed to maximum coercive extraction, and tenants were more secure in their tenure. Where land was of poor quality, tenure was less secure, and the probability of spiraling rents was greater. Where all of these coincided—poor land, distance from commercial markets, and minimal industrialization—as in most of regions 4 and 5, people were maximally under the thumb of landlords and were unlikely to risk voicing appeals to ethnic solidarity.

Throughout the nineteenth century, however, the power of the gentry steadily declined. Extensions of the franchise and reforms of local government undermined their political power; the depression and low agricultural prices diminished their economic profits; and the steady rise of industrial elites challenged their social hegemony. Many of them began selling land, thereby creating a nucleus of freeholders independent of landlords. These trends were occurring throughout Wales, but it was in the west and northwest that they were of greatest import, for it was there that the extended franchise and the unchaining of reactive sentiment was likely to be of greatest consequence. These populations doubtless formed the core of "peripheral sectionalism," oppressed by landlords who were themselves at the margin of their own life-style, located in the economic backwaters of their own regions and in the most disadvantaged portions of Wales as well.

In summary, within each region and subregion there were heterogeneous social groups differentially attracted by the beckon of anglicization, more so in some regions than others as wholes, and within each region more so in the lowland than the upland portions. Mappings of linguistic data (Maps 3 and 4) for 1891 and 1971 provide a visualization of my analysis so far. The maps plot the percentages of Welsh monoglots in the 1891 population and for 1971 the percentages of persons who speak, read, and write Welsh; in both cases, cuts were made at natural breaks in the data to form percentage categories. The data are mapped in their original census districts (solid lines) and are superimposed on regional divisions (dashed lines).[11] Irregularities in the patterns invite comment that limitations of space preclude; overall, the similarities in the two maps are striking. I add that the 1891 data on bilingualism (not mapped) strongly support my analysis of incentives for anglicization: Bilingualism is high (over 30

[11] The data for the 1891 map are presented as they are given in the 1891 British census units. For 1971, however, the data are given in urban and rural districts, the former of which would have been impossible to distinguish on a small-scale map. For all but Monmouth and Glamorgan, I derived percentages for rural districts and included the urban ones in the appropriate hinterland. For Glamorgan and Monmouth, I grouped districts that were adjacent and had roughly the same percentages. For this reason, the boundary lines drawn on Map 4 are not all recognizable to those who know the usual census units of Wales.

The actual percentages for these maps broke into groups as follows. For 1891, Welsh monolinguals 66 percent and over = category 1, 2 = 52–63 percent, 3 = 26–40 percent, and 4 = 0–24 percent. For 1971, percentages of active Welsh users are 1 = 56.7 percent and over, 2 = 41.1–54.5 percent, 3 = 20.1–39.4 percent, and 4 = 1.1–18.5 percent.

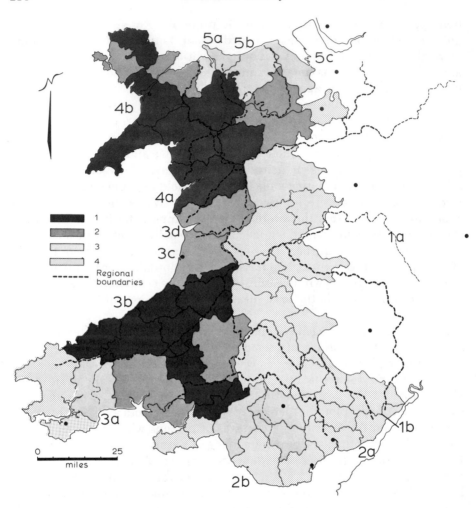

Map 3. 1891 distribution of the Welsh language. Percentage of monolingual Welsh in total population: 1 = 65 percent and over, 2 = 45–64 percent, 3 = 25–44 percent, and 4 = under 25 percent.

percent of the population) in nearly all of region 2, most of lowland 5, most of 3a, upland 2a (the lowland is high monoglot English), 3c, 3d, and the north of 1a—all areas where I hypothesized high or moderate anglicization.

The Spread of Sectarian Differences

The preceding discussion has explored the general consequences of regional structure for ethnicity. But because it is in social structures that

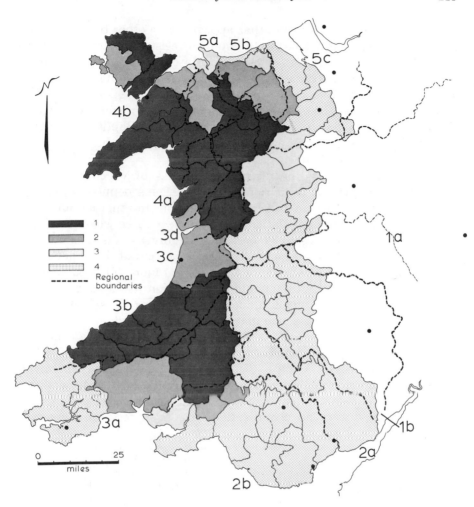

Map 4. 1971 distribution of the Welsh language. Percentage of population aged 3 and older who can read, write, and speak Welsh: 1 = 55 percent and over, 2 = 40–54 percent, 3 = 20–39 percent, and 4 = under 20 percent.

ethnicity is articulated and because I regard religious institutions as the social structure of greatest ethnic import for Wales, I now turn to religion and its spread throughout the Welsh regions. Much of what has already been said is applicable here, for conversion was the obverse of anglicization; but other aspects of the spread of denominations merit separate attention.

The best source of data on the division of the Welsh population into sects is the 1851 census of Great Britain, which included a special addendum on religious worship that appears at no other time.[12] Statistics given in 48 census districts for 13 counties register the total number of people present at all services on Sunday, March 31, 1851, for all religious denominations. From these statistics I derived a subtotal comprising Protestant denominations only and then calculated the percentage of this subtotal accounted for by each denomination's members—Anglican, Wesleyan and Calvinistic Methodist, Independent, Baptist, and various smaller sects.[13] Thresholds were set at natural breaks in the data, yielding a classification with four categories: Category 1 = districts where the largest denomination in the district (regardless of which sect it was) accounts for 50 percent or more of the churchgoing population; category 2 = districts where the two largest denominations together account for 62 percent or more of the population; category 3 = those where the largest three account for 75 percent or more; and category 4 = districts where the largest three sects do not encompass even 75 percent of the population. A fifth category is represented, where 45 percent or more of the population is Anglican, so as to verify the apparent progression in the eastern regions and across the border. I should underline that in my classification one of the two or three largest denominations could be—and in several cases was—Anglicanism. Map 5 shows the data arrayed within the census district boundaries; Map 6 interprets the data within the regional system, eliminating the heavily Anglican districts. (That is, I assume that any district total contains internal variations. This interpretive map analogizes from the overall patterns visible in Map 5 and reinterprets cases that were on the dividing lines of my classification, so as to suggest something closer

[12] This census was considered to have several limitations, which are discussed in Morgan (1963:12–13), but one assumes that the biases were uniform—for example, that Nonconformity was everywhere underenumerated in comparison with Anglicanism. The census gives other data besides the number of people present; it records the number of buildings and the number of locations for seating. I preferred to use the number of persons present because the other data could be skewed by differential *assets*.

[13] I eliminated Roman Catholics, Mormons, and Jews because their distribution correlates with English influence and they are irrelevant to the problem at hand. Ideally, I should also have eliminated Anglicans as well, but a cross-tabulation of percentage of Anglicans with percentage of Welsh-born in the population showed that although Anglicanism tended to correlate with lower-Welsh-born areas, there were several districts with high Welsh-born and high Anglicanism. This necessitated including Anglicans in the subtotals. Also, I might ideally have used *total* population rather than *churchgoing* population as my statistical base, for my final hypothesis would have little validity in an area monopolized by one sect if only 40 percent of the area's population went to church. The earlier elimination of non-Protestants argued aginst my using total population as the base. Furthermore, cross-tabulating the four-category classification with the ratio of churchgoing to total population showed that the ratio was high for nearly all of the one- and two-sect cases and that all the cases with a ratio lower than .75 were border counties with high dispersion among denominations. Thus, there is no reason to think that my use of the churchgoing population as a statistical base will have introduced distortions.

to what the actual distribution might have been. The shadings of Map 6 are merely suggestive and are not keyed precisely to those of Map 5.)

The principal conclusion suggested by Map 6 is that category 1 (50 percent or more of the population concentrated in a single sect) occurs largely along high-altitude watershed lines, or—if seen internally to each region—at the headwaters of river systems; and that category 4 (maximum dispersion across denominations) occurs largely in coastal low-lands. The size of each subregion and the degree of urbanization at its mouth correlate with the number of categorical "steps" through which one will pass in traveling from upriver toward the coast. A small region focusing on a minor center (3c, for example) contains few steps, moving from one denomination in the uplands to two or at most three along the coast; but a highly urbanized and diverse region may have greater denominational spread even at its upland peripheries, and dispersion increases as one moves downriver. This finding is independent of watershed altitudes. In all cases the *degree* of dispersion increases downriver, though the *number* of denominations at the headwaters and coast varies by the region.

Variables of regional position are fundamental to accounting for the religious distributions. Some regions as wholes were more susceptible than others to any sort of outside influence, and within each region the lowland portions were more accessible than the uplands. Because most Nonconformist proselytizing came to Wales via England, these differences in accessibility are important. Regions 1a and 1b were the most open, 5c less so because its river valleys are the narrowest of those that flow into England and were inhospitable to English settlement above the plain. Behind these rank the coastal portions of regions 2a, 2b, and the peninsular head of region 3; coastal 5a and 5b followed, again being centers of some English settlement. The entire western coast was outside the range of much English contact, ranging from greater susceptibility in the southwest to minimum influence in the north. The uplands of the northern regions were the most remote of all.

Within regions, variations in accessibility are linked to the relative urbanization of each area, Englishness always being associated with urban centers. Had the 1851 data been available by settlement rather than by district, I would expect the dispersion of denominations to reflect urban status. Religious data from 1971[14] show that with few exceptions the urban

---

[14] Colin Williams, of the Department of Geography at the University of Wales, Swansea, provided me with 1971 data from his own dissertation research, on the numbers of ministers of each sect for all census units. I have not mapped these data, partly because I do not wish to infringe upon his topic, which is similar to my own, and partly because the data are difficult to compare with my 1851 figures. But the detailed picture this information gave me about current religious behavior aided greatly in my conceptualization of my argument, and I gratefully acknowledge his generosity.

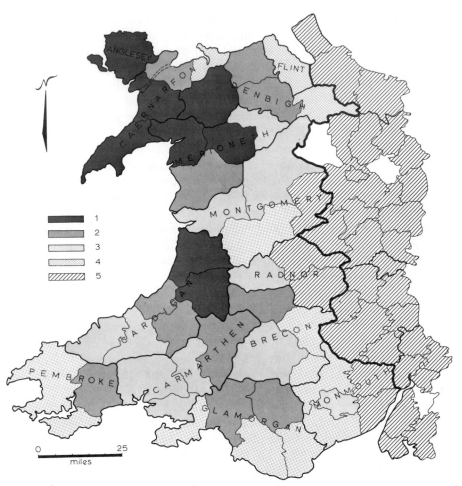

Map. 5. 1851 distribution of population among Protestant denominations. 1 = largest denomination accounts for 50 percent or more of religious population; 2 = two largest denominations together account for 62 percent or more of religious population; 3 = three largest denominations together account for 75 percent or more of religious population; 4 = three largest denominations together account for less than 75 percent of religious population; and 5 = 45 percent or more of religious population is Anglican. (Three unshaded counties on the English side of the border contain 38–44 percent Anglican population.)

districts contain a greater spread across denominations than do rural districts, independent of population size. The English, urban, and border associations of early Nonconformity should not, however, lead one to assume that it was an English population that was being attracted. The converse is proved by the marked growth of Nonconformity in the coalfields, which were overwhelmingly Welsh.

Further insight into the religious distributions emerges from details of the conversion process. Some of these details are specific to regional

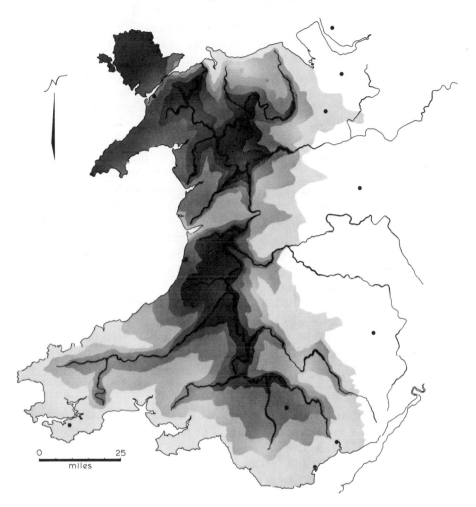

Map 6. 1851 interpretive map of religious data from Map 5. Darker shadings indicate that a large percentage of the population is in one (or two) denominations; lighter shadings indicate that the population is dispersed among several denominations. Width of the regional boundary lines is roughly proportional to altitude of the watershed, wide lines indicating high altitude and narrow lines indicating low.

contexts, while others are not—such as that in all areas Nonconformity came in waves and that nearly all the waves spread from the south, with new denominational successes coming in the wake of older ones. Also, as one might expect, "cultural movements took place principally along the increasingly numerous turnpike roads, by no means all of which followed the ancient valleys and upland ways [Sylvester 1969:186]." Thus, the same dendritic routes that siphoned off goods from the countryside also flushed cultural contact back through the system in the same nonintegrating fashion. Another nonspecific aspect of the routes followed by conversion was that in all regions, dissent probably spread up the valleys, as Jenkins's outline of Nonconformist progress in South Cardiganshire suggests: From its earliest centers in villages of the Teifi valley, dissent spread upward and outward, establishing branches in the valleys of streams tributary to the Teifi but leaving Anglicanism unchallenged beyond the watershed (Jenkins 1960:40).

But these references to watersheds and through-routes necessarily introduce the characteristics of specific regions. The marginality of region 4 and upland region 5 in terms of transport no doubt hindered conversion there. The greater productivity of regions 1, 2, and parts of 3 made for more and better roads there than in the north. To an extent, bad roads and difficult terrain might have inhibited the incursions of itinerant preachers who spread Nonconformity throughout Wales; but the high degree of competition among denominations seeking larger memberships reduces the probability that evangelistic ardor was cooled in proportion to altitude alone.

Other aspects of the interdenominational competition would, however, have caused regionally structured differences in evangelizing and thus in the number of sects present in any one area. All the sects, by virtue of their outlaw status, had no resources except for what they could muster from their local congregations. This meant that each was likely to concentrate its efforts among clustered populations, where the investment of energy would bring maximum returns, rather than in areas of sparse and dispersed settlement; and, further, more intensive efforts would be made in reasonably prosperous areas than in economically marginal ones. The necessities of recruitment therefore intersect with regional economic structure to suggest that regions with poorer land and minimal industry or agricultural commercialization—region 4, upland region 5, and upland region 3—would not have been barraged with religious enthusiasts, and the early successes of one sect in an area might indeed have inhibited the efforts of others [as Owen (1960:191) suggests for Merionethshire], who would have calculated the probability of diminishing returns and gone elsewhere.

These facts, combined with internal organizational differences among the sects, partially explain why it was the Calvinistic Methodists who took over the population in all 8 category-1 districts, most of them in mountainous terrain, and 7 of the 11 category-2 districts, spread through the north, east, and south. Of the denominations in full swing by 1800, only the Calvinists had a hierarchical structure that enabled the pooling and redistribution of resources controlled by the whole denomination; thus, no chapel had necessarily to be self-sustaining, and the threshold of diminishing returns could be set far higher than was possible for the Baptists and Independents. Furthermore, because most of upland Wales remained

Anglican through the first wave of revivals, when Baptists and Independents were making inroads into the rest of Wales, these upland areas constituted nearly virgin territory for the garnering of new resources by the Calvinists.

The sources do not specify why North Wales held to Anglicanism longer than did the south during the early revivals. Itinerant preachers of the earlier dissenting sects did travel through the north; they simply met with little success. Anglican clergymen roused their congregations against the itinerants, who were often driven off or stoned (Rees 1883:371). This reaction could not have been ethnically motivated (the itinerants were Welsh also), nor is it likely that the English origin of the sects poisoned the uplanders against them, for the sects had by this time established strong Welsh credentials. The most probable explanation is that the extreme dependence of the population on their Anglican proprietors, which I have already described in detail, restrained them from conversion. According to Hughes's analysis of the growth of Nonconformity in southern Caernarfonshire, "other Nonconformist denominations only entered our area in the wake of the Methodist success . . . [which had] gained a firm hold amongst the farmers and more especially among the freeholders of the western headland, who could afford to express non-traditional religious viewpoints openly without fear of retaliation [1940:165]." It was also true that workers on estates of the gentry were under obligation to attend the parish (Anglican) church (Hughes 1960:142).[15]

I have suggested that in the uplands of regions 4 and 5, the control of landlords over their tenants was at its strongest. The alliance between landlords and the Church makes it very unlikely that they were unconcerned about the spread of Nonconformity and did not perceive it as a threat to their positions; they probably exerted their influence to slow it, and they were most successful where their influence was greatest. It is my guess that one of the northern waves of Calvinistic Methodism, facilitated by its internal structure, coincided with the shift in the local balance of power that I have already explained; tenants as a result were less coerced by their landlords and less bound to Anglicanism, and they began to convert to that sect which was then active in their midst.

A final speculation on the causes of spatial differences in the dispersion of the populace among sects assumes that conversion *did* constitute a social statement by which one differentiated oneself from someone else. The number of social categories in the population should then relate to the variety of differentiating symbols—that is, the number of sects—that can be utilized. In areas where the principal cleavages were between gentry

---

[15] This sort of spiritual domination is not unknown even today: "In some parts of north Wales a man who has a farm to let in a district where he lives will make sure that his new tenant is a member of the same denomination as himself in order to improve the condition of his congregation (financially and otherwise) [Owen 1960:231]."

and agriculturists, other potential distinctions being underemphasized, there was little to be "said" socially through sectarian affiliation other than that one was nongentry. In the more occupationally varied urban centers, with their populations divided among skilled workers, laborers, foremen, employers, farmers, artisans, and others, larger numbers of denominations provided for greater subtlety in the social statements that could be made. This is another way of reading Owen's point that the early start of one sect sometimes impeded the progress of another, or Hughes's observation that the only elements of the population left, when Baptists and Independents returned to Caernarfon behind the Calvinistic Methodists, were the squatters and the destitute (1960:165). Throughout northern and western Wales, one finds all the denominations represented, but in any one area there are likely to be only two (C. C. Harris, personal communication)—enough for differentiation of the major social groups.

The Religious Mobilization of Ethnicity

Lest I be accused of having so cogently argued the determinative effects of regional physiographic and economic structure that I have obviated the need for my basic thesis—the relationship between variations in ethnic identity and the distribution of religious sects—I should now restate the point of this thesis and expand upon it. Some analysts might contend that social isolation adequately explains the retention of, for example, the Welsh language—although after more than 700 years of increasing contact with and penetration by England, whose border in places is only 50 miles from the Welsh coastline, it is surprising that Welsh persists at all. I have preferred to explain this in terms of regional structure and varying incentives toward anglicizing. But even this sort of explanation is inadequate to account for the organization of purposive, goal-directed ethnic action—or for the fact that learning Welsh is now, for some people, a political act. Having set my discussion of ethnicity and religion firmly in the context of regional systems, I add a special twist to account for the organization of ethnicity by arguing that Nonconformity supplied such an organization at a time when no other institution seemed qualified to do so. But what is the precise link between the spatial distribution of Nonconformity and variations in ethnic mobilization?

By deductive argument one can say that a population will be more effectively mobilized where it is divided among few competing denominations than where it is dispersed among many, for in the latter case unity may fall victim to denominational infighting. This concerns both the populace being mobilized and also the religious leaders, essential to consider in discussing unity in the context of religion, since denominational speciation nearly always resulted from doctrinal disputes among leaders (no doubt reinforced by personal politics), and further fragmentation often stemmed from disagreements between leaders of rival factions in a congregation. Monopoly by one denomination therefore means greater likelihood of unity among the religious elite; it also means that the sect's periodic supralocal events will draw together a larger proportion of the total population than would happen otherwise, thereby reinforcing overall denominational solidarity.

Thus, I hypothesize that the most effective ethnic mobilization will emerge where one Nonconformist sect monopolizes the allegiance of several adjacent areas;[16] where one denomination encompasses the majority in several areas but the monopoly denomination is not the same one for all areas (that is, the religious elite of a region is divided among sects), organization will be less effective; and where the denominational spread is very wide, with none claiming much greater support than the others, ethnic organization will be least effective. Furthermore, the strong hierarchical organization of Calvinistic and Wesleyan Methodists would seem better equipped to unify substantial numbers than would the atomistic Baptists and Independents; therefore, the strongest religious-based mobilization of all should occur where the Methodists dominate large areas.

Ideally, proof of the hypothesis would lie in comparing the religious maps with indicators of ethnic mobilization from the same period. People have noted that the tithe riots broke out mainly in North Wales, that two groups based in Bangor and Aberystwyth united to form the Young Wales movement, and that the Welsh Nationalist Party had its first headquarters in Caernarfon (see Map 1). But this information is not detailed enough, and data of the desired type do not exist. The best that can be done is to present recent voting statistics on the strength of the Welsh Nationalist Party. Map 7 shows the results of the 1970 general election, which are unfortunately aggregated into constituencies (usually whole counties except for the populous southern constituencies) and thus reduce the information for testing my predictions. Still, all but one of the category-1 religious districts are high in Welsh Nationalist voting, as are several of the category-2 districts, and high Welsh Nationalism coincides with Methodist monopolies in all but that one district. There is no case where areas of category 4 (great sectarian spread) are not also very low in Welsh Nationalist voting.

The principal anomalies on Map 7 are the very high degree of Welsh Nationalist voting in Carmarthen and the areas of northeast Glamorgan, which, although they contain areas that had few denominations in 1851,

[16] It might be objected that I have reversed the direction of causality, that a highly mobilized group will not split itself among many sects. Contrary evidence lies in the fact that of all the sects, Calvinistic Methodism—the one that dominates all the one-sect areas—was the *last* to radicalize and to serve as a spearhead of ethnic mobilization.

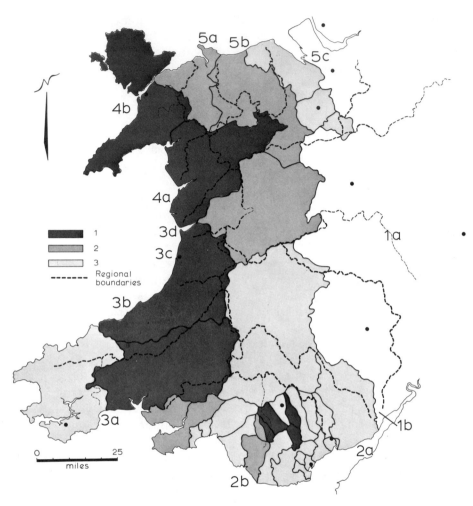

Map 7. 1970 ethnic mobilization. Percentage of the vote won by the Welsh Nationalist Party: 1 = 20 percent and over, 2 = 11–19 percent, and 3 = 10 percent and under.

have some economic characteristics that would have suggested lower ethnic reaction (see pages 209–213). I do not know—or have space to set out—all the details of local politics that might explain the voting patterns in these areas, but both of them illustrate my claim that ethnic mobilization, once achieved, becomes a generally available resource. In the region-4 and -5 counties of Merioneth and Caernarfon, Welsh Nationalists had over 10 percent of the vote as early as 1950, while the party was barely alive in many other areas; but special circumstances gave the first successful Welsh Nationalist candidacy to Carmarthen, in 1966.

The 120-year gap between the data arrayed on Maps 5 and 6 and Map 7 encourages me to refrain from further comment on the disparities. Dif-

ferences in local histories and political situations since the first mobilization of the Welsh in the nineteenth century make it impossible for the
maps to show perfect congruence. But patterns do stand out in these and
the linguistic maps, patterns also evident through time in other maps of
ethnic indicators.[17] It is my opinion that despite local changes within each
area, the spatial framework of these patterns was laid down by developments that created a regional structure still visible today. Had the
accompanying *temporal* framework been different—had the opposition of
those social groups and parts of regions which were maximally reactive to
anglicization been temporally synchronized, as the discussion on pages
209–213 indicates they were not—a more vigorous nationalist movement
might well have emerged.

The object of this exercise has been to show the explanatory power of a
strategy that begins with an a priori division of the countryside,
establishes the geographic and economic structure of the divisions, and
places other data within them. One advantage of the strategy is that it
provides a relatively fixed grid whose lattice has import for the play of
social phenomena upon it and to which these phenomena can be pegged in
charting their course through time. For the analysis of premodern social
systems in particular, a regional division based on topography, with its
strong implications for communication, transport, and the movement of
peoples, as well as for economic development, has perhaps the clearest
intuitive logic for investigating social phenomena. It is hoped that the
present excursion has pointed out a scenic spot or two on this analytical
terrain.

ACKNOWLEDGMENTS

I gratefully acknowledge helpful comments received on early drafts of this paper from
Jane F. Collier, Yvonne Hajda, Christopher C. Harris, Michael Hechter, Julia D. Howell,
Stephen M. Olsen, G. William Skinner, and Carol A. Smith. The final version benefits
greatly from Jane Collier's organizational and editorial skills, Stephen Olsen's help in interpreting the data, and Christopher Harris's and Colin Williams's provision of data that were
otherwise unavailable. I owe particular thanks to G. William Skinner for his assistance in the
manner of arraying the data and his many suggestions for improving the analysis. Katharine
Nigh drafted the maps, with funds generously provided by the Anthropology Department,
Stanford University.

REFERENCES

Barth, Fredrik (Ed.)
    1969 *Ethnic groups and boundaries.* Boston: Little, Brown.
Breton, Raymond
    1964 Institutional completeness of ethnic communities and the personal relations of
        immigrants. *American Journal of Sociology* **70**(2): 193–205.

[17] Other maps have been constructed by Carter and Thomas (1969), Jones and Griffiths
(1963), and Taylor (1973), among others.

Carter, H., and J. G. Thomas
    1969   The referendum on the Sunday opening of licensed premises in Wales as a criterion
           of a culture region. *Regional Studies* **3**(1): 61–71.
Charsley, S. R.
    1974   The formation of ethnic groups. In *Urban ethnicity,* edited by Abner Cohen.
           London: Tavistock. Pp. 337–368.
Coupland, Sir Reginald
    1954   *Welsh and Scottish nationalism: A study.* London: Collins.
Davies, Christopher S.
    1972   A classification of Welsh regions. In *Man, space, and environment: Concepts in
           contemporary human geography,* edited by P. W. English and R. C. Mayfield. New
           York: Oxford Univ. Press. Pp. 481–498.
Davies, E. T.
    1965   *Religion in the industrial revolution in South Wales.* Cardiff: Univ. of Wales Press.
Davies, Morgan L.
    1970   A small town community in mid Wales: An introductory study. In *Urban essays:
           Studies in the geography of Wales,* edited by M. Carter and W. K. D. Davies.
           London: Longmans, Green. Pp. 177–192.
Dunbabin, J. P. D.
    1974   *Rural discontent in nineteenth century Britain.* London: Faber and Faber.
Emmett, Isabel
    1964   *A North Wales village: A social anthropological study.* London: Routledge and
           Kegan Paul.
Evans, Gwynfor, and Ioan Rhys
    1968   Wales. In *Celtic nationalism,* edited by O. D. Edwards, G. Evans, I. Rhys, and H.
           McDiarmid. New York: Barnes and Noble. Pp. 211–298.
Frankenberg, Ronald
    1957   *Village on the border: A social study of religion, politics, and football in a North
           Wales community.* London: Cohen and West.
Gonzalez Casanova, Pablo
    1965   Internal colonialism and national development. *Studies in Comparative Interna-
           tional Development* **1**(4): 27–37.
Harris, Christopher C.
    1963   Church, chapels, and the Welsh. *New Society* **1**(21): 18–20.
Hechter, Michael
    1971   Towards a theory of ethnic change. *Politics and Society* **2**(1): 21–45.
    1973   The persistence of regionalism in the British Isles, 1885–1966. *American Journal of
           Sociology* **79**(2): 319–342.
    1974   The political economy of ethnic change. *American Journal of Sociology* **79**(5):
           1151–1178.
    1975   *Internal colonialism: The Celtic fringe in British national development, 1536–1966.*
           Berkeley: Univ. of California Press.
Hughes, T. Jones
    1960   Aberdaron: The social geography of a small region in the Llyn Peninsula. In *Welsh
           rural communities,* edited by E. Davies and A. D. Rees. Cardiff: Univ. of Wales
           Press. Pp. 119–181.
Jenkins, David
    1960   Aberporth: A study of a coastal village in South Cardiganshire. In *Welsh rural
           communities,* edited by E. Davies and A. D. Rees. Cardiff: Univ. of Wales Press.
           Pp. 1–63.
    1971   *The agricultural community in south-west Wales at the turn of the twentieth
           century.* Cardiff: Univ. of Wales Press.

Jones, David J. V.
    1973 *Before Rebecca: Popular protests in Wales, 1793 1835.* London: Allen Lane.
Jones, Emrys
    1960 Tregaron: The sociology of a market town in central Cardiganshire. In *Welsh rural communities,* edited by E. Davies and A. D. Rees. Cardiff: Univ. of Wales Press. Pp. 65–117.
Jones, Emrys, and Ieuan L. Griffiths
    1963 A linguistic map of Wales: 1961. *The Geographical Journal* **129**(2): 192–196.
Jones Pierce, T.
    1972 *Medieval Welsh society: Selected essays.* Cardiff: Univ. of Wales Press.
Leach, E. R.
    1954 *Political systems of highland Burma.* Boston: Beacon Press.
Morgan, Kenneth O.
    1963 *Wales in British politics, 1868–1922.* Cardiff: Univ. of Wales Press.
Owen, Trefor M.
    1960 Chapel and community in Glan-llyn, Merioneth. In *Welsh rural communities,* edited by E. Davies and A. D. Rees. Cardiff: Univ. of Wales Press. Pp. 185–248.
Pierce, G. O.
    1960 Nonconformity and politics. In *Wales through the ages,* Vol. 2, edited by A. J. Roderick. London: Christopher Davies. Pp. 168–176.
Pool, Kathleen
    1971 Welsh and Irish nationalism in the nineteenth century: A comparative study. Unpublished B.A. thesis, Reed College.
Rees, Alwyn D.
    1950 *Life in a Welsh country side: A social study of Llanfihangel yng Ngwynfa.* Cardiff: Univ. of Wales Press.
Rees, Thomas
    1883 *History of Protestant Nonconformity in Wales.* (2nd ed.) London: Snow.
Skinner, G. William
    1964 Marketing and social structure in rural China: Part I. *Journal of Asian Studies* **24**(1): 3–43.
Stavenhagen, Rodolpho
    1965 Classes, colonialism, and acculturation: Essay on a system of inter-ethnic relations in Mesoamerica. *Studies in Comparative International Development* **1**(6): 53–77.
Sylvester, Dorothy
    1969 *The rural landscape of the Welsh borderland: A study in historical geography.* New York: Macmillan.
Taylor, Alan
    1973 The electoral geography of Welsh and Scottish nationalism. *Scottish Geographical Magazine* **89**: 44–52.
Vallee, Frank G.
    1969 Regionalism and ethnicity: The French-Canadian case. In *Perspectives on regions and regionalism,* edited by B. Y. Card. Edmonton: Western Association of Sociology and Anthropology. Pp. 19–25.
Williams, David
    1950 *A history of modern Wales.* London: Murray.

Chapter 9

Javanese Religious Orientations in the Residency of Surakarta

Julia Day Howell
Stanford University

This paper explores the possibility of accounting for the spatial distribution of Javanese religious orientations in the Residency of Surakarta, Central Java, by the action of regional system variables. It reports and interprets the tentative conclusions that, in two of six regencies of the Residency for which religious orientation data are already available, the regional systems variables—administrative centrality, presence and type of plantations, and transport—are diagnostic. In addition, the performance of the national parties within constituencies of a given value orientation is shown to vary across the region according to the administrative centrality of the local places. If the regional systems variables indeed prove diagnostic in the manner described for the entire Residency when the data become available, the regional systems approach will have expanded and clarified the sociology of Javanese religious orientations and their role in political mobilization.

The importance of volcano-rimmed watersheds as locales for the ecological adaptation of the ancient kingdoms in Java has long been recognized.[1] Basins cultivated with wet rice and fertilized by the gently

---

[1] See Schrieke's documentation of the social definition of physiographic regions of Java from the period of the ancient kingdoms to the nineteenth century. Schrieke argued that political integration of Java beyond these physiographic regions continually disintegrated under conditions of traditional transport and communications technology (1957:102–105).

flowing mineral-rich water from surrounding volcanic peaks supported the Indic kingdoms of Java from the seventh century. Kingdoms located on the treacherous flood plain of Java's north coast and financed by the growing trade of the Java Sea, gained ascendancy over the inland Indic agrarian kingdoms in the sixteenth century. The coastal kings became, like their trading contacts, Muslims, and their coastal sultanates became centers for the diffusion of Islam into the interior of Java. Despite the conversion of the defeated Indic kingdoms of the interior to Islam, the courts of the interior kingdoms have perpetuated Hindu–Buddhist culture to the present day. Islamic institutions remained the religious foci of the north coast following the surrender of the coastal sultanates to the inland kingdom of Mataram. The commercial tradition of the north coast also survived the demise of the sultanates. Small-scale, Javanese-controlled industries and an integrated system of peddler trading based in the north flourished throughout the colonial period and still overshadowed commercial development of the interior in the early republican period (Geertz 1965:89).

Characterization of the social landscape of Java has drawn on the distinction between insular zones: the Islamic coasts and the Hindu–Buddhistic interior (Geertz 1963). On the local level, analysis of a single rural town and its hinterland has associated occupations with religious orientations: petty entrepreneurial activity with a strict Islamic orientation, and peasant agriculture and bureaucratic service with a syncretic Islam in which Hindu, Buddhist and autochthonous traditions are salient (Geertz 1965).

Historical evidence indicates that physiographic regions within the insular zones have been significant units of social integration because of the limits that natural boundaries imposed upon political integration of the traditional kingdoms.[2] But the continuing significance of natural regions as units of contemporary sociological analysis has not been investigated. Transportation prior to the twentieth century was primarily by waterways, and the palaces of the interior kingdoms were located at the center of the basin floors for optimal access to the rice lands, which were the mainstay of the traditional economy of the interior. Hence, the watersheds of river headwaters tended to define administrative regions,[3] with the capital cities of the kingdoms, and later of the Dutch and republican residencies, as coincidental administrative and transport

---

[2] See Schrieke (1957:102–105). Schrieke records the boundaries of natural regions in both the interior and coastal zones of pre-twentieth-century Java. The following remarks apply only to regions of the interior. Patterns of social integration in the coastal zone, as suggested in my concluding remarks, differ from those of the interior.

[3] That is, the negara agung ("the greater capital"). Beyond this administrative sphere was "foreign land" (the mantjanegara), which was "too far off from the center of the kingdom to be included as an integral part of the state" (Selosoemardjan 1962:25–27).

nodes. One might expect the distribution of cultural orientations to be related to regional systems of social integration that have themselves been shaped by physiography.

Moreover, if ecological variation is significantly related to cultural orientations and their political expression on the zonal level of analysis, one might also expect the regular ecological variations within the interior basins to shape the distribution of cultural orientations in these regions. The interior volcanic basins are comprised of several ecological zones. The warm, well-watered basin centers support cultivation of commercially valuable annual crops: irrigated rice, grown by small holders, and sugar, grown on the same land by plantations through rental agreements. At higher altitudes on the volcano slopes, lower temperatures limit the growing season for rice, and in the limestone hills insufficient water supplies and precipitous topography preclude sugar cultivation. Higher yet, the chilly slopes that approach the volcano peaks support cultivation of perennial cash crops such as coffee and rubber, both in plantations and on small holdings.

THE EMPIRICAL SETTING:
THE RESIDENCY OF SURAKARTA

The Residency of Surakarta, a middle-level administrative unit, corresponds closely to a natural physiographic region, the watershed of the upper Solo River. The upper Solo River watershed is formed by volcanoes on the east and west and by low limestone hills to the north and south. The upper Solo River drains to the northeast, where it merges with waters flowing from the volcanic basin of Madiun. The southeastern valley of the Solo watershed adjoins the basin of the Opak and Progo Rivers, which roughly coincides with the Special District of Yogyakarta.

The Progo–Opak watershed had been the site of the ancient Hindu kingdom of Mataram in the eighth century. Again in the sixteenth century the latter-day kingdom of Mataram, then avowedly Islamic, rose to prominence in the upper Solo River watershed. Its capital city was located in Kartasura, several miles from the present-day city of Surakarta, to which the palace of Mataram was shifted in 1742. The inner kingdom[4] of Mataram extended beyond the Solo watershed to include the Progo–Opak watershed, the site of ancient Mataram. When the kingdom of Mataram was divided in 1755, holdings of the king of Surakarta in the Progo–Opak basin were awarded the new sultan of Yogyakarta. The present-day Residency of Surakarta and Special District of Yogyakarta subsume the territories of the former princedoms and correspond roughly to the natural regions of the two basins. Thus, in addition to the close coincidence of the

[4] That is, the *negara agung*. (See Moertono 1963: Map 1.)

bounds of the natural physiographic region with the present borders of the
Residency, there is considerable historical continuity of the basin as a
socially significant administrative unit across the past two centuries and
as a natural stage for political development throughout the history of
Central Java.

While the Residency of Surakarta as an administrative region has had a
stable node and boundary since the nineteenth century, the transport
channels of the area have been altered by the development of land
transport in the twentieth century. Roads,[5] some of which followed
waterways and some of which did not, have facilitated the movement of
goods and communications to and from the Residency capital, intensifying
exchange at the established node of the region. But road development has
also increased the permeability of the region's physical boundaries at
points other than the river valley exits, thereby facilitating communication
with regions neighboring on mountainous borders.

Because Surakarta has considerable historical continuity as a socially
defined region, it is a suitable area in which to test the proposition that
regional systems of integration affect the distribution of cultural–religious
orientations. At the same time, changes in the systems of integration
within the Surakarta region invite a dynamic interpretation of the present
distribution of cultural–religious orientations.

THE DATA BASE AND DEFINITION
OF VARIABLES

The areas to which data on cultural–religious orientations pertain span
the Residency of Surakarta like pieces of pie cut by people sitting at
opposite ends of a table: They are two of the five regencies that fan out
from the City of Surakarta, capital of the Residency. One, Karanganyar,
consisting of 17 subdistricts, spreads out eastward from the capital city
and banks of the Solo River to the peak of the volcano Mt. Lawu. The
other regency, Boyolali, consisting of 19 subdistricts, runs westward from
the Residency capital up the slopes of the twin volcanoes Mt. Merapi and
Mt. Merbabu and northward to low rolling hills. A sixth regency lies to the
south, bordering on two more northerly pie-wedge neighbors.

Map 1 shows the correspondence between the upper watershed of the
Solo River and the Residency of Surakarta. The map shows how the
northern extremity of the Residency's northwesterly regency, Boyolali, lies
outside the Solo watershed. It also shows how the southerly tip of the

---

[5] The routes of the present major roads in Surakarta existed at least from the seventeenth
century. However, the routes were only cleared for passage of vehicles upon the occasion of
"processions, court progresses, and expeditions" (Schrieke 1957:112). Trade was carried on
by waterways.

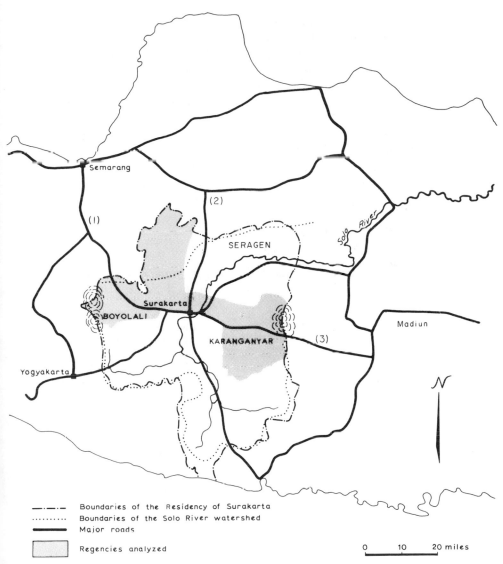

Map 1. The region of Surakarta.

Residency falls outside the watershed where a jumble of calcareous hills abuts the Indian Ocean.

Regional Systems Variables

The analysis distinguishes regional variables of two types: systems of social integration (administration and transport) and systems of ecology that are relevant to commercial agriculture. It also distinguishes periods in which the structure of the transport system differed. Thus, the regional

systems variables tested include: the administrative system;[6] the water
transport system (that is, traditional, pre-twentieth century transport), as
measured by relative access to navigable and partially navigable
waterways within the upper Solo River watershed; the land transport
system[7] as it was in the late colonial period (1930s) and in the early
postcolonial years (1950s); and the ecosystem, as summarized in a
"plantation" variable.[8] Degrees of centrality and peripherality were
specified for all of the regional systems variables except the plantation
variable, which was marked for presence of tree plantations, sugar plantations, or no plantations. Each subdistrict was assigned a centrality-
peripherality score for each of the regional systems variables.

Cultural-Religious Orientations and
Party Performance Variables

Strict Islamic versus Javanistic Orientation

Those who punctuate their daily lives with Islamic religious practices
(the *santri*) have consistently associated with the Islamic political organi-

---

[6] The administrative centrality variable measures distance from a given subdistrict to the
Residency capital in terms of the number of other subdistricts that must be transversed by
road or railway to reach the capital. An initial test of administrative centrality with respect
to the regency capitals showed no relationship with religious orientation, so the variable was
discarded.

[7] The land transport variable reflects degrees of access to rail and road routes connecting
the Surakarta region to major and minor centers outside the region. A score was assigned to
each subdistrict according to the number of branches off a main transport artery that one
must follow to reach the subdistrict. This score was weighted by ranking the main transport
routes according to their relative importance as connectors with major versus minor centers.
So, for example, route 1 (see Map 1) from Surakarta through the regency of Boyolali to
Semarang, the capital of Central Java, was rated as a more important route than route 3 (on
Map 1), which connects Surakarta through Karanganyar with Madiun, a residency capital in
East Java. Road 2 from Surakarta north through Seragen to the provincial capital of Semarang was rated as a better route than route 3 because of its more bustling destination, but not
as good as route 1 because of the circuitous route it follows, its poor condition, and its consequent light traffic. The transport variable was also weighted for distance from Surakarta to
the point of access to the main road from the various subdistricts.

[8] The plantation variable reflects the presence or absence of plantations in each subdistrict
and the type of plantation. Areas in which sugar plantations are located do not sustain the
other types of plantations (tea, coffee, and rubber) common to the Residency because of
constraints of efficiency of land use and growing conditions. The sugar plantations are
located in the rich, well-watered lowlands—the bowl of the volcano-rimmed Solo watershed—
and the tree plantations are located on the mountain slopes (coffee and tea) or on the low rolling and drier northern hills (rubber). The distinction between tree plantations and sugar
plantations connotes differences not only in agriculture but also in the organization of labor
and rights to land. Sugar plantations use rice land rented under duress from peasant farmers
on a rotating basis (after one crop is harvested, planting is moved to a neighboring area). The
peasant owner is, in turn, forced rentier and laborer and then independent operator. Tree
plantations, which require a span of many years to produce, are enclaves of large holdings
upon which the peasant may seek supplemental wage work, but they do not infringe upon the
small holders, from whose operations the tree plantation operations are entirely separate.

zations, and those who orient their lives around Indic–autochthonous traditions and values (the *abangan*) have consistently associated with secular political organizations. From this, Geertz (1959) posited culturally defined constituencies called *alirans*—literally, "streams"—underlying affiliations with the parties and persistent over time.[9] The association between cultural–religious orientation and political affiliation makes feasible the use of election statistics as indices of the relative strength of religious orientations.

While the strict Islamic and Javanist orientations are strongly associated with political alignments, they are not clearly reflected in acknowledgment of religion. The Central Bureau of Statistics figures for 1969 show that 95.8 percent of the population of Java and Madura (geographical areas that include the Javanese culture area and two other more strongly Islamic culture areas) acknowledge Islam (Biro Pusat Statistik 1969:62). However, not all people who acknowledge Islam in the official context of the census vote for Islamic parties[10] or bestir themselves to carry out the duties of a strict Muslim, such as praying five times a day, attending public prayers at a prayer house or mosque on Fridays, and refraining from eating pork. Those who do not are presumably much the same people who would be identified by themselves or neighbors as Javanist (*abangan*).[11] Voting for political parties rather than acknowledgment of religion, then, has been taken as an index of cultural–religious orientations, because of the availability of voting data and because of its stronger association with observed differences in everyday behavior.

[9] Benda (1958: Part I) has discussed the historical background of the differentiation of Javanese religious traditions into the strict and syncretist variants of Islam. Both Jay (1963) and Geertz (1965) have documented the preference of nominal Muslims for the Muslim parties in rural East Java. Jay showed the stability of the *aliran* over time in both the ethnically Javanese provinces of Java, using Feith's (1957) comparison of 1955 and 1956 election statistics and newspaper reports of the 1957 elections. Feith's data showed the constancy of the total vote of the major Muslim and the major secular parties in the regencies of Central and East Java between 1955 and 1956. Jay's comparison of the 1957 election results with those of 1955 showed that changes in party support occurred "almost entirely" from one major secular party to another secular party (from the Nationalist to the Communist Party) or from one major Muslim party to another Muslim party (from Masjumi to NU) (1963:30).

[10] Muslim parties won only a quarter of the votes cast in the 1971 general election, nationwide (Liddle 1973:293), and 43 percent of the votes, nationwide, in the 1955 general election. The Muslim party vote in the 1955 election in Java alone was 37 percent of the total, and in the Residency of Surakarta, 13.0 percent of the total votes (based on Alfian 1971:81–86).

[11] The use of the term *abangan* as one of identification applies more especially to peasants and workers (and perhaps also to well-read intellectuals); however, one is hesitant to apply the term to higher-status Javanese as one of personal identification because of its lower-class connotation. It is proper to say that many higher-status Javanese share the *abangan* orientation (which may be phrased by those individuals as *kejawen*—"Javanese"). Geertz (1960) calls the Hindu–Javanese-oriented aristocratic and bureaucratic upper classes the *priyayi* and distinguishes the *priyayi* "religion" from that of the peasant Hindu–Javanese *abangan* "religion." However, the term *priyayi* is probably better reserved to indicate upper-class position of whatever religious orientation.

The analysis reported here is based on election statistics for the 1971 general election. Voters had a choice of four Muslim parties, two Christian parties, three secular parties, and the government quasi-party, GOLKAR (hereafter referred to simply as a secular party also). Votes for the two Muslim parties Nahdatul Ulama (NU) and the Partai Muslimin Indonesia (PARMUSI), which together won 97.1 percent of the total Muslim party vote in the regencies analyzed (or 21.5 percent of the total vote in the two regencies), were taken as indications of strict Islamic (or *santri*) orientation. Votes for the two secular parties that together won 99.5 percent of the secular party votes in the two regencies (76.8 percent of the total vote for the two regencies) were taken as indicators of Javanist (or *abangan*) orientation.[12]

To summarize the association of religious orientations with parties, Geertz's formula for *alirans* in the 1950s can be updated with the substitution of "PARMUSI" for "MASJUMI" (Islamic reform parties, new and old), and "GOLKAR" for "PKI" (New Order mass organization for a defeated major party of the Old Order), as follows:

> After a . . . [Javanese] said he was an Indonesian and a *santri* [strict Muslim], he was next quite likely to say that he belonged to . . . or leaned toward . . . either MASJUMI [read "PARMUSI"] or Nahdatul Ulama; after he said he was an Indonesian and an *abangan* [Javanist], that he leaned toward PNI or PKI [read "GOLKAR"] [Geertz 1965:128].

(See also Table 1.)

[12] The four Muslim parties are Nahdatul Ulama (NU), the "Muslim Notables Party" Partai Muslimin Indonesia (PARMUSI), the "Indonesian Muslim Party"—heir to the banned MASJUMI; Pergerakan Tarbiyah Islamiyah (PERTI); and Partai Sarikat Islam Indonesia (PSII). PERTI and PSII are minor parties, which in the regencies analyzed took only .14 percent of the total vote as compared with 10.2 percent won by PARMUSI and 11.3 percent won by NU. Votes for the minor parties have been omitted from the analysis. The three secular parties are Partai Nasional Indonesia (PNI), the "Indonesian Nationalist Party"; MURBA; and the Ikatan Pendukung Kemerdekaan Indonesia (IPKI), "Upholders of Indonesian Independence." MURBA and IPKI are minor parties taking only .4 percent of the vote in the two regencies in comparison to the Nationalist Party's 35.4 percent. The Nationalist Party, while ideologically defining itself primarily in terms of nationalism and socialism at the national level, has represented Javanist interests at the local level in ethnically Javanese areas.

Voting for GOLKAR, the government-organized "alternative to the party system," is also treated here as indicating Javanist, or *abangan,* orientation. The association is not as direct as that of the Muslim parties with strict Muslims (*santris*) or Nationalists with Javanists, but it is based on the following considerations: Although GOLKAR was established as an alternative to all the parties, the leadership of GOLKAR has been, if anything, more overtly Javanist in its private behavior and in its public support for Javanist interests than the leadership of the old Sukarno regime and Nationalist party. Moreover, GOLKAR aggressively sought the votes of those former Communist Party sympathizers who were still or again physically and socially active after the destruction of the Communist Party in 1965, lest this predominantly Javanist group give its support to the Nationalist Party. GOLKAR won 41.4 percent of the total vote in the two regencies.

TABLE 1
Conceptualization of Orientations and Political Parties
==

Orientation		Party Affiliation	
English gloss	*Indonesian terms*	*1971*	*1955*
(strict) Islamic or (strict) Muslim	*santri*	Nahdatul Ulama (NU) PARMUSI a	Nahdatul Ulama (NU) MASJUMI b
Javanist or Indic-autochthonous	*abangan*	Indonesian Nationalist Party (PNI) GOLKAR a	Indonesian Nationalist Party (PNI) Indonesian Communist Party (PKI) b

a. *Plus two minor parties.*
b. *Plus numerous minor parties.*

Political Party Performance Variables

An additional "performance" variable measures the relative strength of the two major Muslim parties among the Muslim constituency and the relative strength of the two major secular parties among the Javanist constituency. (1) For each subdistrict, the fraction of votes for the modernist Muslim party, PARMUSI, out of the total votes for both major Muslim parties, represents the strength of the modernist Muslim orientation in comparison with the strength of traditionalist Muslim orientation among the Muslim constituency. (2) Again, for each subdistrict, the fraction of votes for the secular Nationalist Party, out of the total votes for both major secular parties, represents the strength of the Nationalist Party as opposed to GOLKAR among the Javanist constituencies.

HYPOTHESIZED RELATIONSHIPS

For the sake of framing hypotheses concerning the distribution of cultural–religious orientations and their relations to regional systems variables, historical periods of development of each of these orientations are distinguished.

The Religious Orientations Variable

Since Indic culture in Java dates from at least the fifth century, a synthesis of Hindu, Buddhist,[13] and autochthonous culture had been diffused across the entire social landscape of Java by the time the kings of the interior converted to Islam. Islam, which was practiced by enclaves of foreign traders in Indonesia from perhaps the eleventh century, but which was widely propagated only after the rise of the trading sultanates of the north coast in the fifteenth century, has penetrated the landscape of the interior less thoroughly than the Indic religions.[14] Hence, it was hypothesized that the present-day distribution of cultural–religious orientations in Surakarta can be attributed to the premodern systems of communication and control that structured the diffusion of cultural–religious influences across the region.

Since the strict practice of Islam has been associated in Java with the trading and merchant class, it was expected that the distribution of the strict Islamic orientation would be associated with premodern commercial transport networks—the waterways. It was expected that the strict Islamic orientation would be weakest at the rim of the watershed, where access to Surakarta, the commercial center of the region, was poorest.

However, because the commercial center of the region with its large Muslim community of merchants and mosque officials was also the administrative center of the region, Islamic influences radiating from the capital also competed with the Indic–cultural influences from the courts. Thus, in those areas nearest Surakarta a more even mix of Javanist and strict Muslim orientations was expected. A map of the expected distribution of cultural–religious orientations would thus show a fringe of Javanist areas at the rim of the watershed (nearly untouched, or at least little changed, by post-sixteenth-century Islamic influences) and a variegated landscape of Javanist and strict Muslim orientations in areas more central to the capital.

The Political Party
Performance Variables

The performance variables were introduced to measure the success of the parties of the same religious orientation in competition with each other

[13] Of the foreign religious traditions, Hinduism was the more intimately integrated into autochthonous culture. Both Hindu and Tantric Buddhist cults were fostered by the later pre-Islamic kingdoms. However, Buddhism was never widely popular outside the courts. (See Pigeaud 1962:480; Stöhr and Zoetmulder 1965:238.)

[14] In some areas Islamic influences have been so slight that these remote places are spoken of as never having been Islamicized. In the Residency of Surakarta, for example, parts of the subdistrict Jenawi, high on the slopes of Mt. Lawu, are reputedly budo (of the ancient religion); these are areas of recent conversion to Hinduism. In the mountains of East Java there is an ethnic enclave, the Tengger—Javanese who were never Islamicized. The Tengger perpetuate the Indic–autochthonous traditions of the former Hindu-Buddhist kingdom of Majapahit. The Tengger today acknowledge Hinduism and Buddhism.

for support from their religious constituency. Although differences between strict Muslim and Javanist villagers had been politically significant in rural life prior to the twentieth century, it was not until the 1920s, when the nationalist and reform movements began to involve peasants in formal social organizations, that rural Javanese began to distinguish varieties of Javanist and Muslim programs. In the context of electoral politics since independence the rural population has been encouraged to choose between a variety of Muslim stances and secular political philosophies. The early patterns of differentiation of the Javanist and strict Muslim communities around party organizations have, however, been at least partially obscured. The concentration of party strength in certain regional and ecological zones prior to 1965 was blurred by the elimination of one of the major contestants among both the secular and the strict Muslim parties; MASJUMI, which was more popular among successful urbanites and farmer entrepreneurs, was suppressed in 1960. The Communist Party, which also was strong in urban areas, as well as in very poor farming areas and among plantation workers, was eliminated after 1965. Both the new parties—PARMUSI and GOLKAR— had to reach the rural voters who were likely to have migrated in sympathy toward the remaining established parties: the Nationalist Party and the NU. It was thus hypothesized that the performance variables measure ephemeral electoral processes—the use of contemporary systems of social integration to mobilize support within one or the other cultural orientation constituency— rather than the longer-range differentiation and consolidation of party-articulated interest groups in ecologically hospitable regional niches.

It was expected, therefore, that the performance of those parties which have had recent influence in the administrative system—the secular parties—would be correlated with administrative centrality. Since the government issued a directive that civil servants must support the government quasi-party, GOLKAR, the strength of the Nationalist Party, which previously predominated in the civil service,[15] was eroded. One might expect this erosion of Nationalist strength to be greatest in administratively central areas (that is, in areas most vulnerable to government control). GOLKAR should be strongest in areas centrally located within the residency administrative network and gradually give way before entrenched Nationalist strength in more remote areas.

Strict Muslim influence in the civil service has been confined to the Department of Religion, which has branches down to the subdistrict level. Up to the election year the traditionalist Muslims held most important posts in the department. This would lead to the supposition that traditionalist Muslim influence would be strongest at the regional node of the administrative network. However, the traditionalist Muslim party has

---

[15] Prior to 1965, Communists as well as Nationalists were prominent in the civil service of Surakarta. The Communists were, however, removed from their posts after the Suharto regime came to power in October 1965.

been the political vehicle of the rural Muslim notables (the *kiyais*), whose influence did not derive from government office and who were not coordinated primarily through bureaucratic channels. Thus, within a regional system the hypothetical effect of traditionalist Muslim influence in the bureaucracy (greater influence at the center of the bureaucratic network than at the periphery) should be balanced—and thus obscured—by the influence of independent traditionalist Muslim leaders in more peripheral areas.

Modernist Muslim leadership, on the other hand, has come primarily from urban intellectuals,[16] and modernist influence has been extended to rural areas through private modernist organizations: the political party, voluntary associations, and affiliated schools and hospitals. In the Residency of Surakarta in 1955, voting for the old modernist Muslim party MASJUMI (of local origin) was actually heavier than that for the traditionalist Muslim party, NU (based in East Java and new in Central Java). However, in the years after MASJUMI was banned, it was the social organizations that channeled modernist Muslim activities. Thus, although modernists once had a network of party branches in rural Surakarta, that network was no longer intact when PARMUSI, under new leadership, began its campaign. The modernist social organizations provided the single existing network available to PARMUSI in the advent of the 1971 election. Since these modernist organizations have been concentrated in and near urban areas, it was hypothesized that the PARMUSI would be more successful than the traditionalist NU among Muslims in central areas. Further, it was expected that this performance distribution would be related to the measure of recent transport (road and rail) centrality that might reflect the relative strength of urban influences.

The analysis, then, seeks to identify not only mechanisms relevant to the diffusion and social acceptability of cultural practices at various locations in regional systems, but also mechanisms relevant to mobilizing support for organizations that articulate the various cultural orientations— that is, in which regional systems and at what locations in those systems are local communities both accessible and vulnerable to particular kinds of cultural and political communications. Further, the orientation variable and the performance variables measure the results of processes begun in

[16] In the 1955 general election the modernist Muslim party MASJUMI was more successful than the traditionalist party NU in the cities of Central Java's interior and in the City of Tegal. In the City of Surakarta, the MASJUMI vote was 8.9 percent of the total votes cast, and the NU vote was .8 percent; in the City of Yogyakarta, the MASJUMI vote was 13.1 percent, the NU vote 1.7 percent; and in the City of Tegal, the MASJUMI vote was 18.1 percent as compared with 9.9 percent for NU. Of the East Java cities, only Madiun, the most westerly city of East Java, voted higher percentages for MASJUMI (5.1 percent) than for NU (3.5 percent) (based on Alfian 1971:81,91). Note that the NU was founded in an East Javanese city. Also, Yogyakarta, in Central Java, has been a center of development of the modernist Muslim voluntary organization Mohammadiyah.

different historical periods: The Hindu, Buddhist and Islamic orientations diffused across the landscape prior to the twentieth century; and
mobilization of support among the cultural orientation constituencies is
mainly relevant to the 1971 elections.

FINDINGS

The Regional Distribution of Strict Islamic and Javanist Orientations

The regional distribution of the Javanist (*abangan*) and strict Islamic
(*santri*) orientations as measured by percentage of votes cast per subdistrict for the secular political organizations as opposed to the percentage
cast for Muslim parties is related to administrative centrality and land
transport only when presence and type of plantations are specified. The
hypothesized relationship with water transport was not confirmed. Nor
was any correlation demonstrated between water transport and any other
cultural orientation measure.

For relatively central to middle-distant (0–5 on a 10-step scale) subdistricts only, the uncontrolled relationship with the plantation variable
holds; sugar plantation areas are most frequently Javanist, nonplantation
areas are mixed, and tree plantation areas are strict Islamic. (See Tables
2a and 2b.) For more remote areas, which in the regencies analyzed are
either tree plantation areas or nonplantation areas, the relationship
between tree plantations and strong Islamic orientations disappears, indicating outcroppings of strong Javanist orientation in remote tree plantation

TABLE 2a
The Distribution of Abangan *and* Santri *Orientations by Type and
Presence of Plantations: Central Areas*[a]

| | Abangan–Santri Orientations[b] | | | | | | | |
| | A | | B | | C | | Total | |
Plantations	N	%	N	%	N	%	N	%
Sugar	7	86	3	75	0	0	10	71
None	1	13	1	25	0	0	2	14
Tree	0	0	0	0	2	100	2	14
Total	8	99	4	100	2	100	14	99

    a. *Serially correlated.*
    b. *A = High and moderate* Abangan; *B = Moderate* Santri;
C = High Santri.

TABLE 2b
The Distribution of Abangan and Santri Orientations by Type and Presence of Plantations: Middle-distant Areas[a]

| | Abangan-Santri *Orientations*[b] | | | | | |
| | A | | B | | Total | |
Plantations	*N*	*%*	*N*	*%*	*N*	*%*
None	4	100	2	33	6	60
Tree	0	0	4	67	4	40
Total	4	100	6	100	10	100

a. *Serially correlated.*
b. *A = High* Abangan; *B = Moderate* Abangan *to moderate and high* Santri.

and nonplantation areas. This pattern of alteration of the relationship between the Islamic–Javanist variable and the plantation variable in systemically peripheral areas reappears when transport is controlled. (See Tables 3a and 3b.) For relatively good to fair transport access only (1–5 on a scale of 10), tree plantation areas tend to be strongly Islamic. Where transport is bad, the relationship does not hold.

Controlling the plantation variable while testing the relationship between the Islamic–Javanist orientations and transport (Table 4) reiterates the relationship between tree plantation areas where transport

TABLE 3a
The Distribution of Abangan and Santri Orientations by Type and Presence of Plantations: Where Transport Access is Good[a]

| | Abangan-Santri *Orientations*[b] | | | | | | | | | |
| | A | | B | | C | | D | | Total | |
Plantations	*N*	*%*	*N*	*%*	*N*	*%*	*N*	*%*	*N*	*%*
Sugar	1	100	6	100	4	67	0	0	11	79
None	0	0	0	0	1	17	0	0	1	7
Tree	0	0	0	0	1	17	1	100	2	14
Total	1	100	6	100	6	101	1	100	14	100

a. *Serially correlated.*
b. *A = High* Abangan; *B = Moderate* Abangan; *C = Moderate* Santri; *D = High* Santri.

TABLE 3b
The Distribution of Abangan *and* Santri *Orientations by Type and Presence of Plantations: Where Transport Access is Fair*[a]

Plantations	Abangan-Santri *Orientations*[b]									
	A		B		C		D		Total	
	N	%	N	%	N	%	N	%	N	%
Sugar	0	0	0	0	0	0	0	0	0	0
None	2	100	1	33	1	33	0	0	4	40
Tree	0	0	2	67	2	67	2	100	6	60
Total	2	100	3	100	3	100	2	100	10	100

a. *Serially correlated.*
b. *See footnote b above.*

access is good and strong Islamic orientation. It also specifies the orientation of tree plantation areas with bad transport as strongly Javanist.

Controlling the plantation variable while testing Islamic–Javanist orientations against administrative centrality adds a finding concerning the distribution of Javanist and Islamic strength *within* sugar plantation areas: For sugar plantation areas only, more administratively central subdistricts are more frequently strongly Javanist. (See Table 5.)

To summarize the comparative efficacy of the regional systems variables in delimiting the distribution of Javanist and Islamic orientations:

TABLE 4
The Distribution of Abangan *and* Santri *Orientations by Transport Access, Controlled for Presence and Type of Plantation*[a]

Transport Access	Abangan-Santri *Orientations*[b]							
	A		B		C		Total	
	N	%	N	%	N	%	N	%
Good	0	0	4	50	3	75	7	54
Bad	1	100	4	50	1	25	6	46
Total	1	100	8	100	4	100	13	100

a. *Shown for tree plantation areas only and serially correlated.*
b. *A = High* Abangan; *B = Moderate* Abangan; *C = High* Santri.

TABLE 5
The Distribution of Abangan *and* Santri *Orientations by Adminis-trative Centrality, Controlled for Presence and Type of Planta-tion*[a]

Administrative Centrality	Abangan-Santri *Orientations*[b]						Total	
	A		B		C			
	N	%	N	%	N	%	N	%
Central	1	100	5	83	0	0	6	55
Middle-distant	0	0	1	17	4	100	5	46
Total	1	100	6	100	4	100	11	101

   a.   *Shown for sugar plantation areas only and serially correlated.*
   b.   *A = High* Abangan; *B = Moderate* Abangan; *C = Moderate* Santri.

Administrative centrality is useful in differentiating the distribution of these basic cultural–religious orientations within the sugar plantation area and transport access is useful in differentiating the distribution of those orientations within nonplantation and tree plantation areas.

Regional Variations in the Performance of Political Parties

The single variable of administrative centrality accounts both for the performance of the Islamic parties among strict Muslims and the perform-ance of the secular parties among Javanists.

The Secular Parties among Javanists

The relative success of the two major secular parties among Javanist voters is related to administrative centrality. The relationship is curvi-linear: The Nationalist Party performs best among Javanist constituencies in subdistricts near-distant (3–4 on a scale of 10) from the Residency capital. From the near-distant to middle-distant (5) and remote (6–10) areas, GOLKAR's strength increases steadily with peripherality until GOLKAR appears favored over the Nationalist Party among Javanists in three-quarters of the remote areas. In areas closest to the Residency capital, the Nationalist Party performance among Javanists falls off from the strength it demonstrates in relatively close areas: Only one-fourth of the most central subdistricts vote high percentages for the Nationalist Party in comparison with nearly two-thirds (63 percent) registering moderate percentages. (See Table 6.)

TABLE 6

The Performance of the Secular Parties among Abangans *by Administrative Centrality*

Administrative Centrality	Party Performance							
	High % GOLKAR vote		Mixed GOLKAR, PNI vote		High % PNI vote		Total	
	N	%	N	%	N	%	N	%
Central	1	13	5	63	2	25	8	101
Near-distant	1	9	5	46	5	46	11	101
Middle-distant	2	40	2	40	1	20	5	100
Remote	9	75	2	17	1	8	12	100
Total	13	36	14	39	9	25	36	100

The Muslim Parties among Strict Muslims

The single physiographic variable of administrative centrality also accounts for regional variations in the performance of the traditionalist and modernist Islamic parties among the strict Muslim constituency. There is a strong inverse relationship between traditionalist Muslim party strength (as compared to modernist strength) among strict Muslims and administrative centrality. The more central the area, the better the success rate of the modernist Muslim party, PARMUSI, among strict Muslims. So, conversely, the more administratively remote, the higher the success rate of the traditionalist Muslim party, NU, in capturing the strict Muslim vote. The relationship holds when transport access and presence and type of plantation are controlled. (See Table 7.)

An apparent curvilinear relationship of modernist versus traditionalist Muslim success rate among strict Muslims to transport access appears to be an artifact of the presence and type of plantations, since the relationship disappears when the plantation variable is controlled. The relationship with plantations itself disappears when administrative centrality is controlled.

INTERPRETATION OF FINDINGS

The Regional Distribution of Strict Islamic and Javanist Orientations

A direct measure of centrality within the physiographic region of Surakarta—that is, access to water transport, which was the primary

TABLE 7

The Performance of Traditionalist versus Modernist Islamic Parties among Santris by Administrative Centrality[a]

Party Performance

Administrative Centrality	From Strong Traditionalist (A) to Strong Modernist (E)[b]										Total	
	A		B		C		D		E			
	N	%	N	%	N	%	N	%	N	%	N	%
Central	0	0	0	0	1	14	2	22	5	56	8	22
Middle-distant	0	0	2	33	5	71	6	67	3	33	16	44
Remote	5	100	4	67	1	14	1	11	1	11	12	33
Total	5	100	6	100	7	99	9	100	9	100	36	99

a. Serially correlated.

b. Strong traditionalist is high relative percentage of Muslim vote for NU and strong modernist is high relative percentage of Muslim vote for PARMUSI.

means of communications prior to the twentieth century—did not show any relationship to the distribution of strict Islamic and Javanist orientations. But a qualified relationship with administrative centrality, controlling for plantations, did hold, suggesting that pre-twentieth-century processes of diffusion from the region's cultural and administrative center account in part for the present distribution of religious orientations. The administrative centrality variable measures the distance[17] of local systems from the capital city, which has been a stable regional node for several hundred years. Hence, it is still reasonable to interpret the relationship between religious orientations and administrative centrality as evidence of the hypothesized pre-twentieth century pattern of diffusion—albeit modified by later influences. The findings may then be interpreted as follows.

Under conditions of traditional transport technology, Islam did not reach—or contacts with Muslims were not sufficiently sustained to modify—the Indic-autochthonous culture of remote parts of the region. Areas in close contact with the capital city (areas central to intermediate in administrative centrality) were exposed to Islamic traditions of the palace mosque and to the beliefs and culture of Islamic traders. However, not everyone adopted Islamic practices with equal enthusiasm. Given exposure to Islam, then, broad differences in the mode of agricultural adaptation to the various environments of the region determined where Islam was most widely and completely espoused.

The reasons for the strong Javanism of sugar areas may be sought in the structure of relationships between the Dutch plantations and the villagers whose rice land was used by the plantations. As Geertz (1963) has shown, the needs of sugar producers for the same lands Javanese peasants used to grow irrigated rice, and for a self-supporting, seasonally available labor force, were met by the Dutch imposition of a "dual" economy: Dutch administrative capitalism in the export sector and Javanese family-unit subsistence agriculture in the domestic sector (1963:48–49). The commoners' lack of rights to land in the principalities,[18] together with Dutch policies that hampered entrance of Javanese into the commercial sector with their own sugar crop (Geertz 1963:58), undercut the development of indigenous commercial cane farmers. In East Java, where Javanese farmers were able to enter the cane market despite restrictions, the successful native cane farmers turned to strict Islam, which sanctioned thrift and the neglect of costly communal social and ritual obligations (Geertz 1965:40–41).[19] In the principalities the landholders, who were aristocrats,

[17] Distance was measured in units of subdistricts transversed between any given subdistrict and the Residency capital. See note 6.

[18] Javanese farmers in the principalities were granted "inheritable individual rights" to land use in 1918 (Selosoemardjan 1962:219).

[19] This emergent rural middle class of the sugar lands in directly ruled residencies disappeared after 1925, when world sugar prices fell (Geertz 1965:58).

and those others in a position to profit by relations with the Dutch plantation administration (the aristocrats' administrative appointees in the
villages, or *bekels*) derived their authority from Indic–autochthonous
traditions of the feudal states.[20] Local elites in sugar plantation areas were
thus disposed to espouse the Javanist values of the court. This interpretation is supported by the finding that the strength of Javanism in sugar
plantation areas is related to centrality in the administrative system; the
more central the area, the more likely it is to be predominantly Javanist.

In contrast to the sugar plantation system, the colonial tree plantation
system did not exclude small-scale native producers from growing and selling commercial crops (Geertz 1963:56). Since the perennial tree crops were
grown on enclave estates established on previously unsettled land and
semiskilled laborers were employed the year around, tree plantations did
not depend upon traditionalized subsistence economy villages. The tree
plantation areas were thus potential niches for the farmer–entrepreneur
and, hence, for Islam. It is not surprising, then, to find that tree plantation
areas are strongly Islamic in administratively central to intermediate
areas where exposure to Islam was sufficiently intense.

However, not all of the *remote* tree plantation areas are, as expected,
Javanist. The infusion of Islam into these remote areas is evidently related
to twentieth-century improvements in the old overland routes through tree
plantation areas, since it is areas well serviced by new roads that sustain
relatively large strict Muslim communities. When the old overland routes
were paved in the twentieth century, some tree plantation areas on the
periphery of the watershed became well connected not only with the City
of Surakarta but with cities in the more strongly Islamic north coast.
These formerly remote areas that were suddenly opened up to cultural
influences from regional and extraregional centers also gained the commercial advantage of easy (and cheaper) access to markets for their
produce. The improved commercial potential of tree plantations in areas
newly connected to arteries of trade could then support the class of
indigenous small agricultural entrepreneurs who find strict Islam
attractive.

The prevalence of strict Muslims in tree plantation areas with good
transport access contrasts with the prevalence of Javanists in sugar plantation areas with good transport access. Evidently, the structure of social
relationships through which Javanese make their livelihoods predisposes

[20] In the indirectly ruled principalities, Yogyakarta and Surakarta, the Dutch rented rice
land for sugar production from the kings' appanage holders under the seignorial lease system
(Geertz 1963; Selosoemardjan 1962). In directly ruled areas, plantation owners rented land
from corporate villages. Dutch policy in the directly ruled residencies strengthened corporate
villages in sugar areas to foster the subsistence economy of the village labor force and to
rationalize dealings between the companies and the rice farmers. The pressures toward intensification of village traditionalism on sugar plantations of the directly ruled residencies was
thus especially strong in contrast to nonplantation villages of the same regions.

them to make different choices among the cultural–religious currents to which they are exposed. Where the path to prosperity lies through civil service (in the sugar plantation areas), the courtly Javanism of the civil service is prevalent among the peasantry. Where locals do not have access to lucrative positions in the plantation system through civil service, and where commercial opportunities for small producers are conducive to the emergence of individualistic entrepreneurial values, the strict Islamic orientation is prevalent among the peasantry.

The nonplantation areas contrast with both types of plantation areas, since in the nonplantation areas neither civil service nor entrepreneurial opportunities are sufficiently great to foster strong identification with either of the "great traditions." Civil servants in the nonplantation areas are less frequently required to carry out central government directives against local interests than their counterparts in sugar plantation areas, and they lack the opportunities to profit from judicious management of village relationships with the sugar plantations. The peasants in the non-plantation areas farm less productive land than peasants in plantation areas, and the incentive to avoid the expense of solidarity rituals in hopes of building capital is slight in comparison to the incentive to invest in the social security of village ties by carrying out solidarity rituals. So the loyalties of elites in nonplantation areas to their local communities are likely to outweigh their commitments to either of the supralocal systems, administrative or commercial; and consequently they are likely to be less committed to either Hinduistic court culture or orthodox Islam than to the naïve folk blend of the two "great traditions," "Islam Jawa." The mix of Javanist and strict Islamic party strength in administratively central to intermediate nonplantation areas probably indicates less concern in these areas for distinctions among autochthonous, Hinduistic, and Islamic culture. Hence, neither secular nor Islamic parties have an edge in electoral competition.

The remote nonplantation areas are, by contrast, strongly Javanist. Like the remote, inaccessible tree plantation areas, these are areas where folk culture is little influenced by Islam, and peasants are more likely to profess the "Javanese religion" (agama Jawa) than "Javanese Islam" (Islam Jawa).

Regional Variations in the Performance of the Political Parties

The administrative system most powerfully shapes the spatial pattern of the secular parties' performance, with respect to each other, among Javanist voters. This finding is in accord with the supposition that party influence in government administration is a major component of the mobilization potential of the secular parties.

The predominance of GOLKAR over Nationalist strength not only in the center (as predicted) but also at the periphery of the administrative system suggests that more careful attention needs to be given to the *use* of the regional administrative network by supraregional authorities. First, the user of the network may direct the mobilization (or repression) effort at different parts of the region. In the case of the 1971 election campaign, the GOLKAR strategy called for especially intense "campaigning" in former Communist areas. Prior to 1965, Communist party strength was greatest in urban areas.[21] After the destruction of the Communist Party and the elimination of Communists from government posts, fears of underground Communist activity focused on regionally peripheral areas—the sparsely populated arid hills and forested mountain slopes, which might easily hide guerillas. On the one hand, GOLKAR strength in peripheral areas probably shows the effects of the government strategy to assert control over areas of suspected Communist activity. On the other hand, GOLKAR electoral strength in central areas is probably the hypothesized result of effective government manipulation of the civil service (which, after removal of Communists, was predominantly Nationalist).

Second, the modern-day administration has the transport and communications technology necessary to assert control at the periphery of a region. The notion that influences from the center of an administrative network will diminish with distance rests on the assumption that interaction between central areas and the node is more frequent than that between peripheral areas and the node. Modern communications technology compensates for the inhibiting effect of physical distance in the administrative system.

The exclusive and direct relationship of the Muslim parties' performance variable with administrative centrality shows that, as expected, Muslim constituencies in areas near the capital city of Surakarta are more likely to be receptive to modernist Islamic ideology than are Muslims in remote areas. The finding suggests, however, that the role of the government as a channel for modernist influences was underestimated. Thus, the relative strength of modernist Muslims in offices of the Department of Religion near the city, and the perhaps related relative prevalence of government-subsidized modernist schools and clinics in central as opposed to remote areas, need to be examined. A generalized but tentative interpretation of the finding would be that modernists are strong among Muslim constituencies where formal organizations (the government, voluntary organizations) structure a large proportion of social action and that the traditionalists are strong where traditional relationships (such as those with the *kiyais*) are still the predominant forms of social interaction.

---

[21] In the 1955 general election, the Communist Party was the leading party in three of the five cities of Central Java (Surakarta, Yogyakarta, and Semarang) and in all four of the cities of East Java (Surabaya, Madiun, Malang, and Kediri) (Alfian 1971:81,91).

CONCLUSIONS

From the limited data available, it appears that the regions of the interior continue to be significant contexts for cultural diffusion and political integration. Both the patterns of integration of the states in colonial times and the limitations imposed by the physiography of the regions upon social integration of the traditional polities from ancient times until the twentieth century (Schrieke 1957:153) are evident in the present-day distribution of religious orientations.

The success of the contemporary national political parties in calling forth demonstrations of support from among the local religious constituencies in an electoral contest depends upon the parties' access to and control over those constituencies through regional administrative systems. This finding is in accord with the frequent observation that voting is manipulated by inducements and threats that officeholders more than others are in a position to make. However, it is the choice among parties of the same religious orientation that is subject to barter or coercion, not the choice among parties of different religious orientations. Both the association of the orientation variables to other regional attributes—in contrast to the performance variables, which are both associated exclusively with administrative centrality—and the constancy of strict Islamic as compared with Javanist voting strength from 1955 to 1971[22] support this interpretation. The election as a "social document" of the political culture of a region, then, evidences both the ephemeral processes of electoral mobilization and the slow evolution of religious and political orientations.

Taken together, the findings illustrate the multiple ways in which regional systems constrain electoral politics in the new nation of Indonesia. The regional administrative systems provide national political organizations with access to and sanctions to use against local participants. (Or, in the case of traditionalist Muslims, the administrative system fails to provide access to constituencies that informal local leaders provide.) The success of the parties, however, is constrained by voters' commitments to cultural–religious values, the distribution of which evolves under the influences of regional ecology, and regional transport and administrative communications.

To extend conclusions drawn from the study of Surakarta as a region to other regions, it will be necessary to specify the degree of coincidence of

---

[22] In the Regency of Boyolali, votes for the Nationalist Party and the Communist Party combined totaled 67.9 percent of the vote in 1955, and in 1971 the Nationalist Party and GOLKAR together won 72.8 percent of the vote. The Muslim NU and MASJUMI won 26.7 percent of the vote in 1955, compared to 15.8 percent won by PARMUSI and NU in 1971.

In the regency of Karanganyar, votes for the Nationalist Party and the Communist Party combined totaled 72.9 percent of the vote in 1955, and in 1971 the Nationalist Party and GOLKAR together won 85.9 percent of the vote. The Muslim NU and MASJUMI won 8.6 percent of the vote in 1955, compared to 11.6 percent won by PARMUSI and NU in 1971.

natural regions with administrative units as well as transport networks. It would then be possible to test for regular variations in effects of regional systems upon cultural orientations between areas where the coincidence of regional systems is high (for example, in Surakarta) as opposed to those where the boundaries of regional systems widely diverge (for example, in Malang). Given such a regional framework, it might be possible to identify regular variations in the cultural character of local places where system boundaries are not coincident (for example, where a regency falls outside a natural region but is included within the bounds of an administrative unit).

In comparing the physiographic regions of the interior, it will be necessary to recognize that the boundaries of these regions are physical only insofar as geographical features have constituted hinderances to social integration and have been so recognized. It is clear from Schrieke's reconstruction of the boundaries of the traditionally recognized regions that portions of the borders are more permeable than others. Borders are highly permeable where rivers exit from a region (for example, the upper Brantas from the Malang region into the Blitar region); where the headwaters of two river systems lie in close juxtaposition (for example, the Surakarta–Yogyakarta border at Prambangan); or where river systems converge (for example, where the main rivers of the Madiun and Surakarta basins converge before the Solo River flows through the Kendeng Range). In addition, the importance of the trade linkage established through the rivers must be considered in evaluating the permeability of a traditional border. For example, of the rivers in Central Java, only the Solo River was an artery of trade with the north coast. With a broader data base, then, one might find characteristic differences between border areas at relatively impermeable mountain boundaries and those at valley exits. The foregoing analysis demonstrated cultural differences between areas that are both administratively remote (that is, at the periphery of the overlapping administrative and physiographic region of Surakarta) and remote from modern transport, as opposed to those areas that are administratively remote but have ready access to important road exits from the region.

The cultural significance of the regional exits, both traditional and modern, moreover, derives from the character of cultural influences radiating from the centers to which the routes connect. Again, with a broader data base, one might be able to identify "interference patterns" in the cultural influences of the competing regional and extraregional centers in permeable border regions. For example, the Islamic influences of the north coast in the northern regencies of Surakarta were apparent in the 1955 election, whereas the regencies between the royal cities of Surakarta and Yogyakarta were overwhelmingly Javanist.[23] Also, if it is hypothesized that Javanist feelings are strongest where the Muslim reform movement is most intense, the fact that the two regencies of Surakarta that are transversed by the major road between Yogyakarta (the center of reformist Mohammadiyah) and Semarang (on the Islamic north coast) have the most converts to Hinduism of all the regencies in Java seems to dramatize the importance of competing regional centers to the study of regional systems in Java.

Ultimately, one would hope that a systematic understanding of the dynamics of cultural and political integration of the interior regions would make possible more fruitful comparisons with patterns of social integration of the coastal regions, not only northern Java, but elsewhere in the archipelago where trading sultanates emerged. The location of the coastal sultanates near the mouths of rivers to which the trade of the hinterlands flowed and from which sea trade might be controlled have left on the landscape very different patterns of cultural orientations that may yet influence present-day political mobilization.

ACKNOWLEDGMENTS

I would like to express my gratitude to G. William Skinner for his guidance of the statistical analysis upon which this paper is based and to Benedict R. O'G. Anderson, Donald K. Emmerson, and R. William Liddle for their criticisms of early drafts.

REFERENCES

Alfian
    1971   Hasil Pemilihan Umum 1955 untuk Dewan Perwakilan Rakjat (D.P.R.). Jakarta: LEKNAS.
Benda, Harry J.
    1958   *The crescent and the rising sun: Indonesian Islam under the Japanese occupation, 1942–1945.* The Hague: Van Hoeve.
Biro Pusat Statistik
    1969   *Survey sosial ekokomi nasional, tahap keempat (Oktober 1969–Desember 1969), sifat2 demografi Indonesia, laporan No. 1,* Jakarta.
Feith, Herbert
    1957   *The Indonesian elections of 1955.* Ithaca, N.Y.: Cornell Univ. Modern Indonesia Project, Interim Report Series.

[23] In the Surakarta regencies of Sukoharjo, Klaten, Wonogiri, and Karanganyar, and the Yogyakarta regencies of Sleman and Gunung Kidul, the Nationalist Party and the Communist Party polled the first and second highest number of votes in 1955. In the Surakarta regencies of Boyolali and Seragen, a strict Muslim party placed second to a Javanist majority party, and in the Yogyakarta regencies of Kulan Progo and Bantul, a Muslim party placed second to a first-running (but not majority) Javanist party.

Geertz, Clifford
  1959 The Javanese village. In *Local, ethnic and national loyalties in village Indonesia, a symposium,* edited by G. William Skinner. New Haven, Conn.: Yale Univ. Cultural Report Series, Southeast Asian Studies. Pp. 34–41.
  1960 *The religion of Java.* New York: Free Press.
  1963 *Agricultural involution: The process of ecological change in Indonesia.* Berkeley: Univ. of California Press.
  1965 *The social history of an Indonesian town.* Cambridge, MIT Press.
Jay, Robert
  1963 *Religion and politics in rural central Java.* New Haven, Conn.: Yale Univ. Southeast Asia Studies Cultural Report Series No. 12.
Liddle, R. William
  1973 Evolution from above: National leadership and local development in Indonesia. *Journal of Asian Studies* **32**(2): 287–309.
Moertono, Soemarsaid
  1963 *State and statecraft in Old Java: A study of the later Mataram period, 16th to 19th century.* Ithaca, N.Y.: Cornell Univ. Modern Indonesia Project Monograph.
Pigeaud, Theodore G.
  1962 *Java in the 14th century,* Vol. IV. The Hague: Nijhoff.
Schrieke, B.
  1957 *Indonesian sociological studies. Part II: Ruler and realm in early Java.* The Hague: Van Hoeve.
Selosoemardjan
  1962 *Social changes in Jogjakarta.* Ithaca, N.Y.: Cornell Univ. Press.
Stöhr, Waldemar, and Piet Zoetmulder
  1965 *Die religionen Indonesiens.* Berlin: Kohlhammer.
Utrecht, E.
  1969 Land reform in Indonesia. *Bulletin of Indonesian Economic Studies* (Canberra) **5**(3): 71–88.

Chapter 10

Centers and Boundaries of Regional Caste Systems: Toward A General Model

Brenda E. F. Beck
University of British Columbia

In several parts of India, a single dominant caste controls the agricultural activities of a whole region. Under such circumstances, how is a pattern of dominance, or the power of one group to control the members of other groups, structured in space? Under what circumstances will dominance be strongest? Does the control that a single dominant group has over space weaken on the fringes of an area? And can any associated changes in the structure of the social order be observed? These are the questions this paper will address. First the overall issue of dominance and some of the main features of social organization that tend to accompany it are discussed. Then a test case based on data from southern India is examined. Finally, a whole series of social features are related to variations in the basic dominance pattern. Associated components include local food exchange hierarchies, settlement patterns, spatial positioning within the region, and the varied types of historical circumstances that brought particular groups to the area.

THE DEFINITION OF DOMINANCE

In recent years there has been an increased interest in the study of regions in India. Several researchers have now published descriptions of large areas of the subcontinent where a recognized regional subculture exists and where the character of this localized social order appears to be directly linked to the presence of a specific dominant caste (Beck 1972; Pradhan 1966; Srinivas 1952). Such areas are stereotyped in people's minds as the residential locales of particularly large and powerful landowning groups. It is importance to ask ourselves, therefore, what qualifies a caste for regional dominance. And also why we find dominant castes in some areas and not in others.

The status of a dominant caste appears to rest on two things, a near monopoly of management rights in local resources (usually agricultural land) and considerable numerical strength (roughly 30 to 50 percent) vis-à-vis an otherwise fragmented local population.[1] It is a group's right to local resource management that lies at the heart of its members' ability to control the lives of others resident in a given area. Low-status "untouchable" laborers sometimes constitute up to 30 percent of a local population. But such groups do not have an economic power base to back up their sheer numerical strength. Hence, nowhere are they in a position of dominance. Once economic rights are obtained, however, the size of a group does become important. This is because only numerical presence can ensure the occurrence of a maximum number of ranked interactions between members of a controlling group and outsiders dependent on them. Put in other words, resource control must be translated into the face-to-face management of people in order to constitute true dominance. Members of a dominant caste make the day-to-day decisions on who, where, when, and how work is to be done. They must also be able personally to allocate the proceeds that result from labor input. Thus, owners must be managers in substantial numbers if maximum interaction between members of a dominant group and other nonmembers is to occur.

If we consider a very small but wealthy caste, it will immediately be clear that such people will necessarily have to delegate much of their management power to nonmembers. Such a group can maintain its wealth by insisting on a large share of production proceeds but, lacking numbers, its members will never succeed in overseeing most day-to-day activities. The advantage of numbers is that group members with substantial resource rights can delegate the day-to-day management of their affairs to insiders. Wealthier members of large castes in India are observed to delegate management responsibilities in just this ingroup way. On the other hand, a dominant caste cannot constitute too large a proportion of the total population without becoming a tribal group occupying a large tract of land where few other groups reside (Bailey 1961). Tribes control the local resources, but there will be few others in their area over whom group

---

[1] A good summary of the evidence concerning caste dominance in India can be found in Mandelbaum (1970:358–365).

members can assert power. Thus, a tribe can never be described as a dominant group in the sense used here. The relationships suggested above are diagramed in Figure 1.

Research in various parts of India suggests that dominant castes do not exist everywhere. It is only in areas where a landowning group has been able to establish itself in proportionally large numbers and yet maintain its distinctive character (by strictly regulating marriage and descent) that dominance in the sense described here becomes possible. Dominant caste areas, furthermore, do not seem to be located near the oldest civilizational centers but rather in secondary areas of previously low population density. It is into just such areas that well-organized outside groups have tended to expand during periods of political and economic prosperity. The present position of dominance enjoyed by certain groups, therefore, appears to derive from their previous success in the organized conquest of an outlying area. Once established, such castes continue to dominate local social institutions and to structure them to their own advantage. This kind of dominant caste pattern has recently been reported for scattered locales throughout India (Bailey 1957, 1960; Cohn 1955; Dumont 1957; Gough 1955, 1960; Lewis 1955, 1958; Mayer 1958, 1960; Minturn and Hitchcock 1966; Nicholas 1965; Pradhan 1966; Rowe 1963; Schwartzberg 1965, 1967, 1968; Srinivas 1952, 1955, 1959).

Carol Smith (Chapter 8, Volume I) analyzes a somewhat similar situation. She describes the results of the Spanish colonization of western Guatemala where the Ladino descendants of Spanish Indian unions have come to dominate the economy of that area. In both Smith's paper and this one, the power-wielding group constitutes some 30 to 50 percent of the total population of the region. In both cases the group's present power

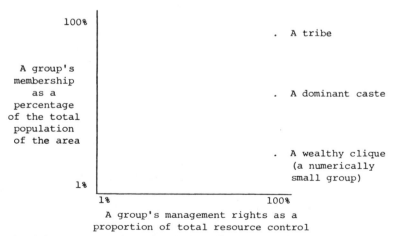

Figure 1. A dominant caste defined vis-à-vis a tribe and a wealthy clique.

derives from successful conquest in the past. Furthermore, in both cases the dominant group has maintained its separate identity through time by a pattern of endogamous marriage and by restricting membership to entry at birth. In the Smith case, however, the descendants of a region's conquerors came to dominate the towns and businesses of the area. The present study deals with a different kind of regional structure, one where the conquering caste has come to control agricultural resources in a large area, but where the market network has remained a competitive arena for many socially distinct groups. Smith goes on to hypothesize that variations in Ladino distribution in her area lead to differing local market structures. In our case, however, we will try to discern how variations in the distribution of the dominant group (in terms of differing settlement patterns) have affected local interaction structures (food exchange hierarchies). Our two papers thus employ a similar type of reasoning, but because of the contrasting nature of dominance in the two situations studied, they attempt to explain quite different dimensions of the resultant local scene.

The following pages will describe a survey of 25 points along the boundaries of a conquest region in southern India. This area, called Koṅku, is now known for its dominant caste, the Kavuṇṭars. It was settled by this group in about the twelfth century. Since then, the fringes of the Kavuṇṭars' original territory have tended to distend in order to accommodate later arrivals. Unable to penetrate to the core of this well-defended area, late comers mostly settled in newly defined marginal areas on its borders. A noticeable out-migration of discontents and political losers from the established center of this Kavuṇṭar area has also taken place. In fringe areas today, therefore, one tends to find two types of groups—relative newcomers and old settlers who have been pushed out. As a result, the area presently referred to as Koṅku extends well beyond its traditional Kavuṇṭar core.

DOMINANCE IN RELATION TO LOCAL INTERACTION HIERARCHIES

In situations of "true" single caste dominance, a very significant patterning of social interaction can be observed. In order to gain social support, a dominant caste will usually agree to share food with a "cluster" of other groups that work closely with its members and whose separate ritual status is not too low. [Descriptions of such food exchanges by a group of allied castes have come from widely different parts of India (Beck 1972; Mayer 1960).] Castes that can maintain an economic base that is relatively immune to manipulation by agricultural interests, however, commonly contest a food alliance. In India these contesters tend to be artisan or merchant communities. As "professionals," they have a certain amount of outside status based on their special skills and their elaborate family networks. Such people enjoy a special situation in an agricultural region, as they are not dependent on primary industry for their links to the market economy. They also tend to use cash (or gold) rather than kind in personal transactions. By such a strategy, they maintain liquid assets that are not easily controlled by their otherwise powerful landowning rivals. Given this special position of artisan and merchant groups, these castes commonly attempt to shift the arena in which local status is contested. They prefer a display of ritual purity to one that stresses political strength. Their most common ploy, therefore, is to refuse all food offered to them by their farming rivals. A landed group can have no satisfactory reply to this kind of exclusive behavior short of snubbing some of their agricultural allies—and endangering some of the local support on which their political hegemony is based. The result is a kind of stand-off, for the leaders of an agricultural alliance wield a great deal of local power. Part of their acceptability in local eyes comes from a strategy of treating some of their important supporters as ritual equals. Groups who find themselves financially secure, however, can ritually snub the dominant group and effectively demonstrate their independence by consistent food refusal.

This pattern of ingroups and outgroups who try to undermine each other's status has been repeatedly noted by observers of the Indian scene (Beals 1964; Hiebert 1971; Nicholas 1965). It suggests one very basic point. Social systems where land is concentrated in the hands of a single group need not be unidimensional hierarchies in other respects; that is contrary to the general assumption, the extreme domination by one group of primary resources does not necessarily lead to a more extreme form of social hierarchy in other arenas. It would seem, on the contrary, that the more oppressive a dominance maintained by a group of agriculturally oriented allies, the more extensive will be the efforts of those having some independent source of livelihood to challenge them. But potential rivals of a dominant landed group cannot themselves be uninformed and unskilled. They must have some independent economic base on which to build. This is what makes artisan and professional groups so commonly suspect and so often vehemently denigrated by territorially oriented power groups. It probably explains why such people are unpopular in many societies. And in India the role of such professionals is made particularly significant by a long-standing tradition that absolutely separates monetary wealth from land (Beck 1970; Pearson 1973; Spodek 1973; Stein 1971). Only recently has this ancient bifurcation begun to break down under the pressure of a modernized economy and Westernized world view. In brief, where a single group dominates primary production, but not secondary manufacture or trade, the social hierarchy is likely to be multidimensional in its structure. This notion is well supported by data gathered from one particular region of southern India, which we will examine soon. First, however, we must ask a preliminary question about the general nature of social dominance in relation to space.

DOMINANCE IN RELATION TO SPACE: A GENERAL MODEL

A dominant caste, just as a dominant species of animal or plant life, once established, tends to expand its domain to fill the space available. This may be an ecologically defined territory bounded by natural features, such as mountains, or a socially defined territory bounded by other equally powerful groups. Once expanded to its natural limit, a group tends to remain stable over time, until outside forces somehow disturb its previous pattern.

One such disturbing force can be the attempt to some new community to penetrate an area previously dominated by someone else. Such attempts usually occur at predictable entrance points such as mountain passes, or along major communication routes like river valleys. It is at such *entrance points* into the territory of a dominant community that one would want to look for the effects of penetration. Some kind of squeeze play often operates in such situations. Those already within a given area unite in an effort to block the new intruders. One would thus expect the general population of an entrance point to be dense, relative to the population density of the central area. It should also be homogenized into a kind of fine-grained mix of species or groups. This "suspension" of particles provides a kind of unstructured social space where dominant relationships are hard to maintain. Coupled with this should be the relative absence of attempts to snub those in power. Similar features should also characterize an area's urban centers. These, just like entrance points, experience social squeeze and are locales from which new groups attempt to penetrate the surrounding social field.

Halfway between the entrance points and the *central area* of the system one would expect an intermediate situation. Here a few groups will have managed to filter through the blockades set up at the entrance points. But these people will have subsequently had to fight with great energy to establish themselves amidst those already settled around them. In such *entrance areas* as opposed to entrance points, one would expect to find a coarse-grained mix of castes where stranger groups will have defensively staked out individual villages or perhaps even larger territories. The overall pattern of settlement here should be spotty and exhibit a "polka-dot" pattern of dominance. One would expect much maneuvering for position and less stable "in" and "out" coalitions than in an area where a uniform dominance by one group extends over a wide area.

The two types of entrance areas I have described are what would be expected in places where new groups have tried to penetrate an established region. Away from the major communication routes, by contrast, should be *cul-de-sac* areas characterized by groups that have been pushed out of the centers of power. In extreme cases these may form almost tribal-like isolates in inaccessible locales (for example, on mountaintops). Such are the places that people find to flee to after defeat in a contest over control of some less remote place. These "tribes," as they are generally classified in South and Southeast Asia, tend to mirror the social structure of the more central area from which they came. The copy of a larger society they provide, however, is often somewhat archaic. Social structure in these culs-de-sac also tends to be miniaturized or simplified because of the reduced number of groups with whom there is an opportunity to interact.[2]

One should also find an intermediate areas between a region's center and the isolated spots on its boundaries. One would expect such *marginal areas* to be peopled by rebellious adventurers, the younger brothers of dominant families or the descendants of previous administrators. These men will likely have come from families that wielded considerable power in the past but who have had no further chance for influence in a central area. Such people will have sought to recoup their fortunes in places where the weight of established power is not so great. They will not likely be members of professional and artisan groups, but rather people who seek power in traditional territorial terms. Hence, one would expect the social pattern in marginal areas to be somewhat like that in the entrance areas. There should be a tendency toward mixed dominance and toward a polka-dot pattern of settlement, difficult to distinguish from the situation created by penetration. However, one might expect a marginal area to have a higher proportion of internally mixed settlements, as newcomers here will have more local contacts, helpful in establishing themselves, than genuine outsiders would have. This pattern would contrast somewhat with the dominance of whole villages by different groups characteristic of entrance areas. One might also find a tendency to stress individual group identity above political alliance formation in such marginal areas.

These five types of microlocales are summarized in Figure 2. Notice that both ends of the scale of types can be seen to evolve from the the basic form (type C), the situation of single group hegemony. Note also that each of the five types of social order depicted has a tail on it. This tail is meant to depict the presence of a few very low-ranking groups. The position of powerlessness and inferiority common to both so-called untouchable communities and many low-ranking service groups in India does not change significantly in any of the five situations outlined.

[2] In a 1957 essay Louis Dumont and David Pocock first suggested the idea that "tribes" in India are merely groups that have "lost contact."

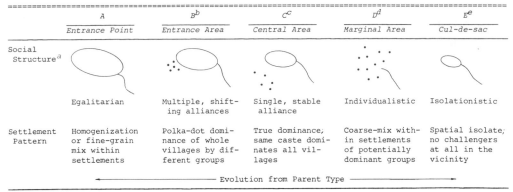

	A	B[b]	C[c]	D[d]	E[e]
	Entrance Point	*Entrance Area*	*Central Area*	*Marginal Area*	*Cul-de-sac*
Social Structure[a]					
	Egalitarian	Multiple, shifting alliances	Single, stable alliance	Individualistic	Isolationistic
Settlement Pattern	Homogenization or fine-grain mix within settlements	Polka-dot dominance of whole villages by different groups	True dominance; same caste dominates all villages	Coarse-mix within settlements of potentially dominant groups	Spatial isolate; no challengers at all in the vicinity

← ———————————— Evolution from Parent Type ————————————→

a. See the text for a fuller explanation of these diagrams.
b. The crucial difference between A and B is the size of the "egalitarian space" at top of system.
c. The crucial difference between B and C is the placement of the non-aligned castes. In B they are near the core group and the shifting of alignments between communities is easy. In C groups in opposition are more easily distinguished from the core of allied castes. Their locations are more scattered (suggesting lack of unity among themselves), resting further down toward the left bottom corner than in B, since the opposition often will accept food from no one and few will take food from them.
d. The crucial difference between C and D is the presence of a pattern. In C there is a group of allies and their opposition, while in D every community seems to establish its interaction rules individually. D resembles C by having a "core" of allied castes near the top. The difference is that this "core" is very weak (or is lacking altogether) as opposed to its relative strength in type B.
e. The crucial difference between C and E is that the latter involves a very small number of castes who live in an isolated environment.

Figure 2.   Proposed types of social hierarchy, by spatial location.

DETAILS CONCERNING DATA COLLECTION

In the summer of 1972, I made a 2-month tour of the edges of a region in southern India to explore these ideas. For this field research I chose a region in which I had already done previous ethnographic work and where I already felt confident about the character of the central area. In my tour I sampled 25 villages,[3] spaced in a more or less equidistant fashion around the boundaries of this geographically distinct region (a plateau surrounded by mountains). I knew the region to be a "naïvely given" cultural area that had had a long-standing political identity of its own.[4] Although this naïve region does not correspond to any particular administrative division at the present time, it is considered to be a socially distinct entity both by long-term residents and by outsiders. It has a name (Koṅku), and people from other Tamil-speaking areas can readily identify residents of this area by various dialect markers in their speech. Koṅku covers an area of

[3] I did this as randomly as was possible given that with each move I had to find a place where I and the "family" of several others with whom I traveled could spend the night.

[4] J. Schwartzberg suggests the term "naïvely given" in his general article on regionalism in India (1967). For details on the political identity of the area under discussion, see Beck (1972).

approximately 7500 square miles and hosts a population of nearly 5 million. For details on the location of the Koṅku region, see Map 1.

On my tour I concentrated on three types of questions, asking these systematically in each of 25 places. The first question concerned the description of 15 to 30 settlements that lay within a 2- to 3-mile radius of each place I stopped.[5] For every settlement named in this way, I next asked: (1) Which castes live here? (2) How many households in this place belong to each of these castes? (3) What do the members of each caste actually (as opposed to traditionally) do for a living? The purpose of this first inquiry was to discover: (1) what castes were present in the area, (2) whether several different landowning castes could be found living in the same village or in neighboring ones, and (3) whether other patterns regarding size or occupational concentration emerged. Some of this information, converted into charts showing the patterning of settlement composition in these areas, is reproduced on the pages that follow.

My next question was simply: Who are the big landowners around here? In the discussion that followed this query, I tried to judge which caste or castes were dominating agricultural activity in that microlocale. To obtain this information, I tried to get informants to generalize about an entire

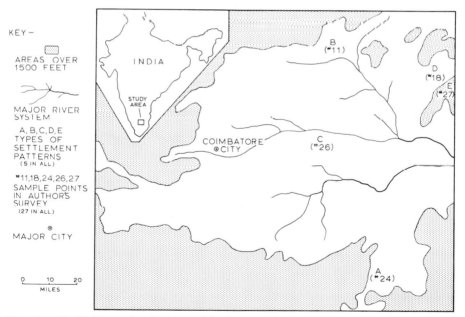

Map 1. The Koṅku region: location of the five sample areas used as examples in the text. (From Beck, *Peasant society in Koṅku: A study of right and left subcastes in South India.* Vancouver: University of British Columbia Press, 1972. By permission of the publisher.)

[5] My goal was to stop about every 15 miles, but the lack of a temple compound to camp in sometimes dictated that I move a few miles further on.

caste or subcaste, though of course some variation between families within any given group was expected. I was especially concerned to know which groups were hiring agricultural laborers on a large scale. These were later identified as major, as opposed to minor, landowners or as those groups most likely to be involved in dominating the agricultural activities of that area.[6] These groups were eventually given a special status in my charts on settlement composition (by using cross-hatching).

My third question was about the traditions of food exchange in each local area. For this I simply listed the names of all the caste groups that had appeared in the sample survey along both the vertical and the horizontal axes of a predrawn matrix of squares. One axis was used to represent food giving and the other food receiving. I next systematically asked whether each caste on the list would habitually accept or refuse food from each other group on the same list.[7] I wanted this information so as to be able to say comparatively, for each sample area, how the local food exchange hierarchy was structured. Food exchange customs in India contain elements (in acceptance patterns) of economic and political power and elements (in refusal patterns) of contested status. Thus, one can use food exchange patterns to say something about: (1) the degree of hierarchy in a local social system, (2) the types of local alliances that have been formed, and (3) the degree of multidimensionality present in the hierarchy more generally. In gathering these data, then, I wanted to examine how the structure of a social hierarchy might vary in response to the presence or absence in a given locale of a truly dominant group.

On completion of the tour, I had collected comparable data for each of 25 sample areas on: (1) the settlement pattern, (2) the degree of dominance of a particular caste as measured by their degree of involvement as directors of local agricultural activities, and (3) the structure of community interaction patterns as measured by food exchange patterns. On my return I was able to supplement this with some information on the historical movements of the various groups I encountered. Some of the historical data came from stories of past history that people had told me during this and previous field trips to the area. In addition, earlier ethnographic reports and historical writings provided scattered hints of past events. It remained

---

[6] Large landowners were defined as castes in which at least some families hired agricultural laborers on a regular basis. Due to time limitations, I sometimes had to rely on simple statements about the extensiveness of a caste's local landholding.

[7] I tried to question a single informant, without onlookers except for my assistant, when dealing with this question. Generally, I did this work late at night. But if it had to be done during the day, I would ask the person to come with me and my assistant to "show" us something, as a means of being alone. The people I chose were usually barbers or non-Brahman priests, both of whom have a "professional" familiarity with community eating habits. Once or twice I suspected that my informants ranked their own group a little higher than was realistic, but generally the presence of my assistant, who was himself a non-Brahman priest, served to make my informants sense that exaggerated descriptions would be disapprovingly received.

to ask how these various types of information were related and whether they showed a plausible correspondence to the more abstract model of regional social organization I had developed. The next section describes the positive results I obtained by matching these two.

ANALYSIS OF SETTLEMENT PATTERNS

My description of the collected data will concentrate on examining five sample locales in some detail. These sample sites provide examples of five different types of microareas with respect to social structure and settlement patterns. After looking at this limited set of data, I will suggest how each of the other sample areas can be grouped with one of the five sample locales on the grounds of general resemblance. This logic will create tentative zones of Koṅku where each of the five variant patterns can be said to generally hold. The next task is to see if these areas correspond geographically to entrance points, entrance areas, and so on of the region, fitting the more general spatial model described earlier. The logical procedure, therefore, will be first to find plausible subdivisions in the dependent variables (dominant caste, settlement pattern, and social hierarchy) that correlate roughly with one another. Then we will see if these differing types correspond in any way to an "independent variable," geographic location. But since a region's geography itself does not do more than provide a setting for human events, I will proceed one step further. The last stage in the inquiry will be to ask whether these dependent variables further correspond with what we know of the history of the area. In the conclusion, therefore, historical developments, as they appear to have been shaped by geographic realities, will be used in an attempt to explain several variant patterns found in the social organization of the Koṅku region today.

Five microareas from my sample survey (numbers 11, 18, 24, 26, 27) have been specially selected. These areas have been identified on Map 1 and are intended to illustrate the following five types of locales:

A. *Fine-grain mix.* Many landowning castes compete within each settlement (24).
B. *Polka-dot mix.* A single but different landowning caste dominates in each neighboring settlement (11).
C. *No mix.* The same landowning caste dominates every settlement (26).
D. *Coarse-grain mix.* Just two or three landowning castes compete within each settlement (18).
E. *Spatial isolate.* A single caste occupies a whole settlement area, and not many other groups are present to compete with or to dominate (27).

The next few pages provide concrete examples of patterns A through D. Comparable settlement data from the one type E sample site (27) were not collected. However, this isolated place can be described verbally.

To reach the representative type E village (27), one must take a winding "ghat" road that leads up a very steep mountainside.[8] This new motor route was opened to traffic just a few years ago. Previously there was only a horse trail. Most residents still choose to climb up and down the cliffs using steep foot paths and root ladders. They carry produce to market on their backs, via these trails. On the tops of these hills there is only one

Figure 3.   Key to settlement charts (Figures 3a–3d), which follow.

[8] There were only 25 villages in my 1972 "sample." Village 27 represents an isolated area that I visited in 1972 but did not think to survey at the time. The value of asking the same systematic questions in this remote spot did not occur to me until afterward. Village 26 represents the village I studied from 1964 to 1966.

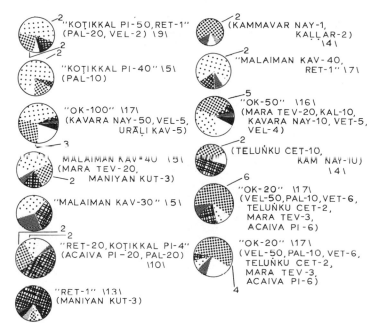

Figure 3a.   Settlement chart, type A (sample area 24): fine-grain intravillage mix.

resident group of any size, the Malai Kavuṇṭars. They have been described as a tribe by the census takers because of their isolation. Malai Kavuṇṭar social organization, however, strikingly resembles that characteristic of the Vēḷḷāḷārs, the dominant caste of the plains below. In particular, the territorial organization of the Malai Kavuṇṭars mirrors on a small scale the traditional organization of the Vēḷḷāḷārs. The main difference, of course, is that the Koṅku or Vēḷḷāḷār Kavuṇṭars live among numerous other groups that they are able to dominate by the fact that they control the majority of the land and resources of the area. The Malai Kavuṇṭars also own land, but since there are few other communities around over which they might exercise control, they are a community largely unto themselves. This social isolation has undoubtedly been important in helping to preserve certain archaic features of their internal organization.[9]

[9] The Ūrāḷi Kavuṇṭars, who live on the fringes of low mountains in the southeastern corner of the Koṅku region, appear to be a similar case of tribelike isolation, though here the details are less clear. Their main organizational features and their relative isolation (some other castes do now live interspersed among them) argue that they also be included as an example of a type E area. Some Ūrāḷi Kavuṇṭars can also be found in the extreme north, near another group of Malai Kavuṇṭars and some Kulasamkaṭṭi Kavuṇṭar enclaves (only the latter are shown on Map 2). This is another area that appears to have tribelike characteristics. Unfortunately, I do not have details. Mauss (1906–1909) and Walker (1965) have argued that the famous Todas (who live in the northwest corner of the Koṅku region) are rather castelike. In my terms, their territory would also represent a type E area.

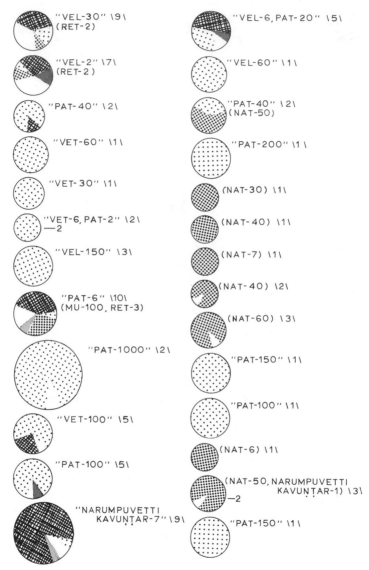

Figure 3b. Settlement chart, type B (sample area 11): polka-dot intervillage mix.

Let us return now to the charts describing the four other types of areas. Notice that the total number of castes present in example A (Figure 3a) is high given the small size of local settlements. Notice also the large number of groups identified as major or minor landowners. No one group even approaches a situation of local dominance. The Vēḷḷāḷārs (also called Koṅku Kavuṇṭars or Vēḷḷāḷā Kavuṇṭars) are present here only in small numbers. Now consider type B (Figure 3b). Here there are still relatively few Vēḷḷāḷārs in the total population. In settlements where they do reside, however, they do so in larger numbers. Other landowning castes, such as the Paṭayācci, Vēṭṭuva, and Nāṭār, clearly control other settlements in the same area. Here there can be little competition for dominance within any one village. Each landowning caste pretty well has a whole village to itself. This is the polka-dot pattern suggested for the second type of area.

A type C area (Figure 3c) is different again. Here the Vēḷḷāḷārs have representatives in every settlement, and no other landowning group is present in sufficient numbers to create any challenge to their hegemony. This is the pattern of true dominance. In a type D area (Figure 3d),

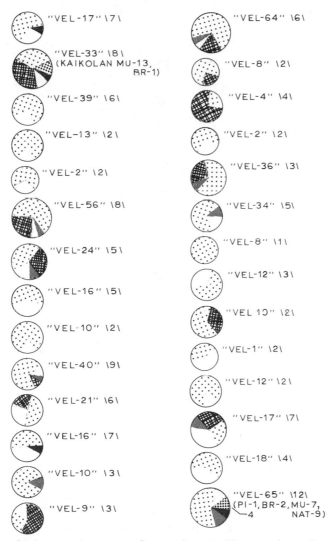

Figure 3c. Settlement chart, type C (sample area 26): no mix, uniform single-caste dominance.

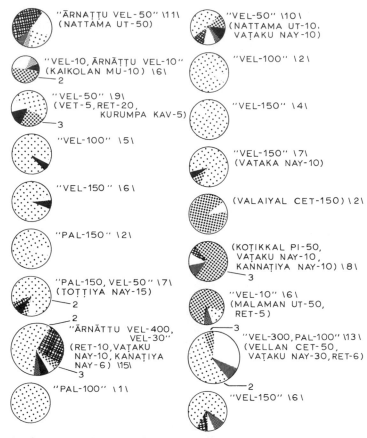

Figure 3d. Settlement chart, type D (sample area 18): coarse-grain intravillage mix.

however, there is a reversion to something more like B. Here again one finds a mixture of landowning castes. But this time the mix within individual settlements is greater. It is not enough to make it "fine grained" (type A), but, on the other hand, only some settlements are dominated by a single caste, so there is not a real polka-dot pattern (type B) either. As in other respects to be pointed out later, type D is the pattern that most resembles disorder. There is a little bit of everything, a kind of coarse mix.

ANALYSIS OF FOOD TRANSACTIONS

Now consider the pattern in the other main type of information gathered on the circle tour, the patterning in food transactions. Each point in the sample survey, as was said earlier, was also the source of a matrix that describes which castes in that microarea would eat or not eat with which other castes present in the same setting. To structure the raw data, each matrix of responses was made into a graph as follows. The number of groups to which a caste succeeds in giving food is transformed into a score on the vertical axis, and the number of groups from which a caste takes food becomes a score on the horizontal axis of the same graph.[10] In this kind of graph, Brahmans are usually found in the upper left-hand corner, as they can give food to everyone but will accept food from none. Untouchables, who take food from all givers but give to none, can usually be found in the extreme lower right-hand corner. Four graphs, one each from microareas A through D, are supplied on the following pages. The main patterns described by these graphs are detailed in the following list. Note that the descriptive terms used match those employed in the general model (Figure 2).

A. *Egalitarian.* So many castes share food that no rank ordering or pattern of alliance is discernible.

B. *Multiple, shifting alliances.* Many castes share food, but there are some differences among them in acceptance and refusal patterns. Attempts at alliance formation and rank ordering are thus clearly discernible. But the distance between these competing "food clubs" is minimal, making shifts relatively easy. Such alliances as do emerge, therefore, are probably unstable.

C. *Single, stable alliance.* A well-defined group of castes (say, three to six castes) shares food. Furthermore, the members of this alliance stand at a marked distance from other groups. Shifts are not easily made. The alliance tends to be stable and its opposition fragmented.

D. *Individualistic.* Each caste has its own transactional rules. Little overall agreement (patterning) is discernible, either with regard to alliances or to simple rank ordering.

E. *Isolationistic.* One caste essentially lives alone in an area. With the exception of a few service groups, there is little opportunity to form alliances or to rank a group vis-à-vis competitors.

Untouchables and low-ranking service groups, such as barbers and washermen, occupy the same inferior position in all five types of structure.

In studying the food transaction graphs, it is important to notice two features in particular. One is the degree to which castes cluster around given points. A cluster is here interpreted to mean that a group of castes has formed an alliance and is giving food to and accepting food from the

---

[10] This method of summarizing the data loses information about which particular castes are involved in given transactions. This is an admitted weakness, but then any method of summarizing data is done at the cost of some detail. At least here one can think of the total score in each dimension as points in a kind of game in which refusal of food or giving food away gains one status and acceptance of food or refusal of one's own cooking by others lowers one's position. I am in agreement with McKim Marriott that there is at least something of this mentality in food transaction logic. I am also indebted to him for his extensive work on this general problem. (See, in particular, Marriott 1959, 1968.)

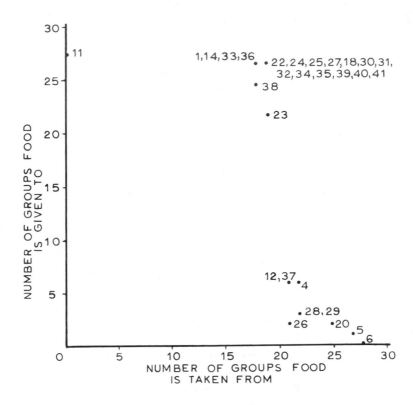

Figure 4a.   Food transaction chart, type A (sample area 24): egalitarian.

ID #	Caste Name	ID #	Caste Name
1	Vēḷḷāḷār Kavuṇṭar	28	Vaṇṇaṉ
4	Boyar	29	Nāvitaṉ
5	Mātāri	30	Malaimāṉ Kavuṇṭar
6	Paraiyār	31	Mara Tevar
11	Vaisnava Brahman	32	Maniyāra Kūṭṭam
12	Maramēri Nātār	33	Kavara Nāyakkar
14	Koṅku Cēttiyār	34	Ūrāli Kavuṇṭar
18	Paṇṭāram	35	Telunku Cēttiyār
20	Kuravar	36	Koṅku Mutaliyar
22	Kamavar Nayakkar	37	Maṇṇuṭaiyār
23	Koṅku Ācāri	38	Kaikoḷa Mutaliyār
24	Kalla Tēvar	39	Ācaiva Piḷḷai
25	Kotikkal Vēḷḷāḷār	40	Vēṭṭuva Kavuṇṭar
26	Paḷḷar	41	Kāppili Kavuṇṭar
27	Reṭṭiyār		

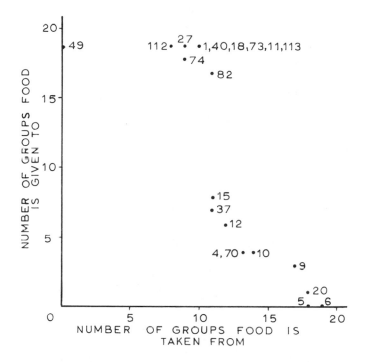

ID #   Caste Name   ID #   Caste Name

 1   Vēḷḷāḷār Kavuṇṭar   27   Rēttiyār
 4   Boyar   37   Maṇṇutaiyār
 5   Mātāri   40   Vēṭṭuva Kavuṇtar
 6   Paraiyār   49   Siva Brahman
 9   Koṅku Vannaṉ   70   Cempatavar
10   Koṅku Nāvitaṉ   73   Vellāṉ Cēttiyār
11   Vaisnava Brahman   74   Ceṅkunta Mutaliyār
12   Maramēri Nāṭar   82   Paṭaiyacci
15   Ācāri   112   Kaṇṇatiya Nāyakkar
18   Pantāram   113   Narampuvetti Kavuṇtar
20   Kuṟavar

Figure 4b.   Food transaction chart, type B (sample area 11): multiple, shifting alliances.

same set of other castes in the system.[11] The other important feature is the degree to which individual points approach any of the four corners of the graph space. A concentration in the lower left corner, for example, suggests

[11] One cannot assume that in any given case two castes that occupy the same point on the graph are necessarily giving food to and receiving food from precisely the same other groups in the system. However, this is certainly true in most cases. In general, Indian transactional matrices that concern food are highly scalable. For the 24 matrices in my sample (I am missing one from sample area 3), the lowest Guttman scalability score is .91, and the average runs about .96. This is despite the obvious discrepancies that appear in the graphs themselves. Hence, we are safe in saying that, in general, castes that share the same point on these graphs are giving to and taking from the same "others." Such similarity represents a kind of food-defined alliance against competitors.

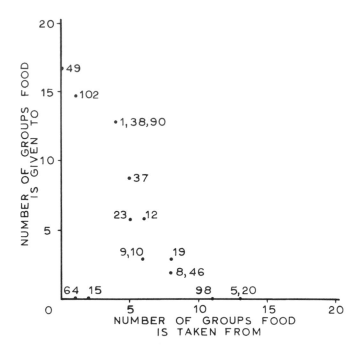

ID #	Caste Name	ID #	Caste Name
1	Koṅku (Vēḷḷāḷār) Kavuṇṭar	23	Koṅku Ācāri
5	Moracu Mātari	37	Koṅku Uṭaiyar
8	Pāṇṭiya Nāvitar	38	Kaikolan Mutaliyar
9	Koṅku Vaṇṇar	46	Vaṭuka Vaṇṇar
10	Koṅku Nāvitar	49	Aiyar Brahman
12	Maramēri Nāṭār	64	Kōmuṭṭi Cēṭṭiyar
15	Cōḷi Ācāri	90	Okaccāṇṭi Paṇṭaram
19	Vaṭuka Nayakkar	98	Koṅku Paraiyār
20	Kuṭai Kuravar	102	Karuṇikar Piḷḷai

Figure 4c. Food transaction chart, type C (sample area 26): single, stable alliance.

disagreement about the local status order and a mutual stand-off in the realm of food transactions. A heavy concentration of points in the upper right corner, on the other hand, represents a high degree of mutual exchange and few stand-offs. The occurrence of scattered points in the lower left corner in combination with a small cluster at some single point high on the graph suggests that the status hierarchy is multidimensional. The occurrence of points only in the upper right quartile indicates that food transactions may be deemphasized altogether as a measure of social status. And, finally, the total spread of points along a diagonal that originates in the upper left corner and terminates in the lower right can be thought of as a measure of the degree of overall hierarchy in the system.

With these generalizations we can now discuss the four examples.

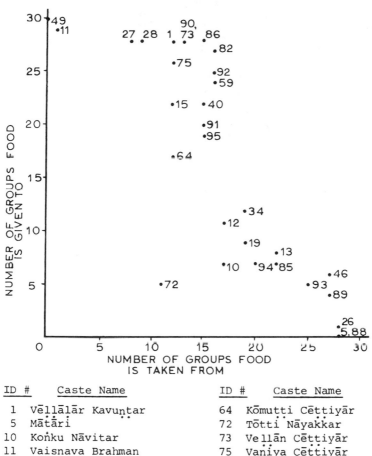

Figure 4d.   Food transaction chart, type D (sample area 18): individualistic.

ID #	Caste Name	ID #	Caste Name
1	Vēllālār Kavuṇtar	64	Kōmutti Cēttiyār
5	Mātāri	72	Tōtti Nāyakkar
10	Koṅku Nāvitar	73	Vellāṇ Cēttiyār
11	Vaisnava Brahman	75	Vaṇiya Cēttiyār
12	Maramēri Nātār	85	Pompaikarar
13	Vatuka Maṇṇutaiyar	86	Ārnāttu Vēllālār
15	Ācāri	87	Nattama Utaiyar
19	Vatuka Nayakkar	88	Coḷiya Paraiyār
26	Pallar	89	Ōttar
27	Rēttiyār	90	Koṅku Pantāram
34	Ūrāli Kavuṇtar	91	Itaiyar
38	Kaikola Mutaliyar	92	Kavaraiyan
40	Vēṭṭuva Kavuṇtar	93	Kannatiya Nayakkar
46	Vatuka Vaṇṇar	94	Uppiliya Nayakkar
49	Siva Brahman	95	Uppānti Pantāram
59	Cōḷiya Vēllālār		

Consider first a microarea of type A (Figure 4a). Here we have a very heavy concentration of castes, not only in the upper right corner but at one particular point. Four more castes are separated from this first group by a margin of just one transaction. Such a situation does not suggest a purposeful alliance so much as a kind of free-for-all in which 17 castes are more or less equal in transactional status. This is not surprising in an area where there is a fine-grain caste mix to the settlement pattern and a kind of overall squeeze effect. Perhaps in such situations status is no longer calculated in food transaction terms at all; instead, fine economic and political distinctions are being made at the family level. I have the impression that the same situation typifies many of the urban areas in the Koṅku region. Such a similarity would be logical given that cities serve as entrance points to regional cultures, just as geographically defined communication routes do.[12]

Now consider a type B area (Figure 4b). Here we find a similar cluster of castes at the top of the food transaction graph. But it is a small cluster and not so far off to the right as in the previous case. Furthermore, there are 4 additional castes located in the same area that are not actually part of the initial cluster but are close to it. This suggests a possible alliance between the 6 castes that do cluster but at the same time some instability in that alliance. It would be easy for realignments to occur by changing a minimal number of transactions. This appears to be a situation of uneasy coalition, where competition in the transaction of food may be fierce and closely watched by status rivals. Here we find 10 different castes that are very nearly (but not quite) alike. Just one or two alterations in local practice could significantly alter their relative transactional ranks. Such a situation seems to fit, as said earlier, with a polka-dot settlement pattern. Each landowning caste has a small domain to itself but is in competition with others for dominance over a larger area.

In the sample area used to illustrate type C, the graph pattern (Figure 4c) has a more stable look to it. Smaller groupings of castes are separated by larger spaces. Furthermore, there is an indication of a clear alliance between castes 1, 38, and 90. Numbers 37, 23, 12, 9, and 10 all perform services for this group and are its satellites. They accept food from almost exactly the same groups as their leaders do, though fewer groups accept food from them. Hence, they lie almost directly under the alliance, in a vertical line with it. Four castes (49, 102, 64, and 15) however, fall significantly to the left of the others. The first of these, the Brahmans, are so placed in all of our examples, but in this case three other castes are follow-

---

[12] Even in premodern eras the local food exchange pattern was probably only one of several means used jointly to establish the relative status of particular castes. As contemporary contestants become more spatially mobile, skepticism about using food in this way seems to be increasing. Greater importance, particularly among youth, is now given to such criteria as clothing, haircut, educated speech, and powerful friends. These "things" (as opposed to transactional norms) can be more easily transferred and recognized when moving from place to place (Marriott 1959). Unfortunately, however, data on these other issues could not be obtained in the course of this particular study, due to severe time constraints. All of these later criteria, it should be noted, vary markedly by individual or by family, in contrast to food standards, which are, in principle, uniform for an entire community.

ing the Brahman example of food refusal. These groups are trying to proclaim their special status in a ritual realm. They serve as a clear countergroup to the agricultural alliance but are different enough from their rivals to allow the situation to stabilize. (See Beck 1972 for a further discussion of this phenomenon.)

In a type D area (Figure 4d), one can notice a significant contrast to all of the previous examples. Food transactions here show little patterning at all. Two castes (90 and 73) may have attempted some sort of alliance, but there are so many other groups scattered in so many positions that the field of competition is undefined. While most nearly resembling type B, this graph is more extreme in its diversity. It suggests a pattern of individual rule building and lacks a genuine alliance or opposition strategy that could lend structure to the whole. This is consistent, of course, with the disordered pattern described for a type D settlement area.

Finally, there is the social structure of a type E microregion. Here a data matrix from which a graph could be constructed is lacking. We can guess, however, that such a graph would have to be very small, as there are very few other groups present with which these isolated landowners could interact. In sum, there would be little multigroup interaction here to structure. The transactions between the Malai Kavuṇṭars and others are so minimal that an opposition to their dominance could hardly develop. Their system presumably replicates a type C structure, but in miniature and without its complexity.

GROUPING THE SAMPLE POINTS

It remains to group the other 22 sample areas by type, using a criterion of resemblance to one of the five locales already discussed. This task was not easy. Settlement pattern types and interaction graph structures did not always quite correspond. Nonetheless, it was possible to arrive at a rough grouping. Settlement pattern classifications were made with the aid of a simple visual examination of the data charts. In the case of the food transaction graphs, a mathematical measure of the degree of clustering was found helpful in distinguishing between types. The formula used required taking each point's share of the total number of castes in the graph, squaring that fractional share, and then totaling the results.[13] This

---

[13] My thanks are due to David Elkins, who suggested the mathematical formula for such a measurement. It is

$$C = \sum_{i=1}^{n} Ti^2$$

where T is any point's decimal share of the total of castes located on the graph and i represents that total. The formula is the inverse of a formula for measuring "fractionalization" in politics and is taken from Douglas Rae (1967).

measure of cluster can be considered a rough assessment of the degree of
competition and of alliance formation present in a local system. Areas having very high cluster scores were labeled A, as the heavy concentration of
points suggested an egalitarian type of interaction setting. Areas having
two or three smaller clusters (and hence a lower score) should be more
intensely competitive; these were classified as type B. Type C areas were
identified as areas having still lower cluster scores than type B locales but
enough point convergence to define one small grouping, that of a dominant
caste and its allies. Type D areas, on the other hand, were taken to be
those with the lowest cluster scores of all. A total lack of clustering was
thus understood to reflect a high degree of caste individualism, such as is
presumed to exist in marginal areas. Cluster scores are not too helpful in
distinguishing type B and C areas, perhaps, but this calculation did
readily distinguish B and D locales, which were hard to separate on the
basis of settlement pattern alone. Differing settlement patterns, on the
other hand, clearly distinguished B and C areas, where the cluster pattern
in social transactions was a less useful guide. With these several factors in
mind, the grouping of sample points shown in Table 1 was made.

Given this grouping, it is now possible to map the findings in relation to
the geographic features of the Koṅku region. This has been done on Map
2. Note that the Koṅku region is clearly defined by a set of high hills that

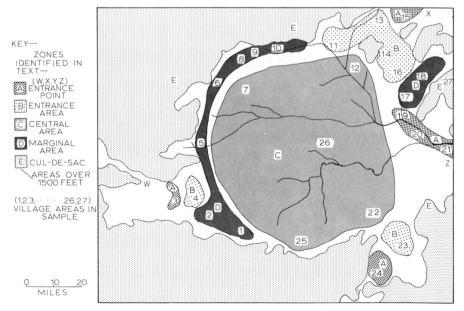

Map 2. The Kóṅku region: geographic and social. Using general impressions, as opposed to
data drawn from particular sample points, one might delimit the region's central area to a
generous southwest quadrant. This is the area where Vēḷḷāḷārs appear to be the truly
dominant group today.

TABLE 1
The Grouping of Sample Points[a]
==

Cluster Score	Settlement Type	Areas Included
.24 - .27	A	(3?), 15, 19, 20, 21, 24
.11 - .15	B	4, 11, 13, 14, 16, 23
.08 - .09	C	7, 12, 22, 25, 26
.04 - .075	D	1, 2, 5, 6, 8, 9, 10, 17, 18, 19
?	E	27 (and other places marked E on Map 2)

a. *The major difficulties in making this "fit" were with*
sample points 7, 22 and 23. First of all, the entire data set
lacked a sufficient number of sample points near the "center"
of the region. Hence category C has been stretched to include
7 and 22,which might, given more points, be better placed in
category D. The settlement patterns of these two areas are not
as dominated by Vēḷḷāḷars as one might wish. There is a related
problem with 23. Here the area is so dominated by the Okkalika
caste that except for the caste name the settlement pattern is
rather like that depicted by Vēḷḷāḷār domination (category C).
Furthermore, according to the historical typology that will be
developed next, the Okkalika belong to category D (because of
having been pushed out of previous administrative and military
foci). Number 23 was categorized by reference to the "cluster
pattern" on its food exchange graph, but using other criteria
it could be included elsewhere. Three other points that raised
a problem were 19, 20 and 21. For a discussion of these see
the text.

surround it on nearly every side. The four main entrance points lie
through a mountain pass on the west (W), among low hills in the northeast
(X) and in the southeast (Y), and along the valley floor directly to the east
(Z). The first finding, then, is that type A areas definitely do lie at the
entrance points labeled by capital letters. Sample area 3, which lies in the
entrance marked W, is probably characterized by the same pattern as the
others in this category, though the data are less complete for this case.
Sample points 19, 20, and 21 fit the predicted settlement pattern for
entrance points very well but are anomalous in one respect: They have the
lowest cluster scores of the entire set of graphs. This finding can perhaps
be explained by the lack of geographic squeeze in a wide river valley in
comparison to a mountain pass.

Thus, type A areas, as predicted, tend to be located at entrance points to
the region. A similar correspondence of pattern to geography can also be
seen in the case of the other model types. Sample areas categorized as B,
for example, tend to be in entrance areas just inside entrance points W, X,

and Y, respectively. Sample areas labeled C are concentrated in the geographically central area. Sample areas classified as D lie in peripheral or marginal areas that are not generally along entrance routes. And areas assumed to have a type E structure lie well up in the hills that border the region—that is, in culs-de-sac. These correspondences suggest that the social types predicted by the model do indeed tend to correspond to particular types of geographic locales. But surely it is not the locale per se that is the fundamental determinant of social types; rather, it is something about the interaction of particular kinds of locations with particular historical processes.[14] Next, therefore, it is important to examine some of the particular groups located in these types of areas, and their social histories, in more detail.

HISTORICAL AND SOCIAL CONSIDERATIONS

Map 3 shows the locations of various important landholding groups that are found along the boundaries of the Koṅku region. The historical background and social characteristics of some of these groups will now be

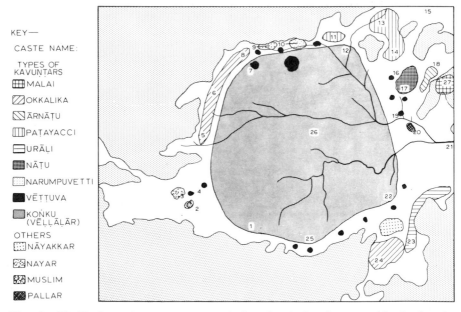

KEY—

CASTE NAME:

TYPES OF KAVUṆṬĀRS

▦ MALAI

◨ OKKALIKA

◩ ĀRNĀṬU

▥ PAṬAYACCI

▭ URĀḶI

▩ NĀṬU

▢ NARUMPUVEṬṬI

■ VĒṬṬUVA

▨ KOṄKU (VĒḶḶĀḶĀR)

OTHERS

▦ NĀYAKKAR

▨ NAYAR

▨ MUSLIM

▨ PALLAR

Map 3. The Koṅku region: concentration of selected agricultural communities, landowning groups only.

[14] B. Cohn (1967) and B. Stein (1967) have both proposed such a correspondence in the Indian context.

briefly described. From the details that follow, it will be seen that this kind of information can also be roughly correlated with the settlement pattern types outlined in Figure 2.[15]

It is useful to begin with the Vēḷḷālār Kavuṇṭars, the dominant caste that gives the Koṅku region its overall character. This group is the one so prominent in the central area and the one most readily identified with the Koṅku region as a whole by outsiders who reside elsewhere in Tamilnadu. These Koṅku Vēḷḷāḷārs, as they style themselves, are generally considered to be an offshoot of the great Vēḷḷāḷār farming class known throughout southern India. There is a fair amount of evidence to suggest that they migrated to the area at the instigation of the Chola kings between the tenth and twelfth centuries and that they were the first to bring extensive areas of the region under the plow. In accordance with Chola administrative policy, and perhaps even before the period of Chola hegemony, the Koṅku region came to be subdivided into 24 smaller units called *nāṭu,* and these into *kirāmams* (revenue villages) and *ūrs* (hamlets). Koṅku Vēḷḷāḷār leaders in the region traditionally spoke of local organization in terms of northern and sourthern halves, four boundary mountains, seven sacred centers, and other such formal features. As a result, these subunits and sacred centers soon came to symbolize the region as a cultural and geographic whole.

The Koṅku Vēḷḷāḷārs (also called Kavuṇṭars) were once governed by an elaborate internal organization, remnants of which remain to this day. For example, their clans were originally matched one-to-one with a set of exogamous *nāṭu* territories (though they are no longer so linked), and each level of administration (*ūr, kirāmam,* and *nāṭu*) had a corresponding headman who oversaw wedding arrangements between clans and arbitrated in cases of dispute. Furthermore, the whole region was (and symbolically still is) headed by four titled families (*paṭṭakkārar*) whose function it was to oversee community business at the highest levels. Although officially this organization existed strictly within the Koṅku Vēḷḷāḷār community, it served many other castes as well. Since these Vēḷḷāḷārs held undisputed sway over the territory as a whole, it was natural that their internal administration be considered by others dependent on them as a final court of appeal. As a part of their role as dominant caste, the Koṅku Vēḷḷāḷārs have always been more than willing to extend their administrative functions in this way. This group will be the sole occupant of category C in the historical typology to be developed next.

When the Koṅku Vēḷḷāḷārs first moved into the Koṅku region and began to bring large parts of it under cultivation, they did not walk into a vacuum. The region was already populated by hunting and gathering

---

[15] Some of this "historical data" is tenuous, much of it is drawn from personal discussions with people in the area about their local legends.

groups and probably by pastoralists who also did occasional farming. The Vēḷḷāḷār immigrants thus had to fight for their new territory, and in the process they seem to have pushed previous residents into the more remote border areas. There is a great epic, sung with some passion by the bards of the region to this day, describing this process of settlement and the ensuing wars. The main antagonists in this story are the Vēṭṭuva (though in fact there were probably other groups as well). The Vēṭṭuva are still found in considerable numbers in the Koṅku area today, though they are (as expected) mainly located in type D marginal areas along the boundaries.[16]

The Okkalika and Nāyakkar caste groups show some similarity with the Vēṭṭuva and have, I believe, a parallel history of being pushed out. The Okkalikas are said to have migrated from Mysore during the period of Hoysala rule over Koṅku (thirteenth and fourteenth centuries), and the Nāyakkar came from Andhra in the same manner during the reign of the Nayaks of Madurai (sixteenth and seventeenth centuries).[17] Both groups, it seems, came into the area as administrators, linked to those in political power at the time. Both were then cast aside during later political struggles in which their benefactors lost out. Now they have become landowners in boundary areas and live interspersed with other landowning groups, as do the Vēṭṭuva.[18] Here we have a coarse mix of landowning castes within individual settlements, a pattern previously associated with a type D area.

The next type of group to be described are those associated with category E. These are the Malai and Ūrāḷi Kavuṇṭars, who are maritally and socially distinct from the Koṅku or Vēḷḷāḷār Kavuṇṭars described earlier. Of these, the Malai Kavuṇṭars clearly constitute the archtype. Three branches or subcastes of Malai Kavuṇṭars live on the tops of three important mountain ranges of the south, the Periyamalai, the Paccaimalai, and the Kollimalai, respectively. Only the third is associated with the Koṅku region, and only the last appears on Maps 2 and 3 (as sample point 27). All three Malai Kavuṇṭar groups are said to be descended from a single set of brothers, the Kollimalai group being the offspring of the youngest of the lot. This last branch claims to have migrated from Kancipuram, an old and very sacred cultural center to the

[16] Other groups that may share a history similar to the Vēṭṭuva are the Nāṭu, the Pālu, and the Centalai Kavuṇṭars. These groups are scattered about in roughly the same areas, but unfortunately I know little about their past movements.

[17] I refer here to the Toṭṭi, Kamava, and Kavara subgroups of Nāyakkar, all of whom own land. There are also groups of stonemasons in Koṅku who, though previously called Ōtan or Bōyar, now style themselves as Nāyakkar, or Vatuka Nāyakkar. Both sets of communities are originally Telugu speaking, and the latter may have come into the area as helpmates or laborers for the former. It would seem that they are not otherwise related.

[18] There are also some areas on the edges of the central core where sons of poor Vēḷḷāḷār Kavuṇṭars forced out by famine or political strife have "homesteaded" new territory. This is the case, for example, with sample area 1.

north, well outside the Koṅku region,[19] and to have settled in their present locale after obtaining the consent of a Chola king. Though, by tradition, these Malai Kavuṇṭars arrived as "outsiders," they say that they became protégés of the same Chola kings who helped the Vēḷḷāḷārs to settle in Koṅku. They also exhibit many of the same features of internal organization as do the latter community. Because of spatial seclusion, they appear to have followed an isolationistic rather than a domineering pattern in their interaction with others (who in any case did not reside nearby until recently). Their territory has thus served as a kind of boundary marker for a much larger and more accessible central area.

Types C, D, and E—that is, the dominant caste of the region and those landowning groups that were either expelled or in some other way remained isolated from the center area—have now been described. It remains to consider types B and A, those who have experienced "compression against" or extended intermingling with the centrally dominant group. These are mainly communities that have tried to penetrate the region, for one reason or another, along its major trade routes after its settlement by a powerful agricultural group. Type B will be considered first, of which type A can be seen as an exaggerated form.

The main examples of type B membership seem to be communities that are originally of warrior ancestry. The specific warrior caste names familiar in this area are the Paṭayācci, who were warriors for the Pallava kings; the Mutaliyar, who fought for the Cholas; and the Muslims, who were converted by the fought for Tippu Sultan. One might also include the Tēvars, who may have fought for the Pandya kings, and the Nayars, who very likely went to battle either for the Ceras or for their successors. All these groups appear to have practiced agriculture on the side when their services were not needed. All were thus interested in establishing themselves as cultivators once their patrons' wars were concluded. Just how these groups managed to acquire land of their own is not always so clear. Some probably obtained grants from their patrons for services rendered, while others, one might suppose, won their land outright with the same martial skills they had previously used in the service of others.

The spatial distribution of these groups suggests that they commonly took up land along the very same trade and migration routes that they had used as warriors. When they did so, they probably came into open competition with other local farming settlements that were likewise expanding. The result produced a polka-dot settlement design in the so-called

[19] The story is consistent and standardized. It has been collected many times and is reported independently in many sources—for example, in Edgar Thurston (1909)—and in several 1961 census monographs on the villages of Tamilnadu, and also in books written in Tamil on the region. I was surprised to hear exactly the same story when I visited the area myself in 1972.

entrance areas. Their residential pattern today suggests that such groups established whole villages for themselves but had to coexist in a larger context with nearby settlements that already belonged to others. Some families from these communities, however, gravitated toward more urban areas. Here they came to live in symbiosis with various merchant communities that had similarly used the trade and communication routes of the region to establish themselves. The two types of groups, similar in some ways, were destined to become bitter rivals (Thurston 1909: Vol. VI, pp. 24–28). Given this kind of historical background, one can easily understand the tendency toward competition for dominance that has developed in type B areas.

The same kinds of castes are also to be found at the region's main entrance points, the type A areas. The difference here is one of geographic squeeze, since entrance points tend to be narrow valleys and thus to be rather sharply defined. In such circumstances the polka-dot pattern has given way to a fine-grain mixture of castes within individual settlements. This close-up competition tended to encourage a kind of openness or free-wheeling situation in which defined lines of group competition did not develop.[20] All of these various historical factors are outlined in Table 2 in order to clarify their correspondence with the various social and structural patterns predicted by the original model.[21] Though these findings are clearly tentative, they do seem worthy of further testing.

CONCLUSIONS

A model of regional organization (Table 2) based on the spatial characteristics of single caste dominance has been proposed. If the center of such a region is characterized by the economic and political hegemony of a single group, then that region should be surrounded by outlying areas displaying two very different kinds of organization. On the one hand, there

[20] It might be possible to link the notion of squeeze and of fine-grain mix, associated here with entrance points and urban areas, with Bernard Cohn's intriguing suggestion (1961) that an increasing convergence of historical images among the several groups of an area measures their movement toward "modernity." The relationship would lie in the squeeze or convergence observable among preexisting groups upon the arrival of some new concept or group in the area. The result would be a "modernization" caused by a convergence of previously distinguishable parts of a structure due to an external "impact" of some sort.

[21] The lack of squeeze at the three sample sites situated in the one river valley entrance to Koṅku (Z) might account for the structural anomaly in their interaction graphs, a lack of clustering. This model, which tries to distinguish central, entrance, and marginal areas in a geographic region, corresponds in a general way to Burton Stein's use (1971) of core, secondary, and periphery zones to describe southern India as a whole at various periods in its history. Although his generalizations apply to a much larger base area, it is reassuring to discover that two conceptual structures, independently developed for the same general material, should so pleasantly converge.

TABLE 2
The Model Complete

	Social Inter-action Type	Geographic Area	Settlement Pattern of Major Landowning Castes	Associated Caste Names	Type of History
A	Egalitarian	Entrance point	Fine-grain intra-village mix	Paṭayācci Muslim Mutaliyar	Warriors' descendants (came from outside region)
B	Multiple, shifting alliances	Entrance area	Polka-dot inter-village mix	Paṭayācci Muslim Mutaliyar Nayar Tēvar Pallar?	Same as above
C	Single, stable alliance	Central area	No mix. Uniform single caste dominance	Koṅku (Vēḷḷāḷar) Kavuṇṭar	Original agricultural settlers and regionally dominant caste
D	Individu-alistic	Buffer or Marginal area	Coarse-grain intra-village mix	Vēṭṭuva Kavuṇṭar Okkalika Nayakkar Vēḷḷāḷar or Koṅku Kavuṇṭar Centalai Kavuṇṭar? Pālu Kavuṇṭar?	Previous occupants or administrators who have been pushed out from the center
E	Isolation-istic	Cul-de-sac	Spatial isolate. Few other groups in area	Malai Kavuṇṭar Urali Kavuṇṭar Ārnātu Kavuṇṭar Naruṁpuveṭṭi Kavuṇṭar?	Early settlers from out-side who established buffer zones between regions with a king's backing

should be entrance areas, lying along trade and communication routes, where other groups have tried to penetrate the area and establish a toehold for themselves. These will be places where an intense competition between castes for the control of land and of other people can be found. In extreme cases, due to geographic squeeze in narrow entrance valleys, a kind of homogenization of social groups may occur, leading to a rather loose or relatively unrestrictive and at the same time egalitarian type of interaction structure. On the other hand, groups that have been pushed out of the central area by those in power will tend to flee to more inaccessible points on the boundaries. Here a kind of individualism reigns, along with a lack of standardization in interaction traditions. In extreme cases certain groups will establish isolated cul-de-sac areas where they interact with practically no outsiders at all.

The explanatory features of this model stress historical processes rather than static conditions. In keeping with this view, regional boundaries are seen to evolve as a response to historical processes as they act in combination with specific geographic restraints. This proposed structure of regional organization has been developed using data collected from the Koṅku region of southern India. Further examination of this proposed pattern is needed, using new information gathered elsewhere.

ACKNOWLEDGMENTS

The field work on which this paper is based was done from May to August 1972. I wish to thank the Shastri Indo-Canadian Institute for its support during this period. In addition, I extend thanks to McKim Marriott, Burton Stein, and Kathleen Gough, all of whom made very helpful comments on an earlier draft. None, however, necessarily concurs with what I have written. For that I alone take responsibility. Finally, I must mention my gratitude to Clarence Maloney, who kindly collected a few missing details for me during his trip to the same area in 1973.

REFERENCES

Bailey, F. G.
　　1957　*Caste and the economic frontier.* Manchester: Manchester Univ. Press.
　　1960　*Tribe, caste and nation.* New York: Oxford Univ. Press.
　　1961　Tribe and caste in India. *Contributions to Indian Sociology* **5:** 7–19.
Beals, Alan
　　1964　Conflict and interlocal festivals in a south Indian region. *The Journal of Asian Studies* **23:** 99–114.
Beck, B.
　　1970　The right–left division of south Indian society. *The Journal of Asian Studies* **29:** 779–798.
　　1972　*Peasant society in Koṅku: A study of right and left subcastes in south India.* Vancouver: Univ. of British Columbia Press.
Cohn, B. S.
　　1955　The changing status of a depressed caste. In *Village India,* edited by McKim Marriott. Chicago: Univ. of Chicago Press. Pp. 53–77.

1961   The pasts of an Indian village. *Comparative Studies in Society and History* **3:** 241–249.

1967   Regions subjective and objective: Their relation to the study of modern Indian history and society. In *Regions and regionalism in south Asian studies: An exploratory study,* edited by R. Crane. Durham: Duke Univ. Monograph Series, No. 5. Pp. 5–37.

Dumont, Louis
1957   *Une Sous-caste de l'Inde du sud.* Paris: Mouton.

Dumont, Louis, and David Pocock
1957   For a sociology of India. *Contributions to Indian Sociology* **1:** 7–22.

Gough, Kathleen
1955   The social structure of a Tanjore village. In *Village India,* edited by McKim Marriott. Chicago: Univ. of Chicago Press. Pp. 36–52.

1960   Caste in a Tanjore village. In *Aspects of caste in south India, Ceylon and northwest Pakistan,* edited by E. Leach. New York: Cambridge Univ. Press. Pp. 11–60.

Hiebert, Paul
1971   Konduru: Structure and intergration in a south Indian village. Minneapolis: Univ. of Minnesota Press.

Homans, George
1950   *The human group.* New York: Harcourt.

Lewis, Oscar
1955   Peasant culture in India and Mexico: A comparative analysis. In *Village India,* edited by McKim Marriott. Chicago: Univ. of Chicago Press. Pp. 145–170.

1958   *Village life in northern India.* Urbana: Univ. of Illinois Press.

Mandelbaum, David G.
1970   *Society in India.* Berkeley: Univ. of California Press.

Marriott, McKim
1959   Interactional and attributional theories of caste ranking. *Man in India* **39:** 92–107.

1968   Caste ranking and food transactions: A matrix analysis. In *Structure and change in Indian society,* edited by M. Singer and B. Cohn. Chicago: Aldine.

Mauss, Marcel
1906–1909   Review of W. H. R. Rivers: The Todas. *Année Sociologique* **9:** 154 158.

Mayer, Adrian
1958   Dominant caste in a region of central India. *Southwestern Journal of Anthropology* **14:** 407–427.

1960   *Caste and kinship in central India.* London: Routledge and Kegan Paul.

Minturn, L., and Hitchcock, J.
1966   *The Rajputs of Khalapur, India.* New York: Wiley.

Nicholas, Ralph
1965   Factions: A comparative analysis. In *Political systems and the distribution of power,* edited by M. Banton. London: Tavistock. Pp. 21–61.

Pearson, K. N.
1973   Merchants and rulers in Mughal India. Paper presented at the 1973 annual meeting of the Association for Asian Studies, Chicago.

Pradhan, M. C.
1966   *The political system of the Jats of northern India.* New York: Oxford Univ. Press.

Rae, Douglas
1967   *The political consequences of electoral laws.* New Haven, Conn. Yale Univ. Press. Pp. 53–56.

Rowe, William L.
1963   Changing rural class structure and the jajmani system. *Human Organization* **22:** 41–44.

Schwartzberg, Joseph E.
   1968   Caste regions of the north Indian plain. In *Structure and change in Indian society,*
          edited by M. Singer and B. Cohn. Chicago: Aldine. Pp. 81–113.
   1965   The distribution of selected castes in the north Indian plain. *Geographical Review*
          15: 477–495.
   1967   Prolegomena to the study of south Asian regions and regionalism. In *Regions and
          regionalism in south Asian studies: An exploratory study,* edited by R. Crane.
          Durham, N.C.: Duke Univ. Monograph Series, No. 5.
Spodek, H.
   1973   Rulers, merchants and other elites in the city-states of Saurashtra, India. Paper
          presented at the 1973 annual meeting of the Association for Asian Studies, Chicago.
Srinivas, M. N.
   1952   *Religion and society among the Coorgs of south India.* London: Asia Publishing
          House.
   1955   The social system of a Mysore village. In *Village India,* edited by McKim Marriott.
          Chicago: Univ. of Chicago Press. Pp. 1–35.
   1959   The dominant caste in Rampura. *American Anthropologist* **61:** 1–16.
Stein, Burton
   1967   Comment on Bernard S. Cohn's paper. In *Regions and regionalism in south Asian
          studies: An exploratory study,* edited by R. Crane. Durham, N. C. Duke Univ.
          Monograph Series., No. 5. Pp. 41–47.
   1971   The segmentary state in south Indian history. Paper presented at the 1971 annual
          meeting of the American Historical Association, New York.
Thurston, Edgar
   1909   *Tribes and castes of southern India.* Madras: Government Press.
Walker, Anthony
   1965   Toda social organization and the role of cattle. Unpublished B. Litt. thesis, Oxford
          Univ.

Section D

POLITICAL ECONOMY: SOCIAL ASPECTS OF ECONOMIC SYSTEMS

The final section of this volume attempts to integrate the study of regional economic systems with the study of regional social systems by focusing on the political economy. In Chapter 11, Appleby examines the social concomitants of the economic system he describes in Volume I, that of Puno, Peru. The economic system is based on export monoculture, a production–distribution system that connects Peruvian peasants with London importing firms. It goes without saying that people in different parts of the system that produces and delivers Peruvian wool play very different economic roles and have very different relations to the production exchange process. By examining the entire process, Appleby relates the organization of one regional system to the world economy, showing the different but complementary economic adaptations of each part and the effects of these on social organization. In so doing, Appleby demonstrates that the Peruvian environment is as conditioned by world variables as by local variables.

In the concluding chapter I use the regional approach to develop a model of stratification for agrarian societies. By concentrating on the exchange economy as a basis for stratification, I suggest several mechanisms by which economic and social inequality can be maintained to which little attention has heretofore been paid. By using regional differentiation of nodal systems as a basis for describing "types" of stratified societies, I can explain much of the variation in stratification systems without recourse to a plethora of ecological variables. Finally, by relating the exchange economy to the spatial distribution of elites, I am able to describe class relations in a new way, showing why differentiation or homogenization of class "cultures" may occur in different systems. Many of the studies in this and the previous volume are used as cases in this paper, demonstrating the utility of the regional approach for comparative studies.

Chapter 11

Export Monoculture and Regional Social Structure in Puno, Peru[1]

Gordon Appleby
Stanford University

THE ORGANIZATION OF
DENDRITIC SYSTEMS

The export of a primary commodity from an area creates a distinctive regional economic organization, commonly labeled a dendritic system (Johnson 1970; Kelley, Chapter 3, Volume I; Smith, Chapter 1, Volume I). This term connotes a hierarchy of commercial centers wherein any center deals with a number of lower-level centers but with only one higher-level center while the whole system focuses on one entrepôt city. Spatially, the pattern of centers resembles a branching tree or dendrite. (See Figure 1, part a.)

Differences in transportation dictate these links. When interregional transport like a railroad is built without improvement in intraregional transport, transport costs at lower levels consume more value than at higher levels. Because the wholesalers must minimize the cost of transport, they can ship only to a center closer to the entrepôt city than themselves. Reversing the commodity flow, a commercial establishment at a lower level must receive goods from a center nearer than itself to the primary

[1] The research on which this essay is based was supported by a NIHM predoctoral fellowship and later by a fellowship from the Organization of American States.

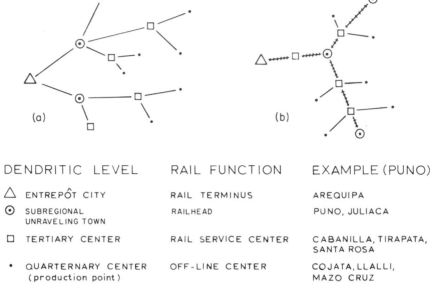

DENDRITIC LEVEL   RAIL FUNCTION   EXAMPLE (PUNO)

△ ENTREPÔT CITY   RAIL TERMINUS   AREQUIPA

⊙ SUBREGIONAL   RAILHEAD   PUNO, JULIACA
   UNRAVELING TOWN

☐ TERTIARY CENTER   RAIL SERVICE CENTER   CABANILLA, TIRAPATA,
                                               SANTA ROSA

• QUARTERNARY CENTER   OFF-LINE CENTER   COJATA, LLALLI,
   (production point)   MAZO CRUZ

Figure 1.   Dendritic structures: (a) standard; (b) under rail transport. Examples from Puno.

redistribution center of the region (Kelley, Chapter 3, Volume I). Otherwise, it could not maintain competitive prices. (See Figure 1, part a.)

Although all dendritic systems are theoretically similar at this level of generality, a number of factors confound the social effects of the economic operation of a dendritic system. First, the amount of land required for production of the export commodity determines the extent of regional reorganization. Second, the aggregation of trade at each higher level requires greater amounts of capital, which limits entry while it may sort merchants into ethnic groups scaled according to their access to capital markets. Third, the organization of the production force conditions the nature of commerce in the area. Not surprisingly, these factors interact and create a complex social situation in any dendritically organized region.

The extent of regional reorganization depends upon the ability of the labor force to produce both the export commodity and its own food requirements. This is possible when the export commodity monopolizes neither all the time nor all the land of the labor force. When the export commodity does monopolize both time and land, however, food production is displaced and the export production area becomes a food deficit area. A trading system arises to move regional staples from the food zone to the export area. The two zones are part of the same system, although the commercial hierarchy typically does not extend into the food production zone. One immediate result of this production distinction is different patterns of land tenure. Investors will purchase land in the export area because low interregional transport costs return high market value for the primary commodity. Conversely, they will not invest in the food-producing area where intraregional transport costs remain high and market values consequently low.[2]

Redfield (1941) reports a typical example of this sequence in the Yucatan. Foreign demand for henequen financed construction of a railroad in the northeastern sector of the state, where lighter rainfall produced a stronger fiber. Henequen estates monopolized this zone, and corn production was displaced to the wetter south. The food zone, however, was peripheral to the commercial hierarchy. For example, Chan Kom, a town in the food zone, had no store until 1938. Rather, the villagers themselves transported their corn to provincial capitals like Valladolid. The difference in land tenure between these two zones was marked: estates in the north, small holder production in the south.

This regional reorganization may predate the export economy due to geographical factors. In the Department of Puno in southern Peru, the highland wool-producing zone historically depended upon more clement agricultural areas for tubers and cereals. The rise in wool exports that occurred with the construction of the Southern Peruvian Railroad reinforced this natural specialization of production. Predictably, towns in the food-producing area lie outside the commercial hierarchy, and land consolidation occurred only on the pastoral *altiplano*.[3]

To the extent that a commercial hierarchy develops, new occupations are created in the export area. Although the numbers and levels of occupations may be a function of the organization of the productive sector, the social identity of merchants at each level relates to their access to operating capital. Merchants at the apex of dendritic systems are typically nationals of the consuming nation. These merchants have access to foreign capital. Meanwhile, local elites underwrite business in the major centers of

[2] Finally, there remains the question of what lies beyond the region. Often the answer is as simple as another system beyond the mountain range or across the international border. While the answer also lies in national geography, both the Yucatan Peninsula and Puno, Peru, illustrate that something more may lie beyond. In both these areas, tropical jungle claims the periphery of the region. Nonetheless, the peoples who inhabit these jungles seem, at times, to form part of a larger economic organization. Although these peoples, colonists in both cases, have little business with the main regional hierarchy, they do produce primary commodities for the international market. In the Yucatan the people of Tusik collected chicle, in Puno they tapped for rubber. Notably, both commodities suffered volatile market conditions of bust or boom. This volatility precluded the construction of transport infrastructure and the development of an urban commercial hierarchy. Still, peddlers appeared periodically. Thus, these tropical areas remained relatively isolated, if not unscathed. This situation, incidentally, points out that the major development in the primary areas of the region is premised upon a steady if bumpy market for the export commodity.

[3] Actually, boat service to lakeside towns extended the reach of the railroad. Stores in these towns bulked regional staples and imported merchandise for *hacendados* (landowning ranchers). In turn, *hacendados* sold their wools to these firms, which shipped the commodity to Puno City. This special extension of the dendritic system premised on rail transport collapsed with the introduction of trucking in the late 1920s.

the producing area, while countrymen (peasants) often enter at the lowest rungs. In other words, a hierarchy of elites parallels the spatial organization of the commercial hierarchy.

Since the commercial hierarchy exists to serve producers, the organization of the production force conditions the nature of commerce and the level of urban development in the export area. The more land concentrated in fewer hands, the fewer the merchants necessary to serve producers, the more local merchants will be by-passed for larger mercantile houses in higher-level centers, and, consequently, the greater the degree of primacy[4] exhibited in the export area.

Redfield's example of the Yucatan appears to illustrate this case. The owners of the large henequen estates depended upon the major commercial houses of Merida and not on local merchants in their area. This situation concentrated urban growth in Merida, which then had a population of 86,000, compared to 10,000 for subsidiary centers like Vallodolid. Puno represents the converse case. Although wool monopolized the *altiplano*, where sheep estates blossomed, countrymen maintained preeminence in the production of alpaca wool. This situation strengthened the commercial hierarchy in the department, so that urbanization was localized through the rail corridor but extreme primacy did not occur.

In sum, the disjunction in transportation underlies the dendritic structure of centers in any region exporting a primary commodity. Transport, however, does not explain the extent of regional reorganization, the patterning of merchants into commercial levels according to ethnic group, the thickness and viability of the commercial hierarchy, or the nature of business in the region. These aspects of dendritic systems vary widely according to access to foreign capital and the organization of local production. Thus, dendritic systems must be considered more broadly as export systems with several components—external demand and foreign capital, interregional transport and its hierarchy of commercial centers, and local organization of productive sectors. In this view, dendritic export systems are not identical, and, therefore, their social consequences for country producers will differ systematically over regions.

THE REGION: HISTORY, PRODUCTION, AND PERIPHERY

The Department of Puno encompasses 27,940 square miles in the southernmost sierra of Peru. Of this area, 4290 square miles are tropical jungle, 1952 square miles are covered by Lake Titicaca, and the remainder, 21,068 square miles, is a very high plain covered with stiff pas-

---

[4] For a discussion of primacy as it relates to dendritic systems, see Smith (Chapter 1, Volume I).

ture grass. The moderating effects of the lake on the 13,000-foot altitude as well as local soil qualities make agriculture possible only along the lakeshore. With distance from the lake, agriculture gives way to a variously mixed farming and herding economy. At the foot of the Andes, which bound the *altiplano* to the east and the west, only herding is possible. This natural specialization in production fostered a traditional rural interdependence between agriculturalists and pastoralists. (See Map 1.)

Economically, colonial Puno was in the middle of everything and in the center of nothing. Cuzco merchants, for example, used the old Incaic road through Puno to provision the mines at Potosí (Gerbi 1941:40). More important, the road made Puno Department a nexus for exchanging Peruvian contraband for that from the south. Merchants from Cuzco and Arequipa brought foodstuffs, including corn, cacao, dried fruit, alcohol,

Map 1.   Department of Puno: administrative boundaries, production, and transportation.

coca, sugar, rice, and flour. Reportedly, ponchos from Otavalo, Ecuador, reached the fairs in Puno. From the south, Argentine muleteers brought their animals, ostensibly for sale on the *altiplano,* laden with merchandise. Silks and other expensive materials from England and France, as well as Cordobán tools and Spanish goods, arrived from Argentina and passed from Puno to the north through a series of annual fairs in Cuzco and Ayacucho (Gerbi 1941:40, 52). Puno thus served as a center of the vast contraband trade that traversed South America in the late colonial era.

Local insecurity after the Wars of Independence, hostile relations among the new nations, and the economic depression in Peru destroyed this transcontinental trade. With the loss of long-distance trade went the economic livelihood of the urban classes. Consequently, very few non-Indians remained in the Department of Puno during the second quarter of the nineteenth century. In the 1820s and 1830s, only 3 to 4 percent of the *altiplano* population was non-Indian (Kubler 1952:11, 18). This ruralization of the department left cellular divisions of the region with few social, political, or economic links. The collapse of long-distance trade, in short, created homogeneous, closed, corporate communities at the lowest political level, the district.

Exports spurred the resurgence of the southern regional economy. Merchants attending the Vilque fair in 1850, then one of the largest in the department, handled 860,000 pesos' business in 2 weeks. While retail sales constituted a third of this total, wholesale bulking of metals, quinine, and wool accounted for more than half the value of all transactions, some 490,000 pesos. Even at this early date, wool was the most actively traded commodity and alpaca the most important fiber. Sheep's wool accounted for a third of the volume and less than a quarter of the value at this time. Although sheep's wool would later gain importance, sizable amounts of wool were already being bulked out of the *altiplano* by 1850. Presumably, small country producers provided most of this supply, despite the closed social and political situation.

The construction of the Southern Peruvian Railroad in the 1870s ushered in a transport revolution that underwrote the expansion of the wool trade, reemphasized natural differentiation of production zones in the department, revivified the urban commercial hierarchy, and restructured the political system.

Southern Peru has always produced wool. Wool export, however, is a modern phenomenon. In 1835 Peru shipped only 8333 quintales of sheep's wool abroad (Tauro 1967:56, 58). In 1892, by contrast, Peru exported 3000 metric tons (66,000 quintales) of both sheep's and alpaca wool, 90 percent of which came from the southern region. The southern port of Mollendo, the coastal railhead, alone accounted for 11 percent of Peru's international sales in 1918, when wool, at its peak, constituted 15 percent of all national exports. Ten years later, wool provided only 2 percent of Perú's external trade because international demand for wool had fallen while industrialized agriculture on the north coast and mining in the central sierra had developed. Nonetheless, diversification of the national economy depended upon regional economies rooted in monoculture. Although wool lost national importance after World War I, it continued supreme in southern Peru. This area has always provided between eight- and nine-tenths of Peru's wool exports. Long unchallenged, wool dominated the economy of southern Peru, particularly of Puno, through the first half of this century.

Pastoralism held a natural predominance on the Puno *altiplano* because agriculture generally fails at these elevations. To supplement their diet, herding peoples traditionally maintained long-distance barter relations with their rural brethren in more temperate areas. Generally, pastoralists throughout the *altiplano* trekked to the agricultural zone around Lake Titicaca to exchange woolens for food staples. Access to fruits and vegetables, however, depended upon proximity. Thus, Huancaneños in the north exploited the Peruvian and Bolivian jungles, as did people along the eastern Cordilleras. Countrymen in northern Melgar Province typically went to the lower country in Cuzco and those in Lampa to areas in the Department of Arequipa. In Puno and Chucuito Provinces, people journeyed to the coastal areas of Moquegua and Tacna to barter. (See Map 1.) In this manner, countrymen throughout the south traditionally provisioned themselves with basic necessities.

Always a food deficit area, the herding zone became more so with the extension of haciendas. Between 1876 and 1915, the number of haciendas increased from 705 to 3219 (Romero 1926:426). Meanwhile, the population of the *altiplano* increased from 200,000 in 1876 to 500,000 in 1940. With less land and more people, the pastoral zone depended more upon the agricultural areas for foodstuffs. The wool boom fostered by the railroad had newly emphasized the traditional interdependence between the two zones.

This dependence of the pastoral area on the agricultural zone led to the different presence of haciendas in each area. Hacienda expansion occurred mainly on the herding *altiplano*. The agricultural lake area did not undergo this massive upheaval in landholding patterns.[5] In part, the sheer mass of countrymen in the agricultural areas with peak densities as high as 250 people per square mile precluded the expansion of haciendas. But, more important, hacienda growth did not occur in the agricultural zone because food from the agricultural zone fed the pastoral labor force. Low

[5] This is not to say that there was no development of haciendas in the agricultural area. As M. A. Quiroga noted in 1915: "*Los pueblos de mestizos y blancos estan esparcidos. Las haciendas van ensanchándose y formandose asombrarsamente á pesar de las resistencias del aborigen* [Quiroga 1915:10]." Nonetheless, the expansion of haciendas in this area was much reduced.

salaries on the *altiplano* meant that workers could not pay much for food. Moreover, primitive transport to the *altiplano* consumed disproportionate amounts of value for bulky foodstuffs. Therefore, investors looked to the wool-producing *altiplano* for new opportunities rather than to the food-supplying lakeside lands. For this reason, *minifundia* continued in the lake area while *latifundia* encroached upon the whole *altiplano*. A similar situation appears to have arisen between the two northernmost zones of the Yucatan Peninsula, as described by Redfield.

THE CORE AREA

The creation of a export system engenders most change in the core area of monoculture production. A simple transport model accounts for many structural changes. Yet many of the functions of a dendritic system are not explained by transport necessities alone. The viability of the commercial hierarchy, the amount of urban and political change, the nature of business—all depend more on the requirements of trade and the organization of production.

Steam transport, for example, requires regularly spaced service centers. Yet, in itself, it engenders little local commercial activity. Rather, these service centers accrete commercial functions because of the disjunction between interregional and intraregional transport. Country goods are brought into these centers for transshipment to the entrepôt city, while merchandise from outside is here broken into smaller lots for distribution in the hinterland. These trade activities support urban commercial development in centers required by steam transport.

Precisely this development occurred in centers along the rail line in the Department of Puno. Entrenched forces in some older provincial centers like Lampa successfully rerouted the railroad away from their towns. The train therefore went through smaller places where little important opposition to steam transport existed. While the older centers declined, the smaller centers grew and were reoriented, resited, and newly founded. Santa Rosa, for example, reoriented to the south, where the rail line passed. The commercial center of Cabana moved several kilometers to the rail line in what is today the district capital of Cabanillas. Finally, José Domingo Choquehuanca and Tirapata, previously small rural communities, evolved into full-fledged political capitals. By the end of the wool era, district capitals existed along the rail line, spaced approximately 30 kilometers apart. Notably, these centers serviced the railroad and performed important commercial functions.

The railroad also underwrote political development at the provincial level. Two provinces that straddle the rail line were created in this century: to the north, Melgar Province in 1901, with Ayaviri as its capital, and, to the west, San Roman Province in 1926, with its seat in Juliaca. In short, the railroad restructured the political hierarchy in its own image.

These political developments reflect the new commercial vitality in urban centers along the rail line. At the beginning of the wool boom, urban size directly related to level in the political hierarchy. In 1876 only five towns in the department recorded populations greater than 1000 inhabitants, and each was a provincial capital. Even Puno City, the departmental capital, then had only 2729 urban residents.[6] By contrast, in 1940, near the end of the wool era, seven towns had populations of at least 2000. Significantly, these all were provincial capitals still. But the urban populations varied widely. Puno City had an urban population of 13,768; Juliaca and Ayaviri, more than 5000, and the others, slightly more than 2000. Thus, population now indexed position in the politicocommercial hierarchy.

Besides restructuring the political hierarchy, the railroad caused important shifts in urban residence. The level of urban residence throughout the department did not increase appreciably in the wool era. In 1876, 11 percent of the 200,000 inhabitants of the department lived in towns; in 1940, 12 percent of the 500,000 Puneños were urban residents. Yet provincial capitals had retained their importance while new centers had arisen along the rail line. Thus, urbanization in the Department of Puno in this period occurred at the expense of older political capitals off the rail line, especially the lower political levels. In other words, the wool trade in the rail era created an urban corridor through the department that made district capitals elsewhere more rural.

Specifically, the disjunction in transportation caused this ruralization. Since transportation consumes most value at the lowest levels when intraregional transportation remains primitive, centers off the rail line can profitably bulk wool only at prices below those of the rail centers. When producers by-pass these noncompetitive centers, commercial activity is concentrated in rail centers, and ruralization occurs elsewhere.

Transport models also predict the number of levels in commercial hierarchies from the functional requirements of the transport system. In southern Peru, for example, four levels of commercial centers existed: The scattered production point, the small rail line center, the subregional unraveling town, and the regional entrepôt city. These correspond in transport terms to the off-the-line center, the rail service center, the rail-head, and the rail terminus. The typical dendritic relation obtained between centers at each level, so that production points dealt with small

___

[6] Ayaviri, which was not yet a provincial capital and still boasted a population of 2563, constitutes an exception to this generalization. This town has always been a major center, situated between the departmental capitals of Puno and Cuzco. In the rail era its importance falls between that of small rail line centers like Cabanilla and Tirapata, on the one hand, and that of unraveling towns like Puno and Juliaca, on the other.

rail line centers or subregional unraveling towns, which in turn dealt with the entrepôt city. (See Figure 1, part b.) The major difference between small centers and unraveling towns lies in the requirements of the wool and merchandise trade. Small centers simply received wool for transshipment, while unraveling towns performed some preparatory operations, such as washing wool. Also, firms in small centers carried general retail merchandise, while commercial firms in unraveling centers proffered more specialized retail merchandise as well as general wholesale dry goods to stores in smaller centers. Thus, the scope of firms' operation corresponds to their level in the commercial hierarchy.

Although transport models may predict commercial and political developments that parallel requirements of particular transportation systems, they cannot predict social consequences that redound upon an area. The ethnic identity of merchants, the strength of the commercial hierarchy, the nature of business, and the evenness of urban development do not depend strictly upon any necessities of transport. To understand these dynamic aspects of dendritic structures, the export system must be considered as a whole.

Export systems have three parts: external demand, with its foregin capital market; interregional transportation, with its hierarchy of bulking and distribution centers; and local organization of production. Thus far, attention has focused upon transport and the commercial hierarchy. Nonetheless, all three parts must be considered if the operation of dendritic systems is to be understood.

External demand and capital operate similarly throughout the world and underlie all export systems. Whether demand is national or international depends upon industrial development in the nation. In Puno, for example, wool was exported for more than 100 years to England and the United States before a strong Peruvian market developed. Yet the system for bulking wool did not change appreciably. Wherever the external market is, knowledge of demand and access to capital provide aliens from the demand area (who reside in the production zone) with an important initial advantage. When the commerce is international, this advantage is even greater because these resident aliens can also control shipping.

Access to capital is particularly crucial because the increased size of operation at each level accordingly imposes greater capital requirements for entry. Ethnic identity appears to have generally determined access to capital in dendritic systems of this period.[7] In Puno initial control of export markets and access to foreign capital markets historically provided resident aliens continuing advantages in commerce. In early republican Peru, for example, foreign houses based in Lima monopolized international trade through a system of agents in major port cities. These agents

---

[7] The more general phenomenon is discussed by C. A. Smith in Chapter 12 of this volume.

possessed local social contacts, knowledge of export production, necessary business acumen, requisite links to firms in the demand area, and extranational support when they were named vice-consuls of their native country to their city of residence. Blessed with these assets, many agents founded independent firms. Guillermo Ricketts, to cite one instance, landed in Islay, a southern Peru port, to work as a bookkeeper for Anthony Gibbs, a major English house in Lima. In time, Ricketts married well locally and established his own mercantile house in Arequipa, the entrepôt city for southern Peru. Ultimately, an oligarchy of Anglo-Peruvian families controlled all international trade in wool and merchandise for this zone. Although this small coterie mixed and married with the national elite, it constituted a distinct ethnic and economic group in the major entrepôt city.

Access to capital similarly ranked merchants in the commercial hierarchy on the *altiplano,* although the system here was not as rigid. Merchants obtain capital in three ways: by birth, by borrowing, and by saving. Those with sufficient inherited wealth, the old regional elite, invested in commercial firms in the unraveling towns or in land. Those who borrowed or earned their capital more often worked in the smaller rail centers. These people generally sprang from the rural agricultural class. Often, they began as itinerant peddlers contracted by stores in rail centers. In time, these individuals gained the ability and confidence to deal directly with firms in the unraveling towns and even the entrepôt city.

The key to these social aspects of commercial establishments lies in access to foreign capital. The Arequipa mercantile houses took short-term loans floated in foreign markets by their English counterparts and allocated this money to local firms on the *altiplano.* The relationship between the two levels of firms was straightforward: "When we give you money, we do no more than facilitate your purchases of wool and contribute to your business which consists of sending us the greatest amount of wool you can."[8] This system naturally led to fierce competition among firms at each lower level, despite collusion at the highest levels. This situation generally characterizes dendritic systems.

Whereas access to international capital sorted merchants into commercial levels according to ethnic identity, access to local capital explains

[8] The following quotations all come from the correspondence of commercial firms and agents in the Department of Puno to the Arequipa mercantile house of Ricketts. This archive is held in the Centro de Documentación Agraria in Lima. Quotations in the original Spanish will be footnoted and the source cited in the following manner: letterbook number, author of letter, date. This citation is thus: 24, F. Garcia, 25–XI–15. In other words, the quote can be found in a letter written by F. Garcia on November 25, 1915, which is in Letterbook 24. The original reads: *"Nosotros al proporcionarle dinero no hacemos otra cosa que darle facilidades para sus compras de lana y contribuir a su negocio que consiste en remitirnos a mayor cantidad de lana que pueda Ud."*

the enigmatic organization of the local production sectors. Puno produces two types of wool: sheep and alpaca. Before the wool boom, the mestizo *hacendados* and small country producers likely participated equally in the production of each fiber. The development of an export system, however, changed this situation. By 1920, sheep's wool production was concentrated on haciendas, which consolidated in fewer hands. By 1930, three families owned 20 percent of the *altiplano* lands, where they specialized in sheep raising and other families also held vast estates. In contrast, indigenous countrymen retained control of alpaca, based in their system of communal lands and smallholding. What had occurred was quite simple. Construction of the railroad facilitated the export of sheep's wool, which had a known international market. Moreover, the government later sponsored experimentation with improved breeds for meat and wool. Those with local capital—the regional *hacendados*—invested in land for sheep. Meanwhile, alpaca, which counted none of these benefits, was left to country producers who lacked sufficient capital. This became a complementary arrangement because alpaca thrive at higher altitudes, where sheep suffer more disease. Thus access to local capital created a production difference between the sheep farms of the vast *altiplano* and individual alpaca flocks in the higher zones.

The two sectors of production dealt differently with the commercial houses, which held distinct consequences for the commercial hierarchy and urban system on the *altiplano*. Consolidation of land in fewer hands undercut the viability of local commercial firms. *Hacendados* with large quantities of wool sold directly to the major mercantile houses of Arequipa. Local firms performed only minimal services, such as transshipping wool. Until the end of World War I, smaller *hacendados* more often dealt with local merchants, which supported local development. And when the wool market stagnated during the interwar period, the commercial houses of Arequipa bought more wool from local merchants in the Department of Puno. Nonetheless, this trade did not provide the major basis for commercial activity on the *altiplano*.

Various mechanisms to assure supply evolved to lessen competition among Arequipa firms for large supplies. These mechanisms also undercut local development. For example, Arequipa firms commonly extended credit throughout the year to *hacendados*. Although the *hacendado* remained free to sell his wool to whichever commercial house offered the best price, manipulation of discounts and interest rates on the debt effectively raised the actual buying price of the creditor firm. In other cases the commercial house in Arequipa actually bought futures. They deposited a stipulated monthly sum in the account of the *hacendado*. The *hacendado,* in turn, contracted to sell all the wool produced at a set price to that commercial house, regardless of the then-current price for wool. Any imbalance at the end of the contract had to be canceled immediately by the debtor party. This mechanism assured the *hacendado* income security and the commercial house a wool supply. Yet it was not a happy arrangement. *Hacendados* broke these contracts when wool prices rose during World War I, and commercial houses stopped offering them when prices fell after that war.

Direct participation in the production of sheep's wool offered another, surer supply of wool for Arequipa firms. In fact, several firms owned large sheep farms on the *altiplano*. One case stands out, that of Enrique W. Gibson, S. A., who organized the Sociedad Ganadera del Sur, a stock company through which Gibson both personally and indirectly owned a number of sheep farms. In all instances the contracts between the farm and the export house stipulated that all wool must be sold to the Gibson company in Arequipa.[9]

In contrast to the direct relation between the entrepôt city firms and sheep's wool production, the Arequipa commercial houses depended completely upon merchants in the *altiplano* rail line centers to bulk alpaca wool. Mercantile houses provided funds and telegraphed price quotations valid for 1 or 2 weeks, depending upon local transport facilities. Local merchants obtained wool for export directly from rural producers or through itinerant peddlers. Either way, the system operated in the same manner.

The unorganized country producer suffered a number of abuses by town merchants. One traveler noted four such prejudices:

> 1. Reduction in price *a fortiori*. 2. Theft on the scales at weighing time. 3. Discount of one pound in twenty-five for dirt, wetness and weight of rope. 4. Finally, the imposition to buy from the agent diverse articles such as alcohol, sugar, unrefined sugar, dates, corn, flour, etc., the prices and weights of which leave a new margin of profit for the agent or forestaller. [Sociedad de Propaganda 1921:209].[10]

Such ruses cost the country producer 5 soles per quintal ($2 U.S. out of $32 U.S. per hundredweight), which created distrust between producer and merchant. Small producers commonly added dung, dirt, grease, and even sugar water to their shearing in order to obtain a 40 percent weight gain. In extreme cases the country producer retaliated smartly. As one

[9] From Title I, Article 2, of the Estatutos de la Sociedad Ganadera del Sur, which Nils Jacobsen has kindly provided. This article reads: *"La adquisición e importación de sementales, maquinarias y viveres y demás para las haciendas, asi como la exportación y venta de lanas y todo cuanto prodúzcan las fincas, se hará unicamente por medio de la firma Enrique W. Gibson, S. A."*

[10] *"1. Rebaja de precio a fortiori. 2. Robo en la romaña al tiempo de pesar. 3. Descuento de 1 lb. en arroba por suciedad, humedad y peso de soga. y 4. en fin, la imposición de comprar al agente, diversos articulos tales como el alcohol, azucar, chancaca, higos, maiz, harina, etc., cuyos precios y pesos deja nueva margen de ganancia para el agente ó alcanzador."*

merchant in Pucara glumly wrote the commercial house in Arequipa:
"During the trip of the Minister of Development [to the experimental
farm at Chuquibambilla], indigenous people surrounded me in the store
and took my weights. Please send me on credit a set of pound weights for a
500-lb. platform scale."[11] This rather hefty theft well illustrates the direct
relationship between the urban commercial corridor and the ruralized
zones of the *altiplano,* where small holder production still held sway.

Despite the animosities between these zones, the country producer was
very much a consumer, and much *altiplano* trade depended upon his
purchases. The wool firms of Arequipa had to maintain agents in each rail
line center or lose this trade,[12] so that often these commercial establishments looked more like bars than businesses.[13] Nonetheless, business
depended upon the country producer, and local merchants catered to their
tastes and buying ability. Lack of country demand was sufficient reason to
return an item,[14] and the Arequipa firms would not substitute more costly
merchandise for items out of stock.[15] In short, countrymen supported the
concentration of commercial establishments in rail centers.

Beyond these constraints, business practices in the same center varied
greatly. One merchant in Santa Rosa dominated commerce there because
"he is serious enough in his dealing with Indians, he gives advances for
wool and very seldom lacks the money to pay on time for the purchases he
makes; moreover, he has a good dry-goods establishment, especially
alcohol, which is what the Indian most consumes."[16] Meanwhile, other
merchants resorted to cut-throat tactics. Ricketts's agent in Santa Rosa at
this same time complained:

> Don Aisicolo Murillo has his store two blocks up from us. He is a person who
> doesn't let a single fiber of wool escape. He grabs every one. In consequence,
> the clientele of Reinoso, Paco Gutierrez, Justo, and others don't go by
> Murillo's door and must take some other street. Six days ago I took possession
> of this store and in that time I haven't been able to buy anything since not a
> single Indian goes by with wool and when they do, they are clients of Reinoso,
> Paco Gutierrez, who has them conducted by store clerks so that Murillo
> doesn't grab them. Even though I've put two men on the outskirts of town to

[11] 493, Vyroubal, 24–VI–27. *"En el viaje del Ministro de Fomento, se me aglomeraron
indígenas en la tienda y me llevaron mis pesos. Les suplico comprar en plaza un juego de
pesas de libras para plataforma de capacidad de 500 lbs."*

[12] 547, Oblitas, 19–VII–29.

[13] No number, Pujault, 19–XI–18.

[14] 340, Parodi, 15–II–21.

[15] 195, Urquiaga, 22–VI–12.

[16] 556, Lazarte, 4–II–30. *"es vastante (sic) serio en sus tratos con el indio, reparte adelantos
para lanas y muy raras [veces] le falta dinero para pagar a su debido tiempo las compras
que hace, además tiene un buen establecimiento de mercaderias, especialmente alcohol que
es lo que mas consume el indio."*

advise people of the existence of my establishment and offering good prices, until now I haven't gotten anything.[17]

As this plaint illustrates, competition among local merchants was fierce, even if it did not necessarily benefit the country producer.

By the turn of this century, countrymen purchased a wide array of foodstuffs and dry goods. Consumption of luxury goods by the small elite *hacendado* class, which nowhere was more than 10 percent of the population, provided too narrow a base for commerce on the *altiplano*. Anyway, most of this trade by-passed local merchants, so that merchants were well aware of the importance of numerous small purchases by countrymen for the success of their stores.

Nonetheless, business declined drastically with the sharp drop in the price of alpaca wool after World War I. Country producers kept their wool in hope of a rise in price, selling only "the most strictly indispensable for their most basic needs." Reportedly, countrymen reverted to more traditional mechanisms of exchange. As many as 20 to 30 women from northern parts of the department attended weekly markets in the more fertile southern agricultural zone to exchange textiles for foodstuffs. This resuscitation of traditional exchange undercut the viability of many commercial establishments.

The collapse of wool prices between the wars led to a consolidation of commercial services into fewer centers along the rail line. The closing of branch offices put Santa Lucia, Santa Rosa, and Tirapata into decline. In Santa Rosa, for example,

> The market was much better to what it is now, since with the establishments of Gibson and Stafford in Ayaviri and Sicuani, and buyers in Nuñoa, Santa Rosa has declined a great deal. At present there are various unoccupied buildings, including those of Stafford, Gibson, Iriberry and others, all of which were in the wool trade before.[18]

[17] 556, Lazarte, 19–VIII–29. "*el caso es que don Aisicolo Murillo tiene su casa dós cuadros mas adelante que nosotros, y es un señor que no deja pasar ni una hebra de lana por adelante, por que toda la acapara, en consecuencia la clientela de Reinoso, Paco Gutierrez, Justo y otros ya no pasan por la puerta de Murillo y se ven obligados a tomar otro camino y hace seis días que he tomado poseción de la casa y durante ese tiempo no he podido comprar nada; por que no pasa ni un solo indio con lana, y si pasan son los clientes de Reinoso, Paco Gutierrez que tienen que ser conducidos por sus muchachos a fín de que Murillo no los ataje. A pesar de haber puesto dos hombres en las afueras del pueblo para que avisen la existencia de mi establecimiento y ofreciendo buenos precios por alpaca, hasta ahora no se ha conseguido nada.*"

[18] 556, Lazarte, 11–II–30. "*este mercado fue muy superior a lo que es en la actualidad, pues con los establecimientos de los señores Gibson y Stafford en Ayaviri y Sicuani, y las firmas compradores en Nuñoa, Santa Rosa ha decaido mucho. En la actualidad, se encuentran varias casas desocupadas como son los de los señores Stafford, Gibson, Iriberry y otras personas particulares; en todas ellas antes se tenía el comercia de lanas.*"

This consolidation of commercial services with the loss of country patronage coincides with the transport revolution in motor vehicles. Although few trucks plied *altiplano* roads until the 1950s, trucking did nonetheless restructure transport requirements. In the late 1920s, merchants already were sending wool overland to Juliaca rather than by boat to Puno.[19] Thus, the lakeside centers lost any role in the wool trade, while commercial services of the *altiplano* contracted into fewer centers.

In sum, change in the core area depended upon access to capital. Capital sorted merchants into levels according to ethnic group and determined the different organizations of production for sheep's and alpaca wool. The presence of many small producers of alpaca in town supported the growth of the commercial corridor along the rail line. Yet it did not create any greater level or urban residence. Presumably, had sheep production not become concentrated in fewer hands, the dendritic commercial hierarchy would have been thicker and more viable, and a greater urbanization might have taken place. As it happened, however, urbanization in the Department of Puno had to await the demise of the dendritic export system and the rise of a regional marketing system moving regional foodstuffs to the cities.[20]

CONCLUSIONS

Transport and trade requirements shape the structure of dendritic systems. Insofar as these requirements are similar throughout the world, the regional structures associated with export economies are identical.

The extent of regional reorganization and the viability and nature of the commercial hierarchy, however, do not depend solely upon transport or trade. When the export commodity monopolizes both labor and space, regional reorganization extends beyond the area tapped by the commercial hierarchy because the export area becomes a food deficit zone. The peripheral food-supplying area remains in small holder production and fails to develop urban centers because investment opportunities are more profitable in the core, export production area.

Investment opportunities therefore account for the development of *latifundia* in the core area. In Puno Department, however, investment paid best in the production of sheep's wool. Alpaca continued to be a less productive and more costly fiber. Thus, production in Puno was organized into two sectors, the sheep *latifundia* and the alpaca *minifundia*.

This difference in organization of the productive sectors directly affected the viability of the commercial hierarchy. Whereas concentration of sheep lands into fewer hands undercut local commerce, the existence of

---

[19] 549, Saravia, 9–XII–29.

[20] Market development in the lakeside agricultural zone is documented in Appleby (Chapter 2, Volume I).

many small producers of alpaca supported the urban commercial hierarchy. The strength of this hierarchy, in turn, created a new pattern of urban distribution in the department and, consequently, a fractionation of political units. Moreover, the presence of many small producers of alpaca also conditioned the nature of business both in and out of town. That stores looked more like bars and that many stores contracted itinerant peddlers related directly to the organization of this sector of production. Finally, when wool prices fell after World War I and country producers reverted to more traditional forms of rural exchange, many firms consolidated services in fewer centers, with a consequent concentration of urban commercial activity in fewer centers.

In sum, as the case of Puno demonstrates, the typical dendritic structure for export depends not only upon transport but also upon foreign capital and local organization of production. These additional factors create more diversity in the thickness and operation of dendritic export systems than has heretofore been suspected through structural analysis alone.

ACKNOWLEDGMENTS

I thank Professors Carol A. Smith and G. William Skinner for the hours they have spent guiding me through anthropology, Professor Benjamin S. Orlove for generously providing me with copies of his reading notes from the Ricketts Archive in the Centro de Documentación Agraria, Dr. Hector Rodrigues Pastor, head of the centro, for his gracious consideration while I worked there, Ing. Atilio Barreda for counterbalancing my views on Puno, and Nils and Terry Jacobsen for reading an earlier version of this essay.

REFERENCES

Gerbi, Antonello
    1941   *Caminos del Perú*. Lima: Banco del Crédito del Perú.
Johnson, E. A. J.
    1970   *The organization of space in developing countries*. Cambridge, Mass. Harvard Univ. Press.
Kubler, George
    1952   *The Indian caste of Perú, 1795–1940*. Smithsonian Institute of Social Anthropology, No. 14. Washington, D.C.: U.S. Government Printing Office.
Quiroga, M. A.
    1915   *La evolución juridica de la propriedad rural en Puno*. Arequipa: Tipografia Quiroz Perea.
Redfield, Robert
    1941   *Folk culture of the Yucatan*. Chicago: Univ. of Chicago Press.
Romero, Emilio
    1928   *Monografia del Departamento de Puno*. Lima: Imp. Torres Aguirre.
Sociedad de Propaganda
    1921   *Guía del sur del Perú*. Arequipa: Sociedad de Propaganda.
Tauro, Alberto (Ed.)
    1967   *Viajeros en el Perú Republicano*. Lima: Univer. de San Marcos.

Chapter 12

Exchange Systems and the Spatial Distribution of Elites: The Organization of Stratification in Agrarian Societies

Carol A. Smith
Duke University

Economic stratification is a defining characteristic of agrarian societies. But agrarian societies are not thereby similar with respect to the number of classes supported, class relations, class mobility, and the amount of stratification found among the peasantry. Although a limited number of agrarian societal types can be isolated by various economic variables, only Marxists have a full explanatory system that can relate differences in the economy to differences in economic stratification. As any rigorous theory must, Marxist theory approaches stratification with a small number of principles, the main ones involving production: Forces and relations of production are seen to structure differential control of the means of production; economic classes are defined in terms of access to or control over the means of production; and variability in class structure is explained by different modes of production. This procedure for examining the basis of stratification is logical, consistent, and in most cases fruitful. Yet agrarian societies exist where control of the means of production does not provide any basis for the division between a powerless producing class and a powerful nonproducing class (Dow 1973; Goody 1971; Lenski 1966;

Smith 1975a). Alternative theories have been found for these cases, but they do not have the general explanatory power of Marxist theory.[1]

This essay proposes that a corollary to the theory of production, anticipated by Marx but ignored by many of his followers and opponents, provides the more general economic explanation for stratification and accounts for the fact that modes of production vary more than modes of stratification and do not always provide the economic basis for stratification. In this corollary production variables are not ignored but are placed within a regional economic framework where the critical variable is the mode of exchange.[2] Stratification is seen to result from differential access to or control over the means of exchange; and variation in stratification systems is related to types of exchange between producers and nonproducers as they affect and are affected by the spatial distribution of the elite and the level of commercialization in the region and beyond. This approach is found to be particularly useful for understanding certain colonial and neocolonial cases of stratification where neither landholdings nor other productive means are alienated from the peasant producers and yet "surplus value" is clearly extracted from the peasantry.[3]

---

[1] This is, of course, my own opinion about the value of various theories of stratification. I should make clear that the discussion here is limited to economic stratification and ignores the whole problem of self-conscious "classes" and strata defined in terms of prestige, honor, or party. In other words, the Weberian niceties about stratification are not considered here, not because I do not consider them important, but because I think they unnecessarily complicate models of "elementary" forces. The discussion here is limited to agrarian (preindustrial) societies, but the same kind of analysis may be applicable to any stratified society.

[2] Marx saw exchange as one aspect of the relations of production, but made exchange strictly subordinate to production as a basis for stratification because he believed along with most scholars of his time that the surplus by which nonproducers exist was determined entirely by the production process (Marx 1971:32–33). Modern evidence suggests, however, that stratification comes first to extract a surplus (through an exchange system) and thereby alter the mode of production. Egalitarian societies fail to produce a surplus not because their technologies do not allow it but because they do not have to support an elite. The old surplus idea did not cripple Marxian analysis in practice inasmuch as in various places Marx defines classes in terms of access to the means of production *and exchange* (1932:13–14), and much of the actual analysis in his major works is devoted to exchange (see Mandel 1970). Indeed, Lenin was able to describe modern forms of imperialism with primary emphasis on the manipulation of exchange (Lenin 1939). Certain recent treatments of Marxist theory (e.g., Meillassoux 1972), however, reiterate the claim that the mode of production is the only important economic process and that to focus on exchange is to focus on relations between things rather than on class relations. Inasmuch as I believe this weakens the generality of the economic model of stratification, this essay was stimulated in part as a corrective to such claims.

[3] My definition of "surplus value" is simply that of Marx, as described in Mandel (1970:82–90), with the caveat that what may be considered absolute necessity by a producer only "becomes" surplus when taken to support a class of nonproducers. In similar vein, my view of peasant "exploitation" (see Dalton 1974) is basically technical, in that exploitation occurs when one group lives off the production of another group, the "morality" of this depending on one's own ethical and political persuasion.

Agrarian societies are societies economically divided between food producers and nonfood producers in which the bulk of the population is engaged in food production. The basis for stratification in all such societies—that which divides the elite[4] from the peasantry and which defines other economic classes—is, without exception, control over some critical resource by select members of that society. The critical resource may be a means of production, such as land, or a means of destruction, such as fire power. But it may also be a simple means of subsistence, such as salt, that cannot be locally procured or produced. In any case, if a stable system of inequality is to be sustained, the stratification system is institutionalized by a system of exchanges in which the elite control the critical nodes or means of exchange. Even in the most obvious situation of control—where a small group exacts tribute from the larger population through use of force—the day-to-day operation of tribute collection is managed in a permanent way by the controlled distribution of one or more scarce resources through an imbalanced exchange system. Where land is a critical resource, for instance, the elite will often use the legal fiction of land ownership to control exchange with peasants, although military means may be an essential ingredient for backing up elite claims and may constitute in some way their part of the bargain. In other words, the classic exploitative production relationship can also be seen as a case of imbalanced exchange: The surplus value created by the producers is "exchanged for" their right to have access to the means of production. Stable stratified societies must always have regular exchanges between producers and nonproducers, if for no other reason than that the nonproducing elite must eat and the producing peasantry must be guaranteed a survival amount of the scarce resource that empowers the elite.[5]

We need not assume that where exchange is used to describe a class relationship, the value that each party receives is equivalent. In fact, where the exchange involves any kind of scarce, critical resource, it is ideological

---

[4] I use the term "elite" throughout as reference to nonproducers who have special access to the means of exchange. This term is an imprecise one, and it may be more useful to specify the means by which a given elite under discussion has control over producers in the term. But since this study is not concerned with production relations per se, terms such as "bourgeois" are not particularly useful; better descriptive terms, such as the "landed" elite of X or the "fish" elite of Y, occasionally sound absurd. Hence, I simply use the term "elite," attempting to specify at some point the means by which the group under discussion becomes an elite class and whether it is a local, regional, national, or even higher-level elite. While merchant and middleman classes are also nonproducers in the technical sense, I set them apart from "the" elite because they typically form a separate class in terms of relations to the means of exchange. When mercantile trade is the major basis of stratification in the system, however, mercantile traders are considered to be the elite.

[5] Clearly, nonproducers' advantage can lie in at least three basic areas: control of critical commodities, control of production, or control of the means of destruction; the point here is that in any event an *economy* forms that operates through an imbalanced exchange system.

nonsense or elite myth to believe that the value the advantaged party gives (patronage, protection, wages, and so on) will balance what he receives (surplus goods, power, prestige, and the like), as suggested by Homans (1961) and more recently Dalton (1974). Even if the disadvantaged party is somehow made to believe that the exchange is balanced, this is hardly evidence that the exchange is in fact balanced. Rather, *because* the elite party controls a critical resource, he is in a position to maintain a system of *imbalanced* exchanges. In this regard, my argument is identical to the standard Marxist argument. Our positions differ in that I see production resources as just one—and not necessarily the most fundamental—of many types of critical resources that can be manipulated by the elite. The lower classes may own or have inalienable rights to the means of production, but the upper classes are always strategically placed in relation to the distribution system created by particular modes of exchange. With this shift in emphasis, imbalanced exchange rather than diversified production becomes the distinguishing characteristic of stratified societies; and the special economic status of the elite is seen to depend upon their control of distribution and exchange rather than production.

The value of casting stratification in the mold of exchange and distribution theories is that one can thereby explain certain regularities of class relations that are independent of the production system. For instance, one may have a feudal clientage relationship where peasants exchange surplus goods in one case for access to salt and in another case for access to land. The stratification system will be identical in both cases even though the production relationship may vary, explained by the fact that in both cases exchanges are organized by the elite without market mediation and without the involvement of other classes such as merchants. Direct rather than market exchange is basic to this particular class relationship, not the mode of production that creates a certain level of surplus. Surplus is a product of exchange, not a fact of production, for its level depends upon the means used to extract it, not just the means used to produce it.[6] The point is that while distribution and production systems are related, the distribution system can be organized in very few ways, thereby constraining the manner in which a host of production systems empower the elite. Furthermore, the way in which the distribution system is organized leads to differences in the mechanisms that elites employ for control; hence, stratification will differ in systems dominated by the same system of production if in one area the product is marketed and in another it is not, and there is nothing intrinsic to the production system that determines if it is to be exchanged through markets. Therefore, I argue that distribution

---

[6] That scarcity rather than surplus has led to intensified production, economic stratification, and complex societies is becoming the new anthropological orthodoxy (see, for example, Lee and DeVore 1968; Spooner 1972).

systems play the critical roles in delimiting types of stratification found in the agrarian world, regardless of whether they allocate use commodities or capital goods, and it is their differences and origins that call for explanation. Inasmuch as the spatioeconomic forms of distribution systems provide a key for differentiating modes of stratification, I will concentrate on these aspects of distribution in my treatment of stratification.

The spatial distribution of people is the other delimiting element of stratification. Peasants, being farmers, are by the nature of their occupation settled and distributed relatively evenly throughout humanly exploitable rural areas. But several possibilities are open to the elite: (1) distribution throughout rural areas where peasants live (but with the option of mobility not available to peasants); (2) exclusive congregation in market towns or urban centers removed from areas where peasants live; and (3) mixed distribution, so that some members of the elite reside among the peasantry while others are physically removed in central places (or the same people move back and forth). Different types of exchange and distribution are not all equally compatible with different spatial distributions of the elite. In fact, some constellations are so much more probable than others that one should be able to predict the spatial distribution of the elite from the organization and spatial extension of the distribution system. This information, together with the fact that each exchange relationship implies certain things about interclass relations, should enable one to determine the general features of stratification in a society—that is, the likely number of classes, class life style distinctiveness, class mobility chances, and the socioeconomic adaptation of peasants.

Before dealing with these aspects of class structure, however, brief attention must be given to the economics and spatial organization of distribution systems, the major intervening variables in the model proposed here. I devote the next section to showing the limited ways in which distribution systems can be organized, constructing a typology of them that justifies my selection of agrarian societal types for analysis. But I reserve discussion of the conditions that give rise to them and the ways in which they maintain economic inequality for later, when I use specific examples of stratified agrarian societies to relate distribution and exchange systems to class structure, pitting this view of stratification against other views.

AGRARIAN DISTRIBUTION SYSTEMS

For both economic and regional–spatial analysis, the most important dimension along which distribution systems can be distinguished is extent of the division of labor or degree of commercialization. This is, in a sense, my independent variable, which I assume without attempting to justify fully here is caused by scarcity of some necessary good(s) in a particular economic system.[7] The greater the resource scarcity, for whatever reasons, the greater the amount of intensification, division of labor, and commercialization of allocation necessary for a viable economy.

Commercialization is clearly a continuous variable, but for heuristic purposes I have divided it into three levels: (a) *uncommercialized,* where distribution systems are based on direct or *nonmarket exchange;* (2) *partially commercialized,* where distribution systems are based on noncompetitive or *controlled market exchange;* and (3) *fully commercialized,* where distribution systems are based on broadly articulated, *competitive market exchange.* These three levels are differentiated not only by amount of commercial integration or division of labor but by the spatial range of the economic system and the degree to which a price-making market allocates commodities and the factors of production. They are not evolutionary levels, however, in the sense that one expects a progression from one level to another with simple increases in population or technology. Rather, they are general modes of economic integration, created by a congeries of economic and political events. In fact, one of the main points to be made here is that most of the complex distribution systems, defined later, are dependent upon the coexistence of one or more of the other distribution types in the broader economic system. It is in this respect that a regional perspective on exchange and stratification is critical.

The spatial organization of distribution can vary within a given level of commercialization. Its features will depend upon the degree to which spatial extension of the system and hierarchical formalization of exchange are required to obtain all the necessary goods for a particular level of commerce. On the basis of available descriptions of agrarian distribution systems, I have isolated two kinds of spatial arrangements compatible with each of the three levels of commercialization.[8] Figure 1 describes them as spatial systems; Table 1 describes them as economic systems. I will argue that each of these distribution systems in otherwise diverse economies determines the economic relations between producers and nonproducers.

As can be seen in Figure 1, the critical structural attributes of distribution systems are networks, hierarchies, and inclusiveness of system integration. *Extended network systems* (1a) have several places related

---

[7] The kind of economic scarcity that leads to inequality may be caused initially by population growth or ecological change; but later, scarcity can be induced by the organization of production, labor, and exchange itself. Certainly the market, which organizes specialization and production so that basic scarcities are overcome, institutionalizes other scarcities that promote intensified production.

[8] The models of spatial economic organization are more fully explained and referenced in Chapter 1, Volume I.

through trade, but the flows are horizontal between equivalent centers, so that exchange is poorly organized. *Bounded network systems* (1b) are well organized by a local hierarchy, but trade outside the small local system is limited and thus cannot affect the local economy. *Solar central-place systems* (1c) have well-organized networks articulated by a strong inclusive hierarchy, but each local system is closed beyond the range of a single major center. *Dendritic central-place systems* (1d) are hierarchical systems without horizontal networks that are open to a theoretically infinite area but are restricted to a narrow range of relationships by ties that are exclusively vertical. *Interlocking central-place systems* (1e and 1f) display both hierarchical organization and network links and are broadly open to a wide range of relationships among all places and thereby all people in the system. The importance of these differences in organization from the economic viewpoint of a food producer is in the implied direction of commodity flow and thus the location of nodes from which price information is communicated. Viewing trade from this perspective explains why each distribution system is associated with a certain level of commercialization.

In extended network systems, each local unit, be it household or community, has multiple links to other equivalent units with which trade is conducted. Goods, people, and information can move along network paths, but because the paths are undifferentiated and poorly articulated with each other, allowing little feedback in demand information, the distribution system has little effect on the economic organization of production.[9] Some extended networks have extremely wide reach—certain Melanesian trade rings (Brookfield 1971; Harding 1967) or the trade networks of lowland South America (Harner 1972; Lathrop 1973) come to mind as examples. But however wide the reach of the trade system, individual nodes or interconnected local economic systems remain at a primitive level of specialization, and the potential regional "market" regulates production decisions minimally. No broader economic system is formed by the links of the network because no nodes become differentiated or hierarchically dominant, and therefore no higher level of integration is attained. It follows that local economies connected by extended networks are uncom-

[9] Rappaport suggests that in simple network systems production "insufficiencies would develop because the production of each of the two commodities [involved] would not be determined by the demand for that commodity, but by the demand for the commodity for which it was exchanged [1967:109]." Simulations of such exchange networks have shown this to be true. On the other hand, Rappaport suggests that if generally scarce items with prestige value were introduced into the system, production could be regulated in a network system. This, in fact, seems to regulate production for exchange in certain parts of New Guinea and certainly the *kula* trade of Melanesia. Hence the common phenomena of partially bounded, prestige-regulated networks with "big men" at their centers; scarcities in these systems, however, are sufficiently unpredictable that fully stratified societies do not emerge.

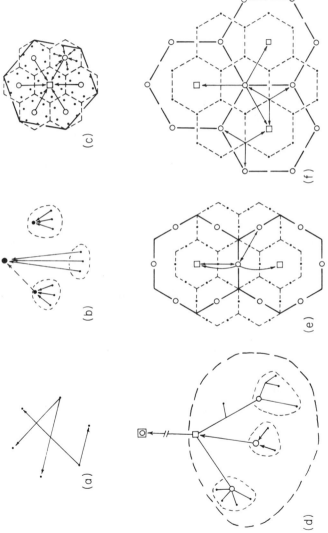

Figure 1. Six ideal systems of nodes or central places. a = an unbounded network system; b = a bounded, hierarchical network system; c = a solar central-place system; d = a dendritic central-place system; e and f = interlocking central-place systems. Dashed lines show boundaries of the system; arrows show relationship of lower-level to higher-level center(s); size of nodes or central places shows order in the hierarchy; open symbols are market centers, closed symbols places without markets.

TABLE 1
Exchange Types and Distribution Systems

	Dyadic, direct	Polyadic, direct	Administered market	Monopolistic market	Competitive market
1. Exchange Type	Dyadic, direct	Polyadic, direct	Administered market	Monopolistic market	Competitive market
2. Division of Labor	None	Very low	Low	Moderate	High
3. Level of Commerce	Uncommercialized	Uncommercialized	Partially commercialized	Partially commercialized	Fully commercialized
4. Stress or Scarcity	Low but some resources unpredictable	Moderate, a few scarce resources	High because of bureaucratic "drain"	High because of limited internal specialization	High because of division of labor
5. Regional Extension	Moderate	Lowest	Moderate	Highest	High
6. Distribution System	Extended network system	Bounded network system	Solar central-place system	Dendritic central-place system	Interlocking central-place system
7. Where Found	Independent "tribal" societies	"Chiefdoms," "feudal" manors	Premodern colonies, developing states and empires	"Peripheries" of "modern" economic systems	"Cores" of "modern" economic systems
8. Spatial Characteristics	Fig. 1a	Fig. 1b	Fig. 1c	Fig. 1d	Fig. 1e, 1f

mercialized, and I will argue that this distribution system does not support stratification.[10]

In bounded network systems, households or communities have links to a nodal center that can allocate specialties among them. But the circumscribed reach and lack of contact among local production systems allow little use of comparative advantage or economies of scale in production without which pricing mechanisms are useless to stimulate diversified production. Indeed, true price-setting markets cannot exist because markets only function to regulate production when at least some factors of production are mobile across local systems. Specialization, therefore, is likely to involve only services that can be allocated by personal agreements—as in some villages in India. The vast majority of people will be engaged in food production for their own consumption. The low level of production assured by limited areas of distribution is guaranteed when the visible hands of people rather than the invisible hand of the market controls production. What is allowed in the way of specialization by hierarchical centralization, then, is restricted by the limited range of the economy, making bounded distribution systems somewhat more specialized but little more commercialized than extended network systems. Certain "chiefdoms," feudal manors, small patrimonial states, and some *jajmani*-organized villages of India provide examples of bounded network systems in which stratification is supported.

Distribution systems in partially commercialized societies are distinguished from those in uncommercialized societies by having one or more central places whose primary function is to organize and articulate production and exchange among several local systems. A central place is not identifiable by population size but by commercial functions—that is, by having a marketplace that provides a locus for price feedback to its dependent hinterland. Hierarchical organization and middlemen, necessary to functioning central-place systems, allow greater specialization and intensification of trade than is possible in local systems where exchange between producer and nonproducer is direct. Both partially and fully commercialized systems have central places. What distinguishes the former are particular central-place arrangements that preclude competition among them for rural trade. Market centers are set apart from the economic systems of their rural hinterlands, so that rural peasants do not reap the benefits of full commercial integration into the regional economy.

In solar central-place systems (Figure 1, part c), urban centers are

[10] Extended network systems are not restricted to small-scale societies, inasmuch as some peasant marketing systems seem to fit the description (see, for example, Bohannan and Bohannan 1968). Although peasant marketing systems always feed into higher-level centers, and thereby are associated with class stratification, when the rural peasant markets are not hierarchically organized, there is no stratification among the peasantry. (See the discussion of Tiv markets in Smith, Chapter 1, Volume I.)

located in the middle of tributary hinterlands, and all rural places are connected to only one of them for marketing. Large centers are without competition from intermediate-sized centers (market towns) on the borders of their territories (as in Figure 1, parts e and f) and themselves fall into the hinterland of a single larger center. Political–territorial or administrative systems are always based on this simple design, although of course most are not so regular in shape. No system of administration can allow overlapping boundaries or competing centers; power and responsibility must be delegated exclusively at each level in a pyramidal chain of command, as provided by this arrangement.[11] But an administrative arrangement is also conducive to monopolistic market control. If only administrative centers conduct trade, and if they are widely spaced or meet on the same day of the week as markets, there will be no possibility for peasant producers to seek other markets with better prices. Hence, the division of labor can proceed only somewhat beyond the local level—normally to include the few places within regular commuting distance of each market. Because each market is in a monopoly position, moreover, division of labor is limited by the fact that producers cannot afford to give up producing their own subsistence requirements or alienate their means of production to the highest bidder without considerable risk. Specialization will therefore involve only simple handicrafts or farm goods that do not require much in the way of labor expenditure or full-time specialization. This type of distribution was common to many historic bureaucratic societies, from which I have chosen colonial Latin American cases as examples.

A dendritic central-place system differs from the solar system by its openness to ever larger areas of trade. Markets form a linear arrangement that is inclusively vertical, oriented to a single point outside the local agrarian region. Collecting points at different levels of the system link to several smaller places, but to only one major, high-level center (Figure 1, part d). Flows are direct, linking levels of hierarchies, but not the local systems that surround each level of the hierarchy, which eliminates competition among high-level markets for a producing hinterland. Thus, while many *places* are connected, they connect to only one price-setting *market*. The arrangement is not efficient for interconnecting markets in the agrarian region but is efficient for channeling the upward flow of raw materials from the agrarian region and the downward flow of specialized goods from the major urban center. Since rural goods do not flow with regularity across rural markets, peasants cannot depend on the market for their food supplies. As a result, peasants at the peripheral ends of dendritic systems

---

[11] Skinner was the first to observe the incompatibility of "administrative" systems with "commercial" systems (1964, 1968). He suggests that where the economy is not administered, the economic and political centers will be independent of one another, so that level in the political hierarchy will not predict level in the economic hierarchy. But in administered *economies*, the two systems should be indistinguishable.

are little more commercialized than those in solar systems: They specialize in producing goods for a broad, often international, market and consume other goods from that market; but at the same time they produce their own subsistence goods. Many agrarian regions in the modern world provide examples of this distribution system, but only western Guatemala has been sufficiently well described for detailed analysis (see also Appleby, Chapter 11, this volume); other possible cases will be suggested, however, the main one being Indonesia.

Fully commercialized systems integrate rural specialization with urban specialization because rural markets are at once connected to urban markets (which sets them apart from uncommercialized systems) and to each other (which sets them apart from partially commercialized systems). As in the partially commercialized systems, multiple market centers are spatially organized by multileveled tiers of places. But they are organized by a *network* of hierarchical relationships rather than a *pyramid* or *chain* of hierarchical relationships. Again there are two basic spatial patterns for fully commercialized systems (Figure 1, parts e and f); while differences in them may structure differences in stratification, information is too limited to allow analysis at this time.[12] Both types are interlocking systems.

In interlocking systems each market center is linked to several higher-level centers (unlike the markets in Figure 1, parts c and d) as well as to several lower-level centers. This creates a network with several levels, several links between levels, and hierarchically organized service to all places in the system. Goods flow to and from other systems and regions but are also exchanged within the local system at each level. Trade areas are overlapping and economic regions unbounded. Hence, supply and demand or price information is communicated across broad areas to ensure coordination of specialization. Under these circumstances the rural consumer can stay put and still enjoy product diversity in his marketplace; he can also depend on a broad market for the goods he produces. This allows specialization within the realm of food production, so that rural areas become as market dependent if not as diversified as urban centers. China and late Tokugawa Japan will provide the major illustrations of this distribution system.

Each of the distribution systems described here provides a basic structure for an agrarian economy that implies certain economic or exchange relationships between food producers and nonfood producers. I argue that they thereby structure a mode of stratification. I take up this argument in the following pages, considering each of the three commercial levels—uncommercialized, partially commercialized, and fully commercialized—

---

[12] These two interlocking systems are known in the literature as $K = 4$ (Figure 1, part e) and $K = 3$ (Figure 1, part f). Their distinctive properties are described in Smith (Chapter 1, Volume I).

as a unit so that my more detailed discussion of exchange and distribution is not far separated from my discussion of stratification and the cases used to support the argument. Each unit is organized as follows. First I consider the conditions under which the two economic systems compatible with a given level of commerce are likely to be instituted, and show the features of each that lead to differential access to the means of exchange. Then I link each economic system to the spatial distributions of the elite that are possible, and within the parameters set by these variables propose the logically consistent mode of stratification. The relationships posited are supported with empirical examples that have been described with enough detail to illustrate my points and by the "solutions" that my model provides for some thorny problems in the analysis of stratification. Because there are so few thoroughgoing descriptions of agrarian exchange and distribution systems, it is impossible to test the various propositions; hence, this essay is programmatic in the extreme. It is hoped that future studies will allow a systematic approach to verification. But for the present, my aim is simply to suggest some of the relationships between regional exchange systems and regional social structure—relationships that clearly require further consideration by students of economic stratification.

UNCOMMERCIALIZED SYSTEMS

In uncommercialized societies that lack markets, exchanges are direct, so that the exchanging parties are in face-to-face contact. Depending on the objectives of exchange and the circumstances under which it takes place, one may have direct *dyadic exchange* (between two equivalent individuals), which creates *extended network distribution systems*; or direct *polyadic exchange* (between a member of the elite and several subordinates), which creates *bounded network distribution systems*. Most uncommercialized societies combine the two types of direct exchange in several different ways. But for purposes of isolating the formal characteristics of direct exchange relevant to stratification, I will concentrate on the two extremes: externally oriented dyadic exchange, which suports egalitarian social structure; and simple localized polyadic exchange, which supports clear-cut and stable differentiation of economic classes.[13] The factors

---

[13] The intermediate forms, usually bounded systems without hierarchical nodes or very unstable, shifting ones, occur where resources are scarce but no one group can control them because of their uncertain or unpredictable distribution in the environment (Kelley 1976). These lead to an intermediate form of stratification, what anthropologists call "ranking" or the phenomenon of "big men" (Fried 1967; Sahlins 1958, 1963); but since anthropologists have dealt with these at length in much the same framework I use, I do not deal with them here. Unfortunately, however, most anthropologists consider the exchange model developed for these intermediate cases to be inapplicable to market societies.

that determine the outcome are scarcity and predictability of critical resources.

If a critical resource is unpredictable in either time or space, it will be exchanged widely among many groups in an extended network (Kelley 1976). For in the face of uncertain supply, when one cannot depend on any one channel to provide help at any given time, one must maintain a variety of channels through which access to the resource is possible. This requires that nonexclusive relationships between multiple dyads be formed on the basis of balanced exchange, which by preventing the development of dependency or hierarchy allows the various parties to seek new sources of supply as the distribution of the resource dictates. Multiple dyadic relationships provide the greatest number and extension of ties, and a balanced contract permits options to be taken as they present greatest benefit.[14] Since all have irregular access to the resource, no inequality results from the quid pro quo exchange of it. Even if the unpredictable resource is also scarce, inequality is at best shifting and unstable. For as long as no party can control a critical resource—and by definition one cannot control an unpredictable one—long-term hierarchical relationships are not possible.[15]

When one party *consistently* controls a scarce resource for which others have need, however, exchanges will take quite another form. The dominant party exchanges the resource he controls, or something he

[14] The marriage exchange system described by Jackson (Chapter 3, this volume) provides a case in point. All settlements in the system she describes produce women and can produce all other necessities—no resources are scarce. But each settlement is so small that it produces marriageable women infrequently and at highly unpredictable rates. Hence, ties must be spread widely and the exchange relationship kept balanced to ensure that people can be distributed in relation to unpredictable need. In accordance with prediction, the marriage system is institutionalized by a rule that requires settlements to seek women outside the language group and thereby further afield than necessary for strictly demographic reasons; and the exchange is kept balanced, the ideal form being direct sister exchange. It is interesting to note that hierarchical organization of exchange, and consequent ranking of groups, may have occurred in the past when "groups with higher rank and more allies—and more numbers among themselves—apparently occupied the larger rivers, particularly sites on river mouths [Volume I:70]." Marriage networks were more restricted then presumably because the allied groups were larger and thus the supply of women more predictable; in addition, higher population density made scarce some trade goods or military advantage at predictable locations (river mouths), which allowed at least the incipient development of hierarchical exchange networks.

[15] The commonplace phenomenon of "generalized" exchange (Sahlins 1965), where a balance is never achieved *in order* to maintain a relationship, would seem to rest on "real" scarcities that are unpredictably reversible. For instance, the Bushman hunter provides a necessary (scarce) good to his band without expectation of an immediate or balanced return because he must maintain a relationship with that group for his own unpredictable needs—he may be unlucky for the next 3 months. On the other hand, the Bushman hunter (male) may have more prestige and power than the Bushman gatherer (female) because he deals in a scarce resource. Notably, most forms of generalized exchange occur within bounded rather than unbounded social groups.

derives from it, for a nonequivalent good from several subordinates. Should he control weapons, for example, he might give his subordinates protection from others like himself in exchange for a regular supply of food. Since his clients need him more than he needs any one of them for survival, the exchange will *not* be balanced—unless the dominant party is unusually altruistic. Nor will the network be extended; continuing scarcity of a critical resource will enforce restriction of the network to those parties who have a formal agreement with respect to its distribution. I term this polyadic exchange to distinguish it from dyadic exchange. The two systems have little in common except lack of intermediaries—although they may be phrased in the same ideological idiom.[16]

Polyadic exchange separates an elite class from the peasantry, but lack of commerce restricts the elite class in numbers and disperses them widely at the nodes of small, closed, rural systems. The size of the systems is determined by the distance over which the elite can control the distribution of the scarce resource. In the absence of markets and middlemen, the distance is limited, typically to the area that food producers are willing or able to traverse on foot at the regular intervals required by food production. Hence, the productivity of the polyadic system cannot be great. Although commerce might raise productivity through the specialization it permits, it might also alleviate the scarcity that empowers the elite; moreover, to the degree that producers trafficked across local systems, so increasing their productivity, the exclusive polyadic contract would lose effect, so curtailing the enforcement of elite privilege. The elite are understandably reluctant to see their power base eroded, so suppress commerce insofar as possible. While low productivity, thus assured, prevents the development of a large retainer class or bureaucracy that might allow the elite to extend their span of control over a more diverse, more productive system, the dangers of commerce are more certain. In this low-energy equilibrium trap, therefore, the amount of hierarchy supported is limited, although what there is of it should be stable, even rigid. Commerce will develop only when further scarcities make the closed polyadic arrangement unviable.

Evolving Polyadic Exchange— Incipient Stratification

As far as stratification is concerned, dyadic exchange is anomalous because it implies little or no exchange imbalance that could lead to the

---

[16] Foster (1967) uses the term "dyadic exchange" to encompass patron–client relationships. I reject this usage on the grounds that it implies that the same kind of balance is achieved in these nonegalitarian relationships as in the egalitarian ones. Clearly, a wholly different dynamic is operating. But it is interesting to note that peasants often conceptualize the relationship as dyadic and balanced, evidence for the power of ideology.

development or maintenance of unequal economic classes. Indeed, many anthropologists (e.g., Mauss 1954; Sahlins 1965) have explicitly linked balanced dyadic exchange or reciprocity to egalitarian social systems. I include it here to provide a contrasting example to exchange systems based on predictable scarcity, all of which differ by supporting distribution systems with hierarchical nodes. To make the contrast more salient, I will describe a situation where a restricted polyadic exchange network grew out of an extended dyadic exchange network under conditions that created differential access to the exchange system. While perhaps not the usual circumstance, if an otherwise balanced trade system regularly provides a select group with scarce goods, which others in their local system need but to which they have no direct access, an elite class will form.[17] The *kula* exchange as it was organized in the northern Trobriand Islands of Melanesia (Malinowski 1922) provides just such a case.

At the interisland level, the *kula* was a classic extended network that linked adjacent islands in a circle that was open at several points. Through formal but nonexclusive trading partnerships between pairs of individuals, special valuables traveled around the network, often passing through the hands of the same individual several times. A kind of false scarcity in these prestige-bestowing valuables, which had to be exchanged in order for prestige to be obtained, was maintained throughout the system so the network that allowed trade of more utilitarian items (which might be needed only now and then or which might involve exchange between islands too distant for direct contact) would stay perpetually open (Brookfield 1971; Uberoi 1962). The balance required in the exchange of the valuables established the trade equality of the partners and different islands, so that otherwise hostile groups could come to terms in the exchange of necessities.

Yet quite by chance an imbalance did occur in the *kula* network, within the northern Trobriand *kula* district. The population of this district was much larger than the populations in the *kula* districts to either side of it. As a result, only some people in the northern Trobriands—those with best access to the sea—could participate in the interisland trade of *kula* valuables (and the utilitarian goods they facilitated). Extralocal trading partners were simply too few in number to allow all northern Trobriand people into the system under the rules of balanced dyadic exchange. Thus, on the one hand, *kula* valuables were relatively common among the smaller *kula* districts that make up the rest of the interisland network, where everyone could be interisland traders, and thereby a basis for stratification did not exist in them; but, on the other hand, *kula* valuables

[17] Rathje (1971) presents a parallel case in his study of the lowland Maya, in which he argues that an imbalanced exchange system led to stratification and the formation of a state. He also shows the political instability consequent on premarket, polyadic exchange systems not based on the control of the means of production (land).

were scarce in the northern Trobriand district, where only a few could be interisland traders, and thereby a basis for stratification did exist in it.

Uberoi, who is not explicit about the population mechanism, otherwise provides ample evidence that the Trobriand "chiefs," who were the main Trobriand participants in the larger network, used their access to *kula* valuables and other trade goods as a basis for local power: "It seems to me evident . . . that in the Trobriand Islands those descent groups which are (a) economically at the nodal point of their locality, and (b) also leaders of overseas expeditions [for *kula* valuables], lay claim to the [chiefly] title . . . [1962:125]." According to Uberoi, chiefly power and privilege rested on two dyadic exchange systems: a marriage system that placed chiefs in a strategic position in terms of the agricultural surplus, and the *kula* exchange system that placed chiefs in a strategic position vis-à-vis "commoner" lineages and villages. It was control of the latter exchange system (*kula* trade) that led to the chiefs' ability to attract wives and through them food surplus. The fact that chiefs had no control over productive resources was of little moment to those unable to obtain necessities from the interisland exchange network: They were quite willing to pay tribute in order to have trade relations with the chiefs who did. Uberoi also makes explicit that the different status groups of the Trobriands attributed by Malinowski to occupation and described by him as castes—chiefs, commoners, and untouchables—were not defined by their actual occupations or productive assets but by their relative access to *kula* trade.

On the other hand, since most people in the *southern* Trobriand *kula* districts did have direct access to interisland trade, they did not have to, and therefore did not, pay tribute or concede their social inferiority to the northern Trobriand chiefs—everyone in them lay claim to the "chiefly" lineage. The northern Trobriand "paramount" chief was only a trade partner to his southern Trobriand counterpart, head of his chiefly lineage. As partners in the broad *kula* network, these two individuals were necessarily equal, for each had equal access to what the other needed— extralocal goods that could fund only local power, and then only where other locals were excluded from the trade network. The equivalence of nodes in the network is important here: The *interisland* exchange system did not provide a basis for stratification because a balance of goods and thereby a balance between nodes was maintained between each two points of the network. *Kula* trade at that level established no political relationship other than that established by reciprocity itself. But *kula* trade at the *local system* level in the northern Trobriands did provide a basis for internal stratification because only certain "centers" had continuing access to scarce and necessary goods. Thus, direct exchanges at the local level could no longer be dyadic; they became polyadic in relationship to the *kula* traders, bounding a local political system whose internal exchanges were isolated from the network. Needless to say, the more necessary trade access in the local system, the more power exercised by controllers of trade—hence the distinction between commoners and untouchables in the northern Trobriands.[18]

The Trobriand case thus neatly demonstrates how trade "balance" maintained by dyadic exchange in a network system establishes egalitarian relationships, while trade "imbalance" maintained by polyadic exchange in a bounded system establishes hierarchical relationships. It also shows a stratification system that in no way rested on control of the means of production. Some have argued that the Trobriand population was not fully stratified on the grounds that production resources were freely available. But this argument allows the definition of stratification to be manipulated by the explanation for it. I would argue that the northern Trobriand districts did have incipient stratification to the extent that the chiefs and their retinue were freed from most productive activities and could exact economic support through some means. Productive means were not scarce but trade access was, so in this case stratification rested very directly on the exchange system.

Stable Polyadic Exchange—
Castelike Stratification

The following examples are less straightforward. For one thing, the polyadic exchange system is found in conjunction with other, broader, exchange systems, and the spatial dimensions of the local system vary a good deal. For another, land is the most common if not the only scarce resource with a predictable distribution in these cases, making standard attention to the means of production quite adequate to deal with them. Finally, some cases are termed "feudal" or "castelike" and others are not, and the literature about the definitions one must use so wildly proliferated that one must throw caution to the winds to even mention them. Nonetheless, the theoretical approach taken here has utility. It can equate similar social systems based on "feudal" clientage relationships, even where landed property rights are not the basis of clientage, thus explaining one effect with a single cause. And it can also explain variability *within* the type with the same general variables that account *for* the type—that is, the spatial

---

[18] The "untouchables" were people from Kuboma who lacked *kula* canoes altogether and were in the lowest and most dependent position: They produced interisland trade goods (pottery and baskets) but could not trade them directly; and they also depended on local trade for agricultural staples that they could only obtain with the interisland trade goods they produced. For them, access to the trade network was critical. Most "commoners," on the other hand, had sufficient agricultural staples and needed access to the network only to trade their agricultural surplus or for occasional times of shortage. Chiefs could exact tribute from both groups in return for access to the trade network, but had more power over the untouchables.

dimensions and nodal development of the distribution system. I hasten to add that the following analysis is offered not as a substitute for more specialized analyses but in the spirit of supplementing and generalizing them.

The simplest case is a very small local system, such as a manor in feudal Europe or a village with a single dominant caste in traditional India, where the critical resource controlled by the elite is land or the products thereof. Relationship to the means of production or to its product can here be seen as leading to economic stratification, although the relationship is also embedded in an exchange contract (but not thereby balanced). In the traditional *jajmani*-organized village of India, for instance, the elite were often the producers or controllers of an agricultural product that they "exchanged" for certain services.[19] The value of examining the exchange aspect of the economy is that it shows how lack of market or commercial distribution leads to fixed class and occupational statuses or castelike stratification. (By the term "castelike" I mean that there is no vertical class mobility within the local system and very limited horizontal mobility across systems; in addition, each occupation, productive or nonproductive, is placed in a finely graded series of fixed positions such that occupational change is difficult, if not impossible, and differential status is accorded to each position.)

Without a market to allocate commodities or factors of production, occupations are ascribed to ensure production of some goods and services that are either necessary or desirable to the elite but that have no general demand value. A fixed system of "rewards" accompanies fixed factors of production (particularly land and labor), both of which are maintained by economic isolation. In addition, a status rank becomes part of the system of local economic rewards, inasmuch as the low level of real specialization and productivity does not allow a great differential in standard of living. Higher rank usually goes to those occupational specialties for which the general market value would be most in doubt—warriors, priests, and the

[19] Neale (1957) has characterized the exchange as "redistribution," a descriptive category for exchange used by Polanyi et al. (1957) for a type of distribution similar to the one I term "polyadic." While my conceptualization of this exchange type (and others) clearly owes a good deal to Polanyi et al., we differ considerably in the interpretation of the "balances" involved; hence my use of other terms. It takes little insight to see that the Indian system of "redistribution" was imbalanced and involved exploitation of those without direct access to critical resources (Mencher 1974). Leach (1960) has argued that in fact the lower castes often had the monopoly powers over critical resources, but it is important to take note that they never had monopoly powers over critical resources: After all, even the "pure" castes could cut their own hair and wash their own clothes—or have their less "pure" women do it for them; but the unlanded barber or washerman was not in a position to force the landed groups to do anything and, like most of the "working" class everywhere, was grateful just to have a job. It is true that in many Indian villages there were fewer people in the lower, untouchable castes than in the higher castes, and the people in the lower castes thereby had the polyadic relationship in services. The land-rich families, however, were almost always fewer than the land-poor families, so that the polyadic relationship as regards the critical resource was imbalanced in favor of a minority in high-status positions.

like—but which might provide alternative means of obtaining the same or competing resources. The economic reward for most producers without such options is usually little more than assurance of livelihood, a significant enough reward in uncommercialized systems where extremes in local fortunes are not evened out by regional exchange systems in basic goods (Epstein 1967). It is at least sufficient to keep producers in the system and producing without a great deal of recourse to physical sanction.[20] What is important in this kind of system is the personal regulation of production and exchange by a *local* elite in a relatively closed local system.

Being directly involved in exchange, the local elite can determine occupation, reward, and rank personally, on a face-to-face basis. They will also be less interested in efficient economic specialization and allocation of rewards than in effective control of their underlings. Because each occupation will have its fixed reward, bettering one's social position is contingent on the degree to which one can provide something special to the elite. Perpetual struggle to exploit every possible occupational niche that might conceivably receive slightly higher rank or a better reward will result, even when all are actually engaged in food production. While a market would discipline this "uneconomic" struggle and proliferation of nonproductive specialties, the elite find it advantageous. Not only does it fragment the class interests of the producers (Mencher 1974), but it provides the greatest possible amount of luxury for the elite in an economy that supports little true division of labor. Competition for "scarce" rank as well as scarce resources will stimulate specialization in nonproductive services as far as the economy will allow.[21]

[20] Orans (1968) argues that the economic imbalance or poor fit between supply and demand in such systems necessitates that the elite use coercive powers to keep production and people in line. But I suspect that isolation of the local economy normally precludes this necessity. Competition and the observable use of coercive power are more likely to be found where different groups control different critical resources (land versus some trade goods, for instance), as in the situation described by Beck (Chapter 10, this volume).

[21] Harper (1959) and Orans (1968) have observed that occupational immobility and identity with rank in Indian *jajmani* systems are seriously jeopardized by commerce and markets, and this is the argument here. Yet "traditional" India, the society most apparently characterized by caste stratification, was at times controlled by major bureaucratic or even mercantile empires and has probably had commerce and markets as long as it has had the caste system. Therefore, it is important to note that castelike stratification cannot be identified with major or high-level social systems; rather, they can be identified only with the small local communities that make up the broader system and that are relatively unaffected by commerce and markets. At higher levels other exchange systems and other forms of stratification exist (Fox 1969). Caste in India is not and has not been a unitary phenomenon, and much of the confusion about caste in India probably stems from this fact. The standard view of stratification in India has been based on community studies that see only part of the picture—localized polyadic exchange and localized caste stratification. But other kinds of exchange processes and other kinds of economic class structure have surely been another part of the picture, as Fox's and Beck's studies (Chapters 4 and 10, this volume) illustrate.

Given settled, rural distribution of the elite and absence of markets, exchanges between lord and peasant must be direct and immediate, the lord forced to live cheek by jowl with peasants, personally removing the peasant surplus for his own consumption. This clearly colors class relations. While exploitation of those unfortunate enough to have no direct access to critical resources is basic here, the personalistic nature of exchange is such that exploitation takes perhaps its most dainty form. Elite recipients of peasant generosity are almost always obligated to "reciprocate" with noblesse oblige, to provide local protection or a source of local pride, and to manifest their equality in human if not status terms by showing personal concern for their clients (Homans 1941; Kolenda 1963; Sahlins 1963). In brief, lack of physical separation between the elite and their inferiors leads to frequent contact and close ties.

Yet when coupled with inefficient economic allocation and low overall productivity—which supports little real difference in standard of living among classes this very intimacy and human equality requires status inequality to be all the more emphatic. To exploit your actual neighbor, so to speak, you must categorize him as a separate kind of being. And to maintain distance, he must be forced by caste regulations (and ideology) to be distinguishable by some difference in life style if not in basic consumption level. Group endogamy—caste barriers to marriage is, of course, the clearest way to sustain differences; and a theory of group "purity" or "impurity" supports the ideology of separation. Hence, I concur with Dumont (1970), who postulates that notions about purity are essential characteristics of caste systems; but I part from his view that India's caste system was uniquely based on this idea or value, submitting that notions about purity should crop up in any intimately stratified system. Support for this argument comes from male-female hierarchies in various parts of the world, which also combine "exploitation" with intimacy together with an ideology of group purity or impurity (see, for example, Rosaldo and Lamphere 1974). In sum, castelike features of stratification basically rest on the wide rural dispersion of the elite and their intimate connection to their inferiors—caste barriers between groups serve the same function that physical distance does in other agrarian societies.

The same reasons that lead one to expect rural distribution of peasants everywhere lead one to expect wide rural distribution of an elite in land-based hierarchical systems and, for reasons already discussed, that such will support the most elaborated forms of castelike stratification. Land-based hierarchies are to be expected in areas where population density is high for the available technology to make land itself the scarce resource. They are also likely to last as long-term systems, as in Europe and India, when local elites are kept in power by regional elites whose power is based on military superiority, or to use Goody's (1971) felicitous phrase, "control of the means of destruction." While enforcing the hold of the local elites

over producers, the militarists will exploit the local elite, pyramiding the
direct exchange relationships. Regional elites, being few in number and
much more widely dispersed than local elites, can rarely operate in terms
of direct control of land and thus are willing for local elites to take a cut of
the surplus in "exchange" for providing the means by which the regional
elite can take some of it.[22] Local elites, of course, have little choice with
respect to the militarists' cut of surplus; for while they have the essential
control of land by virtue of the role they play in local exchanges (see Beck,
Chapter 10, this volume), ultimate power rests with those who control the
use of force. But when the two elites work hand in hand—controlling land
by controlling force—both local and regional elites can stay in almost perpetual power over producers. Hence the common association of the two, in
pyramidal relationships termed feudal.

If the military base of the regional elite is secure for some time, the
relationship between them and the local elite is likely to be more intimate
than that between local elite and producer. Military leaders with their
local elite cadres make an efficient team for quelling local rebellions while
extracting a high rate of surplus. Thus, in Europe and perhaps Japan in
their feudal ages, where local elites were often absent from their domains
and in more frequent contact with their superiors, status ranks proliferated at the elite level, and caste elaboration at the local, manorial level
was less developed.[23] But if the military base of the regional elite is not
secure, one would expect the opposite. In India, for example, a long history of "political upheavals, dynastic changes, local rebellions, invasions
and counter-invasions, and at times severe anarchy [Fox 1969:43]" led
status rank to proliferate at the local land-based level instead of at the
elite level. Discontinuity at the upper level forced local elites to a permanently settled, rural adaptation where they collected their own tribute
directly from producers in a stable system relatively unscathed by broader
events. In turn, the regional zamindar or potentate of whatever name,
when in power, did not collect tribute by means of a highly differentiated
retainer class or in terms of the village-level castes (*jati*); he collected
tribute from an undifferentiated set of rural elite underlings, physically
set apart from him and from one another. Often, in fact, the zamindar
utilized his own kin as collectors of tribute, there being minimal differentiation of elite classes (Fox 1971; Chapter 4, this volume). The more
often described *jajmani* system in India, with its extreme differentiation
of occupation and rank and its elaborate distance-maintaining symbolism,

---

[22] For documentation of this view, see the articles in Frykenberg (1969).

[23] This argument is supported by Homans' (1941) discussion of stratification on feudal
manors in thirteenth-century England. Manors typically encompassed a larger area than the
local-level, land-based systems in India, the elite were more frequently absent from their
domains, and hence stratification was more elaborated at the upper rather than the lower
levels of the system.

had meaning only at the lowest level, the land-based system with resident local elites.

Polyadic exchange need not be land based at some level, however. Goody (1971) and Kottack (1972) have described several East African "patrimonial" kingdoms that illustrate how polyadic exchange operates with other bases. Goody asserts that in most of precolonial, class-stratified Africa, class relations appear feudal inasmuch as personal clientage defined them, but that class relations were not based on control of the means of production. Land was simply not valuable or scarce enough and production techniques not conducive enough to fixed territorial controls. Given their inability to control land, Goody suggests that the power base of most "feudal lords" in these systems was "control of the means of destruction," often cavalry or fire power (1971:39-56). His own evidence and that of others (e.g., Beattie 1964; Kottack 1972), however, indicates that in many instances control of critical trade goods or trade routes was equally important, if not more so. Often the important trade goods were slaves, sometimes iron, and in Buganda, Kottack hypothesizes that it may have been fish in a region where the staple diet was notably deficient in other sources of protein. In these cases, then, unlike feudal Europe and much of traditional India, trade networks at the supralocal level were manipulated to give a power base over a local level—as in the Trobriands. That is, by controlling a long-distance trade network and the scarce goods it provided, the elite were able to establish clientage relations with sedentary producers who were willing to give tribute in exchange for the scarce resource. Tribute would consist of food staples, but could also and frequently did consist of wives for the polygynous elite—again as in the Trobriands. When wives numbered in hundreds, even thousands, they were used both as hostages from distant producer families and as agricultural producers themselves on the elite estates.

Because land was not sufficiently valuable (that is, scarce) to support local elites, these systems were basically two-level systems—sometimes broad but always thin. The population was so sparse and unproductive that the elite class was small and had to be mobile in order to collect tribute. Physical separation between elite and producers, and small numbers in the elite class, did not provide the prerequisites for a fully proliferated and elaborated caste system. Being less effective at controlling production, moreover, these trade-based or purely military-based systems could support few specialist groups. On the other hand, the few fully specialized occupations carried out in the East African kingdoms (such as blacksmithing) were usually held by endogamous out-caste groups. Women might also be considered a special occupational and status category, or caste, since often they alone were ascribed at birth with the occupation of basic farming, and since exploitative relations between males and females, especially in larger polygynous households, were laden enough with distance-maintaining symbolism.[24] Goody makes a further suggestion: The mobility of the elite, coupled with the low productivity of agriculture, may encourage the use of multipurpose (multioccupational) slaves, who could be moved about in relation to both resources and the elite more easily than sedentary serfs. One might expect, therefore, in wide-ranging polyadic network systems based on the control of goods rather than land, a collapsed and vastly simplified caste system where a few fixed occupational groups did most of the productive tasks but actual caste mechanisms were played down to the extent that the elite were physically removed from the producing classes.

Sahlins, perhaps the first to relate stratification to distribution systems (in somewhat different form),[25] observed the basic logistic problems of any larger system not based on localized control of the means of production:

> A lesser chiefdom, confined say as in the Marquesas Islands to a narrow valley, could be almost personally ruled by a headman in frequent contact with the relatively small population. But the great Polynesian chiefs had to rule much larger, spatially dispersed, internally organized populations. . . . Now, such extensive chiefdoms would have to be coordinated; they would have to be centrally tapped for a fund of power, buttressed against internal disruption, sometimes massed for distant, perhaps overseas, military engagements. All of this to be implemented by means of communication still at the level of word-of-mouth, and means of transportation consisting of human bodies and canoes. . . . A tendency for the developed chiefdom to proliferate in executive cadres, to grow top-heavy, seems in these circumstances altogether functional, even though the ensuing drain on wealth proves the chiefdom's undoing [1963:299].

But the problem that Sahlins describes is a problem of political centralization, not of stratification, and this particular problem occurs in virtually all premarket societies—land-based systems as well as others. The problem for stratification in two-level polyadic systems, exemplified perhaps by Polynesian chiefdoms as well as East African kingdoms, is that when the leader fails or the military base weakens, there are no means by which the unequal exchange system can be maintained. Hence, stratification in premarket societies tends to be a stable and enduring condition only where there is control of local resources—usually when land rather than something else is the critical scarcity.

The general relationships and the sources of variability in polyadic

---

[24] Boserup (1970) discusses the laboring role and special status of women in traditional Africa, observing that women often did the bulk of farming and that men acquired economic power by acquiring many wives.

[25] With his acute powers of observation, Sahlins saw that premarket stratified societies based on imbalanced exchange systems were quite fragile; but he did not explore the possibility that market exchange could lead to less fragile systems that were also imbalanced.

exchange systems can be summarized as follows. Polyadic exchange isolates a local system by creating a boundary around all the parties to exchange who relate to a single, but sometimes internally differentiated, elite "center." Because of elite monopoly in the exchange relationship, the local-level social system integrated by polyadic exchange will be isolated whether or not the elite engage in some kind of network or even market trade, which may fund their power. Without a local market to allocate factors of production, stratification will be rigid and castelike, yet status positions little differentiated in standard of living. The exchange relationship is without question exploitative, but in small-scale systems personal ties between peasant and elite, together with caste ideology and the proliferation of status groups, prevent the formation of self-conscious classes. Spatial extension of the system on the basis of control over factors other than land will not lead to more caste or status positions but to fewer of them, since a large system will separate the elite and their specialist retainers from the peasant mass. When long entrenched, however, the elite class itself may proliferate in status positions. In either case, the only classes really formed are two: producers and nonproducers. Spatial extension may be great in land-based systems, if a militarily based regional elite controls a local elite. But in systems based on other resources or military control alone, spatial extension is limited, given the very low level of production expectable when a local-level elite does not personally supervise production by peasants—to the degree that the single elite class extends the system by mobility, their overall control diminishes.

Instability of polyadic—feudal, if you will—systems based on resources other than land may explain why they are often ignored by students of economic stratification. But political fragility is not synonymous with economic equality. A chiefdom based on the control of scarce fish can be fully as exploitative as a feudal manor based on the control of scarce land. This fact indicates more than that various mechanisms exist for creating stratification; it shows that control of the means of exchange is a real phenomenon. I will argue that it is increasingly important as exchange systems are based on market distribution. The market, by institutionalizing scarcities of various kinds, can cement unequal exchanges to maintain a stable hierarchy of classes. And it can control production at the lower levels at the same time that it allows extensive pyramiding and centralization of power, suffering few of the limitations of polyadic exchange systems. I turn to these more complex systems now.

PARTIALLY COMMERCIALIZED SYSTEMS

When markets come into being, and with them urban centers, the spatial organization of a society takes on considerable complexity. So too does the organization of the elite, in related fashion, making it impossible to talk in terms of one or two elite classes as before. Given the programmatic nature of this essay, I cannot hope to give full specification of elite levels and relations; I will indicate only briefly the elite differentiation possible in these more complex systems, concentrating as before on the relations between the general classes of food producers and nonfood producers.

Market exchange and direct (polyadic) exchange are often coupled in "archaic" economies or in historical bureaucratic societies, as Polanyi *et al.* (1957) observed some time ago. I term this coupling *administered trade,* placing emphasis on the market imperfections that prevent full commercialization of the food-producing classes rather than on the motivations of the actors involved, as Polanyi was wont to do. Most people are "rational maximizers" in the context of market or any other trade; but a market does not have to integrate an economy fully in Adam Smith's sense, particularly when the conditions of its use are determined by the polity. *Administered market trade,* where politics dominates commerce rather than vice versa, leads to imperfect market penetration through *solar central-place systems.* Even when a market is free of political controls, as in the type I term "general monopolistic trade," its own imperfections can prevent the full commercialization of an economy, producers and even traders maximizing their economic survival by circumventing the market mechanism in some domains. Systematic *monopolistic–monopsonistic market trade,* where commerce dominates politics rather than vice versa, leads to imperfect market penetration through *dendritic central-place systems.* Table 1 and Figure 1, pp. 316–317, recall to mind the basic spatioeconomic characteristics of these two systems.

Markets exist in virtually all large hierarchical social systems because, after a certain size is reached, the elite and their retainers (themselves hierarchically organized) must be fed by a system more efficient than direct exchange or tribute collection. Tribute is costly to collect and time consuming because administrators must continually struggle against low rates of production or nonparticipation; but in a "free" marketing system, peasants will compete among themselves to produce more goods, thereby driving down the costs of production and increasing the surplus. Moreover, the peasants require little policing and no one need administer production. For these very reasons, political administrators are likely to allow a marketing system to evolve in politically secure regions when commerce cannot erode elite powers, most likely when the technology of weaponry and the organization of military force is developed enough that smaller groups with their own localized economic resources have no means by which to compete with or remain independent from a centralized state apparatus. By allowing a "free" marketing system under these conditions, the administrators do not relinquish economic control. The marketing system is an organ of the state when markets and the bureaucracy are concentrated in a few administrative centers, and the much smaller class than the peasantry, merchant–artisans, is policed.[26]

How administrators control a market at the local level can be seen from the following description of colonial markets in Ecuador:

> Particular attention is given to *controlling market location and periodicity,* preventing forestalling outside the market-place, controlling monopolies and speculators, checking weights and measures, ensuring certain minimum hygienic and quality standards, disposing of refuse, maintaining law and order, *selling and checking trading licenses,* and collecting market taxes. . . . Often, either consciously or unconsciously, the municipal *governments protect and ·assist urban traders against the competition of rural entrepreneurs* [Bromley and Bromley 1975:91; emphasis added].

By controlling who is to trade, and by proscribing when and where, administrators can keep close tabs on the economy. In particular, if only administrative centers hold markets and if they all meet on the same day—quite commonplace in administered economies, especially of colonial Latin America—only the urban monopolies fostered by administrators will flourish, and no uncontrollable rural class of merchants will develop. This will of course make marketing for rural peasants a time-consuming and rather costly business. Nonetheless, town administrators can call forth the necessary surplus from the peasantry by controlling monopolies over some goods and services that peasants need—tools, cloth, ritual-political services, and so forth. Since rural goods are priced through competition among all local peasants, their prices are quite low (although transport costs for peasants might be high enough that they would not necessarily depend on the market for their own food supply). But since the prices of urban goods are not established by competition among market centers, an efficient urban administration should have no difficulty regulating the monopolies necessary to peasant survival and thereby not only assure themselves a sufficient supply of food—the main urban problem—but considerable monopoly profits. As modern colonial administrators have found, it takes a very short period of holding necessary goods in a market (or insisting on cash payment of taxes) to make a peasantry sufficiently market dependent that no other form of coercion or taxation is necessary

[26] Eisenstadt (1963) makes a similar argument in explaining the evolution of historical bureaucratic societies, and I acknowledge his influence on my analysis. Appleby (Chapter 5, Volume I) and Bromley (Chapter 3, Volume I) describe the operation of administered markets in some detail without labeling them such. From their studies it seems that a major indicator of market administration would be lack of periodic market articulation—virtually all major markets held in administrative centers on the same day. Under these circumstances, traders are restricted in operation to the local system, arbitrage between systems is not possible, and price controls are easily administered.

to sustain a large urban class. In earlier times, urban monopolies on religious and ritual paraphernalia seem to have been the more common mechanism. All direct forms of tribute collection and taxation can wither away, although some of it may linger.[27]

The essence of administered market economies is that *rural* commodity prices are established by the urban market through *competition* among rural producers, while most *urban* commodity prices are established by urban *monopolies.* In addition, many factor prices (land, many kinds of labor) are not set by any market—in the presence of an often arbitrary pricing mechanism, producers would be foolhardy to respond to market prices for their means of production. Thus, the market that exists is highly imperfect, prices are sticky, and the regulation of exchanges is quite inflexible. But it is "the market" rather than direct tribute collection that gathers surplus from the peasantry.

No marketing system is fully competitive. But systematic monopoly and monopsony in agrarian markets by large, external, commercial firms develop under a special set of circumstances. The most likely circumstance is when merchants in a fully commercialized economy seek new sources of raw materials or new markets for their goods, in most cases in an agrarian region that has a comparative advantage in producing some primary good or goods and has a large and already partially commercialized population. Commercial firms born in developed economies will gain natural monopolies by bringing markets and more efficient transport to less well-organized economies. Differences in the energy controlled in terms of capital and communications between merchants in the developed subsystem and producer–consumers in the less developed subsystem will allow the terms of trade to be dictated by the distant merchants. If the trading firms also form cartels with respect to buying and selling in the agrarian region, the energy–organizational difference that supports the monopolies can be maintained almost perpetually. A dendritic arrangement of markets is achieved, indeed is natural, when the merchants determine the alignment of transport with the objective of servicing their own rather than the local economy at the lowest possible transport cost. Transport nets may be spread to many agrarian regions but will connect

---

[27] Most modern versions of administered economies have elite market control coupled with elite control of some of the production resources (land)—most stratified societies, in fact, are composed of a mix of exchange types. But I would like to emphasize that administered trade can be the single most important basis for elite control of the economy. Where land is held by the elite it is often not even in production, being held mainly to force market dependence on the peasantry who are not otherwise taxed. In colonial Guatemala, for example, land control was minimally necessary because many peasants were already heavily market dependent. The colonial elite had only to take charge of the markets. In a later period when additional Indian labor was necessary on the plantations, forced taxation was the means by which it was initially obtained, but later the market mechanism alone could garner it since meanwhile peasant wage laborers had become heavily market dependent.

them all to a single dominant metropole in the developed economy, keeping transport costs low by requiring the fewest number of connecting paths between ultimate producer and ultimate consumer.

When markets are thus aligned by external market forces, development and autonomy in the agrarian region are limited by the kinds of goods the external economy requires and delivers. External markets are in most cases specialized enough that crops that meet external demand (for example, spices, sisal, wool, coffee, sugar) do not also meet the subsistence requirements of the producers. Yet transport costs for bulky subsistence goods are so high that the external market does not meet local subsistence requirements either. Hence, the producers tied to an external market must continue to produce their own food along with the specialized crop. Sometimes production in the agrarian region for the external market is by capitalist enterprises (such as plantations), but just as often it is by small-scale peasant producers. In either case, the producers have little withholding power in the market because they produce goods for which they have no demand and for which general demand is extremely elastic, and whose price therefore will be determined more by the incomes of external consumers than by the costs of production. To survive, plantations must be sufficiently capitalized to expand and contract with the state of the external economy. But in the case of peasant producers, it is their bellies that must be able to expand and contract; for if they are dependent on the market for some necessities, they must produce even more of the commercial crop when prices drop, cutting into their food supply (cf. Appleby, Chapter 11, this volume).[28]

On the other hand, the external market competes successfully with local production of handicrafts and the like, because they are light in weight and more cheaply produced in the developed economy. This cuts down demand in the agrarian region for the local support services that might otherwise have provided an economic basis for an efficient local marketing system. And in the absence of locally organized markets to meet local needs, the producers in the agrarian region become all the more dependent on the external market for goods their individual holdings cannot produce

[28] One might argue that because peasants would not have to produce for or buy from the external market they must be getting what they want from it. The answer to this is given by Kelley (Chapter 7, Volume I). The most "rational adaptation" for peasants distant from a market is to be self-sufficient, engaging in extensive production for their own consumption. But peasants cannot produce extensively if population growth has put too many people on the land; and they must intensify production for the external market if no local market exists for their goods, as will be the case with peasants this close to the subsistence margin. Distance from the external market will mean they will have to accept lower prices for their goods, which will lead them to intensify production all the more. In addition to Kelley's work, I have used insights from the work of Baran (1957), Frank (1967), and Dow (1973) in this analysis. Appleby details the various possibilities for dendritic systems given different production systems and organizations of labor.

and thus much more vulnerable to price control in the monopolistic center that both supplies them and buys from them. Since capital will therefore not be accumulated in the peripheral agrarian economy, no higher-order systems in the periphery will coordinate potentially specialized niches of the related agrarian subsystems that feed the external market. Low-cost primary goods will be delivered to distant urban consumers but not to neighboring agrarian regions. Hence, when peasants are both external market producers and subsistence farmers, they will be caught in a high-energy equilibrium trap, their economic adaptation involuntary. Population growth to produce labor will follow intensification of production for the market, which will chase population growth; economic growth in the external developed sector will take place at the expense of economic growth in the agrarian underdeveloped sector. Under these circumstances, who "owns" the means of production—it will often remain the peasant producer—makes little difference for peasant economic opportunity and life chances. Peasants will play no entrepreneurial roles in an economy where the exchange system is controlled by external metropoles.

Administered Solar Systems— Stratification by Estate

Administered economies have partially commercialized distribution systems, and they have partially stratified social systems. They are typically associated with a kind of "estate" stratification, where peasants are unstratified, the administrative elite forms a distinct group superior to peasants in every way—especially in their standard of living—and merchants and artisans are set apart as a special group, closely observed and controlled by the administrative elite and distrusted by the peasantry. For certain kinds of analysis, mainly political analysis, one might want to separate a fourth estate, the clergy. While in political struggles they have a power base different from actual administrators, I lump them with administrators here because as an economic strata they work hand in glove with administrators, helping them manipulate the economy and in turn being supported by it in the same way that administrators are, sharing the same life style and standard of living. There may be a small or remnant class of rural gentry, but this group flourishes in more commercialized economies.[29]

Members of the elite (by which I mean the administrative class) almost always live in the central places, often fair-sized urban centers, physically removed from the peasantry; merchant–artisans invariably live there. As

[29] A large rural gentry class is likely to coexist with major urban centers when the latter develop in response to external trade. See the discussion in the section on fully commercialized systems.

urban centers are few and dispersed in a rural landscape that lacks inter-mediate-sized towns, they are fully differentiated from the rural–peasant hinterland and are many times larger than any other places in the system. Urban centers are the places that have to be supported, places to which most market activity is directed. Various exchange systems will be found in solar systems, but the primary ones regulating class relations are those focused on the markets in the major urban centers. Most exchanges *between* food producers and nonfood producers are market exchanges, while most exchanges *among* food producers and *among* nonfood producers are direct, nonmarket exchanges.

Good examples of administered trade could be found not long ago in the most isolated remnants of the Spanish empire of the Americas. The follow-ing description of stratification and peasant social organization is based on descriptions of a region in Chiapas, Mexico—San Cristobal las Casas, an old colonial town of about 20,000 people and its purely rural hinterland of about 200,000 people—as it probably was some 25 years ago. But this analysis is meant to be general and applicable to other administered solar systems, especially of Latin America: the Patzcuaro hinterland of Mi-choacan, Mexico (Kaplan 1965), and western Guatemala (Smith 1973) at the turn of the century; highland Peru (Appleby, Chapter 5, Volume I) and Ecuador (Bromley and Bromley 1975) more recently. The organiza-tion of all these regions resulted from Spanish colonial policy in marginal areas of the New World where the principal economic support for the elite was peasant labor and the major means of extracting it, especially after independence, was through the market.

The elite of highland Chiapas gained their initial preeminence through conquest, their power based on military strength and their economic interests oriented toward exporting wealth to the home country, Spain. Uninterested in the land itself, Spanish administrators settled in towns; later, upon the vast reduction of the Indian population, together with the depressed European market for their goods, they were forced to turn to landed enterprises (haciendas) for their wherewithal. These enterprises—based on localized polyadic exchange, which led to castelike stratification at the local hacienda level—were to remain important sources of elite income during subsequent times of economic closure. Yet along with them, the heirs of the Spanish empire have attempted to maintain urban residence, using the market mechanism—and their control over imports, exports, the local marketplace, and wage levels—to support a citadel of "civilization" even during long periods of relative isolation, when there was little outside stimulus to the economy and little contact with major administrative centers. Indeed, the market rather than their own land pro-vided most of their income. Administered extraction of peasant-produced surplus describes the economy they controlled for the entire colonial period (McLeod 1973).

The administrative elite in this system are today only a pale reflection of former times. Where there was once a large urban class of political officials, legal specialists, clergy, and army officers that staffed the administrative apparatus, there are now only a handful of bureaucrats, some impoverished clergy, and a paltry number of professionals and lawyers—still an extravagant number for the services performed, however. Yet even in their present reduced situation, this class controls the economy. While nearly all of the elite families have landholdings, what gives them economic clout in the system is administrative power; and it is this power, as it is expressed in market exchange, that structures class relations. A member of the elite would never be found in the marketplace except as a buyer, but until recently no other class would be involved in external trade. When it is a matter of importing tools, industrial goods, or luxuries, or of exporting gold, cattle, or even corn, this group brooks little interference from the "merchant" class. Petty market trade is fully depreciated, but high-level mercantile trade is not—the administrative elite monopolize high-level trade, which provides the greater part of their incomes, and are in no way demeaned by it.

People who run the local marketplace and small shops, peddle in the rural Indian hinterland, and produce specialized goods (cloth, liquor, furniture, iron tools, and so forth) form a distinct urban class. Many urban trades are restricted by a type of guild, monopolies of kin-related or localized segments (*barrios*) of the urban center (Plattner 1975; Siverts 1969). Wealth differences among merchant–artisans are pronounced— some poorer than most Indian peasants, some as rich as members of the elite; and there is considerable turnover or movement from rags to riches in even the lifetime of an individual (Plattner 1975). But there is little possibility of moving from the merchant class to the elite class—at least within the same community. The primitive level of regional trade and the basically narrow division of labor generates little urban growth that might change the distribution of resources between the two urban estates.

Market trade is necessary to the operation of the economy—the means by which both urban classes gain their livelihood—but, if uncontrolled, is dangerous to the administrative class. The administrators, therefore, guard market trade carefully in the manner described earlier and dispense trade monopolies to urban groups they can control while protecting these monopolies from rural competition. The merchant class is controlled not only in this direct form but by elite disparagement of them as a class. Strictly separated in the status system, forced into class if not occupational endogamy, the merchant is the urban pariah. His rewards are mainly those things that money can buy, and even these are often restricted by sumptuary laws. Most important, his commercial operations are kept at the petty level, trade outside the local economy being the privilege of the administrative elite. Exchanges between elite and merchant are direct rather than market exchanges—clientage relations formed between a large-scale importer or exporter of goods and his merchant agents. In addition, the marketplace and merchant–artisan shops are taxed heavily, this often being the only direct form of taxation in the system. (The burden, of course, is shifted to peasants who must utilize the market.) Inasmuch as class relations between merchant and elite are determined by direct polyadic exchanges, it is castelike: endogamous merchant segments specializing in certain commercial occupations as described earlier, striving for greater privilege from the elite and thereby providing the elite with much of the surplus.

Relations between the merchant and peasant class, however, are conditioned by the market. Owning the basic means of production, land and their own labor, peasants are somewhat buffered from the vagaries of the imperfect market but are committed to it for some tools, ceremonial goods, and perhaps a few peasant-produced specialties—pottery, baskets, salt, and the like. As a result, prices of urban goods and urban transactions of any kind are usually very high relative to their costs of production, for the income provided by the urban market and other monopolies is the primary support of the urban classes. Moreover, the food necessary for the subsistence of these classes will be available in the market only to the extent that peasants must sell it to provision themselves with urban goods. So, if they are to survive, the urban merchants *must* have monopoly control of some goods necessary for peasants and *must* price them high enough to call forth sufficient surplus foodstuffs, for both themselves and the administrative elite (who will take their cut in market and other urban taxes). As a result, merchants expend considerable effort attempting to "convert" the peasantry to the use of some urban monopolies—often religious–ceremonial goods (Collier 1975; Plattner, Chapter 2, Volume I). They are supported in this by the administrative elite who have the same interests and who force peasants to use urban markets by suppressing horizontal peasant marketing arrangements, among other means.

Merchants disparaged by the elite heap contumely, of course, on the peasants. But while mistreated and insulted in the market, peasants spend the greater part of their lives in communities where the urban status system does not touch them. Their relations to other classes being market relations, disparagement is not so personal. Yet the socioeconomic adaptation of the rural peasantry is related to the operation of the administered market. Peasants are unstratified as a class but are divided into communities with different economic means. Access to rural economic resources is restricted by community membership, peasant communities are distinguished from each other by badges of ethnic identity, and movement across peasant communities is limited. Peasants specialize in certain market commodities, generally on a community-wide basis; but at the same time they attempt to provide themselves with basic subsistence goods. From these imperatives follow the characteristics of "closed, corpo-rate" (homogeneous but pluralistic) peasant communities (Wolf 1957): restricted sale of land, restricted community membership, "leveling" mechanisms, and local oligopoly in market production. The phenomenon of peasant community specialization by identical family "firms" in an identical market product is common to economies with administered markets and perhaps unique to them. An analysis of how it operates shows some of the inner workings of market administration.

In community-wide specialization, everyone in the community produces the same market goods, which completely contradicts the market principle of space utility in the division of labor. Producers are not located where there is demand for their goods but are located where everyone else produces the goods, and therefore do not need them—rather than each village having a potter, as in India, one village produces pottery for the whole regional system. Ecological diversity of resources does not explain this phenomenon (Collier 1975; Smith 1975b). The effect of this kind of production system is to place community members, all producing the same goods, in the same relationship to the market, thus regulating com-munity access not only to the means of exchange but also to the means of production. By equalizing the members' access to the market, no one member will have sufficient market profit windfalls to distort the group relationship to the means of production—local land and labor. (Peasant community specialization is only exclusive or monopolistic in goods for which demand is relatively elastic; all peasant communities produce goods of inelastic demand—food—for their own protection and sell any windfall or surplus in competition with one another. From this one must conclude that exclusive production of *some* goods is only for purposes of maintain-ing community homogeneity of income and thus equalizing access to local factors of production, rather than for purposes of market power.) This is clearly advantageous to the peasant, for his own local needs. But it is also advantageous to the urban merchants, who buy and resell these peasant-produced goods to other peasants.

Needless to say, community regulation of production is only effective if deviations from communal norms are strongly sanctioned by a face-to-face group—hence the closed corporate community.[30] But because peasant unionization vis-à-vis an unpredictable monopoly market is quite limited spatially in these circumstances, peasant "class" interests are frag-mented—peasant communities are like separate potatoes in a sack of potatoes, to paraphrase Marx. Its net effect is to protect local communities

[30] A number of students of Meso-American corporate communities have observed that com-munity specialization is not only constrained to a single product but to a highly standardized version of it, innovators being punished. This "noneconomic" behavior is explained in my interpretation of production regulation, inasmuch as an innovative producer of the same product is as dangerous as a producer of a different or competing product.

but at the cost of pitting peasant communities against each other in the subsistence sphere as they compete for land and in food production for the urban centers. Rather than leading to peasant class stratification, it leads to economic homogeneity of the peasant class but plural or heterogeneous cultural groupings without class identity.

The point of note in the overall "estate" system is not its rigidity but rather the flexibility *within* estates and the fact that the three basic estate divisions do not rest on wealth or differential control of the means of production.[31] Peasant communities have widely varying local resources, and as a group *own* many of the productive resources; but all produce for the market and have the same generally poor access to it. The merchant–artisan class again has widely varying resources and incomes, but what defines them as a single group is that they run the market and are tainted by it. Finally, the administrative elite may or may not own productive resources and may follow very different occupations with different economic rewards, but what makes them a single class is that they "control" the market by all the various means that the different administrative occupations have. On the other hand, the spatial distribution of these groups affects their specific relations to the market and their relations with each other. The urban elite and urban merchant–artisans form a strong coalition vis-à-vis rural peasants, because both classes need the provisions that the peasants bring to market. In addition, because both classes live in centers separated from the peasantry, they share a general urban life style that differentiates them from the peasantry more strongly than they are differentiated from each other. From the peasant point of view, there is little difference among the urban classes, in the "cultural" sense there being only two estates. This has the following consequence for stratification in a place like Chiapas.

The Chiapas system of stratification operates and is usually perceived by both outsiders and rural participants as if it were a two-"caste" system—rural peasants and urban elite (Collier 1975). This perception persists even in the face of greater mobility *across* the caste line than across peasant communities or across urban occupational and status groups (Colby 1966). That is, under some circumstances peasants—all culturally defined as "Indian"—easily become the lowest status group in the urban classes—both urban estates culturally defined as "Ladino"— while the Ladino urban merchant rarely becomes either an Indian or a member of the Ladino administrative elite, and Indian peasants never become members of Indian communities they are not born into. While Indians and Ladinos are thus in no way castes, the perceived two-caste

---

[31] In Chiapas some land is controlled by the elite, some by the peasantry; but elite land was held until recently to force peasant production for the market rather than for commercial production; see note 27.

system is real from the rural point of view and reflects actual economic differences based on differential relations to the means of exchange—the imperfect market of the urban center. Whereas rural Indians are market provisioners whose livelihood and income remain partially independent of the market, all urbanites are fully dependent on the market for both food and income. And at the same time, urbanites control the market. That is, the economic fortunes of both urban estates determine market conditions and prices, amount of specialization that takes place in rural communities, the number of positions for unskilled labor (through which Indians "become" Ladinos), and the wages paid to labor. The different relations that Indians and Ladinos have to the market determines the fundamental differences in income, culture, and life style between the two groups, so that this relationship overrides wealth and productive resources as a criterion of "caste" membership.

Under conditions of isolation from external economic forces, the only mobility possible in this type of economy would be downward mobility—assuming differential class fertility—from leisured bureaucratic positions to skilled urban crafts and trade, and from that to unskilled labor; and from landed peasant to unlanded serf on some noncommercial elite estate. Population brakes would be provided by the unskilled urban and rural serf elements, who would be "expendable" in times of economic closure and would not reproduce themselves. At such times one would not expect rural migration of peasants to join the lowest ranks of the urban classes. The only market-determined wage—that of unskilled labor—would regulate an otherwise immobilized occupational structure, providing the slack in an otherwise tightly constricted, noncompetitive economy. This occupational opening would also lend flexibility to the system in periods of growth, for under these conditions—determined by outside forces—the urban classes would be open to upwardly mobile peasants. The fact that the line between the rural and urban classes is thus occasionally permeable in no way contradicts the basic division between them. The essential life conditions of each would still be determined by their relationship to the market, the market would determine the wage for unskilled labor, and peasants would therefore never flood the urban centers and change their character. Major changes in stratification would only accompany those economic changes that broke the self-preserving urban and rural monopolies that stultify both economy and stratification in administered market systems.

Administered market economies were once common, but today outside of a few isolated regions of Latin America they are rare, dissolved by the industrial revolution and the vast expansion of mercantile trade that accompanied it (Wallerstein 1974). Even highland Chiapas has been transformed, making the above description relevant to another era there, as elsewhere. It is probably a faithful picture of early Tokugawa Japan, for instance, and the parallels will be drawn later when the changes that took place in Japan then are chronicled. It may also describe some of the precolonial kingdoms of West Africa (Goody 1971; Morton-Williams 1969; Polanyi 1966), precolonial Java (Geertz 1963; Howell, Chapter 9, this volume), and many of the historical bureaucratic societies described by Eisenstadt (1963) What Eisenstadt found characteristic of these societies is the unvarying presence of markets and a price mechanism but control over the economy by an administrative elite. He also found broadly ascriptive class structure, with considerable flexibility within the classes—what I call "estate" structure. He relates this phenomenon to the growing autonomy of both the economy and polity but the basic dominance of the polity over the economy, as I do. But where he emphasizes the political definition of class and status, I find it possible to put continued emphasis on exchange and distribution systems as the forces that determine class structure. For the polity controlled the economy, essentially, by controlling critical economic resources through the market. And the spatial organization of distribution had a good deal to do with class relations.

Dendritic Market Systems— Stratification by Ethnic Group

The dendritic market system is a creature of colonialism. It is the movement of trade across political–cultural boundaries, controlled from a well-organized core, penetrating less highly organized peripheries. Wallerstein (1974) argues that this kind of trade came into its own with the European discovery of the New World and was essential to the development of industrial capitalism in the West. While his point about the development of modern capitalism is well taken, it is unlikely that dendritic marketing systems are new to the world. More likely is Wallerstein's other main argument—that lack of political controls over this trade system in the West allowed it to flower to an extent never seen before, hence permitting unprecedented economic growth in the West. In the past, extensive mercantile trade, under political control, led to the growth and expansion of bureaucratic empires. But empire systems, in the process of controlling trade, either killed the geese that laid the golden eggs (special trade goods) or allocated the new resources into noneconomic channels. The fragmented polities of postfeudal Europe, by contrast, allowed trader groups to move freely and trade centers to be moved freely, channeling most of the immense wealth gained in trade into further economic expansion. As Wallerstein notes, this development of the West was at the same time the underdevelopment of much of the rest of the world, which constituted the geese whose eggs were to be taken.[32]

To a striking degree, class structure in dendritic distribution systems is

[32] Wallerstein's argument rests heavily on previous analyses of the bases of modern capitalism, particularly those of Marx (1967:I), Dobb (1946), and Braudel (1961), as he acknowledges.

related to the formation of ethnic groups and ethnic stratification. Once pluralistic and culturally differentiated, peasant communities lose their individuality to become "lumpen-peasants" of a particular ethnic stripe. (In simpler societies, also fragmented into small communities with little unity among them except perhaps language, groups of people become politically identified as "tribal" units.) While this process may encourage cultural unification of previously separate groups, just as often it fragments them politically even further, so that the relevant social unit becomes nothing more than a localized group of related families—that is, the corporate character of peasant or tribal communities expires. In related fashion, local elites become identified with the peasant ethnic group that surrounds them, losing political and economic power to the external elites in distant metropoles. They may remain local leaders, but their status even within the local system drops several notches. Finally, a third group, "resident strangers" with connections and relatives in the external control centers, takes control of the local exchange economy. Their cultural identification with the external world plays a major role in transforming the local people into one or more generalized ethnic groups distinct from them. Examination of several empirical cases will show the dynamics of this process.

Northwestern Guatemala is the ultimate periphery in a dendritic system with at least three "core" levels: a western regional center and the developed subsystem in its immediate hinterland; a national center and its even more developed hinterland; and an external metropole located in the United States. Except for the top one, each level can be identified as a periphery with respect to a higher-level core. The export "crop" in northwestern Guatemala is seasonal labor for plantations in the south coast of the country, which produce export crops for the industrial world. I will concentrate on the class and ethnic relations at the regional level—a tiny microcosm of world trade—although I emphasize that the ultimate core is outside the national economy, as is typical for most dendritic systems.[33]

Major merchants and businessmen who deal with northwestern Guatemala are concentrated in the regional and national centers. Their intermediaries in the periphery consist of a group of "resident strangers" and a group of "mobile strangers." The resident group constitutes 20 percent of the population in the periphery; they are Ladinos and town dwellers, both culturally and physically set apart from the local peasantry, who are rural Mayan Indians. What defines Ladino status in the area, aside from cultural emulation of the core population, are economic roles in the businesses of the larger core economy. As vehicles for outsiders rather than as

---

[33] The economy of western Guatemala is more fully described in Smith (1975a; Chapter 8, Volume I).

independent entrepreneurs, they dominate local shops, transport, and the few production enterprises other than agriculture. They also regulate and purchase the area's major export, seasonal labor, providing a local staff for distant plantations. The mobile group from the regional core area are other Mayan Indians, culturally distinct from the peripheral Indians. Working in small marketplaces or peddling house to house, they supply the peripheral Indians with consumables produced in the core and buy a few raw materials not produced in the core. These Indian traders are also agents of the core—although unknowing ones—because by selling their intensively produced specialties for high profit but at cheaper prices than could locals without a developed system of specialization, they fill all the potential niches by which the less highly organized economy of the periphery might develop. In this situation, there is no penalty for taking the lead, the underdevelopment of the periphery feeding into the further development of the core and thus its greater control over the periphery.

The irrelevance of production control for economic power in this market-dominated system is demonstrated by the fact that northern Indians have much better agricultural resources than either northern Ladinos or core-area Indians. Yet because their local marketing system is superior, peasants in the core are able to produce a surplus, afford a higher standard of living, and compete successfully with peripheral-area Indians in both trade and production. The marketing system in the core is organized to feed the regional urban centers housing the regional Ladino elite; in consequence, it is oriented toward domestic rather than external demand, articulates rural specialization, and thereby allows a higher level of production. In the periphery, by contrast, the marketing system is organized for the convenience of external rather than internal suppliers, which thereby *precludes* a high level of local production. Peasants in the periphery must leave their land seasonally to work on the plantations for cash enough to buy imported food—at very high prices from monopolist distributors, the same local Ladinos who buy their labor; they farm extensively when they can and so do not realize their potential agricultural wealth. This makes peasants in the periphery all the more dependent on the market but unable to develop their own market infrastructure; their needs are met by Ladino monopolists or the more efficient and productive core-area Indians.

The plantations that undergird the regional and national economies are owned by core-area Ladinos who derive considerable profit from them. But the profit they derive from owning the means of production is much less than that derived by the large commercial firms that market the product and control the means of exchange. At each level of the system, then, it is market power that is critical to the economic position of each group. In the most clear-cut instances of market power, peasants produce the export crop on their own land (cf. Appleby, Chapter 11, this volume), and nothing but dendritic market distribution organizes the agrarian economy and establishes the system of stratification.

Four economic classes and four ethnic groups are forming in relation to the exchange systems of western Guatemala: two of them Ladino, two Indian. (Stratification in the plantation area, determined by other exchange and marketing systems, is something else again and will not be treated here.) The Ladino elite live in a few major centers and control the regional import–export economy—some but not all of them own plantations as well. A class of rustic Ladinos, those who live in the periphery as agents for the dominant Ladinos, is clearly separated from the elite in economic means, life style, and manners. The ethnic division that separates elite from rustic Ladino is not sharp inasmuch as Ladino culture in general sets both classes apart from Indians, but the rustic Ladinos have a more archaic version of this culture. To the extent that Ladinos in the periphery emulate Ladino culture in the core, Ladinos in the core differentiate themselves further by emulating the general Western culture of the external elite in the United States. Trend setters at the top keep the cultural system in motion, cultural symbols of status going out of style among the high-level elite as they are picked up below. Rustic Ladinos are just now discovering the elegance of snap-brim hats and plastic tablecloths. Should any rustic individual succeed in emulating the more dominant group, he becomes part of it, moving away from his less successful confreres. Hence, physical distance and this kind of physical cooption maintain the general differences of the two or three strata.

While status mobility with physical mobility and cultural change is therefore possible, the highest-level positions are not generally open to parvenus. To engage in successful import–export trade not only requires more capital than that to which rustic Ladinos have access but also assumes political sophistication and personal ties with those who control this trade outside the country, neither of which is easily acquired without a generation or two of acculturation. Monopoly controls are most stringent where potential monopoly profits are highest, so few of the national elite move out of their own economy to join the highest-level elite. While more Westernized than other nationals, the national elite have more in common with their countrymen than with outsiders.

People who work the land with their hands, Mayan Indians, are sharply separated from all Ladinos in status and culture. But once equally peasants under an administered economy, Mayan Indians are now divided by the dendritic economy into two opportunity groups: Indians in the core, who by dominating domestic markets and production rival rustic Ladinos in standard of living; and Indians in the periphery, who control no important resources and are fragmented into several cultural groupings, equally poor. The economic differences are restructuring Indian sociocultural systems as Indian corporate communities adapted to an administered economy dissolve in both areas. In the core area a single ethnic group is forming—Quicheans for want of a better term. Quicheans have become less culturally plural and more internally stratified than they were in the past, as a result of competition in the market arena to support the domestic economy. The most successful often becomes Ladinos, although many do not—perhaps to better control the Indian wage labor in their large enterprises. When they do not become actual Ladinos, rich Quicheans emulate certain Indian groups in the Quiche-speaking heartland who are bicultural. Thus, able to operate in some parts of the Ladino economy as well as their own, Quicheans have developed a separate set of wealth and status symbols by which they claim a different rather than an inferior status with respect to local Ladinos. The group is not a well-organized one, their general ethnic identity barely discernible; yet locals almost always make a clear behavioral distinction when they are dealing with a Quichean as opposed to a peripheral-area Indian. Ladinos of the region, in fact, have several racial theories to account for the obvious differences between the two Indian groups; they do not, however, concede Quicheans political or status equality.

In the peripheral area corporate Indian communities are on the wane for other reasons and to other ends. Community differentiation and internal status hierarchies have progressively diminished under stress of poverty, mobility, and wage labor to the point that local Indians no longer provide leadership for their own communities. Even where Ladinos have not forcefully taken over community political offices, Indian figureheads in these positions have little control of their communities, there being little to control. In the absence of a partially autonomous economy, there is no basis for a partially autonomous political community—the relevant social unit being nothing more than a hamlet of related families linked by kinship and proximity. A successful Indian, moreover, is not one who leads his community, but one who leaves it to become a Ladino in another community (Colby and van den Berghe 1969). Separate Indian cultural groupings, often with distinct languages, are found at the ends of each penetration road from the core. These groupings may be expected to form more self-conscious ethnic interest groups in the future, but at present neither this nor pan-Indian identity has developed. Although some Quichean styles are slowly filtering into the periphery, Quichean Indians are seen there as strangers only somewhat less rapacious than local Ladinos. In sum, the relationships among different groups of Indians are even more fragmented than relationships among different groups of Ladinos, who at least have their unity vis-à-vis Indians.

The literature contains few descriptions of dendritic marketing systems (for an exception, see Chapter 11 in this volume). Some cases, however, fully described as to social organization and general economic conditions would seem to fit the market model very well, a prime example being

Geertz's analysis of colonial and postcolonial Java (1963), from which I draw a few parallels. Geertz observes that the export orientation of the usual tropical luxuries in this colony was paradoxically coupled with peasant self-provision of food: "The Javanese cane worker remained a peasant at the same time that he became a coolie, persisted as a community-oriented household farmer at the same time that he became an industrial wage laborer [1963:89]." Geertz also makes clear that land tenure patterns did not determine economic stratification (1963:97–100). While peasants owned the land, the colonists had put a market lien on it, first through the "Culture System," a form of taxation that forced peasants to produce for the market, later through the market mechanism alone that pushed peasant production for external demand. Peasants required certain goods they could obtain only in the market, and it was relatively easy to manipulate prices in such a way that peasants were on a dead run just to feed themselves while producing specialties for external demand and external profit. The high-level elite were Dutch, removed from the agrarian areas and concentrated in the metropoles of Indonesia and Holland; by controlling trade they did not have to control the means of production once peasants were involved in a cash economy. As far as internal trade was concerned, Javanese peasants were no more than marketers, while imported Chinese became the local-level merchants and resident strangers in the Javanese market towns and cities (Dewey 1962).

Geertz is somewhat elusive about the effects on social organization, noting an "advancement toward vagueness" and a "monotonous poverty of social substance" (1963:103). What these phrases seem to mean is that Javanese peasant communities lost the internal integrity they once had and became increasingly blurred as local social systems, much like the northern Indian townships in western Guatemala. What seems most important is that the local Javanese elite had lost power, so that local systems became less internally differentiated with respect to the overall system of stratification. This is not to say that the local Javanese elite disappeared into the peasantry—although some may have. More often they became town-based elites co-opted into administering the colonial apparatus. But their previous roles of lending coherence and leadership to local systems no longer existed. The end result was a social system with four separate compartments: the absent Dutch elite; the town-based local Javanese elite in the role of bureaucrats or local "princes"; the segregated town-based Chinese merchants and tradesmen; and an undifferentiated mass of rural Javanese peasants. The final "involuted" stage saw a proliferation of rural ethnic groups, most of them localized (cf. Howell, Chapter 9, this volume). A dendritic market structure has not been demonstrated for colonial or postcolonial Java, but it doubtless existed.

The main feature of stratification to be noted in both of these examples is a perceptible shift from three basic estates, each fragmented into self-contained homogeneous segments, to a multiple class system that is layered in space to produce multiple interest and ethnic groups. Each peripheral end of the system encompasses a distinct ethnic group, within each of which there are layers having differential access to the market and different degrees of cultural assimilation to the dominant group, located in the main outside the agrarian region. (See Verdery, Chapter 8, this volume, for another description of this latter aspect in the subregions of Wales.) As in the solar system, the high-level elite are concentrated in urban centers removed from places where peasants reside, but the major urban center in this case is removed from the entire agrarian region. Around the major urban center and local feeder centers exist privileged groups, members of which often become traders or merchants in the marginal areas remote from the centers. The group least privileged in its relationship to the means of exchange is, of course, the peasantry in the marginal feeder ends of the dendritic system.

Coexisting with spatial layering of interest groups is the regular alternation between a town-based trader class and rural-based peasantry. But at each remove from the core center, this town-based class becomes less able to identify with the core elite and more enveloped by the surrounding peasants. Sometimes the town-based traders will be resident strangers not only among peasants but in the region as a whole; regardless of origin, however, the town-based class is distinct from both the peasants and the removed mercantile elite, perhaps not as obviously as the Chinese in Southeast Asia, but at least as clearly as the Ladinos in northern Guatemala. Under these circumstances, ethnicity is of high salience at even the local level, and class interests are often perceived in these terms. When seen in large scale and from the perspective of the major metropole, however, one has what Hechter (1975) has termed a "cultural division of labor," for which André Gunder Frank (1967) has provided forceful analyses with respect to stratification. From the point of view of outsiders or the external elite, the class and cultural divisions below them have low salience, their tendency being to see the entire region as relatively undifferentiated but each agrarian region with which they deal as different: all Guatemalans temperamental, coffee-producing Latins; all Indonesians inscrutable, sugar-producing Orientals. When the core elite, made arrogant by their complete control over the system, refuse the local elites the dignity of an identity separate from that of the surrounding peons, localized interests—national or ethnic—can unite against the core.[34] But if

[34] Using insights from Barth (1969), Hechter sees cultural "boundaries" as accounting for the ability of the dominant group to impose role restraints on the peripheral peoples. But he notes that ethnicity may be turned to other ends, for "if at some initial point acculturation did not occur because the advantaged group would not permit it, at a later time acculturation may be inhibited by the desires of the disadvantaged group for independence from a situation increasingly regarded as oppressive [1975:38–39]." Hence a "cultural division of labor" is not simply based on preexisting differences but brings about some differences that may not have existed in the past.

a core elite reaches the point of being able to afford such disdain, in most cases their power is sufficiently entrenched to make local rebellions inefficacious for realigning the exchange system.

It does not follow, moreover, that gradual cultural homogenization of an agrarian region creates ongoing class solidarity within. Substituting for local peasant community pluralism as a mechanism for fractionalizing class interests is spatial layering of economic opportunity. Two groups are found at each dendritic tier, each directly exploiting the other, and each tier is part of a more elaborate stratification system. Peasants in and near major centers who reap the benefits of greater and more diverse commerce see more in common between themselves and the core elite than they do between themselves and peasants who are economically disenfranchised by distance and poor market development. Peasants at the periphery, in turn, see the advantaged groups as allies of the core elite, the more so when those advantaged groups are prominent in rural trading activity. Also, peasant cultural simplification at the periphery makes class differentiation at the local level a much starker reality, dividing the two lowest-level groups (rural peasants and town-based traders—in Guatemala, Indians and Ladinos) absolutely. As a result, interest groups throughout a region remain parochial in view and divided with respect to economic and political power.

In terms of mobility, overall stratification is much less rigid in dendritic systems than in solar systems. For one thing, rural peasants may enter the trader classes, at least theoretically, for there is no single urban monopoly on this occupation. As export commerce penetrates the countryside, trade niches proliferate, and people at the lower-level parts of the system can move into them. For another, class change is readily accomplished by changing one's residence and ethnic identity. In fact, class mobility depends on just such physical mobility and cultural assimilation, insofar as success can be measured in terms of actual location of the trade or production enterprise and cultural ties to the core. The closer to the metropole, however, the greater are the constrictions on entrance: Class mobility becomes a mere trickle, for the external trade structure is open only to the core monopolists who have all the advantages of capital, scale, political power, and ethnic culture already defined as the dominant one. In addition, distance is a powerful constraint on mobility. The peripheral ends of dendritic systems usually remain regional and cultural isolates, although tied to and tapped by a broader trade structure than that found in solar systems. External goods flow to and from the isolated areas with relatively little movement of personnel to provide less direct contact between the far peasant producer and the elite consumer than in any other kind of agrarian exchange system. It follows that peasant culture in the far periphery is little affected by elite styles and core culture. Peasants at the end of dendritic systems, therefore, will be among the most "backward," "traditional," and "primitive" to be found in the world even though connected to and part of advanced economic systems.

FULLY COMMERCIALIZED SYSTEMS

At several different times and places in the world, many more than assumed by those who see the industrial revolution as necessary for true market development, fully commercialized systems have come into existence.[35] Almost always they have developed in localized areas (whether from the perspective of the region or the world), and the causes behind their development have been more or less the same. For one reason or another, administrative control over trade in partially commercialized systems has slipped, allowing commerce to move out of tightly constricted channels. Often the process begins when mercantile traders enter a peripheral region, sometimes at administrative instigation, to restructure its markets dendritically. Enormous profits flow into a core area, and a new type of marketing structure builds up in the core on that foundation. Wallerstein (1974) has described the industrial development of the West with this basic model, but one can see the same process at various levels of organization throughout the world—the development of the core area of western Guatemala is a case in point. The instances I have chosen for analysis here were the much further developed core areas of traditional Japan and China. I had reached the following conclusions about them before I encountered Wallerstein's analysis of the world-system; but his perspective allows me to include sixteenth-century western Europe as the most outstanding example.

Expansion of trade from a core area into peripheries first leads to growth of core-area urban centers, whose locations are dictated by administrative requirements. These centers grow not only in population (from rural migration) but in wealth, increasing their demands for rural foodstuffs and for more specialized goods. In response, production and specialization in the immediate rural hinterland of the core area intensify. At some point it becomes advantageous for the administrators of the urban

[35] Polanyi et al. (1957) argue that all preindustrial economies were in one way or another partially commercialized economies because factor prices were not set by the market—that is, by supply and demand crowds. While Polanyi has correctly identified some preindustrial societies as having administered economies, the assertion that the modern industrial revolution was necessary to free labor and land from administration is patently absurd. All that is necessary is a competitive market organization, such as one of those described here. There is no doubt that preindustrial China, Japan, even Europe, contained some localized systems where the market was competitive and did price all factors of production. Parts of the preindustrialized Third World today also have such markets, as many anthropologists have shown. Polanyi is correct, however, in his assertion that not all markets have all the market functions, as I have argued for the partially commercialized systems.

centers to encourage further rural specialization in the immediate area by fostering (or at least not suppressing) an integrated rural trade system. Periodic peasant marketplaces in which peasants exchange some goods may exist in any of the economies already described: In feudal economies where polyadic exchanges are based on control of a scarce commodity, that commodity is simply not forthcoming in the peasant marketplace; where the scarce resource is land, peasants may exchange most of the commodities they produce themselves as long as they do not produce exclusively for the market; and in administered and dendritic economies, periodic marketplaces tied to a single urban center for its supply allow localized horizontal peasant exchanges of some goods as well. But in none of these economies is the peasant marketing system designed to articulate broad specialization among the peasantry, being little more than an undifferentiated network system without higher-level nodes or market specialists to arbitrage a division of labor. As Bohannan and Bohannan put it for the Tiv network markets, which seem to feed into an external dendritic structure, "although Tiv market places are overtly institutionalized, the market system is not [1968:219]." Rural marketing *systems* only come into their own under special circumstances that conspire to keep large firms and administrators from interfering with rural trade.

When untrammeled by monopolies of one kind or another or by administrative decrees, a rural marketing system will develop in a core area as follows. Rural market towns spring up wherever demand calls them forth, so that their pattern of growth is strongly competitive. Those markets that serve rural demand with efficiency because of location and comparative advantage flourish, while less competitive centers diminish or die out. In short order, the core area has nonadministrative towns at an intermediate level in the central-place hierarchy located for the express purpose of facilitating rural commerce; that is, fully *competitive exchange* creates *interlocking central-place systems*. Competitive, redistributive trade in rural environs, articulated by high-level market towns without administrative function, assists the rural producers in specialization and intensification of production by providing them with necessities dependably and at cheap enough prices that they can forego producing their own. While this means lost monopoly revenue to the urban elite, it also ensures them a cheap and plentiful supply of food. Meanwhile they can collect their accustomed "tribute" from places other than the local markets.

Given that a large territory will be fully and competitively serviced by an interlocking central-place system, one can expect rural as well as urban distribution of the elite. On the other hand, if indeed the elite always locates itself in terms of advantage in the exchange system, one would expect concentration of the most powerful members of the elite in the major central places of the system. Empirical cases suggest that in fact both distributions are possible and related to the operation of the inter- locking system. If the competitive rural marketing arrangement develops at roughly the same time that major administrative and commercial centers also arise, true for sixteenth-century Europe, or if the administra- tive elite of an administered economy alternate between rural and urban residence, true for much of traditional China, a rural gentry class— "feudal" in origin and based on the land—will be maintained, will even flourish, involved in local-level governance and commerce. A smaller group descended from the same rural families will staff the major political offices and merchant houses at some remove from their rural base. Aristocratic pretensions based on a previous golden age without competi- tion will die slowly here, and the rural and urban elite may not be in strict agreement over political matters. But there will be so much elite move- ment back and forth from rural places to urban centers accompanied by occupational change that one cannot point to two estates, one rural and the other urban; instead, there are multiple interest groups in a single class that has finely tuned status and power gradations within. As resources from which commercial advantage might stem are put into motion by the penetration of the market mechanism throughout, no one of the old estates controls them; any entrepreneur with capital enough can exploit the opportunities that come his way. Shifting power bases and need for capital break down the barriers between old elite and merchant classes, the latter able to buy their way into elite status.

In other instances, stemming from previously administered economies where the elite is fully removed from the countryside, the rural "gentry" are the entrepreneurs that develop from the peasantry; in time they become the new middle classes throughout the system. As the engines of commerce make local rural trade profitable and draw away business from the urban centers, little will distinguish the rural entrepreneurs from the urban merchant class. Individuals from either group may develop com- mercial enterprises large and efficient enough to overpower the adminis- trative monopolies, the highest-level elite unwilling or unable to curb the activities of business from which they benefit.

In either case, when trade and production opportunities both at home and abroad proliferate, people of various origins in the core system will take advantage of them. Traders will lose their commercial taint to join the highest-level elite of the system, and cultural boundaries that separate the various classes will disappear, the mobility process homogenizing the regional and class cultures of the system. On the other hand, differential advantage in the exchange system is not eliminated, so class differentia- tion based on access to the means of exchange is still supported. The most successful competitors must exploit every opportunity, which includes exploitation of those people unable to cope with, or without the basic resources to engage in, the rigors of cut-throat competition. The position of the nonproducing elite, however, must to some degree be based on economic contribution, or competitors will take their positions from them.

High rates of mobility, cultural homogenization, and the new dignity acquired by merchant classes *throughout* a system, of course, presuppose that the central-place hierarchy is organized competitively from top to bottom in one of the interlocking patterns. This need not be true, and the evidence suggests that in fact it is unlikely—fully competitive systems gracing only economics textbooks. A complex urban hierarchy may have anywhere from five to nine levels in it, and each of the levels may be aligned in different fashion. New rural markets may align themselves in a competitive and efficient pattern vis-à-vis preexisting administrative centers, which themselves do not change their alignment with regard to high-level commerce—as in western Guatemala. Hence, one may find a pattern that has peasants in competition with one another (tending toward cultural homogeneity as they seek both horizontal and vertical mobility within the rural system), but excluded from the higher-level urban system by the organization of the higher levels. That is, rural market-town growth may be encouraged, but higher-level town growth might be completely suppressed, thereby precluding the full development of the interlocking pattern and restricting rural–urban mobility to its traditional form—cheap labor. This would keep high-level urban merchants and peasant traders distinct from one another rather than finely graded in wealth and status, and might also prevent full cultural acceptance of the rural merchant classes—the case in western Guatemala. In other cases the situation could be reversed, with high-level markets in competition but peasant markets still administered. But wherever competitive exchange is institutionalized by an interlocking system—whether in an entire region or at several levels of a region—the effects on stratification should be those described above. Examination of the two empirical cases will show the processes involved.

Competitive Exchange at the Lower Levels

I begin with the simpler case—whose simplicity no doubt rests on lack of information. Recently a number of publications on marketing during the Tokugawa era of Japan have appeared in English (Rozman 1973; T. C. Smith 1973). These describe the rapid growth of urban centers and rural market towns that seem to have played a major role in the consequent economic development of Japan as well as in the diminution of the earlier rigidly ascriptive status–class hierarchy. From the descriptions of both Smith and Rozman, it is certain that with the Sengoku and Tokugawa regimes, Japan moved from an earlier feudal phase to an administered economy.[36] As Smith puts it, the new central administration concentrated the warrier (samurai) class, including family and retainers, in and around the daimyo's castles, which led to centralized control by an administrative class (daimyo and their samurai), a spurt of urban growth, and the development of a large merchant–artisan class in the many sizable castletowns. In addition, major markets were located nowhere but in these towns, and trade outside their purview was ruthlessly suppressed. Rozman observes that there was an urban hierarchy of sorts, but there were many "holes" in it and a virtual vacuum at the intermediate level—that is, the level of nonadministrative market towns that would articulate rural peasant marketing systems with each other (1973:52, 109). The ordering of central-place levels that Rozman describes is precisely what one would expect for a solar central-place system.

Hence, along with a central administration, Japan achieved in very short order a classic administered solar system of central places: Administrative towns became the primary market centers, rural trade oriented to these centers as peasant periodic markets were drawn into the hinterland of a *single* castle town, and castle town merchants were physically segregated, closely observed, controlled, and taxed. There was also the classic estate system of classes: warrier daimyo and their samurai running the show by administering the economy; merchants forming a separate group of widely varying fortunes but invariant low status; and an economically undifferentiated but locally pluralistic peasantry, organized into closed, corporate communities.

In the latter half of the same era, however, Smith notes an interesting shift in the urban pattern: Castle towns in the more developed areas (he singles out Kinki and the Inland Sea regions) diminish in size and commercial power, while other places—Smith calls them "country places"—not legally designated as urban but in effect constituting intermediate-sized towns with markets, grow in profusion (1973:136). Rozman finds that during this time the Japanese central-place hierarchy fleshes out with a huge increase in intermediate-sized towns and growth of smaller nonadministrative market towns (1973:109–110).[37] Neither author attempts a spatial

---

[36] According to Rozman, the feudal central places were primarily peasant periodic marketplaces, poorly articulated with each other because of lack of intermediate-sized centers. Toward the latter part of the feudal period, other market centers developed, but they did not coalesce into an administered system until the "warring states" period forced previously independent local systems (the feudal manors) into hierarchically organized systems.

[37] Rozman's chronology seems to be about a century ahead of Smith's. But Rozman appears to look for the first emergence of a central-place level for his chronology (and one intermediate-size center does not a system make). Given Smith's more careful analysis of the emergence of country places (Rozman's fifth level), I am following Smith's chronology.

analysis of the developing central-place system, but from their descriptions it is clear that the nonadministrative towns growing during this
period were in strong competition with castle towns, functioning to articulate local rural systems with each other. At the critical level where rural
commerce was interrelated with town commerce, it is reasonable to
assume that an interlocking central-place hierarchy was developing.

In considering why this phenomenon should have taken place when it
did, Smith argues that growing rural productivity and market dependence,
together with rural freedom from taxation and guild restrictions, enabled
country places to attract merchants and labor away from castle towns. Yet
it seems equally evident that rural productivity and market dependence
would be enhanced by a competitive, interlocking marketing system,
reversing causality—that is, country places were competitive and therefore
permitted the necessary growth in rural productivity. These positive functions may explain why the elite allowed country places to develop. For, on
the one hand, the castle towns had grown so large and so fast with
centralization of administration that they required considerably more
volume and more efficient supply of rural surplus than a completely
administered system could provide; but, on the other hand, the urban
traders and administrators were not at all happy about the turn of events
because it meant lost monopoly revenue. According to Smith:[38]

> Government attempted to block this development, which it regarded as likely
> to divert labor from farming and to make the peasants lazy, quarrelsome and
> greedy. Also, it sought to confine trade and industry to the towns in order to
> assure their provisioning, and to facilitate price control and the taxation of
> non-agricultural income [1973:139].

> The government increasingly attempted to confine the sale of certain staples
> in each region to licensed wholesalers in towns who paid for their monopolies
> handsomely in financial "contributions," "thank-money" and taxes. . . . The
> establishment of the monopolies, however, inevitably created incentives for
> producers and buyers to circumvent them in order to avoid rigged prices, taxes
> and the high transport charges consequent upon circuitous shipping. Despite
> this, monopolies were relatively well enforced in towns, where guild organiza
> tions could be harnessed for the purpose and the surveillance area was limited
> in extent and swarming with samurai officials and police [1973:144-145].

But it seems there was little that government could do about *rural*
market development, given the need for rural goods and the fact that the
administrative apparatus was concentrated in towns and could depend on
rural policing only by people who would themselves have to be policed.
The reaction of government, therefore, was to compensate for lost revenue
from administrative towns by cutting down expenditures where most con-

---

[38] World Copyright: Past and Present Society. These excerpts are reprinted with the permission of the Society and the author from T. C. Smith, "Pre-modern Industrial Growth:
Japan and the West," *Past and Present* no. 60 (August 1973).

venient—largely in samurai stipends. This, of course, impoverished a great many samurai, who, to make ends meet, themselves began taking up the "demeaning" trades.

Smith documents far-reaching changes in the old estate system of stratification produced by these developments. For one, peasants entered trade with a vengeance, not to become just "peasants with an abacus [1973:151]" in Smith's words, but major merchants. In addition, rural industries developed that divided peasants into workers and managers. Urban merchant monopolists lost ground, so that the gulf between them and rural traders was considerably diminished. Finally, the samurai, forced into various expedients by their loss in income, became less and less of an elite class. Smith observes that this was a major factor in the eventual overthrow of the Tokugawa and the ushering in of a new period where old-fashioned estate distinctions withered away. What capped it was that while per capita incomes rose enormously in this period, "the resulting benefits were not very evenly distributed and large numbers of Japanese were not better off [1973:128]." The new era did not change this, but it did bring an end to many of the arbitrary controls of the previous administered economy. Class mobility became commonplace, economic class and status competitively achieved, and the regional and estate cultures homogenized.

Japan is notable for commercialization without stimulation by external colonial expansion until rather late in its development and for an unprecedented rate of growth. Both Smith and Rozman point to several unique features of its central-place develpment that may have been critical in this, especially the speed of general urbanization pushed by the Tokugawa. But it is worth observing that development was not regionally homogeneous, for while administrative centers diminished in size and power in the commercialized regions, they were developing in size and power in peripheral regions (Smith 1973:136), trade apparently pushing outward from the developed cores into the undeveloped peripheries. Until these regional patterns are better documented, we cannot be sure of the process; but given that Smith and Rozman both note a definite regional pattern of urban and commercial growth in Japan, the model that postulates core development with expansion into peripheries is not contradicted by this example. It is also worth noting that the modern period sees the complete commercial dominance of Tokyo (the administrative center of the Tokugawa) over the country, an immense administrative center that encompasses all of Japan as its hinterland. An associated phenomenon is that the highest-level administrative elite never lost economic power or ran into serious competition for it. So, in a sense, Japanese development seems to have produced a competitive level of organization at the lower levels with monopolistic organization at the highest level, hindering the competitive process for some economic strata. That is, I suggest very tentatively that at the highest level Japan has remained an "administered economy," with a distinctive Tokyo-based bourgeois elite stemming from the same families as the old administrative elite.[39]

Competitive Exchange at the Upper Levels

China also seems to involve a mixture of competitive and administrative exchange systems. In fact, because of its many regions and subregions, each with varying levels of development in any period, it probably could provide examples of any exchange system. Hence, this description of the traditional Chinese economy is of necessity selective rather than general and is based primarily on G. William Skinner's regional analysis of Chinese economic and central-place development of more developed systems [presented in Chapter 10, Volume I, and elsewhere (in press a, in press b)]. Skinner divides agrarian China into eight macroregions (nine if one includes Manchuria) defined physiographically, each with a core and a periphery. Most of the cores are in river basins, and most were far more developed than their higher-altitude peripheries. Several regional systems in late traditional China achieved full commercialization, some doing so very early. The lower Yangtze regional system in the environs of Nanking, Yangchow, Soochow, and Hangchow seems to have been commercialized from the twelfth century on. Certainly in later epochs this area evidenced all of the features of full commercialization: a wide division of labor, heavy market dependence even by rural peasants, a high degree of urbanization, and a fully fleshed-out, interlocking central-place hierarchy (Rozman 1973; Skinner 1965:220, in press a). In the following short discussion I generalize from descriptions of various developed cores of late traditional (Ch'ing) China, the period for which information is most complete, though I emphasize that regional variation was pronounced.

Throughout much of late traditional China, the elite consisted of rural-based gentry as well as urban-based administrators. While most of the rural gentry owned land, it provided only a portion of their incomes and in the developed areas a *small* portion at that (Chang 1962); land was a commodity in developed areas, sublet through many owners, bought and sold by peasants and elite alike (Perkins 1969:88–98). Besides providing leadership to the local peasant communities and giving them collective representation in higher-level politics (Skinner 1964), the rural gentry through various means controlled the local economies—more so in peripheries, less so in cores. Yet opportunities for even these residents of villages and small market towns were concentrated in higher-level central

---

[39] Supporting this point, Lockwood (1954) has argued that economic development during the Meiji period was led by the national elite, who combined entrepreneurial activity with administration and who promoted monopoly development in many national industries (based in Tokyo).

places. Those who climbed the central-place hierarchy to better their chances were generally one of two types, merchants or political administrators. They went either to exploit business opportunities in economic central places or to take advantage of opportunities for education and bureaucratic service in the administrative central places. Notably, these were not always the same places, as is true in solar central-place systems (Skinner, Chapter 10, Volume I, in press a). Rates of mobility along both tracks were exceptionally high in china (Chow 1966; Eberhard 1962), but the most successful in both tracks usually came from developed core areas (Skinner, Chapter 10, Volume I).

According to Skinner, traders and economic specialists tended to pursue their callings away from home because particularistic demands of kin and neighbors would have made business relationships difficult for merchants operating on home ground and because it was easier to exercise unseemly practices on unknown, unknowing faces. Major merchants could, of course, undertake major business operations only in large urban centers. But the centers in which they would ply their trades were frequently not even the major centers of their own regional systems. The most commercialized regions of China, such as the lower Yangtze, tended to provide merchants and financiers of particular specialties for the whole country (Jones 1974; Skinner, Chapter 10, Volume I). Although this may have narrowed the range of competition within a business, it certainly did not eliminate it, for by working outside the region of local ties merchants were required to achieve success on the basis of offering a competitive product. In Skinner's words, "upward mobility in any sector involved testing and tempering sojourners in a context of competition with their same-native-place fellows. In the long run, relevant merit played a major role in success [Volume I:354]."

A similar but more directly competitive situation prevailed in political–bureaucratic mobility. The opportunity structure consisted of an open examination system by which bureaucratic governor–administrators were selected. While relatively few were in a position to take the examinations and the process selected out even fewer for positions of power, the system was theoretically open to all. Moreover, local systems stood so much to gain from having a person from their locale in a position of power that many of them collectively subsidized the education of promising young men whose resources would otherwise have been inadequate (Chapter 10, Volume I). Officials were required to serve in administrative systems remote from their own, again in order to evade particularistic demands. But because the upwardly mobile Chinese did not sever ties to home, like the wide-ranging merchants he saw the locality in which he served as a place to be plundered for the benefit of his own. The competitive nature of politics, therefore, also supported a highly mobile stratification system. But here too, as Skinner points out, the successful tended to come from the commercialized regions, where there was broad economic support for them—and presumably more local-level competition by which competitors could sharpen their skills.[40]

Central-place and marketing data are most complete on the upper Yangtze region, somewhat less so for the lower Yangtze. In both cases the data are fullest on the core areas, one partially, the other fully, commercialized. These provide sufficient information for the following preliminary analysis. Skinner has shown that in the upper Yangtze region, in the hinterland of Chengtu (Szechuan), rural market organization was at once competitive and administrative (in my sense of the term). Peasant communities were organized into a solar arrangement around a single standard market, but the standard markets were themselves arranged into competitive interlocking patterns—both of those shown in Figure 1 (Skinner 1964). Skinner also noted that while peasant horizons were limited to their own local marketing community, the rural gentry regularly participated in the higher marketing levels, and in more than one. In another context, Skinner argues that throughout most of agrarian China the basic class division was between the rural peasantry and the gentry of whatever level, who were landed, leisured, and literate, but that even here the line was not sharp (1968:18). I will be so bold as to guess that the line between peasant and gentry was sharper in these "traditional" marketing areas than in the more commercialized areas where peasant villages themselves were part of competitive, interlocking central-place systems. The Chengtu hinterland had been commercialized, but only within a traditional context (Skinner 1965:223). In such areas it seems likely that most economic (and political) opportunity was available only to the rural gentry, who moved with ease between the higher-level, competitive marketing levels carrying dossiers of information on everyone and everything noteworthy. Peasants, however, were excluded from external opportunity by their marketing community parochialism.

The hinterland around Ningpo in the lower Yantze regional core, whence came many of the successful merchants and bureaucratic degree candidates, provides the more commercialized example. This area is cited by Skinner as one that had become "modernized" by the end of the Ch'ing, as had about 10 percent of agrarian China in his estimate.

---

[40] Skinner (Chapter 10, Volume I) argues that the most successful degree candidates came not simply from the most commercialized areas but from counties that supported central places that were at once high-level commercial centers and high-level administrative centers. Elsewhere (in press) he notes that congruence of the two is most likely in more commercialized, urbanized, densely populated areas where the administrative span of control was broad and relatively weak. (There would be fewer administrative centers but more commercial centers per capita than in undeveloped, sparsely populated areas, so fewer administrative centers need be situated in small towns lacking commercial development.) The core area of the lower Yangtze regional system exemplifies this situation and provided more degree holders to the country than any other area of comparable size.

Modernization, according to Skinner, "can commence only when [a traditional marketing system] is linked by economically efficient transport to outside systems of production which are likewise economically efficient [1965:213]." "True modernization occurs only when a modern transport network is developed within an already commercialized central marketing system to the point where the standard [peasant] markets of the system are obviated and die [1965:216]," as had happened in Ningpo's immediate hinterland by 1937. And, "it will be noted that such modern trading systems are by definition indiscrete [1965:220]," so that "inevitably the social horizons of the peasant—now in the process of becoming a farmer are extended toward the limits of the larger modern trading area [1965:221]." Here, one would guess, the line dividing peasant and elite might become so blurred as to be nonexistent. Not that there would not remain rich and poor; but upper-level peasants would be distinct from lower-level elites only in the memories of living people.

The central-place organization of the lower Yangtze is not yet fully described, but Skinner notes that in this most urbanized region of China the amount of both extra regional and intraregional commerce was at least double that of agrarian China taken as a whole (in press a; see also Rozman 1973). Moreover, the administrative component of central-place development was small—smaller than that of any other macroregional system of China (Skinner in press a:24). Without question, both regional and extraregional trade had slipped far out of "administrative" control in the area by the end of the imperial period; in fact, commerce seems never to have been fully controlled here since the medieval urban revolution that began in the eighth century (Skinner in press b). From Skinner's earlier work we know that the rural area around Ningpo had been modernized by the end of the imperial period; and from various sources (Perkins 1969; Rawski 1972; Rozman 1973) we know that purchasing power was widely distributed and not limited to the politically powerful—a marked contrast to the situation in purely administered systems. That this may have been a completely interlocking system, from top to bottom, and from very early on, would go far to explain the entrepreneurial success of people from this particular region—tempered not only in competition with their fellows where they sojourned but in their very places of origin. A competitive rural marketing system would also account for the lead of the lower Yangtze region over the rest of China on almost any indicator of economic development one could choose.

According to the causal model advanced here, a completely developed, competitive, interlocking marketing system would lead to considerable class mobility and allow for a good deal of variability and differential opportunity among rural peasants as well as the urban-based strata. Stratification would not be eliminated; in a sense, it would be intensified. Economic–political advantage would still stem from access to and control over the means of exchange, which the elite based in major centers would have an especially advantageous situation for monopolizing. For one thing, their communication networks would be broader than those of peasants; for another, they would have more initial means by which they could position themselves and their members in the economic–political networks. But in this kind of system, unlike the previous systems described, peasants would not be sharply separated from the elite. One would expect peasants to be themselves stratified and there to be considerable upward class mobility from the peasant classes to various levels in the elite classes. One would not expect a high degree of "class solidarity" among any particular occupational or status groups because differences in economic expectations, opportunities, and success would fragment each group. One would expect more cultural homogeneity across classes and across local systems than is typical of most agrarian societies. One would not expect ethnicity to be of high salience in the system, unless parts of the system were integrated by other exchange systems. One would expect, in brief, a finely graded series of classes and statuses, considerable competition among and within economic classes, and a high rate of class turnover. This provides an important contrast to stratification in monopolistic or administered economies, where one finds relatively few economic classes that are wholly divided, little competition among classes although more of it among peasants, and virtually no significant class turnover.

These expectations stem from the nature of exchange in an interlocking distribution system. A hierarchy of nodes would create a basis for class stratification, based on position in the system. But the competition among nodes at each level would allow for open economic niches in the system, so that an able entrepreneur could make his way regardless of class or regional origin. Since no part of the territory would be seriously disadvantaged in terms of opportunity for economic growth, given the dynamic nature of competitive exchange, one would expect the elite to be distributed throughout the territory—situated in frontier areas and rural pockets as well as in major central places. The wide distribution of the elite would mean wide distribution of specialized knowledge, information, and cultural life styles, which would allow talented and ambitious peasants to acquire the special attributes necessary for upward mobility. Articulated exchange among all parts of the system would allow local specialties to be translated into general expertise, and thus allow each part to have some of its members in positions of special power in both the economy and the polity. Finally, competition among centers would involve competition among local systems and thus among specialties, so that ultimately there emerges a class system based on relative economic contribution, rather than one based on position in an unchanging, administered, or monopolistic central-place hierarchy, characteristic of most agrarian societies. To say that stratification in this kind of system leaves room for merit is not to say that all meritorious people are successful. But by leaving even *some* room for merit, this system distinguishes itself from other agrarian exchange systems.

While China stands as an example of an agrarian society with perhaps more interlocking, competitive marketing systems at different levels than any other and with a more competitive, nonascriptive stratification system than any other (with the possible exception of sixteenth-century western Europe), it was not organized in interlocking fashion throughout.[41] One of the interesting features of China is that its immense frontier and areas of non-Han Chinese gave it internal territories to colonize and exploit, so that some areas—that of the lower Yangtze, for example—could become fully commercialized, developed, and competitive. An examination of the exchange and marketing systems in the less developed areas of China would almost certainly show these were the areas that the successfully mobile Chinese from commercial areas "plundered" most mercilessly for the benefit of their own local, or regional, systems. The coexistence of substantial development in some parts of China with underdevelopment in other parts may account for the fact that some analysts see every aspect of modern commerce in traditional China, while others see only various stages of feudalism. It undoubtedly had both, within an economy that was in essence administered. The central administrative apparatus, however, was located almost continuously in one corner of an immense country. Given China's size alone, much less this anomalous placement of its administration, it is hardly mysterious that trade could regularly break out of administrative restrictions within the country, exploiting parts of the realm for the benefit of other parts. Skinner suggests:

> a unified empire could be maintained on into the late imperial era only by systematically reducing the scope of administrative functions and countenancing a decline in the effectiveness of formal government [in press b:38].

[41] This, of course, brings up the old question "Why was Europe rather than China the first to develop industrially?" Two answers have been given within the analytical framework developed here. Wallerstein argues that China, unlike Europe, was an empire system, so much of the development of China fed into noneconomic channels determined by the polity and mercantile trade outside the system was not encouraged. Rozman suggests that the central-place system of late Imperial China was proliferating at the lower levels (peasant markets), instead of consolidating at the higher and intermediate levels as happened in Japan. It could be that competitive marketing at the local peasant level had been regularly stifled by the rural elite (hence the modal administrative pattern of the peasant marketing community found by Skinner), which prevented their full articulation in the economy. These two notions are clearly compatible with each other and also with Elvin's argument (1973) that late traditional China was caught in a "high-energy equilibrium trap" whereby increased production fed mainly into increased population.

I see a long-term secular trend beginning in the T'ang whereby the degree of official involvement not only in commercial matters but also in social regulation . . . and in administration itself steadily declined, a retrenchment forced by the growing scale of empire [in press b:43].

China's distinctive type of stratification system, then, seems to have rested on centralized control of basic administration and high-level trade, along with administrative control of the peasantry, never fully removed from the hands of the rural gentry, but wide competition and freedom of movement at the middle to higher levels. This created a significant gulf between gentry and peasant in most parts of the realm—those parts not fully commercialized—and the sharp separation of the central apparatus from its bureaucracy, but left considerable latitude for class mobility, entrepreneurship, and so forth to its very large middle to upper classes.

The history of western Europe is so much a part of our cultural heritage that it needs little review here. Suffice it to say that Wallerstein (1974) has demonstrated (to my satisfaction at least) that its development rested on two basic foundations: the exploitation of much of the rest of the world through trade in the sixteenth century and onward; and its inchoate political organization in the sixteenth century that allowed trade to expand across political boundaries without any interference from a single core empire, which might have restricted this trade for administrative designs. The central-place hierarchies of Europe have not been fully explored for the sixteenth century, but it is reasonable to assume that they formed interlocking networks in many regions and at several levels, then and even earlier (Pirenne 1958; Russell 1972). On the other hand, T. C. Smith (1973) notes that the development of the West did not lead to urban diminution of old administrative or trade centers, presumably because the tremendous wealth provided by world trade allowed lower-level centers to grow up around them without robbing the major centers of either power or population.

What may have happened is that a competitive, interlocking system developed at the lower levels that did not compete with the higher levels of the system, where mercantile trade and traders were concentrated. As Wallerstein points out, however, major European trade centers may have had no *local* competition, but during at least the initial phase of growth these centers were in strong competition with each other. And any trade center in which monopolies developed that threatened to choke off growth was quickly disciplined by the competition of trade centers in other parts of the system. For these reasons, for instance, trade centers moved from Spain and northern Italy to Flanders and Great Britain. When the system eventually matured and capital was concentrated in industrial development, internal competition diminished, so that the ultimate design of the West was one that had several enormous metropoles that "administered" both local and distant economies. Parts of Europe that had led expansion—Portugal, Spain, northern Italy—became part of the periphery. With this in mind, an important point should be made about the nature of competition and growth in interlocking systems, based on insights from Marx. Just as competition occurs only in the early phases of capitalism before concentration of industrial power leads to monopoly, so competition in interlocking systems can occur only when the market system is expanding and before it has reached natural boundaries of one kind or another; that is, no market exchange system can expand infinitely. Once a boundary is reached, the system stabilizes in such a way that growth through commercialization and competition will as inevitably lead to the development of trade concentration, and thereby monopoly, as competition in industry leads to industrial concentration, and thereby monopoly. Competition will reoccur only when a new form of technology or a new type of scarcity develops to shift the exchange advantage in other directions. One major shift occurred with industrial distribution. Another may occur with energy distribution.

A final point that the three preceding examples make is that competitive exchange systems require a special set of circumstances to break earlier entrenched elite interests, for old elites are in the best position to take control of any new situation. In Japan it was the rapidity of growth, which required new commercial personnel. In China it was the enormous span of empire, which made it too costly for a centralized administration to keep tabs on all commercial enterprises. And in western Europe it was the huge flow of overseas wealth, which allowed trade and traders in local systems to proliferate. Even in these cases, old elites only shared power, and the new groups became quickly entrenched.

CONCLUDING REMARKS

As Sahlins remarked at the end of his well-known article on exchange (1965), it is difficult to end this kind of analysis with a flourish—one can only restate the main argument. My restatement and conclusion consist simply of a table of the main variables considered here (Table 2). This outlines for comparison different distribution systems resultant upon certain exchange mechanisms and levels of commerce (Table 1), together with the important stratification variables: spatial distribution of the elite, basic type of stratification, rural social organization, and mobility chances within the stratification system. The examples used for each type are then listed in the table.

One important point remains, however. The problem of origins has not been resolved, nor has the basis for the exchange and distribution systems posited been fully drawn out. I have suggested scarcity as a fundamental

TABLE 2
Distribution Systems and Stratification

	Extended network system	Bounded network system	Solar central-place system	Dendritic central-place system	Interlocking central-place system
1. Distribution System	Extended network system	Bounded network system	Solar central-place system	Dendritic central-place system	Interlocking central-place system
2. Distribution of the Elites	Not relevant (undifferentiated)	Concentrated, rural (settled or mobile)	Concentrated, urban (settled or mobile)	Absent from peasant region (settled)	Even, rural *and* urban (settled or mobile)
3. Type of Stratification	Egalitarian; no life-style differences	Castelike; few life-style differences	Estates; great life-style differences	Ethnically defined; culturally plural	Complex, competitive; culturally homogeneous
4. Rural Social Organization	Open, corporate communities; egalitarian	Closed, corporate communities; internally segmented	Closed, corporate communities; egalitarian	Open but isolated communities; noncorporate; egalitarian	Open, regionally integrated communities; noncorporate; internally stratified
5. Mobility Rate	Not relevant	Lowest	Low--only with physical mobility	Low--only with ethnic change	High
6. Examples	Indig. New Guinea, Australia; lowland S. America	Kiriwina, Trobriands; feudal Europe; parts of India; E. Africa	Chiapas, Mexico; W. Africa; pre-Tokugawa Japan	Pastoral Puno; N.W. Guatemala; U.S. Navajo; Java	Premodern W. Europe; core areas of Japan, China, Guatemala

causal variable, but this too must have its origins. The problem here, as with the origins of any major institution, is that causation is not likely to be linear and simple, but rather to be circular and complex. This is particularly true of the phenomenon of scarcity, which may bring on one particular institution to handle one kind of scarcity, which then brings on other kinds of scarcities. The market certainly has this characteristic. When it comes to ultimate origins, I suspect that by and large any given ecological adaptation—production system, if you will—leads to particular kinds of scarcities that constrain the basic possibilities for exchange systems. The elegance of production when used as a theoretical basis for stratification is that production can be seen as the first term, center, and last term of an entire causal chain. Yet this insistence on a fully unitary theory results in difficulty in explaining some empirical cases and fails to handle the effects of wide variability in production systems. It also implies that when differential control of the means of production is eliminated, so too will stratification be eliminated. Modern events tell us that this is not true, that an elite class can remain in power by their control of an exchange system even when they do not directly control the means of production. Class economic equality is only assured when access to the means of exchange is equalized, decentralization of an elaborate division of labor is achieved, local production is determined by local needs, or full rotation among high- and low-level nodes of the distribution system is compelled.[42]

The very emergence of inequality depends on the development of nodes for the accumulation of resources giving rise to imbalance in the exchange process. Hence, it is logical to expect some correlation between fundamental types of exchange systems and fundamental types of stratification. It has been my aim to argue and illustrate this logical possibility for agrarian societies.

ACKNOWLEDGMENTS

I would like to thank a number of people for reading and commenting on an earlier draft of this paper: Gordon Appleby, Richard Barrett, Brenda Beck, Jane Collier, Richard Fox, Naomi Quinn, and Ronald Smith. To the degree that this version withstands the scrutiny of empiricists, they deserve the credit. I would also like to thank for specific help as well as general comment the following: Klara Kelley for permitting me to use her written but unpublished work on nonhierarchical network systems; Steve Olsen for putting me onto Wallerstein (who is well worth being put onto); and G. William Skinner for pointing out the

[42] Russian and Chinese practitioners of Marxism differ on how they weigh the importance of access to the means of exchange as a basis for stratification. Russia has a highly centralized exchange system that appears to support a fully differentiated elite bureaucratic class in the absence of individual or class control of the means of production. The Chinese have at least experimented with ways to decentralize the exchange system and consider it necessary to rotate individual bureaucrats between high-level and low-level nodes to prevent the development of an entrenched elite.

(embarrassing) lack of a regional perspective in the first draft and for permitting me to draw on his unpublished papers. Katherine Verdery deserves special mention both for forcing me to think about elite levels and for her careful editorial comments on the original draft. Obviously, I did not follow every suggestion and am responsible for all of the present content.

REFERENCES

Baran, Paul A.
    1957   *The political economy of growth.* New York: Monthly Review Press.
Barth, Fredrik
    1969   Introduction: In *Ethnic groups and boundaries,* edited by F. Barth. Boston: Little,
         Brown.
Beattie, J. H. M.
    1964   Bonyoro: An African feudality? *Journal of African History* **5:** 25–35.
Bohannan, Paul, and Laura Bohannan
    1968   *Tiv economy.* Evanston, Ill.: Northwestern Univ. Press.
Boserup, Ester
    1970   *Woman's role in economic development.* London: Allen and Unwin.
Braudel, Fernand
    1961   European expansion and capitalism, 1450–1650. In *Chapters in Western civilization*
         (3rd ed.) New York: Columbia Univ. Press.
Bromley, R. D. F., and R. J. Bromley
    1975   The debate on Sunday markets in nineteenth century Ecuador. *Journal of Latin*
         American Studies **7:** 85–108.
Brookfield, H. C., with Doreen Hart
    1971   *Melanesia: A geographical interpretation.* London: Methuen.
Chang, Chung-li
    1962   *The income of the Chinese gentry.* Seattle: Univ. of Washington Press.
Chow, Yung-teh
    1966   *Social mobility in China.* New York: Atherton Press.
Colby, Benjamin
    1966   *Ethnic relations in the Chiapas highlands of Mexico.* Santa Fe: Museum of New
         Mexico Press.
Colby, Benjamin, and Pierre van den Berghe
    1969   *Ixil country.* Berkeley: Univ. of California Press.
Collier, George
    1975   *Fields of the Tzotzil: The ecological bases of tradition in highland Chiapas.* Austin:
         Univ. of Texas Press.
Dalton George
    1974   How exactly are peasants "exploited"? *American Anthropologist* **76:** 553–561.
Dewey, Alice
    1962   *Peasant marketing in Java.* New York: Free Press.
Dobb, Maurice
    1946   *Studies in the development of capitalism.* London: Routledge and Kegan Paul.
Dow, James
    1973   Models of middlemen: Issues concerning the economic exploitation of modern
         peasants. *Human Organization* **32:** 397–406.
Dumont, Louis
    1970   *Homo hierarchicus.* London: Wiedenfeld and Nicolson.
Eberhard, Wolfrom
    1962   *Social mobility in traditional China.* Leiden: Brill.

Eisenstadt, S. N.
   1963   *The political systems of empires.* New York: Free Press.
Elvin, Mark
   1973   *The pattern of the Chinese past.* Stanford, Calif.: Stanford Univ. Press.
Epstein, Scarlett
   1967   Productive efficiency and customary systems of rewards in rural south India. In
           Themes in economic anthropology, edited by R. Firth. London: Tavistock.
Foster, George M.
   1967   The dyadic contract: A model for the social structure of a Mexic peasant village. In
           Peasant Society: A Reader, edited by J. M. Potter, M. N. Diaz, and G. M. Foster.
           Boston: Little, Brown.
Fox, Richard G.
   1969   *Varna* schemes and ideological integration in Indian society. *Comparative Studies
           in Society and History* **2:** 27–45.
   1971   *Kin, clan, raja and rule: State–hinterland relations in pre-industrial northern India.*
           Berkeley: Univ. of California Press.
Frank, André G.
   1967   *Capitalism and underdevelopment in Latin America.* New York: Monthly Review
           Press.
Fried, Morton H.
   1967   *The evolution of political society.* New York: Random House.
Frykenberg, R. E. (Ed.)
   1969   *Land control and social structure in Indian history.* Madison: Univ. of Wisconsin
           Press.
Geertz, Clifford
   1963   *Agricultural Involution: The processes of ecological change in Indonesia.* Berkeley:
           Univ. of California Press.
Goody, Jack
   1971   *Technology, tradition and the state in Africa.* New York: Oxford Univ. Press.
Jones, Susan Mann
   1974   The Ningpo *pang* and financial power at Shanghai. In *The Chinese city between two
           worlds,* edited by M. Elvin and G. W. Skinner. Stanford, Calif.: Stanford Univ.
           Press.
Harding, T. G.
   1967   *Voyagers of the Vitiaz Strait.* Seattle: Univ. of Washington Press.
Harner, M. J.
   1972   *The Jívaro.* Garden City, N.Y.: Doubleday.
Harper, Edward B.
   1959   Two systems of economic exchange in village India. *American Anthropologist* **61:**
           760–778.
Hechter, Michael
   1975   *Internal colonialism: The Celtic fringe in British national development.* Berkeley:
           Univ. of California Press.
Homans, George
   1941   *English villagers of the thirteenth century.* Cambridge, Mass.: Harvard Univ. Press.
   1961   *Social behavior: Its elementary forms.* New York: Harcourt.
Kaplan, David
   1965   The Mexican marketplace: Then and now. In *Essays in economic anthropology,*
           edited by J. Helm. Seattle: Univ of Washington Press.
Kelley, Klara
   1976   Murngin and Gidjingali land use and social organization. Unpublished manuscript.

Kolenda, Pauline
    1963 Toward a model of the Hindu *jajmani* system. *Human Organization* **22:** 11–33.
Kottack, Conrad P.
    1972 Ecological variables in the origin and evolution of African states: The Buganda
          example. *Comparative Studies in Society and History* **14:** 351–380.
Lathrop, D. W.
    1973 The antiquity and importance of long-distance trade relationships in the moist
          tropics of pre-Colombian South America. *World Archaeology* **5:** 170–186.
Leach, E. R.
    1960 Introduction. In *Aspects of caste in south India, Ceylon, and northwest Pakistan,*
          edited by E. R. Leach. Cambridge, Mass.: Cambridge Univ. Press.
Lee, Richard, and Irven DeVore (Eds.)
    1968 *Man the hunter.* Chicago: Aldine.
Lenin, V. I.
    1939 *Imperialism: The highest stage of capitalism.* New York: International Publishers.
Lenski, Gerhard
    1966 *Power and privilege.* New York: McGraw-Hill.
Lockwood, William W.
    1954 *The economic development of Japan.* Princeton, N.J.: Princeton Univ. Press.
Malinowski, B.
    1922 *Argonauts of the western Pacific.* London: Routledge and Kegan Paul.
Mandel, Ernest
    1970 *Marxist economic theory,* Vol. I. New York: Monthly Review Press.
Marx, Karl
    1932 *Manifesto of the Communist Party.* New York: International Publishers.
    1967 *Capital,* Vol. I. New York: International Publishers.
    1971 *The Grundrisse,* edited by David McLellan. New York: Harper.
Mauss, Marcel
    1954 *The gift.* New York: Free Press.
McLeod, Murdo J.
    1973 *Spanish Central America: A socioeconomic history, 1520–1720.* Berkeley: Univ. of
          California Press.
Meillassoux, Claude
    1972 From reproduction to production. *Economy and Society* **1:** 93–105.
Mencher, Joan P.
    1974 The caste system upside down, or the not-so-mysterious East. *Current Anthropology*
          15: 469–495.
Morton-Williams, Peter
    1969 The influence of habitat and trade on the polities of Oyo and Ashanti. In *Man in
          Africa,* edited by M. Douglas and P. Kaberry. London: Tavistock.
Neale, Walter C.
    1957 Reciprocity and redistribution in the Indian village: Sequel to some notable dis-
          cussions. In *Trade and market in the early empires,* edited by K. Polanyi, C. Arens-
          berg, and H. Pearson. New York: Free Press.
Orans, Martin
    1968 Maximizing in jajmaniland: A model of caste relations. *American Anthropologist*
          70: 875–898.
Perkins, Dwight H.
    1969 *Agricultural development in China, 1368–1968.* Chicago: Aldine.
Pirenne, Henri
    1958 *A history of Europe* (2 volumes). Translated by B. Miall. Garden City, N.Y.:
          Doubleday.

Plattner, Stuart
  1975   The economics of peddling. In *Formal methods in economic anthropology,* edited by
         S. Plattner. Washington, D.C.: American Anthropological Association.
Polanyi, Karl
  1966   *Dahomey and the slave trade.* Seattle: Univ. of Washington Press.
Polanyi, Karl, C. Arensberg, and H. Pearson
  1957   *Trade and market in the early empires.* New York: Free Press.
Rappaport, Roy A.
  1967   *Pigs for the ancestors.* New Haven, Conn.: Yale Univ. Press.
Rathje, W. L.
  1971   The origin and development of lowland classic Maya civilization. *American
         Antiquity* **36:** 275–285.
Rawski, Evelyn S.
  1972   *Agricultural change and the peasant economy of south China.* Cambridge, Mass.:
         Harvard Univ. Press.
Rosaldo, Michelle, and Louise Lamphere (Eds.)
  1974   *Woman, culture and society.* Stanford, Calif.: Stanford Univ. Press.
Rozman, Gilbert
  1973   *Urban networks in Ch'ing China and Tokugawa Japan.* Princeton, N.J.: Princeton
         Univ. Press.
Russell, J. C.
  1972   *Medieval regions and their cities.* Bloomington: Indiana Univ. Press.
Sahlins, Marshall
  1958   *Social stratification in Polynesia.* Seattle: Univ. of Washington Press.
  1963   Poor man, rich man, big-man, chief: Political types in Melanesia and Polynesia.
         Comparative Studies in Society and History **5:** 285–303.
  1965   On the sociology of primitive exchange. In *The relevance of models for social
         anthropology,* edited by M. Banton. New York: Praeger.
Siverts, Henning
  1969   Ethnic stability and boundary dynamics in southern Mexico. In *Ethnic groups and
         boundaries,* edited by F. Barth. Boston: Little, Brown.
Skinner, G. William
  1964   Marketing and social structure in rural China: Part I. *Journal of Asian Studies* **24:**
         3–45.
  1965   Marketing and social structure in rural China: Part II. *Journal of Asian Studies* **24:**
         195–228.
  1968   The city in Chinese society. Paper prepared for Research Conference on Urban
         Society in Traditional China, Wentworth-by-the-Sea, N.H.
  In press a   Regional urbanization in 19th century China. In *The city in late Imperial
         China,* edited by G. W. Skinner. Stanford, Calif.: Stanford Univ. Press.
  In press b   Urban development in Imperial China. In *The city in late Imperial China,*
         edited by G. W. Skinner. Stanford, Calif.: Stanford Univ. Press.
Smith, Carol A.
  1975a   Examining stratification systems through peasant marketing arrangements: An
         application of some models from economic geography. *Man* **10:** 95–122.
  1975b   Production in western Guatemala: A test of Boserup and von Thünen. In *Formal
         methods in economic anthropology,* edited by S. Plattner. Washington, D.C.:
         American Anthropological Association.
Smith, Thomas C.
  1973   Pre-modern economic growth: Japan and the West. *Past and Present* **60:** 127–160.
Spooner, Brian (Ed.)
  1972   *Population growth: Anthropological implications.* Cambridge, Mass.: MIT Press.

Uberoi, F. P. Singh
  1962   *Politics of the Kula Ring.* Manchester: Manchester Univ. Press.
Wallerstein, Immanual
  1974   *The modern world-system.* New York: Academic Press.
Wolf, Eric
  1957   Closed corporate peasant communities in Mesoamerica and central Java.
         Southwestern Journal of Anthropology **13:** 7–12.

Index[1]

A

Administered economies, *see* Solar systems

Administered exchange, 317, 319, 334–336, 338–341, 342–344, 345, 353, 358, 359–360, *see also* Solar systems

Administered markets, in Ecuador, 335

Administrative centrality, as a regional systems variable, 233–234, 239–240, 249–253

Administrative systems, 319

Agrarian societies
definition, 311
economic distribution systems in, 313–321
markets in, 318–321, 327, 333–338, 346–347, 353–354, 357–358, 362–363, *see also* Distribution systems
position of peasants in, 341, 343–344, 349, 351–353, 355–356, 363–364
stratification in, 309–369
types of, 315–321

American South, as a region, 29–31, 43

B

Balanced exchange, *see* Imbalanced exchange

Berry, Brian J. L., 36–37, 38–40.

"Big men," 321n

Bounded network systems
economic distribution in, 316–317, 318, *see also* Polyadic exchange
formal characteristics, 315, 316–317, 368
social organization in, 322–333, *see also* Castelike stratification

Brokers, between local systems and regional systems, 16, 48, 96–97

C

Canonical analysis, 37n

Castelike stratification
class mobility in, 327–329
definition of, 326–327
economic base, 327–328
elites in, 327, 328–330, 333
influenced by elite mobility, 329–330, 331–333

[1] Scholars are indexed only if their works are discussed. For references readers are referred to the individual reference lists at the ends of chapters.